Dynamic Modeling and Econometrics in Economics and Finance

Volume 26

In recent years there has been a rapidly growing interest in the study of dynamic nonlinear phenomena in economic and financial theory, while at the same time econometricians and statisticians have been developing methods for modeling such phenomena. Despite the common focus of theorists and econometricians, both lines of research have had their own publication outlets. The new book series is designed to further the understanding of dynamic phenomena in economics and finance by bridging the gap between dynamic theory and empirics and to provide cross-fertilization between the two strands. The series will place particular focus on monographs, surveys, edited volumes, conference proceedings and handbooks on:

- Nonlinear dynamic phenomena in economics and finance, including equilibrium, disequilibrium, optimizing and adaptive evolutionary points of view; nonlinear and complex dynamics in microeconomics, finance, macroeconomics and applied fields of economics.
- Econometric and statistical methods for analysis of nonlinear processes in economics and finance, including computational methods, numerical tools and software to study nonlinear dependence, asymmetries, persistence of fluctuations, multiple equilibria, chaotic and bifurcation phenomena.
- Applications linking theory and empirical analysis in areas such as macrodynamics, microdynamics, asset pricing, financial analysis and portfolio analysis, international economics, resource dynamics and environment, industrial organization and dynamics of technical change, labor economics, demographics, population dynamics, and game theory.

The target audience of this series includes researchers at universities and research and policy institutions, students at graduate institutions, and practitioners in economics, finance and international economics in private or government institutions.

More information about this series at http://www.springer.com/series/5859

Herbert Dawid · Jasmina Arifovic
Editors

Dynamic Analysis in Complex Economic Environments

Essays in Honor of Christophe Deissenberg

Springer

Editors
Herbert Dawid
Department of Business Administration
and Economics
Bielefeld University
Bielefeld, Nordrhein-Westfalen, Germany

Jasmina Arifovic
Department of Economics
Simon Fraser University
Burnaby, BC, Canada

ISSN 1566-0419 ISSN 2363-8370 (electronic)
Dynamic Modeling and Econometrics in Economics and Finance
ISBN 978-3-030-52969-7 ISBN 978-3-030-52970-3 (eBook)
https://doi.org/10.1007/978-3-030-52970-3

This Springer imprint is published by the registered company Springer Nature Switzerland AG
The registered company address is: Gewerbestrasse 11, 6330 Cham, Switzerland

Contents

Contributors

Francisco Alvarez Departamento de Fundamentos Análisis Económico y Economía Cuantitativa, Universidad Complutense Madrid and ICAE, Madrid, Spain

Jasmina Arifovic Department of Economics, Simon Fraser University, Burnaby, Canada

William A. Barnett University of Kansas, Lawrence, USA;
Center for Financial Stability, NY City, USA;
ICEMR Institute for Nonlinear Dynamical Inference, Moscow, Russia

Alain Bensoussan Naveen Jindal School of Management, University of Texas at Dallas, Richardson, TX, USA;
City University of Hong Kong, Kowloon Tong, Hong Kong

Herbert Dawid Department of Business Administration and Economics, Center for Mathematical Economics, Bielefeld University, Bielefeld, Germany

Giovanni Di Bartolomeo Facoltà di Economia, Sapienza University of Rome, Rome, Italy

Manfred Gilli School of Economics and Management and Swiss Finance Institute, University of Geneva, Geneva, Switzerland

Andrea Gurgone Economics Department, Bamberg University, Bamberg, Germany

Philipp Harting Department of Business Administration and Economics, Bielefeld University, Bielefeld, Germany

Jingxian Hu Boise State University, Boise, USA

Giulia Iori Department of Economics, City, University of London, London, UK

Michael Neugart Department of Law and Economics, Technische Universität Darmstadt, Darmstadt, Germany

Enrico Saltari Facoltà di Economia, Sapienza University of Rome, Rome, Italy

Marcello Sartarelli Departamento de Fundamentos Análisis Económico y Economía Cuantitativa, Universidad Complutense Madrid and ICAE, Madrid, Spain

Enrico Schumann CPV/CAP Pensionskasse Coop, Basel, Switzerland; University of Basel, Basel, Switzerland

Willi Semmler New School for Social Research, New York, NY, USA; University of Bielefeld, Bielefeld, Germany

Suresh P. Sethi Naveen Jindal School of Management, University of Texas at Dallas, Richardson, TX, USA

Ngo Van Long Department of Economics, McGill University, Montreal, Canada

K. Vela Velupillai Solna, Sweden

Introduction

Jasmina Arifovic and Herbert Dawid

Abstract This is the introductory chapter to the book "Dynamic Analysis in Complex Economic Environments", which collects essays in honor of Christophe Deissenberg. It briefly reviews the achievements of Christophe Deissenberg and gives an overview of the different papers included in the book.

This volume is written to mark the 75th birthday of Christophe Deissenberg. It collects a series of papers analyzing dynamic and complex economic problems and thereby reflects the broad range of interests and methodological approaches characteristic for the work of Christophe Deissenberg. The main theme in his long academic career has been the aim to develop and exploit dynamic modeling frameworks that allow us to gain a better understanding of complex economic dynamics and to carry out policy analysis in such challenging environments. Christophe Deissenberg has made contributions to this field of research employing a wide range of methodological approaches including stochastic and deterministic optimal control (e.g., Deissenberg 1981; Deissenberg et al. 2004), dynamic games (e.g., Deissenberg and Alvarez Gonzalez 2002), and agent-based simulation (e.g., Deissenberg et al. 2008).

Fostering interdisciplinary approaches and combining analytical and computational methods is an important aspect of Christophe Deissenberg's work and his research agenda. Apart from his own contributions, Christophe Deissenberg has been an important facilitator of research in the areas of economic complexity and computational economics as an organizer of workshops and conferences, in particular a highly visible series of COMPLEXITY workshops in Aix-en-Provence, as editor of several books and journal special issues or as long-term chair of the selection committee for the Graduate Student Contest of the Society for Computational

J. Arifovic
Department of Economics, Simon Fraser University, Burnaby, Canada
e-mail: jasmina_arifovic@sfu.ca

H. Dawid (✉)
Department of Business Administration and Economics, and Center for Mathematical Economics, Bielefeld University, Bielefeld, Germany
e-mail: hdawid@uni-bielefeld.de

H. Dawid and J. Arifovic (eds.), *Dynamic Analysis in Complex Economic Environments*, Dynamic Modeling and Econometrics in Economics and Finance 26,
https://doi.org/10.1007/978-3-030-52970-3_1

Economics. In all these roles, Christophe Deissenberg had an important impact on the profession pushing economists to keep updating and enlarging their toolbox in order to deal with the complexity and uncertainty of our economic environment.

The different research papers in this volume, contributed by former students, co-authors, and close colleagues of Christophe Deissenberg, although addressing a wide range of economic topics, are all related to his research agenda. They all deal with issues of optimal individual behavior or policy design in complex environments. The paper by Alvarez and Sartarelli examines cross-bidding behavior in eBay like second-price auction environments. They build a computational model of several parallel auctions and study the implications of different bidding strategies on the (distribution of) generated surplus in such a setting. Their results based on extensive Monte Carlo simulations suggest that behavior like nibbling, i.e., incrementally increasing bids, and cross-bidding reduces the variability of obtained surplus without reducing the expectation compared to a strategy of truthful bidding for the most highly valued object. In this way, the paper provides a theoretical explanation for the frequent empirical observations of nibbling and cross-bidding in auctions. Also, the paper by Gilli and Schumann considers a complex problem, namely, the design of optimal portfolios under different objective functions and constraints. The main agenda of their paper is to carry out a replication exercise, i.e., to check findings from a previous paper using different data and also a different implementation of the numerical optimization algorithm. Although it is widely accepted that the reproducibility of results is an important issue in many areas of (economic) research including computational work, unfortunately, few systematic studies on this issue are published. Gilli and Schumann in their study indeed confirm qualitative insights from previous studies, in particular with respect to the appeal of investing in low-risk assets of using risk measures differentiating between losses and gains. The contribution by Bensoussan and Sethi considers an optimal investment and consumption problem in a dynamic setup with multiple securities. They distinguish between scenarios where inflation is fully observed and where the decision-maker only obtains an inflation signal and apply dynamic programming to characterize optimal investment strategies in both scenarios. The main insight from their analysis is that in both cases the optimal strategy induces investment in the risk-free fund as well as in the same two risky funds. Only the weights in the optimal allocation differ between the two information scenarios.

The next two papers address dynamic issues in resource and environmental economics, another area of research to which Christophe Deissenberg has contributed. The paper by van Long extends the established literature on dynamic resource exploitation games with the tragedy of the commons properties by incorporating moral scruples of players into such a dynamic framework. In particular, he considers a differential game of resource exploitation in which agents do not only care about their material well-being but also about their self-image which is affected by the difference between their chosen action and the 'Kantian action' which is optimal from a social planner's perspective. A main insight of the analysis is that under an appropriate self-image function behavior under a Markov-perfect equilibrium of the game induces the socially optimal outcome. Whereas van Long focuses on the role of moral scruples for dynamic exploitation of a common resource Di Bartolomeo, Saltari and Semmler analyze how the planning horizon of a policy-maker affects its design of pollution control measures and the resulting induced dynamics of the stock of pollution. They consider scenarios where the policy-maker governs the transition to a higher as well as to lower pollution levels and show that shorter planning horizons of the policy-makers lead to quicker but costlier transitions. These results are obtained using numerical analysis relying on a Nonlinear Model Predictive Control approach.

The issue of policy design in complex dynamic environments is also examined in the next group of papers of this volume. Barnett and Hu employ an open economy New Keynesian model to analyze the implications of capital controls in combination with different exchange rate regimes and monetary policies. They identify conditions under which the model exhibits multiple equilibria and unstable dynamics. Based on this, they derive insights on how a policy-maker can stabilize the economy. Gurgone and Iori study the implications of different kinds of macroprudential capital requirements for the dynamic of the financial and real side of the economy in the framework of an agent-based macroeconomic model incorporating financial distress propagation. They show that capital requirements that are derived from vulnerability measures of systemic risk can improve financial stability without having negative implications on the real side. Also, Dawid, Harting, and Neugart employ an agent-based macroeconomic model for policy analysis. In particular, they use the Eurace@Unibi model, which is an advanced version of the original Eurace model, which was conceptualized and developed in parts by Christophe Deissenberg, in order to study how different degrees of decentralization in the wage-setting influence economic growth and wage inequality. Their extensive simulation analysis shows that increasing the degree of wage centralization does not only reduce wage inequality but also implies higher market concentration in the consumption goods sector and faster economic growth.

The concluding chapter of this volume in honor of Christophe Deissenberg is a discussion by Vela Velupillai of what he, based on an unpublished Deissenberg paper from 1977, calls the '*Deissenberg problem*'. This problem is formulated as finding the optimal point in the efficient set and Velupillai analyses the algorithmic complexity of the problem and its solvability. The paper illustrates nicely how early in his career Christophe Deissenberg was already concerned with issues of computability and also man-machine interaction.

All papers in this volume have been peer-reviewed and revised in light of the reviewer's comments. We are most grateful to all the colleagues who have provided helpful and critical feedback on the submissions.

References

Deissenberg, C. (1981). Optimal stabilization policy with control lags and imperfect state observations. *Zeitschrift fuer Nationaloekonomie (Journal of Institutional Economics)*, *41*, 329–352.

Deissenberg, C., & Alvarez Gonzalez, F. (2002). Pareto-improving cheating in a monetary policy game. *Journal of Economic Dynamics and Control*, *26*, 1457–1479.

Deissenberg, C., Feichtinger, G., Semmler, W., & Wirl, F. (2004). Multiple equilibria, history dependence, and global dynamics in intertemporal optimization models. In W. Barnett, C. Deissenberg, & G. Feichtinger (Eds.), *Economic complexity: Non-linear dynamics, multi-agents economies, and learning*. ISETE, Vol. 14 (pp. 91–122). Amsterdam: Elsevier.

Deissenberg, C., van der Hoog, S., & Dawid, H. (2008). EURACE: A massively parallel agent-based model of the European economy. *Applied Mathematics and Computation*, *204*, 541–552.

Cross-Bidding in eBay-like Environments

Francisco Alvarez and Marcello Sartarelli

Abstract Bidding in different (single object) auctions, or cross-bidding, and bidding incrementally within one auction, or nibbling, are two phenomena observed in platforms like eBay. This paper tests with numerical methods the validity of a theoretical setting that rationalizes such behavior, while bidders are assumed to observe privately and without error, their valuations from the onset and the objects are imperfect substitutes. Our analysis shows that cross-bidding and nibbling might reduce significantly the variability in the bidder's surplus.

Keywords Auction · Cross-bidding · eBay · Montecarlo · Multiple auctions · Nibbling

JEL Classification: C15 · D44 · D90

1 Introduction

Single object auctions have led to a vast—and fruitful—body of theoretical literature in economics over decades. From a theoretical viewpoint, an auction is an adverse selection problem in which a side of the market has some informational advantage and is allowed to send messages—which determine assignment and payments—to the other side. In the most extensively used model, buyers have private information about their valuation of the good on sale and submit individually bid prices to the

Financial support from the Spanish Ministerio de Economía y Competitividad (Alvarez: ECO2017-86245-P; Sartarelli: ECO2016-77200-P, ECO2015-65820-P and ECO2013-43119) is gratefully acknowledged.

F. Alvarez (✉) · M. Sartarelli
Departamento de Fundamentos Análisis Económico y Economía Cuantitativa,
Universidad Complutense Madrid and ICAE, Madrid, Spain
e-mail: fralvare@ccee.ucm.es

M. Sartarelli
e-mail: marcellosartarelli@gmail.com

H. Dawid and J. Arifovic (eds.), *Dynamic Analysis in Complex Economic Environments*,
Dynamic Modeling and Econometrics in Economics and Finance 26,
https://doi.org/10.1007/978-3-030-52970-3_2

seller. The seller assigns the object to the bidder who submitted the highest bid. With a number of variations, the bids also determine the winning bidder's payment.

While a great deal of the existing theoretical literature considers *an* auction in isolation, real-life markets are ahead of the theory, as evidence from eBay shows that the same bidder either bids several times in the same auction, called nibbling (Ockenfels and Roth 2006; Alvarez and Sartarelli 2020), or bids in multiple auctions running simultaneously, called cross-bidding (Anwar et al. 2006), or both. As it is well-known, all auctions in eBay are second price auctions. Typically, many auctions for similar goods are held simultaneously. Within each auction, any given buyer is allowed to revise her bid upwards as much as desired. Of course, switching between auctions is also allowed. If anything, these bidding platforms have set to virtually zero search and switching costs among auctions. Consequently, the selection of auctions and the timing of bidding are a part of the bidder's strategy, at least in what we are to name informally as eBay-like environments.

This paper contributes to build a bridge between theory and eBay-like environments. Our approach has two essential characteristics. First, we lay on a behavioral—as a synonymous to non-fully rational—ground. Generally speaking, rational agents anticipate the consequences of their actions as much as their information set allows for and choose the action that maximizes their conditional expected utility. A vast literature has studied a number of departures from rationality. We take an intentionally simple approach: our bidders just play the current best move every time they are called to play. Second, we rely on numerical methods, which have a clear potential for combining theory and data.[1]

Our model mimics the features outlined above. A fixed number of auctions are held. We give the sellers a passive role: a single object is inelastically supplied in every auction. On the demand side, we consider a fixed set of bidders. Valuations of each object are privately observed at the start of the game and differ along two dimensions: objects and bidders. Each bidder only derives utility from her most valued object she is awarded with (if more than one). All auctions run in parallel for a fixed number of periods. Bidders are allowed to increase—but not to withdraw—their bids over time within an auction or to switch among auctions. Like eBay auctions, we take the second price auction rule. Only the standing prices at the end of the last period are taken into account.

The underlying motivation for this model is to explain two facts that have been consistently reported in the empirical literature on eBay-like environments. First, within an auction, bidders bid incrementally, i.e., *nibble*. Second, the same bidder bids in different auctions for goods that are probably perceived as imperfect substitutes, i.e., *cross-bid*. There is a compelling theoretical prediction for second price auctions, such as eBay: it is weakly dominant to bid *truthfully*, that is, the true valuation. The

[1]The analysis and implications of departures from rationality in decision-making has acquired a markedly cross-disciplinary "flavor" over decades. For example, Tesfatsion (2003), reviews the literature on agent-based modeling which received contributions from scientists and social scientists alike; Camerer et al. (2011) reviews the economics literature which has tried to rationalize a number of puzzling predictions thanks to insights from other disciplines in social science; finally Chernev et al. (2015), reviews research on choice overload in psychology.

canonical model that leads to that prediction considers just a single object on sale. The extension to a multi-object setting when each bidder wants only one—but no one in particular—object is rather straightforward.

The first part of our analysis focuses on whether truthfully bidding still survives as a robust prediction when any given bidder perceives the objects on sale as imperfect substitutes. We have explored, through Monte Carlo (MC) simulations, the outcome delivered by two different scenarios. In the first scenario, we assume that all bidders bid truthfully, just once, and for their highest valued object (assuming valuations are i.i.d. across bidders and objects). This is an intentionally simple bidding strategy and, perhaps more importantly, as close as it can be to the strategy suggested by the single-auction models. We denote this strategy as second price. In the second scenario, we assume that all bidders nibble. More specifically, each time a bidder is called to play, she bids incrementally for the good that is currently offering her the highest surplus, i.e., the difference between valuation and winning price. Each MC run is defined by a set of valuations. For each set, we simulate separately both scenarios. Our findings, averaging across MC runs, show that there is not a clear better strategy between second price and nibbling in terms of expected bidders' surplus. Interestingly, there are differences in the second order moments: the surplus under nibbling has lower variability than under second price. Our analysis suggests that nibbling generates a cross-auction correlation between winning prices, and that reduces the variance of surplus with respect to second price.

The second part of our analysis deals with a somehow *smoothed* version of second price bidding. Under the nibbling scenario, we assume that two kinds of nibblers coexist: *hard* and *loose*. Hard nibblers restrict themselves from the onset to participate in a subset of auctions for objects that they value highly and, each time they are called to play, they bid aggressively, that is, close to their true valuation of the corresponding object. In contrast, loose nibblers do not impose themselves any *ex-ante* participation constraint and, whenever they bid, they bid just slightly above the current winning price. In a nutshell, hard nibblers are more similar to second price bidders or, more precisely, more similar than loose nibblers are. Our results again show that there is not a clear best strategy in terms of surplus but, if anything, there is a slight out-performance of loose over hard nibblers.

The rest of the paper is organized as follows: Section 2 puts our paper in perspective in the related literature. Section 3 describes the model. Section 4 defines precisely the strategy space under consideration. Section 5 contains the analysis and results and, finally, Section 6 concludes.

2 Related Literature

Our paper is related to at least two strands of the literature on online auctions. One strand analyzes deviations in observed bidding behavior relative to what is predicted by canonical models of second price auctions when multiple bids are allowed, i.e., intra-auction bidding or nibbling, and the close time is fixed and known, i.e., hard close, as in eBay. The second strand focuses, instead, on multiple auctions, motivated by the fact that bidders may simultaneously be bidding on different but similar goods being sold in different auctions, i.e., inter-auction bidding or cross-bidding.

Empirical evidence from (non-)experimental studies on online auctions overall shows that the nature of bids heavily depends on the timing of bidding, e.g., early or late bidding. Roth and Ockenfels (2002) test whether the share of last minute bidders, called snipers, differs in eBay and Amazon auctions since the former uses a hard close, i.e., the end time is known from the onset, while the latter a soft close, i.e., the end time is extended if a bid is placed within the last three minutes from the current end time. In line with predictions, the empirical evidence shows a larger share of snipers under the eBay hard close rule. Similarly, Ockenfels and Roth (2006), prove that sniping may hold in equilibrium as the best reply to nibbling and find empirical support for this prediction using eBay data.

In related work, Ely and Hossain (2009) test whether sniping increases bids and surplus in an auction by conducting a field experiment which consists in placing early and late bids in an auction and measuring whether the experimental bids alter its outcome. They find that sniping leads to a larger average surplus. In our own related work, we leveraged data from the Hossain and Morgan (2006) field experiment in eBay auctions to test whether the shipping cost, defined as a share of the reserve price and the reserve price affect sniping and also nibbling. We find that nibbling is significantly higher when the shipping cost is a high share of the total price but only for music CDs auctions, while no effect is observed for Xbox games auctions (Alvarez and Sartarelli 2020). A growing body of empirical literature reports that bidders bid incrementally over time within an auction in eBay-like environments (Roth and Ockenfels 2002; Backus et al. 2015; Alvarez and Sartarelli 2020), i.e., *nibble*.

A number of theoretical papers have attempted to rationalize nibbling observed in eBay auctions. Rasmusen (2006) is the first study proposing a two-bidder model with an *ex-ante* asymmetry. One of the bidders is standard in that she knows her own valuation (but not her rival's). The other fails to know even her own valuation but can costly learn it throughout the auction. The paper characterizes equilibria under which the standard bidder snipes while the other bidder plays an incremental bidding strategy that interacts with her learning process, for auctions with hard and soft close rules. Hossain (2008) uses a similar framework, with an *ex-ante* informational asymmetry in a two-bidder dynamic game, although only for hard close auctions. The uniformed bidder learns whether her value is larger than the current price or not costlessly by observing the current auction price, just like in an eBay auction. The key result is that the informed bidder snipes while the uninformed one nibbles.[2]

A somewhat different model with no *ex-ante* differences among bidders and no value discovery process is proposed by Ambrus et al. (2013). Bidders can bid (or wait) only at random instants throughout the duration of the auction, which gives rise

[2]The departure point of multi-object single bid auction settings is classically represented by Milgrom and Weber (1982). They assume that bidders submit bids for no particular object and they are allowed to bid just once. In short, the choice of an auction and the timing of bidding is absent in the bidder's decision process. A number of branches in the theoretical literature have been developed thereafter.

to multiple equilibria. While under each equilibrium bidders behave symmetrically, equilibria differ from one another in the extent of nibbling. More importantly, bidders might implicitly collude either in the extent of nibbling or by abstaining from bidding. In equilibrium sellers' revenues are lower than under the standard truthful bidding strategy.

To the best of our knowledge, Vadovič (2017) offers the most recent theoretical contribution to rationalize behavior observed in online auctions by adding to the idea of value discovery used in previous studies two novel ingredients: a market in which goods are not auctioned and a search cost to find in the market substitute goods to those being auctioned. Bidders are *ex-ante* identical but nature assigns each bidder a different search cost to find a market for a close substitute to the good being auctioned. Additionally, since auctioned goods have a common and known value, then bidder's type is unidimensional and is given by the search cost. Then, bidders with high search cost bid early to signal they are aggressive while those with low search cost observe early bids and search for alternative markets. In short, early bidding helps bidders to coordinate their decisions to either leave or stay in the auction.

In addition to rationalizing multiple bids in a single auction, Vadovič (2017) also suggests that while some bidders can only obtain the good they are interested by winning an online auction, because a bidder may live in a remote location or may not search for the good in other markets, other bidders may try to buy the good from a different seller. For simplicity, Vadovič (2017) considers a market in which the good is not auctioned, thus ignoring the case in which two similar goods are each sold in a different auction and a bidder may simultaneously or sequentially bid in any of the two auctions, i.e., cross-bidding.

In related theoretical work, Backus et al. (2014) study the relationship between price dispersion for a good auctioned and search costs and establish that they are negatively related. The intuition is that the lower the search cost the easier or quicker it is for bidders, first, to find if multiple auctions of the same good (or of substitutable ones) are run simultaneously and, second, to bid on the cheapest good. When they test their prediction using data on eBay auctions they find that visible goods, which have a lower search cost, have a higher probability of being sold and, when they consider only those goods who are sold, visible ones are sold at a higher price.

However, perhaps the only empirical study offering evidence of cross-bidding is by Anwar et al. (2006). They test by using data on eBay auctions the hypothesis that auctions of substitutable goods are run independently of one another. Their results reject this hypothesis in favor of 19–30% of bidders submitting bids in competing auctions. In addition, they find that cross-bidders tend to bid in the auction with the lowest bid, in line with theoretical predictions. Finally, they find that those subjects bidding in multiple auctions pay lower prices, by about 10% relative to those who bid in a single auction.[3]

3 Model

Our theoretical model captures some characteristics of eBay auctions with the aim of reproducing essentially the environment in which buyers take decisions. We consider K single object auctions being held simultaneously and N bidders, or buyers, with $N > K$. In the sequel, n and k denote an arbitrary bidder and auction, respectively.

Auctions evolve over discrete time. We denote by *period* the object of time. Periods are indexed by t. All eBay auctions are *hard close* auctions: the end time is known from the onset and independent of the bidding record. In line with this, we assume all auctions start at period $t = 0$ and finish at $t = T - 1$. In eBay, bids take place in continuous time, which implies that each bidder knows exactly the winning bids every time he bids. To account for that, we assume within each period there are N rounds. Exactly one bidder is allowed to bid at every round, and each bidder is allowed to bid exactly once per period. The ordering in which bidders are allowed to bid within a period is purely random and changes from one period to the next, thus no bidder has *ex-ante* informational advantage due to her position in the bidding ordering.

Regarding payments, eBay auctions are second price auctions: the highest bid wins and pays the second highest bid. Thus, we must distinguish winning bid (highest) from the payment (second highest). At the time of bidding, each bidder observes the current winning bid in every auction, but not the current payment or winner, unless for the auction(s) in which she is precisely the current winner. Payments and assignments are based on prices observed at the end of the last period. Withdrawing one's own bid is not allowed: at any given period, the current winner is committed to pay the current second highest price unless some other bidder outbids it.

In our model, sellers do not play any role, i.e., supply is inelastic and exogenous. Regarding the buyers, let $v_{n,k}$ denote bidder n's valuation of the object being sold in the auction k. We further assume that each bidder only wants one object. Thus, more precisely, $v_{n,k}$ represents the corresponding valuation if—and only if—bidder

[3]Our paper is also related to studies on multiple auctions in operational research, whose common objective is maximizing the efficiency of algorithms which, on behalf of bidders, bid in multiple auctions, i.e., proxy bidding. Byde et al. (2002), Anthony and Jennings (2002) develop an algorithm which can bid for multiple units of a good is sold in different types of auctions, e.g., English or Dutch, with different start or end times. In related work Ma and Leung (2007) develop an algorithm to bid in multiple continuous double auctions, which are common in commodities markets and have the peculiarity that bidders and auctioneers can continuously update their bid and ask throughout the trading period. Finally, Chang (2014) creates a proxy measure of heterogeneity in cross-bidding behavior by using statistical methods in entropy analysis and finds that it is positively correlated with revenues.

n only wins auction k. Formally, if bidder n wins a subset of $\mathcal{K}$ auctions, her utility is $\max\{v_{n,k} \mid k \in \mathcal{K}\}$. As usual, we assume valuations are privately observed by each bidder at the start of period 0. We will further assume for most of the analysis that valuations are i.i.d. draws from a uniform distribution in [0, 1].

4 Strategy Space

As mentioned, eBay is a second price auction, and we have assumed that valuations are known from the onset. A well-known result for the single object auction setting is that it is weakly dominant to bid *truthfully* (true valuation). The underlying reason is that in a second price auction your bid determines your likelihood of winning but, in case of winning, your payment is independent of your bid (save that you know that it will be below). Obviously, if I am to bid truthfully, I will bid only once, and with no defined preference over timing.

Truthfully, bidding in eBay-like environments has an additional complexity since we are assuming that if a bidder happens to win more than one auction he only obtains utility from his most valued object among those he has been awarded with. A standard argument then induces to bid only for the most valued object. We denote that bidding strategy as *second price bidding*, as its justification is essentially based on the second price character of the payment rule.

Definition 1 Under a **second price bidding**, the bidders bid truthfully, only once, and each bidder bids for her highest valued object.

One of our main objectives in this paper is analyzing to what extent this strategic signaling does improve the bidders' surplus when those outside options are in fact other auctions running simultaneously and—more importantly—with an endogenous price. As mentioned in the introduction, our approach is behavioral. We consider a nibbling strategy under which, whenever each bidder is called to bid, she bids:

1. incrementally and only in the auction which currently offers her the highest surplus;
2. only if she is not the current winner of that auction;
3. only if the valuation of the object on sale in that auction lies above some threshold value.

Formally, let $\mathbf{w} = (w_1, \ldots, w_K)$ and $\mathbf{v}_n = \left(v_{n,1}, \ldots, v_{n,K}\right)$ denote the vector of current winning price and bidder n's valuations, respectively, where the time subscript is omitted in $\mathbf{w}$. So that, bidder n's current surplus is $\mathbf{s}_n = \mathbf{v}_n - \mathbf{w}$. Furthermore, let k^* be the index of the highest entry in $\mathbf{s}_n$, that is, the auction offering highest current surplus for bidder n, and let $\hat{n}(k^*)$ denote the current winner in auction k^*. Then bidder n's bid at the current period is only in auction k^* and it is:

$$b_n(\mathbf{v}_n, \mathbf{w}, \hat{n}(k^*)) = \left(\alpha w_{k^*} + (1-\alpha)v_{n,k^*}\right) \times \mathbf{1}(\hat{n}(k^*) \neq n) \times \mathbf{1}(v_{n,k^*} \geq \beta), \quad (1)$$

where **1** is an indicator function, $\alpha \in (0, 1)$ and β lies in the support of the valuations. The first term on the right-hand side of Eq. (1) accounts for the incremental bidding described in point 1 in the numbered list above.[4] Increments are a convex linear combination, parametrized by α, of the current winning price and valuation.[5] The second and third terms in Eq. (1) refer to the points 2 and 3 in the numbered list above, respectively. In particular, β defines the threshold below which that auction is disregarded.

Definition 2 Under a (α, β)-**nibbling strategy**, or simply nibbling, each bidder follows Eq. (1) each time she plays.

Of course, the above nibbling strategy allows for a number of different bidding behaviors. We will focus on two extreme cases, which we will denote as *hard* and *loose* nibblers, or H and L, respectively. Hard bidders *select* a priori just a few auctions (high β) to participate in, while then they bid relatively *aggressively* (low α).[6] In contrast, loose bidders are not a priori selective nor aggressive, thus, they have low β and high α, respectively. In other words, hard nibblers bid more than once, but cross-bid less than loose nibblers. When nibbling is assumed, both H and L are assumed to coexist.

5 Analysis

Our analysis is divided into a number of subsections. We first present the parameter values that define our benchmark scenario (Sect. 5.1). Then we compare second price and nibbling bidding strategies from the buyers' perspective (Sect. 5.2) and present descriptive statistics of the nibbling behavior (Sects. 5.3 and 5.4). Finally, some robustness analysis is presented (Sect. 5.5).

5.1 Setting and Computation Time

We perform a numerical analysis of the model using Monte Carlo (MC) simulations. Table 1 summarizes the parameter values used for this section, which will be generically labeled as the benchmark values. In Table 1, the first block of rows define the auction environment: number of bidders, objects, hard nibblers, number of periods and the probability law that generates the valuations. The second block defines the

---

[4] $\mathbf{1}(\mathscr{A}) = 1$ if event $\mathscr{A}$ occurs, while $\mathbf{1}(\mathscr{A}) = 0$ otherwise.

[5] Notice that Eq. (1) implicitly assumes $w_{k^*} < v_{n,k^*}$. Otherwise the bid would be below the current winning price and thus it would be irrelevant.

[6] The term a priori refers to the fact that the condition $v_{n,k} \geq \beta$, which defines whether bidder n wants to participate in auction k or not, can be checked before the bidding time starts.

Table 1 Benchmark parameter values

Parameter	Value	Brief description
N	20	Number of bidders
K	5	Number of objects
N_H	`round(0.3*N)`	Number of hard nibblers
T	5	Periods
$v_{n,k}$	i.i.d. draws U(0, 1)	Valuations
(α_H, α_L)	(0.7, 0.9)	Aggressiveness
(β_H, β_L)	(0.5, 0)	Selectivity
`MCtot`	2000	No. Montecarlo runs

nibbling strategy. Finally, the last row shows the number of MC simulations.[7] In the Appendix we compare some parameter values in Table 1 with evidence from eBay auctions. While some values are larger the difference is not huge once it has been taken into account the fact that we assumed a fairly heterogeneous pool of bidders, i.e., second price bidders, Hard and Loose nibblers and not all N bidders in our model bid in all auctions.

The computation time increases approximately linearly with the number of MC runs and the number of periods, while it increases quadratically with the number of bidders and objects. All other parameter values—within reasonable bounds—do not have a major impact on the computation time. Some numerical exploration shows that increasing the number of MC runs does not lead to sizable gains in terms of robustness of our results. We have also found that the results are qualitatively invariant as long as the ratio between the number of objects and the number of bidders is kept constant.

5.2 *Second Price Versus Nibbling*

This subsection deals with the comparison between second price and nibbling. More precisely, for each MC, we run for T periods with all bidders playing nibbling (H and L nibblers coexisting) and—for the same realizations of the valuations—we compute the corresponding outcomes when all bidders play second price. The fact that the same realizations are used under two different strategies generates paired samples, thus ensuring that the difference in the outcomes is not due to *more favorable* realizations for a specific strategy.

Let us consider bidders' surplus (valuation minus payment) as the starting point. The choice between second price and nibbling in terms of surplus is not trivial. The driving forces are emphasized in Tables 2 and 3. Both tables consider a setting with

[7]The code, written in `Python 3.6.5`, will be made available by the corresponding author upon request.

Table 2 Nibbling outperforms second price

Bidder	Object 1	Object 2
A	10	9
B	8	0
C	0	1

Table 3 Second price outperforms nibbling

Bidder	Object 1	Object 2
A	10	0
B	0	9
C	8	7

two objects on sale and three bidders. The numbers in the cells are the corresponding valuations. For instance, Table 2, shows that bidder A's valuation of object 1 is 10.

Consider first Table 2. Under the second price strategy, each bidder bids truthfully for his most valued object. Thus, A and B bid for object 1, A wins and gets a surplus $10 - 8 = 2$. Bidder C is the only bidder bidding for object 2, so she gets it for free and her surplus is 1. Summing across bidders, the total surplus is $2 + 1 = 3$. The key reason for which there is room for improvement is that A's valuation for object 2 and B's for object 1 are both *missed* while they have a huge advantage over the next highest valuation. In contrast, the valuations associated with the winning bids have a tight margin over its rivals.

Now, let us apply over those valuations a nibbling strategy in which all bidders have $\beta = 0$ and α is arbitrarily close to one. In words, all bidders consider participating in all auctions and the increments are very small. Still, B and C will only bid for object 1 and 2, respectively. Bidder A will start bidding for object 1 and, once she realizes that her opponent for object 1 is stronger than for object 2, she will switch to object 2. More specifically, C will stop bidding when the winning price for object 2 is 1. At that price A's surplus at that auction is $9 - 1 = 8$. Thus, when the race for object 1 between A and B hits the winning price 2, which delivers A surplus of 8, A will switch definitely to object 2, to obtain that surplus, thus B gets object 1 at price 2, which delivers her a surplus $9 - 2 = 7$. The total surplus is now $8 + 7 = 15$. It is worth noting that the nibbling strategy is based on private observation of the valuations and public observation of the current winning price, which is the standard in eBay auctions.

The valuations in Table 3, reverse the surplus-based ranking of strategies. Under second price, A gets object 1 with a surplus of $10 - 8 = 2$ while B gets object 2 with a surplus of 9, since C goes for object 1. The total surplus is $2 + 9 = 11$. The key point for having a higher total surplus under second price than under nibbling is that C, who is bound to loose in both auctions, under second price only increases the winning price in one auction, while by nibbling she increases the wining price in both. In effect, C will keep switching and bidding while rivals are bidding and her surplus is positive in some auction, which means that she will definitely quit auctions for objects 1 and 2 when the corresponding prices hit 8 and 7, respectively. That implies a total surplus of $10 - 8 + 9 - 7 = 4$.

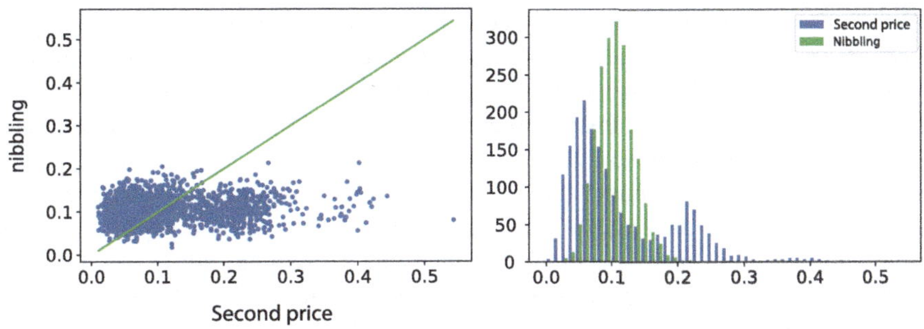

(a) Second price vs nibbling surplus. (b) Histogram of Second price vs nibbling surplus.

Fig. 1 Second price versus nibbling surplus

Table 4 Summary statistics for second price and nibbling surplus

	Mean	Std	Min	25%	50%	75%	Max
Second price	0.115	0.080	0.010	0.055	0.085	0.168	0.544
Nibbling	0.104	0.028	0.018	0.084	0.103	0.121	0.213

The outcome from the MC simulations regarding bidder's surplus is shown in Fig. 1. Each point in panel (a) in Fig. 1 is a MC run or, equivalently, a table of valuations since our data are from paired samples. Points above (below) the 45° line correspond to a MC run in which surplus under the nibbling strategy is greater (smaller) than under second price bidding.

The first essential message from Fig. 1, is that numerical analysis seems necessary, as there is not a clear ranking between second price and nibbling in terms of bidders' surplus. More precisely, such ranking is not clear in terms of *expected* surplus. Moreover, there is no correlation between surplus under the bidding strategies under consideration. Still, the figure reveals that surplus under second price (horizontal axis) has a much larger variability than under nibbling (vertical).

Panel (b) in Fig. 1, plots the (marginal) histograms of surplus under both strategies, thus disregarding the pairing. From the figure, it is apparent that the surplus has a much larger standard deviation under the second price than under nibbling, while the expected values are quite close to one another.

Finally, Table 4, summarizes Fig. 1. The table shows marginal statistics, thus ignoring pairing. There is no significant difference between the average surplus under the second price and nibbling at conventional significance levels (p-value 0.552), while—as a measure of dispersion—the inter-quantile range under second price is, roughly, three times higher than under nibbling. The same conclusion follows from the corresponding standard deviations. In a nutshell, our numerical analysis suggests that in real auction bidders do not nibble in order to attain a larger expected surplus but a lower variability in surplus.

Why is there more volatility under second price than under nibbling? Nibbling is a mechanism under which there is a transmission of information—through bids—across auctions. Our claim is that the correlation of bidding over different auctions tends to stabilize the surplus. Instead, second price bidding does clearly not generate any cross-auction correlation.

We report in the Appendix shows evidence for the comparison of payments. Essentially, the basic message follows analogously. The average payment is not significantly different under second price than under nibbling, while the standard deviation under second price bidding is much larger than under nibbling.

5.3 *Morphology of Nibbling*

This subsection analyzes the assignment generated by nibbling. The first question is to what extent this assignment is similar to the one generated by second price. We must first notice that the difference in assignments between these bidding strategies can be due to the fact the second price might leave objects unassigned. It might be the case, for instance, that object 1 is the most valued for all bidders, which implies that—under second price bidding—no bidder will bid for an object other than object 1. If so, except object 1, the others will be unassigned.

By using the valuations in Table 2, we can assess whether there are coincidences between assignments—or winners—under second price and nibbling. We report this in Table 5, which shows that there are no coincidences in winners: though A wins an object under both bidding strategies, they are different objects.

In addition, we report in Fig. 2, the percentage of coincidences for the same object over MC runs. The figure shows that the modal value is slightly lower than 40% of coincidences, which is labeled as 0.4 on the horizontal axis, among the assignments under both bidding strategies in 700 MC runs (out of 2000). The histogram is unimodal and approximately symmetric, with the largest percentage of realized coincidences, 80%, occurring in less than 100 MC runs.[8]

Next, we turn our attention to switching, that is, the same bidder bidding in different auctions (within a given MC run or, equivalently, for a given set of valuations). We pose two questions: how much switching does actually occur? Does switching pay off? The first question is just a matter of counting. The second is more subtle since switching might pay off to other bidders than the switcher. For instance, taking again the valuations in Table 2 and the nibbling bidding, bidder A switches from object 1 to 2 and that greatly benefits B (while it harms C). This suggests that measuring externalities precisely can be a complex task.

We answer the first question by using the evidence reported in Fig. 3. This shows in panel (a) the average number of switches. For each MC run, the number of switches for each bidder goes from 0 to $T-1$. For instance, a bidder that bids for object 1

[8]Recall than under the benchmark parameter values, in Table 1, it is $K=5$, so 0.4 means 2 out of 5 possible coincidences.

Table 5 Winners for the valuations reported in Table 2

	Object 1	Object 2
Second price	*A*	*C*
Nibbling	*B*	*A*

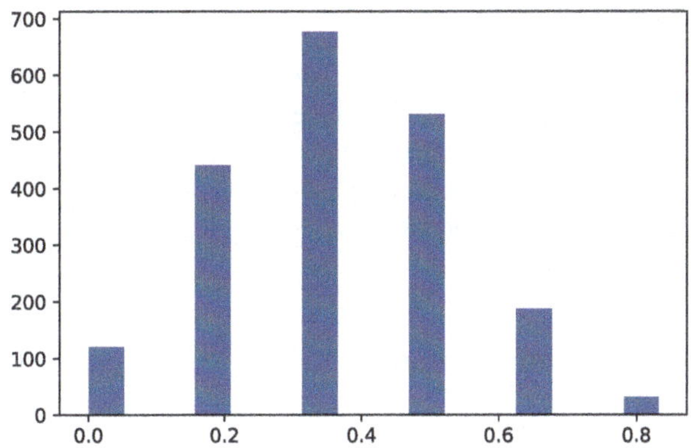

Fig. 2 Histogram of coincidences in winners between second price and nibbling

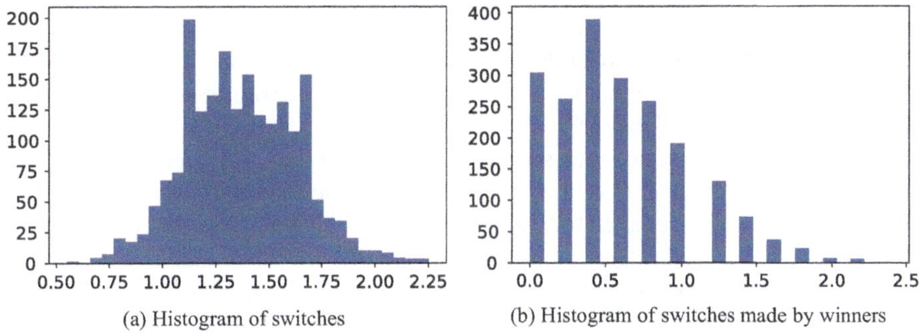

Fig. 3 Switches

in even periods and bids for object 2 in odd periods, switches $T - 1$ times. For the benchmark values, with $T = 5$, the number of switches ranks from 0 to 4. For each MC run, we compute the cross-bidder average of switches. The figure shows that, roughly, 1.3 is the median. The important message is the comparison with panel (b), which shows that winners tend to switch less.

Figure 3 does not account for externalities. It is important to remark at this point that switching decisions are purely based on the own interest of the switcher and just based on observed prices (rather than valuations). Furthermore, in our nibbling bidding strategy, defined in Eq. (1), all bidders act as price-takers in the sense that they do not anticipate the effect of switching in future rival behavior. In short, the mechanism has quite a *competitive* rather than *strategic* flavor. To answer the sec-

Table 6 Regression of surplus on average switching

	Coef.	Std. err.
Switch	0.0238***	0.0023
Const	0.0712***	0.0032

$^{*}p < 0.10$, $^{**}p < 0.05$, $^{***}p < 0.01$

ond aforementioned question, i.e., whether switching increases surplus, we use the evidence in Table 6. This table reports estimated coefficients of the regression of surplus on the average number of switching times and it shows a positive and significant association between switching and surplus. This suggests a positive and significant association between switching and surplus.

5.4 Hard Versus Loose Nibblers

So far in our analysis, we have analyzed nibbling without taking into account that the nibbling strategy is not homogeneous. Hard nibblers, denoted by H, are very selective, they just choose a priori to participate in auctions for which their corresponding valuation is high enough and they bid aggressively in those auctions, in the sense that their bids are always relatively close to their valuations. In contrast, loose nibblers, denoted by L, are not a priori selective and their bidding is less aggressive. Which strategy performs better?

As in the comparison between second price and nibbling, we can think of simplified examples in favor of H or L nibblers. Clearly, the (comparative) drawback of H is that they miss the chance to win low-price low-valued objects even though the higher valued ones lead to lower surplus. In contrast, their advantage is that they are *faster* in inducing rivals to quit their targeted auctions. Table 7 provides valuations under which H outperforms L's.

Table 7 shows three bidders' valuations for two objects. Bidder A is a H nibbler while bidders B and C are both L's. Assume that, prior to bidding, the value of β, which is larger for H than for L, is such that A decides to go only for object 1 while B and C are willing to go for both objects. Whenever they bid, let α_H and α_L denote the corresponding bidding parameters for H and L, respectively (see Eq. 1). The argument that follows does not really depend on the ordering of bidding, but it can

Table 7 H nibbler outperforms L's

Bidder	Object 1	Object 2
A (hard)	10	2
B (loose)	10	5
C (loose)	10	2

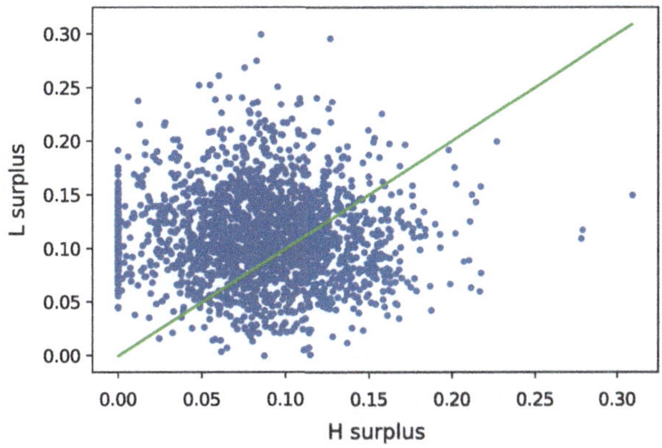

Fig. 4 Intra-group cross-bidder average of H versus L nibbler surplus. The green line is the 45° line. Each point is an MC run

be made simpler if we assume that the ordering is A, B, C in the first period and then any ordering in subsequent periods. Following Eq. (1), A starts bidding $(1-\alpha_H)10$ for object 1. Clearly, if $\alpha_H \leq \frac{1}{2}$, then B and C will not bid for object 1 thereafter, which gives A object 1 and a surplus $\alpha_H 10$. In turn, B and C engage in a competition for object 2. If α_L is close enough to one, C will quit when the winning price is close enough to 2, which gives B object 2 and a surplus of $5-2=3$. Thus, for any α_H in $\left(\frac{3}{10}, \frac{1}{2}\right)$ and $\alpha_L \rightarrow 1$, H has higher surplus than B and C despite A's valuations for each object are not higher than *any* of her rivals. The key is that A has "expelled" her rivals from object 1 with just her first bid, while B, who is bound to win the race for object 2 thereafter, is not able to make her rival quit until the corresponding price hits her rival's valuation.[9]

Figure 4 reports for each MC shown as a point the intra-group cross-bidder average surplus for L on the horizontal axis and for H on the vertical one, analogously to panel (a) in Fig. 1. Points above the 45° line are MC runs (set of valuations) under which surplus for L is larger than for H. The further away from the diagonal, the larger the difference. The figure reveals a greater mass of points above the diagonal. There is a number of MC runs under which the H do not get any object, which means their surplus is zero, and the corresponding points lie on the vertical line at zero on the horizontal axis. Table 8 complements Fig. 4 by reporting only the number of wins, regardless of the surplus for each win. Again, it shows a clear dominance of L's over H's strategy.

[9]Of course, not only the valuations but the choice of $\alpha_H \in \left(\frac{3}{10}, \frac{1}{2}\right)$ is essential for the result. A lower value of α_H would expel A's rivals from auction 1 in A's first bid as well, but A's surplus would also be lower. A higher value of α_H would not expel B in A's first bid, which would imply also a lower surplus for A.

Table 8 Number of wins for H and L nibblers across MC runs

Value	H wins	L wins
0	134	1
1	546	84
2	830	404
3	404	830
4	84	546
5	1	134

5.5 Robustness

A number of variations to the benchmark parameter values have been explored, all them showing that findings are qualitatively robust. We split our robustness analysis into two parts, that we label as fixed and random effects. Fixed effects have to do with deterministic elements: the percentage of Hard versus Loose nibblers or how much difference is there between both types of nibblers. Random effects deal with variations in the distributional assumptions on the valuations. In order to shorten the presentation, we focus on the comparison of surplus.

5.5.1 Fixed Effects

In Fig. 5, we report surplus from a setting with a large percentage of Hard nibblers, panels (a) and (b) and the opposite setting, that is, with a low percentage of hard nibblers (equivalently, a large percentage of loose), panels (c) and (d). Specifically, we have changed the row for N_H in Table 1, containing the benchmark values, to `round(0.7*N)` and `round(0.1*N)` for the case of large and low percentage of hard nibblers, respectively, while all other parameters are kept at the benchmark values. Results in panels (a) and (b) are in line with the ones in Fig. 1, and so are (c) and (d). An increase in the percentage of Hard nibblers reduces the variance of nibblers' surplus.

Figure 6 keeps the percentage of Hard nibblers at its benchmark value, while it increases the difference in behavior between Hard and Loose nibblers. That difference has two dimensions: aggressiveness and selectiveness. Hard bidders are more aggressive than Loose as the former bid closer to their valuations. We have parametrized aggressiveness with α, in Eq. (1), such that nibblers are more aggressive as α decreases. Panels (a) and (b) of Fig. 6 are obtained under $\alpha_H = 0.2$, while its benchmark value, in Table 1, is 0.7 for Hard and 0.9 for Loose nibblers.

A second dimension in which Hard and Loose nibblers differ is selectiveness. Hard nibblers focus on a smaller range of auctions than Loose nibblers or, equivalently, Hard nibblers just bid when the valuation is large enough. We parametrize

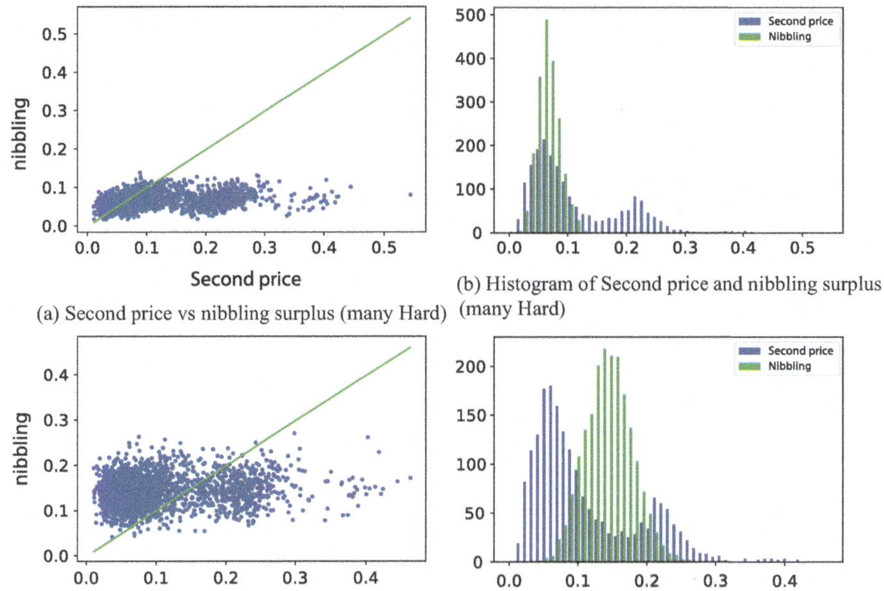

(a) Second price vs nibbling surplus (many Hard)

(b) Histogram of Second price and nibbling surplus (many Hard)

(c) Second price vs nibbling surplus for (few Hard)

(d) Histogram of Second price and nibbling surplus (few Hard)

Fig. 5 Fixed effects variations I: many versus few hard nibblers

selectiveness with β, in Eq. (1), with selectiveness increasing with β. Panels (c) and (d) of Fig. 6 are obtained under $\beta_H = 0.8$, while its benchmark value, in Table 1, is 0.5 for Hard and 0 for Loose nibblers. Finally, panels (e) and (f) show results for simultaneous variations in selectiveness and aggressiveness.

5.5.2 Random Effects: Distributional Assumptions

Next, we present results for different distributional assumptions on the valuations. In particular, we have considered Beta-distributed valuations. The benchmark model assumes that valuations are uniformly distributed, which is a $Beta(1, 1)$ probability distribution. More generally, all $Beta(a, b)$ distributions with $a = b$ are symmetric. In addition, when $a = b < 1$ holds, the distribution is bi-modal, the modes being 0 and 1. In turn, the cases $a = b > 1$ are unimodal, thus the mode is $\frac{1}{2}$. We have assumed that valuations are distributed as $Beta\left(\frac{1}{2}, \frac{1}{2}\right)$ and $Beta(2, 2)$, which we simply refer to as *bimodal* and *unimodal* valuations hereafter.

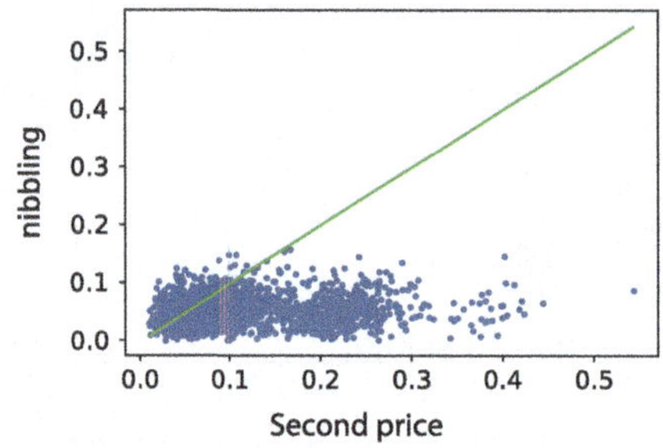

(a) Second price vs nibbling surplus (very aggressive)

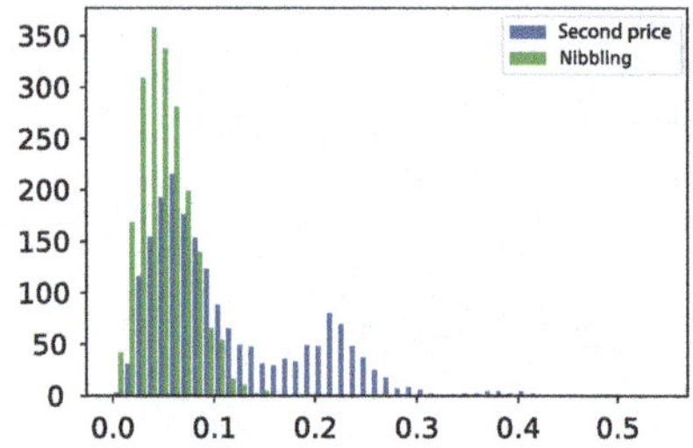

(b) Histogram of Second price and nibbling surplus (very aggressive)

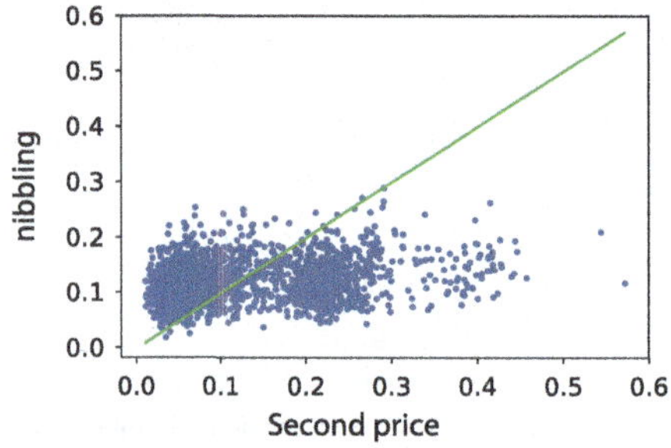

(c) Second price vs nibbling surplus for (very selective)

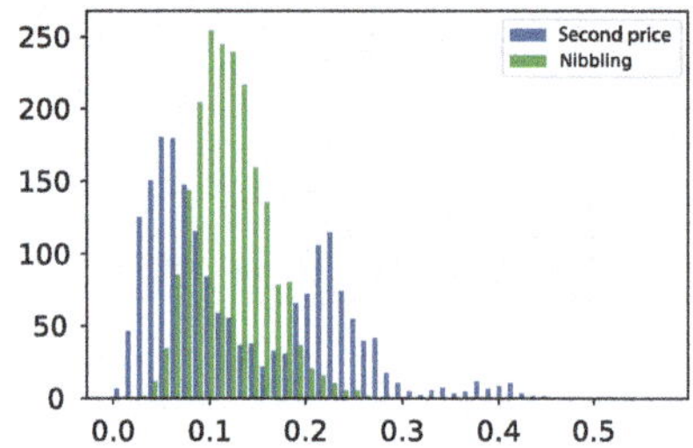

(d) Histogram of Second price and nibbling surplus (very selective)

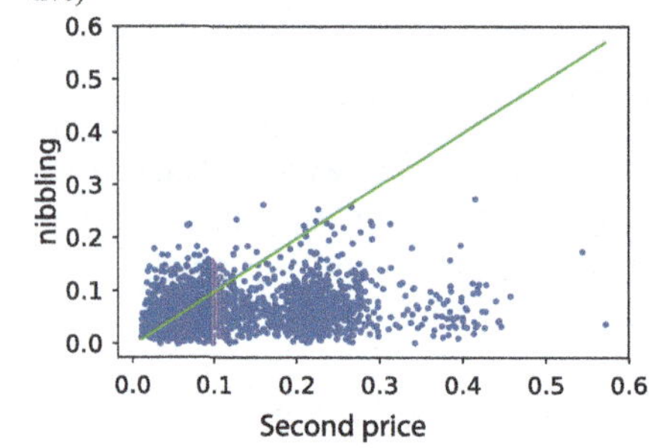

(e) Second price vs nibbling surplus for (very aggressive and selective)

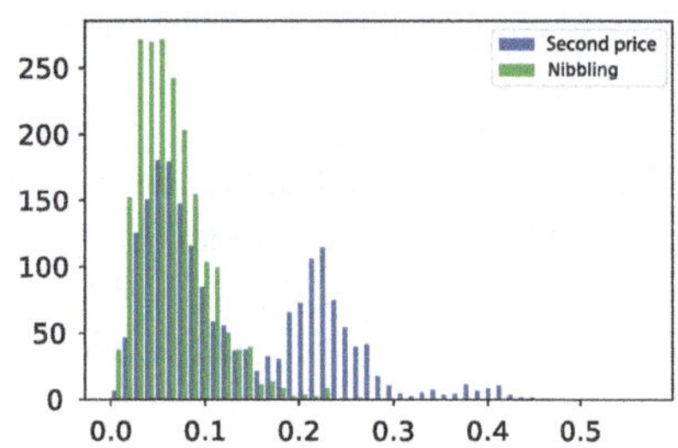

(f) Histogram of Second price and nibbling surplus (very aggressive and selective)

Fig. 6 Fixed effects variations II: aggressiveness and selectiveness

Results are reported in Fig. 7. Panel (a) and (b) are the counterparts of Fig. 1 for the case of unimodal valuations, with the green line in the panel being the 45° line and each point an MC run. Panel (c) and (d) present the analogous results for the bi-modal case. As mentioned before, surplus under nibbling strategy exhibits considerably less variability than under second price bidding in all cases.

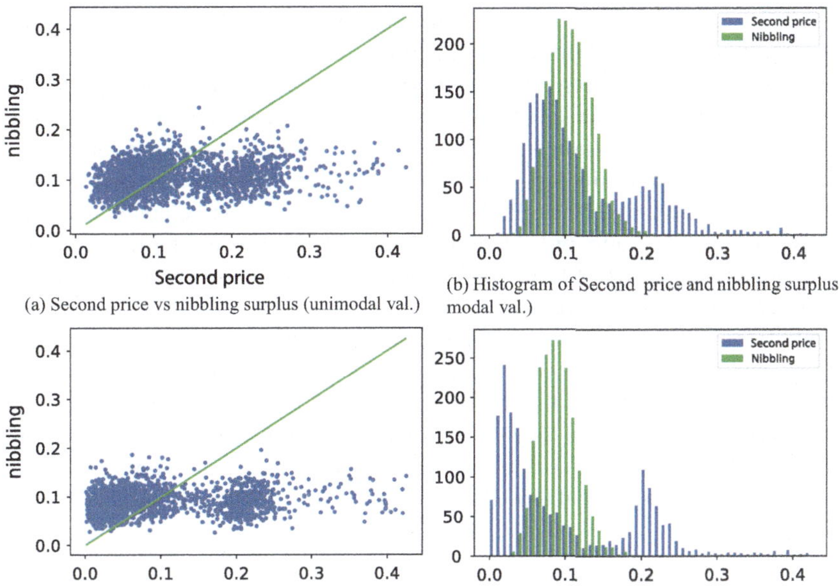

(a) Second price vs nibbling surplus (unimodal val.)

(b) Histogram of Second price and nibbling surplus (unimodal val.)

(c) Second price vs nibbling surplus for (bimodal val.)

(d) Histogram of Second price and nibbling surplus (bimodal val.)

Fig. 7 Random effects variations: Beta distributed valuations

6 Conclusion

This paper aims to provide a theoretical framework to study a market composed of several single object auctions that run simultaneously over time, in each auction bidders are allowed to update bids over some bidding period and the objects on sale are perceived as imperfect substitutes by the pool of bidders, who face no search nor switching costs to cross-bid in different auctions. Following one of the most worldwide known such markets, we have named this as eBay-like environment. Our main motivation is to explore justifications underlying two observed facts in bidding behavior in this environment: bidders bid incrementally in an auction, which is usually termed as nibbling, and the same bidder bids in different auctions over time, that is, there is cross-bidding.

Our results, obtained using standard numerical methods, suggest that a certain combination of nibbling and cross-bidding reduces the variability of bidders' surplus, while it has a low marginal impact in terms of expected surplus, as compared to a sharper bidding strategy under which bidders commit themselves to participate in just the auction for their highest valued object (which eliminates cross-bidding) and to bid truthfully in that auction (which eliminates nibbling).

Although we have explored the qualitative robustness of the main results to a number of variations in the values of parameters and distributional assumptions in the numerical methods we used, we consider this as a first step. Particularly, we believe that a fruitful path for future research is testing our predictions with experimental and nonexperimental data. Within eBay auctions, it would be interesting to explore the capacity of our setting to predict the observed amount of cross-bidding, ideally by creating a large meta-dataset obtained by combining existing datasets on eBay auctions used in different studies. Furthermore, our model assumes the coexistence of behaviorally different nibblers, that is, nibblers who differ not in their ex-ante valuations but in their strategies. Probably, this heterogeneous behavior is present in any given set of real auctions. One interesting exercise would be to use data to calibrate our modelization of heterogeneity and then use the model to predict their impact on the auction's outcome.

An additional extension might be of interest. Three stylized facts have been consistently reported in empirical works: nibbling, cross-bidding, and sniping. The latter consists of submitting last minute bids. Thus snipers are not nibblers and are not cross-bidders in the sense that they do not participate in different auctions simultaneously. Sniping has not been considered in this paper. To the best of our knowledge, to rationalize the coexistence of those three bidding strategies in real markets remains an open question.

Appendix

Benchmark Values and a Sample from eBay

Alvarado Guevara (2019) analyzes a dataset of two hundred eBay auctions which were randomly selected between March and April 2019. The auctioned items were secondhand mobile phones, which makes the sample relatively homogeneous. For each auction, the whole bidding record was downloaded by the author just after the termination of the auction.[10] This subsection discusses to what extent the benchmark values used in our paper are in line with statistics computed from that sample.

In our model, N is the number of bidders within an auction. Figure 8 plots, for each auction in the sample, the number of bidders against duration, computed as the difference between the opening of the auction and the last bid. While the red line shows that the average number of bidders is 10.84, it is higher for auctions using the eBay standard 7 days closing rule and closer to our benchmark $N = 20$.

In our model, T is the number of times each bidder bids under nibbling (assumed exogenous in our model). Any given bidder in our model does not bid all of the T rounds in the same auction. Thus, the observed sample statistic of bids per bidder within an auction should be taken as a lower bound for T. Table 9 shows some percentiles of the distribution of bids per bidder. Our benchmark value is $T = 5$.

Finally, K is the number of auctions that each bidder considers simultaneously. Clearly, some bidders might bid in auctions within our sample and in bids in other

[10]The raw data can be supplied on request from the corresponding author of this paper.

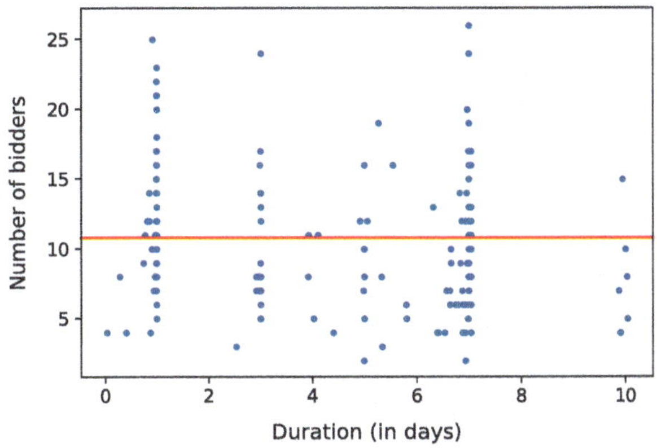

Fig. 8 Number of bidders versus duration (in days). Each dot corresponds to an auction. Duration is computed as the difference between the opening time and the time when the last bid was submitted. The red line is the average of the number of bidders, which is 10.84

Table 9 Percentiles of bids per bidder

0%	25%	50%	75%	100%
1	1.83	2.26	3	7.44

auctions. Thus, the cross-bidding within our sample must be understood as a lower bound of the actual cross-bidding. Only 14% of the bidders of the sample bid in more than one auction (among the auctions in the sample). Among those bidders, the average number of auctions is 2.85, while we have taken $K = 5$ as benchmark value.

We do not try to justify all other benchmark values using sample statistics. The percentage of hard nibblers, α and β essentially define the strategy space under consideration. To elicit behavioral rules from observed bids constitutes an interesting—and not trivial—question in itself, which we consider beyond the scope of this paper. A similar comment applies to the probability distributions generating valuations.

Second Price Versus Nibbling Payments

See Fig. 9 and Table 10.

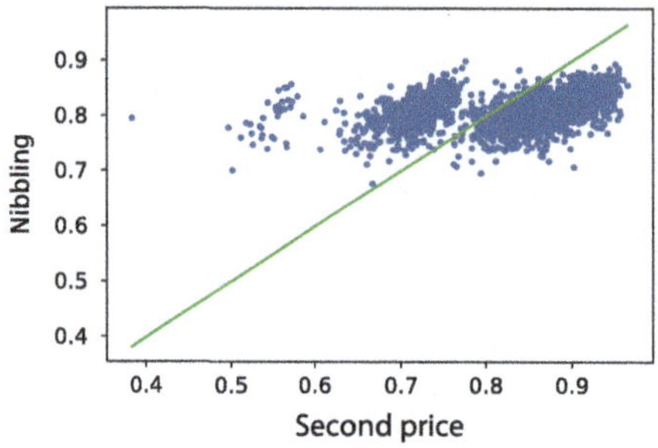

(a) Second price vs nibbling payment

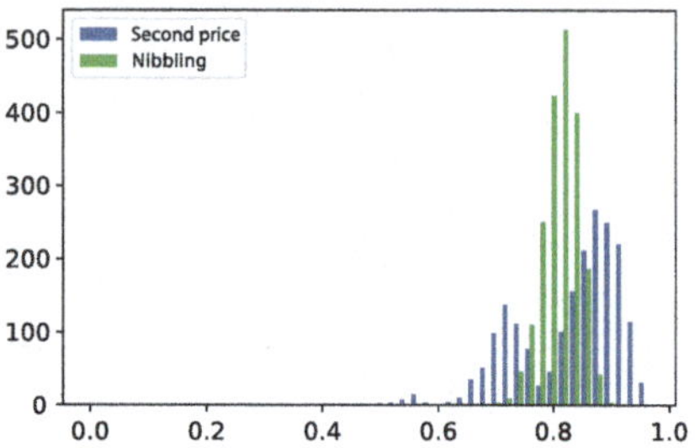

(b) Histogram of Second price and nibbling payment

Fig. 9 Histograms of second price and nibbling payment

Table 10 Summary statistics for second price and nibbling payment

	Mean	Std	Min	25%	50%	75%	Max
Second price	0.827	0.089	0.383	0.750	0.857	0.895	0.965
Nibbling	0.811	0.031	0.685	0.792	0.813	0.833	0.906

References

Alvarado Guevara, E. (2019). *Efecto sniping y nibling sobre el precio de subastas en ebay*. mimeo Universidad Complutense de Madrid.

Alvarez, F., & Sartarelli, M. (2020). *Nibbling and sniping in eBay auctions*. Documentos de Trabajo del ICAE 2020-04, Universidad Complutense de Madrid.

Ambrus, A., Ishii, Y., & Burns, J. (2013). *Gradual bidding in eBay-like auctions*. Economic Research Initiatives (ERID) Working Paper 129, Duke University.

Anthony, P., & Jennings, N. R. (2002). Evolving bidding strategies for multiple auctions. In *European coordinating committee for artificial intelligence* (pp. 178–182). IOS Press.

Anwar, S., McMillan, R., & Zheng, M. (2006). Bidding behavior in competing auctions: Evidence from eBay. *European Economic Review*, *50*(2), 307–322.

Backus, M., Blake, T., Masterov, D. V., & Tadelis, S. (2015). *Is sniping a problem for online auction markets?* Working Paper 20942, National Bureau of Economic Research.

Backus, M., Podwol, J. U., & Schneider, H. S. (2014). Search costs and equilibrium price dispersion in auction markets. *European Economic Review*, *71*, 173–192.

Byde, A., Preist, C., & Jennings, N. R. (2002). Decision procedures for multiple auctions. In *Proceedings of the First International Joint Conference on Autonomous Agents and Multiagent Systems: Part 2* (pp. 613–620). ACM.

Camerer, C. F., Loewenstein, G., & Rabin, M. (2011). *Advances in behavioral economics*. Princeton University Press.

Chang, S. A. (2014). Multiple overlapping online auction market: Bidder strategic mixture analysis using entropy. *Decision Support Systems*, *64*, 57–66.

Chernev, A., Böckenholt, U., & Goodman, J. (2015). Choice overload: A conceptual review and meta-analysis. *Journal of Consumer Psychology*, *25*(2), 333–358.

Ely, J. C., & Hossain, T. (2009). Sniping and squatting in auction markets. *American Economic Journal: Microeconomics*, *1*(2), 68–94.

Hossain, T. (2008). Learning by bidding. *The RAND Journal of Economics*, *39*(2), 509–529.

Hossain, T., & Morgan, J. (2006). Plus shipping and handling: Revenue (non) equivalence in field experiments on eBay. *The B.E. Journal of Economic Analysis & Policy*, *5*(2).

Ma, H., & Leung, H.-F. (2007). An adaptive attitude bidding strategy for agents in continuous double auctions. *Electronic Commerce Research and Applications*, *6*, 383–398.

Milgrom, P. R., & Weber, R. J. (1982). A theory of auctions and competitive bidding. *Econometrica*, 1089–1122.

Ockenfels, A., & Roth, A. E. (2006). Late and multiple bidding in second price internet auctions: Theory and evidence concerning different rules for ending an auction. *Games and Economic Behavior*, *55*(2), 297–320.

Rasmusen, E. (2006). Strategic implications of uncertainty over one's own private value in auctions. *The B.E. Journal of Theoretical Economics*, *6*(1), 1–22.

Roth, A. E., & Ockenfels, A. (2002). Last-minute bidding and the rules for ending second-price auctions: Evidence from eBay and Amazon auctions on the internet. *American Economic Review*, *92*(4), 1093–1103.

Tesfatsion, L. (2003). Agent-based computational economics: Modeling economies as complex adaptive systems. *Information Sciences*, *149*(4), 262–268.

Vadovič, R. (2017). Bidding behavior and price search in internet auctions. *International Journal of Industrial Organization*, *54*, 125–147.

Risk–Reward Ratio Optimisation (Revisited)

Manfred Gilli and Enrico Schumann

Abstract We study the empirical performance of alternative risk and reward specifications in portfolio selection. In particular, we look at models that take into account asymmetry of returns, and treat losses and gains differently. In tests on a dataset of German equities, we find that portfolios constructed with the help of such models generally outperform the market index and in many cases also the risk-based benchmark (minimum variance). In part, higher returns can be explained by exposure to factors such as momentum and value. Nevertheless, a substantial part of the performance cannot be explained by standard asset-pricing models.

1 Introduction

The primary goal of this chapter is not exciting to non-scientists: we want to redo something we already did; we want to replicate a previous study. (We said primary goal: we add some new material too.)

In Gilli and Schumann (2011b), we examined a large number of alternative specifications for portfolio-selection models. The key results were: (i) primarily risk-based and even completely risk-based investing lead to portfolios with attractive risk–reward characteristics, and (ii) risk definitions that captured asymmetry, i.e. differentiated between losses and gains, worked better than symmetric risk definitions such as volatility.

In this chapter, we attempt to replicate these findings. Replication does not mean that we rerun old code and try to come up with the very same numbers. It is meant

M. Gilli
School of Economics and Management and Swiss Finance Institute, University of Geneva, Geneva, Switzerland
e-mail: Manfred.Gilli@unige.ch

E. Schumann (✉)
CPV/CAP Pensionskasse Coop, Basel, Switzerland
e-mail: es@enricoschumann.net

University of Basel, Basel, Switzerland

H. Dawid and J. Arifovic (eds.), *Dynamic Analysis in Complex Economic Environments*, Dynamic Modeling and Econometrics in Economics and Finance 26,
https://doi.org/10.1007/978-3-030-52970-3_3

in a qualitative sense. That is, we see whether we can confirm (i) and (ii), but with a new data set, which also covers the time after Gilli and Schumann (2011b) and in particular the financial crisis 2007–2008, and with a new implementation of all algorithms.[1]

1.1 Risk-Based Investing

It all starts with Markowitz (1952), who argued persuasively that investors should (and do) care about risk. Hence, risk should be one key element when constructing a portfolio. Early on, his choice of a risk measure—variance of portfolio return—was criticised. After all, not all return variation is perceived as bad by investors. Still, because it was simple and tractable, it was quickly adopted in research and practice. (In practice mostly for measuring investment performance ex-post; it would take many years before it was also used in computer programmes that actually implemented Markowitz's decision rule.)

Irrespective of how risk is measured, it turned out that including and even emphasising risk was beneficial not only in a normative, 'a rational investor should do this' sense.

For one, there is the literature on the troubles of 'estimating' the input parameters in the portfolio optimisation. Several studies, e.g. Broadie (1993) or Chopra and Ziemba (1993), showed that the much-criticised choice of variance as the risk measure was not really the cause of trouble, but the expected returns were.

It is by now a stylised fact of equity markets that risk—in the sense of return variability—is persistent. That makes sense: whether volatility is driven by the fundamental riskiness of a business, or by fads and fashions (Shiller 1984): neither cause is completely erratic. Investors who have preferences about risk (and most have) can exploit this persistence to build portfolios that suit their preferences.[2]

But it is not only that we can control risk. Empirical studies also showed that the CAPM-implied relationship between risk and reward—more reward comes with more risk—does not hold. Indeed, in the cross section of stocks, risk-bearing is not rewarded.

---

[1]Software and implementations matter a great deal for reliable results; see Merali (2010). The computations for Gilli and Schumann (2011b) were implemented in MATLAB, making use of the Myrinet Cluster of the University of Geneva. For more details see http://spc.unige.ch/doku.php?id=computing_resources. In this study, all optimisation algorithms are written in R (R Core Team 2017) and we make them freely available in the NMOF package (https://github.com/enricoschumann/NMOF; Gilli et al. 2019; Schumann 2011–2018). For the walk-forward backtests, we use the PMwR package (Schumann 2008–2018); again, we make the software freely available (https://github.com/enricoschumann/PMwR). All computations are done on a work station running Lubuntu Linux with an Intel Core i7-5820K CPU @ 3.30 GHz (12 cores) with 64 GB RAM.

[2]Many institutional investors, notably pension funds, work under tracking-error restrictions. For such investors, being able to control portfolio risk is important to fulfil their mandate.

The first chapters that documented this apparent anomaly date back to the 1970s (e.g. Black et al. 1972). The results have been interpreted in two ways: The mild—or modest—interpretation is that return differences in the cross section of stocks cannot be explained by risk at all. Whether one buys low-risk or high-risk stocks, one gets on average the same return. As a consequence, one should buy low-risk stocks, because then risk-adjusted returns will be higher (Black et al. 1972; Chan et al. 1999). The more aggressive interpretation says that returns from low-risk stocks are not only comparable with those of high-risk stocks, but even higher (Haugen and Heins 1972).

This more aggressive interpretation has received empirical support in recent years, in several forms: in the good performance of low-β stocks (Frazzini and Pedersen 2014), and conversely in the bad performance of stocks with high (idiosyncratic) volatility, as described in Ang et al. (2006, 2009).

These advantages of low-risk investing motivated much research into better ways to estimate/forecast risk; see, for instance, Ledoit and Wolf (2004). Alternative approaches provide improvements, indeed, though it seems hard to identify a best method (Chan et al. 1999; Disatnik and Benninga 2007). This research, however, considered exclusively variance as a measure for risk.

1.2 Alternative Measures of Risk

There is much less research that addresses the long-standing criticism of Markowitz's choice of a risk measure: only a few studies have reported results when variance is replaced by alternative specifications of risk, which take into account the asymmetry of returns. One important reason for this lack of research is the difficulty to optimise portfolios with such objective functions, in particular in conjunction with constraints and real-world data, since the resulting optimisation problems are often not convex and cannot be solved with standard techniques (such as linear or quadratic programming). The few existing chapters (e.g. Biglova et al. 2004; Farinelli et al. 2008) consequently either use only a small number of assets and do not include realistic conditions such as transaction costs, or restrict themselves to those models to which standard solvers can be applied (e.g. Racheva-Iotova and Stoyanov 2008).

In sum, there exists little evidence regarding the general value-added of alternative measures when applied in portfolio optimisation. On the contrary, there are studies that compare the rankings of funds (hedge funds, in particular) according to downside risk measures with those obtained from Sharpe ratios. Rankings ignore correlations and may thus not be equivalent to a full portfolio optimisation; yet, the results of these studies are quite clear: while funds' returns often do not have Gaussian distributions, the Sharpe rankings are virtually identical to rankings based on alternative performance measures (Eling and Schuhmacher 2007; Brooks and Kat 2002).

1.3 *Outline of the Study*

To summarise: much empirical evidence is in favour of risk-based investing, which has also been recognised by the industry in recent years. There are many details to this (e.g. the way data are handled to come up with forecasts of risk), but in this study we wish to ask a narrower question: how does the definition of risk affect portfolio performance? To provide an answer, we follow Gilli and Schumann (2011b) and analyse the results of a number of risk measures that take into account asymmetry of returns, i.e. risk measures that differentiate between gains and losses.

Our aim is not to find a 'best' risk measure; rather, we look whether particular classes of functions—partial moments, say—are useful building blocks for portfolio optimisation.

The remainder of the chapter is structured as follows: in Sect. 2, we briefly outline the various models that we test. Section 3 describes the dataset that we use and our general methodology; results follow in Sect. 4. Finally, Sect. 5 concludes the chapter.

2 Models

We use one-period optimisation models. We are endowed with an initial wealth v_0 and may choose from a universe $\mathcal{A}$ of $n_{\mathcal{A}}$ assets. The cardinality of the selected subset of assets we denote by k.

Next, we outline different rules and models by which portfolios can be selected. We generally refer to these methods as 'strategies'.

2.1 *Constructive Rules*

2.1.1 1/N

The equal-weight portfolio, made popular by DeMiguel et al. (2009). We invest in every asset in $\mathcal{A}$ and all weights are set to $1/n_{\mathcal{A}}$.

2.1.2 SORT-20

As in Schumann (2013), we compute the volatilities of all assets and invest 5% into each of the 20 stocks with the lowest volatility. (There is nothing special about 20; there could be SORT- 25, SORT- 33, and so on, as well.)

2.2 *Optimisation Models*

The generic model that we solve is

$$\min_{w} \phi(w). \tag{1}$$

The objective function ϕ also depends on the available data and other parameters; but for an optimisation run, these other arguments are fixed and we write ϕ as a function only of portfolio weights w. The objective function is subject to the budget constraint: since we assume fully funded investments, it takes the form

$$\sum_{i=1}^{n_{\mathcal{A}}} w_i = 1 . \tag{2}$$

Furthermore, we enforce lower and upper bounds on weights:

$$0 \leqslant w_i \leqslant w_i^{\max} \quad \forall i . \tag{3}$$

We implement UCITS-compliant weight constraints, which means that

$$w_i^{\max} = 10\% \quad \forall i , \tag{4}$$

$$\sum_{\{i \,:\, w_i > 5\%\}} w_i \leqslant 40\% . \tag{5}$$

These holding-size constraints are often referred to as the 5/10/40 rule, as set by the UCITS directive. Additionally, we set a cardinality constraint and require

$$k \leqslant 33 . \tag{6}$$

A lower cardinality of 16 assets is implied by the 5/10/40 rule.[3,4]

2.2.1 Minimum Variance

Our primary benchmark model is the long-only minimum-variance (MV) portfolio, for which

---

[3]In practice, a portfolio manager will often fix maximum weights slightly below these limits. Otherwise, the limits may too easily be exceeded as a result of changing market prices. While such so-called passive breaches may be treated more leniently, they may nevertheless force the manager to trade eventually.

[4]A small number of assets in the portfolio is sometimes preferred by portfolio managers as it reduces operational effort, and also allows to maintain an intuitive grasp of the portfolio.

$$\phi(w) = w'\hat{\Sigma}w\,, \tag{7}$$

with $\hat{\Sigma}$ being a forecast of the variance–covariance matrix. Section 3.2 describes the data used to compute unknown quantities. For completeness, we also compute a minimum-MAD portfolio.

2.2.2 Risk/Reward Ratios

As in Gilli and Schumann (2011b), we define generic risk/reward ratios as objective functions:

$$\phi(w) = {}^{\text{risk}}/_{\text{reward}}\,. \tag{8}$$

Such ratios are widely accepted in the financial industry, and they offer a straightforward interpretation as required risk per unit of return. For risk and reward, we use various building blocks:

Partial Moments

Partial moments are a convenient way to capture return asymmetry around a threshold θ. For a sample of n return scenarios, partial moments $\mathcal{P}_\gamma(\theta)$ can be computed as

$$\mathcal{P}_\gamma^+(\theta) = \frac{1}{n} \sum_{\{i\,:\,r_i>\theta\}} (r_i - \theta)^\gamma\,, \tag{9a}$$

$$\mathcal{P}_\gamma^-(\theta) = \frac{1}{n} \sum_{\{i\,:\,r_i<\theta\}} (\theta - r_i)^\gamma\,. \tag{9b}$$

The superscripts $+$ and $-$ indicate the tail (i.e. upside or downside). Partial moments take two more parameters, an exponent γ and the threshold θ. The partial moment of order zero is simply the probability of obtaining a return beyond θ.

Partial moments have a long tradition in the financial literature—see e.g. Fishburn (1977)—and are used as risk functions in ex-post measures such as the Sortino and the Upside Potential ratio (Sortino et al. 1999).

Conditional Moments

Conditional moments can be calculated as

$$\mathcal{C}^{+}_{\gamma}(\theta) = \frac{1}{\#\{r_i > \theta\}} \sum_{\{i\,:\,r_i>\theta\}} (r_i - \theta)^{\gamma}\,, \tag{10a}$$

$$\mathcal{C}^{-}_{\gamma}(\theta) = \frac{1}{\#\{r_i < \theta\}} \sum_{\{i\,:\,r_i<\theta\}} (\theta - r_i)^{\gamma}\,. \tag{10b}$$

Again, + and − indicate the tail; and '$\#\{r_i > \theta\}$' stands for the number of returns greater than θ.

Conditional moments measure the magnitude of returns around θ, while partial moments also take into account the probability of such returns.

Quantiles

A quantile of a sample $r = [r_1\ r_2\ \ldots]'$ is defined as

$$\mathcal{Q}_q = \text{CDF}^{-1}(q) = \min\{r \mid \text{CDF}(r) \geq q\}\,,$$

in which CDF is the cumulative distribution function and q may range from 0 to 100% (we omit the %-sign in subscripts).

Quantiles can also be used as reward measures; we could maximise a higher quantile (e.g. the 90th). We need to be careful when we construct ratios of quantiles, since ideally we would want to maximise all quantiles (i.e. move the return distribution to the right). We use quantiles far in the tails, so we can form ratios of the form $-\mathcal{Q}_{\text{lo}}/\mathcal{Q}_{\text{hi}}$; nevertheless, we check that $\mathcal{Q}_{\text{lo}}$ is below zero, and $\mathcal{Q}_{\text{hi}}$ is above.

Drawdown

Let v be a time series of portfolio values, with observations at $t = 0, 1, 2, \ldots T$. Then the drawdown (DD) of this series at time t is defined as

$$\text{DD}_t = v_t^{\max} - v_t \tag{11}$$

in which $v_t^{\max}$ is the running maximum, i.e. $v_t^{\max} = \max\{v_{t'} \mid t' \in [0, t]\}$.

DD is a vector of length $T + 1$, and different functions may be computed to capture the information in the drawdown vector, for instance, its maximum or standard deviation. The definition of Eq. (11) gives DD in currency units. A percentage drawdown is often preferred, obtained by using the logarithm of v or by dividing Eq. (11) by $v_t^{\max}$. (We opt for the latter.)

2.2.3 Maximum Diversification

Choueifaty and Coignard (2008) suggest to maximise what they call the diversification ratio. We minimise, so we multiply by -1:

$$\phi(w) = -\frac{w'\sqrt{\text{diag}(\hat{\Sigma})}}{\sqrt{w'\hat{\Sigma}w}}\,. \tag{12}$$

$\sqrt{\text{diag}(\hat{\Sigma})}$ is a column vector of the assets' standard deviations.

2.2.4 Minimum β

Low-β strategies became popular recently with Frazzini and Pedersen (2014). So we have

$$\phi(w) = \beta(w)\,, \tag{13}$$

i.e. we minimise the portfolio's β.

2.2.5 Equal-Risk Contribution

Equal-risk contribution (ERC; Maillard et al. (2010)), more commonly known as risk parity, also represents a risk-driven allocation method, yet we do not test it in this study. ERC is a scheme for asset weighting; by contrast, the models described before rather select subsets of assets from a larger universe. With ERC, there is no natural way to enforce cardinality constraints.[5]

3 Data and Setup

3.1 Data

The dataset consists of share-price series of those German firms that make up the so-called HDAX, corrected for splits, dividends and other corporate actions, over the

[5]To be sure, we could conceive ways to use ERC. For instance, we might minimise another risk measure, subject to the constraint that the weights are 'as ERC as possible', perhaps even with respect to the specific risk measure. Nevertheless, we feel that with the weight constraints we have, ERC would not add much, since a strategy more likely stands or falls with the selected assets, not with these assets' weights.

period from January 2002 to May 2017.[6] The HDAX originally comprised 100 stocks (the H stands for *hundert*, German for one-hundred): there were 30 large caps from the DAX and 70 mid caps from the MDAX. Since March 2003, the index has had up to 110 components: those of the DAX (30), MDAX (50) and TecDAX (30; large and mid caps). These stocks typically represent about 95% of the German stock market capitalisation.

We construct a dataset that is free of survivorship/look-ahead bias (Daniel et al. 2009) in the following way. At the end of each calendar year, starting with 2003, we compile a list of the constituents of the HDAX. During the following calendar year, the strategies are only allowed to invest in these index constituents. In this way, our results are not influenced by survivorship/look-ahead bias, and we may compare them with the returns of the HDAX. In the Appendix, we estimate the size of this survivorship bias.

3.2 Setup

We implement a rolling-window backtest, better known as a walk-forward. At point in time t, we compute an optimal portfolio that may use data from t − historical window to $t - 1$ day. For the historical window, we use 250 business days, i.e. roughly one year. The portfolio is then held for a specified period, at the end of which we compute a new portfolio and rebalance the old portfolio into the new one. As a holding period we choose 3 months; more specifically, we rebalance the portfolio at the end of every quarter. Transaction costs are assumed to be 10bp of the notional amount traded.

In this manner, we 'walk-forward' through the data to compute a wealth trajectory. All results presented later are computed from the out-of-sample paths of these walk-forwards, which run from 30 December 2003 to 17 May 2017.

Whenever quantities need to be forecast or estimated, we always rely on standard estimators on historical data. This choice is (and should) be a point of criticism. There is ample empirical evidence that the forecasts of many quantities such as β coefficients or variances may be improved; for instance, by way of shrinkage methods. Nevertheless, we wish to stress the differences between different objective functions, and try not to confound possible effects with those of alternative ways to handle data. Since we compute long-only portfolios, such a 'data policy' should still work (as the results confirm), though we agree at once that results could be improved by better ways of handling the data.

---

[6]The exact period is 2 January 2002 to 17 May 2017. All strategies and the benchmarks run over exactly this period.

3.3 Algorithm

We use a single method, Threshold Accepting (TA), for all optimisation models; specifically, we use the R implementation `TAopt` provided by the NMOF package (Gilli et al. 2019; Schumann 2011–2018). TA was first described in Dueck and Scheuer (1990) and Moscato and Fontanari (1990); it also was, to the best of our knowledge, the first general-purpose heuristic used for portfolio optimisation (Dueck and Winker 1992).

TA is a Local-Search method. A Local Search starts with a random feasible portfolio w, which we call the current solution. Then, again randomly, a new solution close to w is selected: for this, we pick two assets from the portfolio, increase one weight and decrease the other. In this way, the total amount invested stays unchanged. If this new portfolio, called a neighbour portfolio, is better than the original portfolio, it becomes accepted, and becomes the current solution. If it is worse, we reject it and select another neighbour instead. This whole process is repeated many times over.

TA adds a simple feature to such a Local Search: whenever the new solution is worse than the current one, it still becomes accepted, but only if it does not degrade the solution quality by more than a specified threshold. In this way, the algorithm may walk away from local minima. For more information on the procedure, see the Appendix.

All constraints are implemented in a model-specific neighbourhood; the code is available from http://enricoschumann.net/risk-reward-revisited/. For the difficulties of ensuring UCITS-compliant weights, see Scozzari et al. (2013).

4 Empirical Results

4.1 Statistics

We compute several statistics for all strategies:

return: Annualised returns.
maximum drawdown (in %): Computed from daily data.
volatility p.a. (in %): Computed from monthly returns and annualised by multiplication with $\sqrt{12}$.
reward/volatility: Annualised return divided by annualised volatility.
maximum drawdown (in %): Computed from daily data.
tracking error: Computed from monthly returns. We report tracking error against the HDAX and also against the MV portfolio.
β: Computed from monthly returns. We report β against the HDAX and also against the MV portfolio.

We also regress the strategies' returns on the—by now traditional—Fama-and-French factors: the market excess return (M), the excess returns of small caps against large caps (*small minus big*, or SMB), and the excess returns of value against growth stocks (*high minus low*, or HML). We also add momentum (*winners minus losers*, or WML), so the regression resembles the specification suggested by Carhart (1997).

We use the factor dataset described in Brückner et al. (2015) and provided by the authors.[7] Summary statistics of the factor series are provided in the following table:

		Annual return in %	Volatility in %	Ret./vol.
HDAX		7.9	18.0	0.44
SMB		−1.8	10.7	Neg.
HML		7.0	9.7	0.72
WML	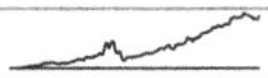	11.3	15.7	0.72

Figure 1 displays the time series of the factors. As is clearly visible, the returns of the factor portfolios vary markedly: small caps performed negatively over the period, compared with strong returns for momentum.

For all strategies, we report for completeness two β-coefficients against the market index: one against the HDAX and one against the broad-market return as provided in the dataset of Brückner et al. (2015), denoted M. The two time series of market returns are almost identical[8]; we rather add the second β coefficient because the HDAX-β comes from a univariate regression, whereas the M-β comes from the multivariate regression. Note that for the factor regression coefficients, we provide 90% confidence intervals (i.e. parameter estimates plus/minus 1.7 standard errors) and the R^2.

4.2 General Remarks

All results can be found in Table 1 at the end of the chapter. Figure 2 shows the time series of several strategies. Before we go into details, a number of general observations can be made. The overall time period, even though it comprises the financial crisis 2007–2008, was a good one for German equities. The HDAX returned 9.5% annually, with a volatility of 17.6%. Essentially all risk-based strategies delivered high absolute and risk-adjusted returns over the period, often handily outperforming the market index.

All strategies that emphasise risk come with substantially lower volatility than the market, and with β coefficients to the HDAX in the range 0.5–0.7.

---

[7] See https://www.wiwi.hu-berlin.de/de/professuren/bwl/bb/data/fama-french-factors-germany/fama-french-factors-for-germany. We use the monthly dataset TOP with tax credit, which spans the period July 1958 to June 2016. Accordingly, all regressions use strategy data up to June 2016.

[8] Monthly returns have a correlation of 0.99 and annualised returns are almost identical (7.90% *v* 7.86%). However, the time series of Brückner et al. (2015) is slightly less volatile, with annual volatility of 16.7% as compared with 18.0% for the HDAX. Thus, in Table 1, you will find that the HDAX has a M-β slightly greater than one.

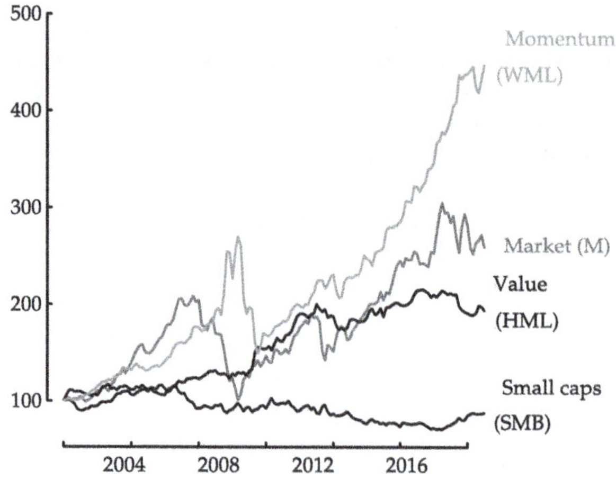

Fig. 1 Time series of Fama/French factors for the German equity markets. The series are created from the monthly return series provided by Brückner et al. (2015)

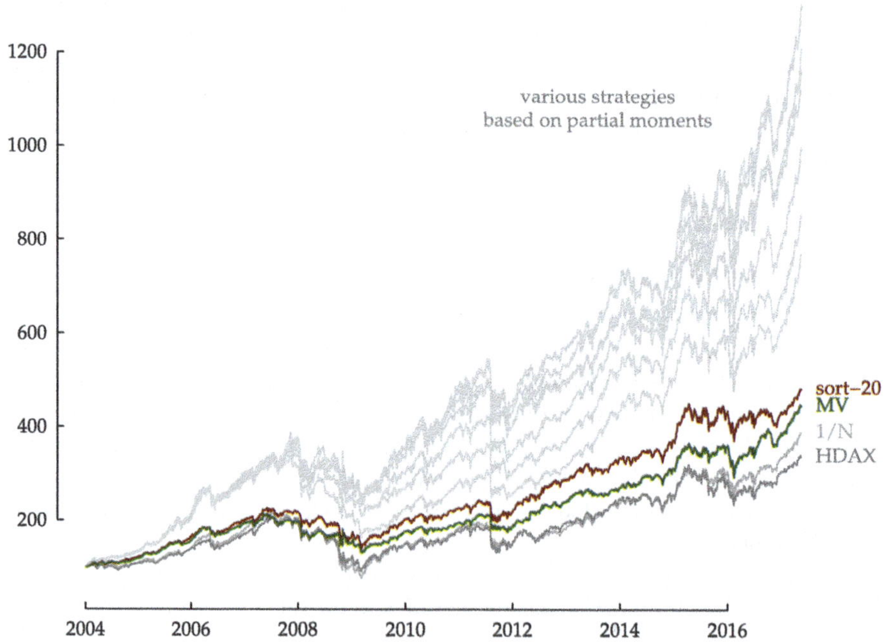

Fig. 2 Time series of several strategies and the HDAX. 1/N performs very similarly to the market, with only a slight outperformance starting in 2015, which matches the uptick in the performance of small caps (SMB) visible in Fig. 1. MV performs better, though it is dwarfed in terms of returns by strategies based on partial moments

Most strategies come with a sizeable tracking error against the index—often more than 10% per year—, which is consistent with the argument of Baker et al. (2011) that low-risk strategies perform well because they are practically infeasible for portfolio managers who work under tracking-error constraints (i.e. are bound to a benchmark).

Most strategies load meaningfully on small caps (SMB); many well-performing strategies, such as those based on partial moments, also have substantial loadings on momentum (WML). Altogether, R^2-values for many strategies are in the range 60–80%, i.e. a good portion of variability remains unexplained.

All strategies are rebalanced quarterly, and there were no restrictions at all on turnover. The lowest trade requirements had 1/N, with an average turnover of about 10% per quarter. Turnover is measured two-way: 10% means that a notional amount of 5% of the portfolio value had to be sold, and 5% were bought. For the SORT-20 strategy, turnover was in the range 30–40% per quarter; for MV and Maximum Diversification, it is was 40–50. For other strategies, turnover was higher. For risk-only ratios based on partial moments (i.e. without a reward measure), the average quarterly turnover was in the range 50–60%; adding a reward measure increased turnover to 80–90% per quarter. Turnover for portfolios based on quantiles was typically about 100% of the portfolio (i.e. 50% sold; 50% bought).

It is also useful to look at those assets that remain in the portfolio during a rebalancing, i.e. assets for which the rebalancing only changes weights. For such positions, constraints can often easily be added. For MV and Maximum Diversification, we found that about 80% of the positions remained stable (i.e. for a portfolio of 30 assets, say, 24 assets would remain in the portfolio, though perhaps with different weights). For partial moments without reward measure, it was 70–80% of assets, and with a reward measure this range dropped to 50–60%. Even for strategies based on quantiles, which proved less stable than other strategies, there typically was a 'core' of about half the positions which remained stable across rebalancing dates.

4.3 Results

4.3.1 Benchmarks

We compare all strategies with two benchmarks: the HDAX and the long-only MV portfolio. See Table 1 for more statistics.

The MV portfolio provided a return of 11.9%, more than two percentage points higher than the index, the HDAX, which returned 9.5% p.a; see Table 1. The advantage is even higher when risk is taken into account: the MV portfolio came with a volatility of only 11.6%, compared with the HDAX's 17.6%. Altogether, MV would have been a very successful strategy over the period.

4.3.2 Constructive Strategies

The 1/N portfolio provided less clear-cut results. While its returns were higher than those of the index (10.7% v 9.5%),[9] it also came with a slightly higher volatility of 18.9%. Noticeable is the higher SMB coefficient, which is as expected since 1/N overweights small caps compared with the index.

SORT-20 performed well: its volatility was less than half a percentage point higher than that of MV (11.9% v 11.6%); yet, it provided a return 0.7% higher per year (12.6% v 11.9%). Even if one considered these differences too small to be meaningful (in particular in light of the results in Sect. 4.4), it is remarkable how similar SORT-20 performed to MV, given how much simpler the strategy is. Noteworthy may also be that it showed lower factor loadings on SMB, HML and WML than MV.

4.3.3 Strategies Based on Partial Moments

Risk–reward ratios with partial moments for both their risk and reward function yielded the highest returns across all objective functions. Volatilities were often 3–4 percentage points higher than those of MV, though still lower than the market. These strategies loaded on small caps, momentum and value.

Risk-only strategies, i.e. strategies that minimise a ratio risk/constant, that use a partial moment as a replacement for variance yielded portfolios similar to MV, often with slightly higher returns.

Risk-only strategies also loaded less on HML, SMB and WML than those strategies with a reward function. But in turn, the strategies with a reward function came with substantially higher returns.

4.3.4 Strategies Based on Conditional Moments

Minimising a conditional moment of negative returns, i.e. $\mathcal{C}_\gamma^-(0)$, resulted in portfolios very similar to MV, even for different values of γ.

Choosing a lower threshold and minimising $\mathcal{C}_\gamma^-(\mathcal{Q}_{10})$ or $\mathcal{C}_\gamma^-(\mathcal{Q}_{25})$, increased returns but also volatility.

Risk–reward ratios typically beat the index in terms of return and/or volatility, though they had lower risk-adjusted returns than MV; they also came with higher β-coefficients to the market index.

---

[9]The sensitivity checks described in Sect. 4.4 indicate that the return may have been somewhat lucky.

4.3.5 Strategies Based on Quantiles

For strategies based on quantiles, simply minimising (the negative of) a lower quantile gave good results: volatility was higher than for MV, but still substantially below the HDAX's volatility.

Forming ratios $-\mathcal{Q}_{\text{lo}}/\mathcal{Q}_{\text{hi}}$, i.e. adding a reward function, increased returns somewhat. It did, however, increase volatility, too.

4.3.6 Strategies Based on Drawdown

Portfolios that minimised drawdown behaved similarly to MV, with both returns and volatility marginally higher.

4.3.7 Other Strategies

Minimum β performed better than the index, though inferior to MV.

Maximum diversification performed well, very much on par with MV, with realised volatility as low as that of MV.

4.3.8 Chasing Returns

The results we presented so far were of strategies that emphasised risk. Even when there was a reward measure, as in $\mathcal{P}_2^-/\mathcal{P}_1^+$, the risk was weighted at least as high as the reward. In $\mathcal{P}_2^-/\mathcal{P}_1^+$, for example, risk takes a higher coefficient than reward.

We also provide results when only reward is maximised. It turns out that chasing returns lead to comparatively poorly performing strategies; see Table 1, Section *Chasing returns*. Essentially, such strategies go against the idea of minimising risk: upper partial or conditional moments may capture reward, but they confound return and risk, since maximising an upper moment inevitably also increases return variability. This is confirmed by the data: the strategies came with realised volatility that was substantially higher than that of the index.

It is remarkable, nevertheless, that a number of these strategies came with returns that were comparable with the index's return. It may be tempting to attribute this to the rather strong performance of the momentum factor during the period. However, the strategies generally load negatively on WML.

4.4 Sensitivity Analysis

The way we presented the results in the previous section is commonplace in financial studies. Yet it suggests a level of accuracy that is not really present. All of the statistics that have been computed reflect the outcomes of decisions or realisations of random processes.

The most obvious cause of randomness is the optimisation method that we have used. Threshold Accepting is a stochastic algorithm, and hence its results are stochastic. We have set up the algorithm so that any remaining randomness is extremely small; see the Appendix. For instance, for the objective function that minimises volatility, the in-sample variation of the final solutions was less than 1 basis point.

So the noise that is added by the algorithm is not our main concern here.[10] Rather, it is the data and the setup that we have chosen. Many decisions have been made, such as when to rebalance, or what historic window to choose. Different choices would have led to—often substantially—different results (Acker and Duck 2007; Dimitrov and Govindaraj 2007; Gilli and Schumann 2016).

To give an idea of the overall sensitivity, we run 100 walk-forwards[11] with these adjustments:

- We use random historical windows and random rebalancing days. The rebalancing dates are randomly spaced between 20 and 80 business days apart; the historical windows span between 120 and 500 business days.
- We perturb the historic data in each period by randomly deleting 5% of the observations. So at a given point in time, the algorithm will 'look back' over between 120 and 500 days. We take the data from these business days, compute returns and randomly delete 5% of the returns.

This confounds the different sources of randomness, but the purpose here is to illustrate the uncertainty that is hidden behind seemingly precise numbers.

To keep the discussion brief, we choose a small subset of strategies (MV plus 12 others). For each strategy, we compute the same statistics as before (as in Table 1). But now, there is not a single number for volatility, say, but 100 numbers. Hence, we compute the range of each statistic. For regression coefficients, we now also report the range, not the confidence interval. All results are in Table 2. For reading convenience, we have added the single-walk-forward numbers, too. Graphical displays of the resulting wealth trajectories are in Figs. 3, 4 and 5.

All strategies are very sensitive to changes in the data, with annual returns often varying by 5 percentage points or more. This is most pronounced for strategies that also have reward functions. For instance, minimising $\mathcal{P}_2^-(0)$ leads to returns from 11.2 to 14.9%, i.e. a range of roughly 3½ percentage points. Adding a reward function and minimising $\mathcal{P}_2^-(0)/\mathcal{P}_1^+(0)$ lets returns vary between 14.6 and 20.5%, i.e. a range of about 6 percentage points. See Fig. 5. We should stress that this sensitivity is not unique to our dataset or our setup, but in line with the findings of other studies such as Acker and Duck (2007), Dimitrov and Govindaraj (2007).

---

[10] LeBaron and Weigend (1998) and Gilli and Schumann (2016) argue and provide evidence that the noise added by numerical procedures, e.g. when fitting a model via a non-deterministic method, is much smaller than the uncertainty that comes from the data.

[11] 100 may not seem a large number; but the purpose of these tests is not to trace out the distribution, but to provide intuition—an idea—about the variability of results given small changes in the setup.

Table 1 Results of single walk-forwards as discussed in Sect. 4.1. Volatility is computed from monthly returns and annualised by multiplication with $\sqrt{12}$. β coefficients are computed from univariate regressions of monthly returns; we report β against both the HDAX and the MV portfolio. Tracking error (t.e.) is computed from monthly returns; we report tracking error against both the HDAX and the MV portfolio. Fama–French factors are denoted M (market minus risk-free rate), SMB (excess returns of small caps against large caps; *small minus big*), HML (excess returns of value stocks over growth stocks; *high minus low*). WML is momentum (*winners minus losers*). The factor dataset is described in Brückner et al. (2015) and provided by the authors. For the factor regression, we report 90% confidence intervals for the coefficients and the adjusted R^2

Strategy	Return p.a. (in %)	Volatility p.a. (in %)	Reward/ volatility	Maximum drawdown	β HDAX	β MV	t.e. HDAX	t.e. MV	M	SMB	HML	WML	R^2
HDAX	9.5	17.6	0.54	56.3	1		0		1.05	−0.01	−0.01	−0.07	0.98
MV	11.9	11.6	1.02	39.9	0.48	1.00	12.0	0.0	0.57–0.72	0.17–0.40	−0.05–0.16	0.09–0.22	0.62
1/N	10.7	18.9	0.56	64.6	1.00	1.20	7.0	13.0	1.06–1.19	0.28–0.47	−0.06–0.12	−0.27–−0.16	0.90
SORT-20	12.6	11.9	1.06	37.8	0.59	0.88	9.3	6.3	0.60–0.72	0.03–0.23	−0.09–0.10	−0.07–0.05	0.74
$\mathcal{P}_1^-(0)$	13.6	12.7	1.07	44.9	0.52	1.06	12.3	3.3	0.64–0.80	0.20–0.44	−0.08–0.14	0.14–0.28	0.63
$\mathcal{P}_2^-(0)$	11.8	12.2	0.97	39.7	0.48	1.02	12.6	2.7	0.59–0.75	0.18–0.42	−0.09–0.13	0.13–0.28	0.61
$\mathcal{P}_3^-(0)$	11.7	12.1	0.97	38.1	0.47	1.01	12.8	3.0	0.56–0.73	0.15–0.40	−0.10–0.13	0.11–0.26	0.57
$\mathcal{P}_4^-(0)$	11.5	11.9	0.97	36.8	0.48	0.99	12.5	3.0	0.56–0.71	0.13–0.38	−0.10–0.12	0.08–0.23	0.58
$\mathcal{P}_1^-(0)/\mathcal{P}_1^+(0)$	16.4	15.1	1.09	51.5	0.60	1.11	12.8	7.9	0.79–0.98	0.33–0.62	−0.05–0.21	0.21–0.38	0.65
$\mathcal{P}_2^-(0)/\mathcal{P}_1^+(0)$	18.7	15.3	1.22	44.2	0.60	1.10	13.2	8.4	0.75–0.94	0.25–0.55	0.05–0.33	0.19–0.37	0.61
$\mathcal{P}_3^-(0)/\mathcal{P}_1^+(0)$	21.1	14.9	1.41	36.9	0.60	1.08	12.7	8.2	0.74–0.94	0.27–0.57	0.00–0.27	0.14–0.32	0.61

(continued)

Table 1 (continued)

$\mathcal{P}_3^-(0)/\mathcal{P}_2^+(0)$	17.6	14.4	1.22	28.1	0.56	1.03	13.0	7.9	0.70–0.89	0.23–0.52	−0.11–0.16	0.20–0.37	0.60
$\mathcal{P}_4^-(0)/\mathcal{P}_1^+(0)$	20.0	14.9	1.35	36.2	0.60	1.08	12.7	8.1	0.74–0.93	0.24–0.54	−0.01–0.26	0.16–0.34	0.61
$\mathcal{P}_4^-(0)/\mathcal{P}_2^+(0)$	18.0	14.7	1.22	34.3	0.59	1.06	12.8	8.1	0.75–0.93	0.29–0.59	−0.08–0.19	0.15–0.33	0.62
$\mathcal{C}_1^-(0)$	12.3	12.7	0.97	46.2	0.59	1.02	10.3	4.5	0.67–0.82	0.19–0.41	−0.06–0.14	0.03–0.16	0.70
$\mathcal{C}_2^-(0)$	12.5	12.2	1.03	40.9	0.50	1.01	12.2	3.2	0.61–0.76	0.18–0.41	−0.07–0.15	0.13–0.28	0.63
$\mathcal{C}_3^-(0)$	12.1	12.0	1.00	40.3	0.47	1.00	12.8	3.2	0.56–0.72	0.14–0.39	−0.09–0.14	0.10–0.25	0.57
$\mathcal{C}_4^-(0)$	12.3	12.0	1.02	36.7	0.49	0.99	12.4	3.5	0.58–0.73	0.14–0.38	−0.09–0.14	0.09–0.24	0.60
$\mathcal{C}_1^-(\mathcal{Q}_{10})$	14.4	13.7	1.06	51.3	0.63	1.05	10.4	6.1	0.74–0.89	0.24–0.47	−0.04–0.18	0.06–0.20	0.71
$\mathcal{C}_1^-(\mathcal{Q}_{25})$	13.0	15.3	0.85	56.5	0.75	1.12	8.9	8.2	0.90–1.04	0.31–0.53	−0.06–0.14	0.07–0.20	0.80
$\mathcal{C}_2^-(\mathcal{Q}_{10})$	15.3	13.6	1.13	48.5	0.62	1.06	10.5	5.9	0.75–0.90	0.27–0.50	−0.04–0.18	0.07–0.21	0.72
$\mathcal{C}_2^-(\mathcal{Q}_{25})$	12.5	16.2	0.77	60.9	0.77	1.18	9.7	8.9	0.93–1.09	0.29–0.55	−0.08–0.16	0.07–0.22	0.77
$\mathcal{C}_1^-(\mathcal{Q}_{25})/\mathcal{C}_1^+(\mathcal{Q}_{75})$	12.7	16.5	0.77	56.8	0.81	1.14	9.0	10.0	0.97–1.11	0.40–0.63	−0.02–0.19	−0.04–0.10	0.82
$\mathcal{C}_1^-(\mathcal{Q}_{10})/\mathcal{C}_1^+(\mathcal{Q}_{90})$	14.6	17.9	0.82	65.8	0.87	1.22	9.4	11.1	0.98–1.15	0.24–0.50	−0.06–0.18	−0.12–0.04	0.79
$\mathcal{C}_1^-(\mathcal{Q}_{25})/\mathcal{C}_1^+(\mathcal{Q}_{90})$	14.2	18.1	0.78	61.6	0.89	1.18	9.4	12.1	0.96–1.14	0.27–0.55	−0.20–0.06	−0.19–−0.01	0.77

(continued)

Table 1 (continued)

$\mathcal{C}_1^-(\mathcal{Q}_{10})/\mathcal{C}_1^+(\mathcal{Q}_{75})$	13.9	16.9	0.82	58.5	0.81	1.21	9.9	9.8	0.92–1.10	0.32–0.60	0.02–0.28	−0.05–0.12	0.74
$\mathcal{C}_2^-(\mathcal{Q}_{25})/\mathcal{C}_1^+(\mathcal{Q}_{75})$	15.4	16.0	0.97	54.2	0.75	1.13	10.0	9.2	0.91–1.07	0.32–0.57	−0.11–0.13	0.06–0.21	0.76
$\mathcal{C}_2^-(\mathcal{Q}_{10})/\mathcal{C}_1^+(\mathcal{Q}_{90})$	19.6	18.0	1.09	63.1	0.86	1.21	10.2	11.5	0.92–1.11	0.21–0.51	0.00–0.28	−0.17–0.01	0.74
$\mathcal{C}_2^-(\mathcal{Q}_{25})/\mathcal{C}_1^+(\mathcal{Q}_{90})$	15.2	16.6	0.91	60.0	0.80	1.16	9.6	9.8	0.90–1.07	0.26–0.53	−0.03–0.22	−0.06–0.10	0.75
$\mathcal{C}_2^-(\mathcal{Q}_{10})/\mathcal{C}_1^+(\mathcal{Q}_{75})$	16.7	17.4	0.96	60.7	0.83	1.19	10.0	10.9	0.91–1.09	0.30–0.59	−0.01–0.26	−0.16–0.02	0.73
$\mathcal{C}_2^-(\mathcal{Q}_{25})/\mathcal{C}_2^+(\mathcal{Q}_{75})$	14.2	16.4	0.87	60.9	0.80	1.16	9.2	9.5	0.93–1.09	0.31–0.56	−0.06–0.17	−0.01–0.13	0.78
$\mathcal{C}_2^-(\mathcal{Q}_{10})/\mathcal{C}_2^+(\mathcal{Q}_{90})$	16.6	19.1	0.87	66.9	0.89	1.24	11.1	12.8	0.96–1.16	0.31–0.63	−0.06–0.24	−0.27–−0.08	0.73
$\mathcal{C}_2^-(\mathcal{Q}_{25})/\mathcal{C}_2^+(\mathcal{Q}_{90})$	16.4	17.8	0.92	59.1	0.88	1.21	9.2	11.2	0.97–1.15	0.29–0.56	−0.13–0.12	−0.14–0.03	0.78
$\mathcal{C}_2^-(\mathcal{Q}_{10})/\mathcal{C}_2^+(\mathcal{Q}_{75})$	16.5	16.8	0.98	59.3	0.80	1.20	10.0	9.8	0.93–1.10	0.32–0.59	0.04–0.29	0.00–0.16	0.75
$-\mathcal{Q}_{10}^-/\mathcal{Q}_{75}^+$	18.2	15.8	1.16	52.9	0.73	1.09	10.4	9.4	0.85–1.03	0.33–0.60	0.03–0.28	0.00–0.16	0.72
$-\mathcal{Q}_{25}^-/\mathcal{Q}_{75}^+$	15.2	16.9	0.90	61.1	0.82	1.18	9.4	10.1	0.93–1.10	0.30–0.57	−0.09–0.16	−0.06–0.10	0.77
$-\mathcal{Q}_{10}^-/\mathcal{Q}_{90}^+$	16.0	17.9	0.89	66.8	0.87	1.18	9.6	11.8	0.93–1.11	0.25–0.54	−0.08–0.18	−0.21–−0.04	0.76
$-\mathcal{Q}_{25}^-/\mathcal{Q}_{90}^+$	15.2	17.0	0.89	58.5	0.83	1.18	9.4	10.3	0.96–1.12	0.27–0.52	−0.22–0.01	−0.05–0.10	0.79

(continued)

Table 1 (continued)

$-\mathcal{Q}_{10}^{-}$	14.8	13.4	1.11	45.8	0.61	1.05	10.7	5.7	0.72–0.87	0.20–0.44	0.00–0.21	0.10–0.24	0.70
$-\mathcal{Q}_{25}^{-}$	14.5	14.6	0.99	52.1	0.68	1.04	10.1	8.2	0.80–0.96	0.27–0.52	−0.08–0.15	0.05–0.20	0.72
Drawdown: maximum	12.0	12.6	0.96	43.8	0.51	0.99	12.4	5.1	0.63–0.78	0.20–0.44	−0.07–0.15	0.11–0.26	0.63
Drawdown: volatility	10.9	12.4	0.88	45.3	0.50	0.97	12.4	5.1	0.61–0.76	0.17–0.41	−0.05–0.17	0.12–0.26	0.63
Drawdown: mean	13.5	12.8	1.05	43.2	0.54	1.00	11.7	5.5	0.66–0.81	0.19–0.43	−0.06–0.15	0.11–0.25	0.67
Minimum β	10.1	13.0	0.77	44.1	0.51	1.08	12.9	3.7	0.58–0.76	0.17–0.46	−0.03–0.23	0.06–0.23	0.53
Maximum diversification	12.0	11.5	1.05	39.5	0.49	0.97	11.7	1.8	0.57–0.71	0.19–0.41	−0.06–0.15	0.05–0.18	0.64
Minimum MAD	12.0	14.1	0.85	53.4	0.67	1.05	9.6	6.9	0.76–0.91	0.20–0.43	−0.08–0.13	−0.03–0.11	0.75
Chasing returns													
$1/\mathcal{P}_1^{-}(0)$	11.4	28.7	0.40	77.5	1.35	1.48	17.3	23.7	1.37–1.70	0.22–0.73	−0.22–0.25	−0.39–−0.08	0.70
$1/\mathcal{P}_2^{-}(0)$	3.6	29.3	0.12	77.6	1.33	1.49	18.7	24.3	1.39–1.74	0.36–0.91	−0.16–0.35	−0.37–−0.04	0.67
$1/\mathcal{P}_3^{-}(0)$	5.3	29.3	0.18	75.4	1.29	1.40	19.2	24.8	1.32–1.69	0.37–0.94	−0.16–0.38	−0.45–−0.11	0.64
$1/\mathcal{P}_4^{-}(0)$	5.0	28.5	0.18	77.3	1.27	1.43	18.2	23.6	1.32–1.67	0.38–0.92	−0.24–0.26	−0.44–−0.11	0.66

(continued)

Table 1 (continued)

$-\mathcal{Q}^-_{75}$	9.9	26.5	0.37	75.3	1.29	1.44	14.8	21.2	1.33–1.61	0.31–0.73	−0.25–0.14	−0.40–−0.15	0.76
$-\mathcal{Q}^-_{90}$	9.4	25.1	0.37	71.2	1.21	1.35	14.0	20.1	1.25–1.51	0.29–0.69	0.01–0.39	−0.37–−0.13	0.76
$1/\mathcal{C}^+_1(\mathcal{Q}_{75})$	11.3	26.6	0.42	67.4	1.29	1.39	14.9	21.6	1.29–1.56	0.27–0.69	−0.08–0.31	−0.49–−0.24	0.76
$1/\mathcal{C}^+_1(\mathcal{Q}_{90})$	9.0	28.4	0.32	78.7	1.36	1.44	16.6	23.5	1.30–1.59	0.12–0.56	−0.13–0.28	−0.62–−0.35	0.77
$1/\mathcal{C}^+_2(\mathcal{Q}_{75})$	8.1	27.4	0.30	75.1	1.34	1.50	15.3	21.9	1.31–1.59	0.10–0.54	−0.21–0.20	−0.46–−0.19	0.75
$1/\mathcal{C}^+_2(\mathcal{Q}_{90})$	4.4	26.6	0.16	79.5	1.28	1.37	15.1	21.8	1.29–1.56	0.25–0.66	−0.10–0.28	−0.51–−0.26	0.78

Table 2 Results of sensitivity tests as described in Sect. 4.4. The columns are as in Table 1, but we report the ranges of outcomes of 100 walk-forwards with randomly chosen settings. For every strategy, we report first the results of a single walk-forward without any perturbations; then, we also report the ranges of the statistics

Strategy	Return p.a. (in %)	Volatility p.a. (in %)	Reward/ volatility	Maximum draw-down	β HDAX	β MV	t.e. HDAX	t.e. MV	M	SMB	HML	WML	R^2
Results from single walk-forwards–same as in Table 1–and ranges of outcomes													
HDAX	9.5	17.6	0.54	56.3	1		0		1.05	−0.01	−0.01	−0.07	0.98
MV	11.9	11.6	1.02	39.9	0.48	1.00	12.0	0.0	0.57–0.72	0.17–0.40	−0.05–0.16	0.09–0.22	0.62
	10.7–14.0	10.9–12.3	0.94–1.25	29.8–43.1	0.37–0.51	0.89–1.00	11.3–15.1	0.0–6.0	0.51–0.65	0.12–0.30	0.00–0.10	0.10–0.26	0.38–0.66
1/N	10.7	18.9	0.56	64.6	1.00	1.20	7.0	13.0	1.06–1.19	0.28–0.47	−0.06–0.12	−0.27–−0.16	0.90
	9.2–10.1	18.3–18.8	0.5–0.55	62.7–66.0	0.97–0.99	1.14–1.16	6.8–7.2	12.9–13.6	1.07–1.09	0.29–0.33	0.02–0.05	−0.25–−0.21	0.88–0.90
SORT-20	12.6	11.9	1.06	37.8	0.59	0.88	9.3	6.3	0.60–0.72	0.03–0.23	−0.09–0.10	−0.07–0.05	0.74
	11.2–13.9	11.2–12.1	0.94–1.22	31.0–42.4	0.53–0.60	0.81–0.89	8.9–10.4	5.6–7.7	0.61–0.68	0.04–0.14	0.00–0.07	−0.02–0.09	0.69–0.79
$\mathcal{P}_2^-(0)/\mathcal{P}_1^+(0)$	18.7	15.3	1.22	44.2	0.60	1.10	13.2	8.4	0.75–0.94	0.25–0.55	0.05–0.33	0.19–0.37	0.61
	14.6–20.5	13.7–15.6	0.99–1.45	30.3–55.0	0.51–0.69	0.99–1.14	11.2–13.7	7.3–8.9	0.74–0.95	0.30–0.50	0.02–0.22	0.17–0.35	0.57–0.71
$\mathcal{P}_3^-(0)/\mathcal{P}_1^+(0)$	21.1	14.9	1.41	36.9	0.60	1.08	12.7	8.2	0.74–0.94	0.27–0.57	0.00–0.27	0.14–0.32	0.61
	14.2–21.8	14.0–15.6	0.95–1.52	30.5–45.8	0.50–0.66	1.02–1.16	11.1–14.8	7.1–9.5	0.73–0.90	0.27–0.49	0.02–0.22	0.15–0.38	0.50–0.69

(continued)

Table 2 (continued)

$\mathcal{P}_1^-(0)$	13.6	12.7	1.07	44.9	0.52	1.06	12.3	3.3	0.64–0.80	0.20–0.44	−0.08–0.14	0.14–0.28	0.63
	11.9–16.3	11.6–12.9	0.94–1.26	30.0–47.4	0.43–0.52	0.97–1.06	11.7–14.4	3.2–5.4	0.59–0.71	0.17–0.33	0.00–0.09	0.17–0.30	0.49–0.67
$\mathcal{P}_2^-(0)$	11.8	12.2	0.97	39.7	0.48	1.02	12.6	2.7	0.59–0.75	0.18–0.42	−0.09–0.13	0.13–0.28	0.61
	11.2–14.9	11.5–12.4	0.92–1.2	28.1–44.3	0.41–0.49	0.96–1.05	12.0–14.5	2.8–5.2	0.56–0.67	0.15–0.29	−0.02–0.07	0.18–0.30	0.49–0.64
$\mathcal{C}_1^-(0)$	12.3	12.7	0.97	46.2	0.59	1.02	10.3	4.5	0.67–0.82	0.19–0.41	−0.06–0.14	0.03–0.16	0.70
	9.7–15.2	11.6–13.4	0.77–1.26	33.6–51.5	0.53–0.63	0.93–1.05	9.6–11.4	4.1–6.5	0.66–0.78	0.17–0.36	−0.01–0.15	0.06–0.17	0.65–0.76
$\mathcal{C}_2^-(0)$	12.5	12.2	1.03	40.9	0.50	1.01	12.2	3.2	0.61–0.76	0.18–0.41	−0.07–0.15	0.13–0.28	0.63
	10.6–14.4	11.4–12.8	0.9–1.22	29.9–45.0	0.39–0.53	0.93–1.07	11.3–15.2	2.9–6.4	0.53–0.70	0.10–0.28	−0.03–0.07	0.14–0.30	0.42–0.68
$-\mathcal{Q}_{10}^-$	14.8	13.4	1.11	45.8	0.61	1.05	10.7	5.7	0.72–0.87	0.20–0.44	0.00–0.21	0.10–0.24	0.70
	11.9–17.5	12.3–13.9	0.89–1.29	35.5–54.5	0.49–0.65	0.97–1.12	9.7–13.7	4.9–7.6	0.63–0.82	0.11–0.37	−0.02–0.13	0.04–0.24	0.48–0.75
$\mathcal{C}_1^-(\mathcal{Q}_{10})$	14.4	13.7	1.06	51.3	0.63	1.05	10.4	6.1	0.74–0.89	0.24–0.47	−0.04–0.18	0.06–0.20	0.71
	12.5–17.1	12.4–14.1	0.9–1.33	36.7–53.3	0.47–0.65	0.97–1.12	9.8–14.7	4.7–7.9	0.60–0.81	0.10–0.34	−0.02–0.17	0.06–0.24	0.41–0.74

(continued)

Table 2 (continued)

$\mathcal{C}_2^-(\mathcal{Q}_{10})$	15.3	13.6	1.13	48.5	0.62	1.06	10.5	5.9	0.75–0.90	0.27–0.50	−0.04–0.18	0.07–0.21	0.72
	12.0–17.6	12.2–13.8	0.91–1.4	34.2–54.3	0.52–0.64	0.97–1.11	9.7–11.8	4.7–7.2	0.68–0.82	0.21–0.37	−0.01–0.12	0.07–0.22	0.60–0.75
Maximum	12.0	11.5	1.05	39.5	0.49	0.97	11.7	1.8	0.57–0.71	0.19–0.41	−0.06–0.15	0.05–0.18	0.64
Diversification	10.6–15.1	11.0–12.3	0.94–1.22	32.3–42.9	0.38–0.50	0.92–1.01	11.4–15.0	1.7–6.0	0.51–0.64	0.13–0.28	0.02–0.11	0.11–0.28	0.40–0.65

Fig. 3 1/N and SORT-20. Wealth trajectories from 100 walk-forwards with randomly perturbed data. The grey shades indicate different quantiles: lighter shades mean farther away from the median

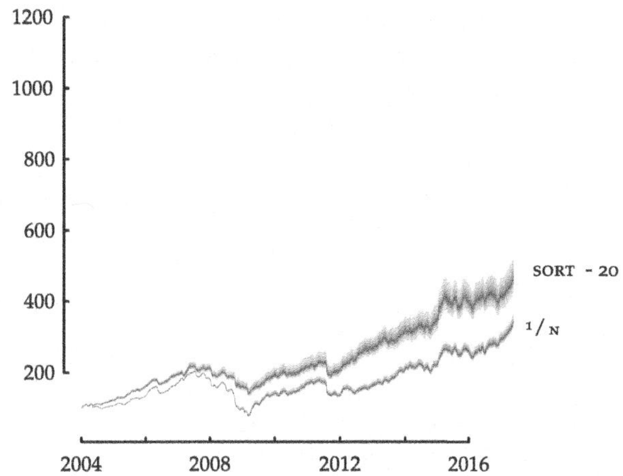

Fig. 4 MV. Wealth trajectories from 100 walk-forwards with randomly perturbed data

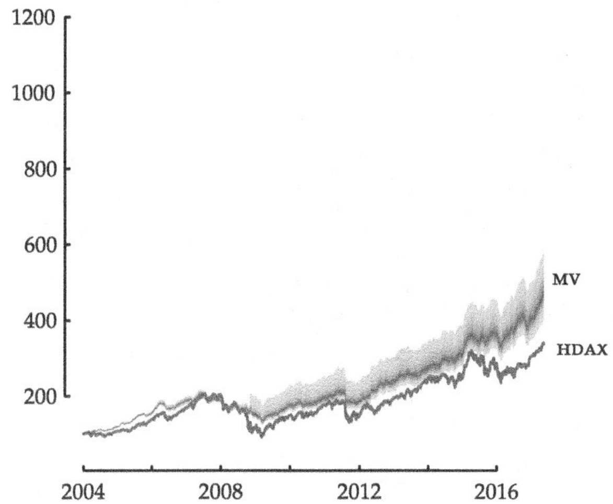

Fig. 5 $\mathcal{P}_2^-(0)$ and $\mathcal{P}_2^-(0)/\mathcal{P}_1^+(0)$. Wealth trajectories from 100 walk-forwards with randomly perturbed data

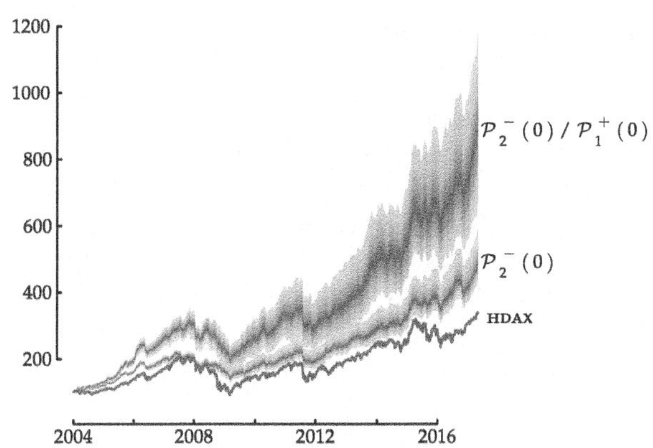

The constructive strategies are least affected. The results of 1/N vary little when the data are perturbed; see Fig. 3. After all, the strategy completely ignores historic data; but it is affected by changes in rebalancing dates. SORT-20 is slightly more sensitive, which is as expected, since it is essentially a more-selective (more-concentrated) version of 1/N.

In sum: while the sensitivity analyses clearly suggest not to put too much emphasis on specific numbers, they do confirm the overall results as presented in Table 1.

5 Conclusion

Richard Hamming once quipped that in academic research, a result is ‘well known’ if one can find it in the literature. That investing in low-risk assets works well has been well known in this sense since the early 1970s; yet, it took more than three decades before investors and the asset-management industry took it up.

Our results broadly confirm the low-risk effect: many different specifications, as long as they emphasise low risk in the sense of low return variability, work well. That does not mean, of course, that there would exist a myriad *different* strategies that are all better than the market. All these strategies simply exploit the good performance of low-risk stocks during the period.

Our results also confirm those of Gilli and Schumann (2011b): Alternative risk measures, notably those that differentiate between losses (risk) and gains (reward), in many cases work better than the MV-benchmark. As we said in the introduction, there are many details to low-risk investing. Choosing an appropriate risk function should be one detail worth looking into.

Appendix

Survivorship Bias

We run an equal-weight portfolio on the stocks that made up the HDAX at the end of 2016. The backtest runs over the same period as the other tests described in the chapter, but it suffers from survivorship bias: the test exploits the fact that the index components in 2016 were companies that had performed well in prior years, and which were accordingly included in the index. Companies that performed badly, on the other hand, were excluded from the index over time and hence are invisible to the test. Figure 6 shows the results. The difference is a staggering 6.7% p.a. (10.7% for 1/N compared with 17.4% for the variant with survivorship bias).

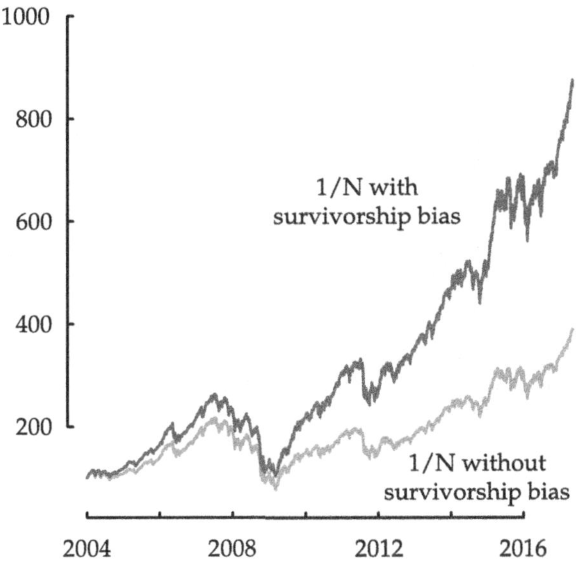

Fig. 6 Time series of equal-weight portfolios with and without survivorship bias

Calibrating Threshold Accepting

Threshold Accepting (TA) is a stochastic algorithm: running the algorithm two times, even from the same initial solution, may lead to two different solutions. TA is not alone in this regard: almost all heuristic methods, e.g. Genetic Algorithms or Simulated Annealing, are stochastic.

It is instructive to consider the result from a single run of TA as the realisation of a random variable that has a distribution $\mathcal{D}$. By 'result' we mean the objective-function value ϕ that is associated with the returned solution. (It is useful, too, to analyse the decision variables given by a solution, i.e. the portfolio weights.)

It is straightforward to analyse $\mathcal{D}$: run a reasonably large number of restarts, each time store ϕ_j, and finally compute the empirical distribution function of the ϕ_j, $j = 1, \ldots,$ number-of-restarts as an estimate for $\mathcal{D}$.

For a given model or model class and for our implementation of TA (notably the neighbourhood function), the shape of the distribution $\mathcal{D}$ will depend on the settings that we have chosen; most obviously, on the number of iterations to the search time to that we allow for. With more iterations, $\mathcal{D}$ should move to the left and become steeper. Ideally, its whole mass should collapse on a single point, the global optimum.

To determine the required number of iterations we ran such experiments for all strategies. Figure 7 shows results for two objective functions. Altogether, we can essentially make the randomness of a solution as small as we want (see also Gilli and Schumann (2011a)).

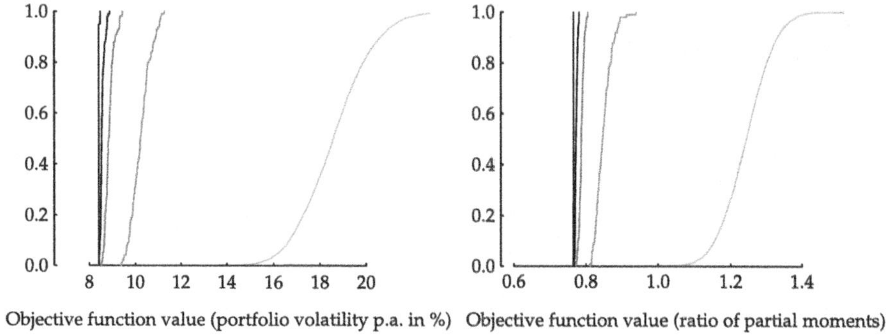

Fig. 7 Empirical distributions of objective-function values for increasing number of iterations (100, 1000, 2500, 5000 and 25,000 iterations). Left: MV; Right: $\mathcal{P}_2^-(0)/\mathcal{P}_1^+(0)$. The rightmost distribution is the one with the fewest iterations, not much better than random portfolios. As the number of iterations increases, the distributions move to the left (i.e. the solutions become better) and become steeper

References

Acker, D., & Duck, N. W. (2007). Reference-day risk and the use of monthly returns data. *Journal of Accounting, Auditing and Finance*, *22*(4), 527–557.

Ang, A., Hodrick, R. J., Xing, Y., & Zhang, X. (2006). The cross-section of volatility and expected returns. *Journal of Finance*, *61*(1).

Ang, A., Hodrick, R. J., Xing, Y., & Zhang, X. (2009). High idiosyncratic volatility and low returns: International and further U.S. evidence. *Journal of Financial Economics*, *91*, 1–23.

Baker, M., Bradley, B., & Wurgler, J. (2011). Benchmarks as limits to arbitrage: Understanding the low-volatility anomaly. *Financial Analysts Journal*, *67*(1), 40–54.

Biglova, A., Ortobelli, S., Rachev, S., & Stoyanov, S. (2004). Different approaches to risk estimation in portfolio theory. *Journal of Portfolio Management*, *31*(1), 103–112.

Black, F., Jensen, M. C., & Scholes, M. (1972). The capital asset pricing model: Some empirical tests. In M. C. Jenson (Ed.), *Studies in the theory of capital markets*. Praeger Publishers Inc.

Broadie, M. (1993). Computing efficient frontiers using estimated parameters. *Annals of Operations Research*, *45*(1), 21–58.

Brooks, C., & Kat, H. M. (2002). The statistical properties of hedge fund index returns and their implications for investors. *Journal of Alternative Investments*, *5*(2), 26–44.

Brückner, R., Lehmann, P., Schmidt, M. H., & Stehle, R. (2015). *Another German Fama/French factor data set*. Working Paper. https://ssrn.com/abstract=2682617.

Carhart, M. M. (1997). On persistence in mutual fund performance. *Journal of Finance*, *52*(1), 57–82.

Chan, L. K. C., Karceski, J., & Lakonishok, J. (1999). On portfolio optimization: Forecasting covariances and choosing the risk model. *Review of Financial Studies*, *12*(5), 937–974.

Chopra, V. K., & Ziemba, W. T. (1993). The effect of errors in means, variances, and covariances on optimal portfolio choice. *Journal of Portfolio Management*, *19*(2), 6–11.

Choueifaty, Y., & Coignard, Y. (2008). Toward maximum diversification. *Journal of Portfolio Management*, *35*(1), 40–51.

Daniel, G., Sornette, D., & Wöhrmann, P. (2009). Look-ahead benchmark bias in portfolio performance evaluation. *Journal of Portfolio Management*, *36*(1), 121–130.

DeMiguel, V., Garlappi, L., & Uppal, R. (2009). Optimal versus Naive diversification: How inefficient is the 1/N portfolio strategy? *Review of Financial Studies*, *22*(5), 1915–1953.

Dimitrov, V., & Govindaraj, S. (2007). Reference-day risk: Observations and extensions. *Journal of Accounting, Auditing and Finance*, *22*(4), 559–572.

Disatnik, D. J., & Benninga, S. (2007). Shrinking the covariance matrix. *Journal of Portfolio Management*, *33*(4), 55–63.

Dueck, G., & Scheuer, T. (1990). Threshold accepting. A general purpose optimization algorithm superior to simulated annealing. *Journal of Computational Physics*, *90*(1), 161–175.

Dueck, G., & Winker, P. (1992). New concepts and algorithms for portfolio choice. *Applied Stochastic Models and Data Analysis*, *8*(3), 159–178.

Eling, M., & Schuhmacher, F. (2007). Does the choice of performance measure influence the evaluation of hedge funds? *Journal of Banking & Finance*, *31*, 2632–2647.

Farinelli, S., Ferreira, M., Rossello, D., Thoeny, M., & Tibiletti, L. (2008). Beyond Sharpe ratio: Optimal asset allocation using different performance ratios. *Journal of Banking & Finance*, *32*(10), 2057–2063.

Fishburn, P. C. (1977). Mean-risk analysis with risk associated with below-target returns. *American Economic Review*, *67*(2), 116–126.

Frazzini, A., & Pedersen, L. H. (2014). Betting against beta. *Journal of Financial Economics*, *111*(1), 1–25.

Gilli, M., & Schumann, E. (2011a). Optimal enough? *Journal of Heuristics*, *17*(4), 373–387.

Gilli, M., & Schumann, E. (2011b). Risk–reward optimisation for long-run investors: An empirical analysis. *European Actuarial Journal*, *1*(1, Suppl. 2), 303–327.

Gilli, M., & Schumann, E. (2016). Accuracy and precision in finance. In O. Hieronymi, & M. L. Cascio (Eds.), *A new social market economy for the 21st century*. Aracne.

Gilli, M., Maringer, D., & Schumann, E. (2019). *Numerical methods and optimization in finance*, 2nd ed. Elsevier/Academic Press. http://nmof.net.

Haugen, R. A., & Heins, J. A. (1972). *On the evidence supporting the existence of risk premiums in the capital market*. University of Wisconsin-Maddison/Graduate School of Business Working Paper.

LeBaron, B., & Weigend, A. S. (1998). A bootstrap evaluation of the effect of data splitting on financial time series. *IEEE Transactions on Neural Networks*, *9*(1), 213–220. http://citeseer.ist.psu.edu/lebaron98bootstrap.html.

Ledoit, O., & Wolf, M. (2004). Honey, I shrunk the sample covariance matrix. *Journal of Portfolio Management*, *30*(4).

Maillard, S., Roncalli, T., & Teïletche, J. (2010). The properties of equally weighted risk contribution portfolios. *Journal of Portfolio Management*, *36*(4), 60–70.

Markowitz, H. M. (1952). Portfolio selection. *Journal of Finance*, *7*(1), 77–91.

Merali, Z. (2010). ERROR: Why scientific programming does not compute. *Nature*, *467*, 775–777.

Moscato, P., & Fontanari, J. F. (1990). Stochastic versus deterministic update in simulated annealing. *Physics Letters A*, *146*(4), 204–208.

R Core Team. (2017). *R: A language and environment for statistical computing*. R Foundation for Statistical Computing, Vienna, Austria. http://www.R-project.org/.

Racheva-Iotova, B., & Stoyanov, S. (2008). Post-modern approaches for portfolio optimization. In *Handbook on information technology in finance*. Springer.

Schumann, E. (2008–2018). *PMwR: Portfolio management with R (Package version 0.10-0)*. http://enricoschumann.net/PMwR/.

Schumann, E. (2011–2018). *Numerical methods and optimization in finance (NMOF): Manual (Package version 1.5-0)*. http://enricoschumann.net/NMOF.htm#NMOFmanual.

Schumann, E. (2013). Take-the-best in portfolio selection. http://enricoschumann.net.

Scozzari, A., Tardella, F., Paterlini, S., & Krink, T. (2013). Exact and heuristic approaches for the index tracking problem with UCITS constraints. *Annals of Operations Research*, *205*(1), 235–250.

Shiller, R. J. (1984). Stock prices and social dynamics. *Brookings Papers on Economic Activity*.

Sortino, F., van der Meer, R., & Plantinga, A. (1999). The Dutch triangle. *Journal of Portfolio Management*, *26*(1), 50–58.

Optimal Investment–Consumption Decisions with Partially Observed Inflation: A Discrete-Time Formulation

Alain Bensoussan and Suresh P. Sethi

Abstract We consider a discrete-time optimal consumption and investment problem of an investor who is interested in maximizing his utility from consumption and terminal wealth subject to a random inflation in the consumption basket price over time. We consider two cases: (i) when the investor observes the basket price and (ii) when he receives only noisy signals on the basket price. We derive the optimal policies and show that a modified Mutual Fund Theorem consisting of three funds holds in both cases, as it does in the continuous-time setting. The compositions of the funds in the two cases are the same but, in general, the investor's allocations of his wealth into these funds differ.

1 Introduction

We study a discrete-time optimal investment and consumption decision problem of an investor when the consumption basket and real (inflation adjusted) asset prices are partially observed. Traditionally, the investment literature has assumed that the basket price, a measure of inflation, is fully observed. In reality, the basket price is difficult to assess, as it requires collecting the prices of all the consumption goods in the basket and their weights. Moreover, these prices may not be unique as discussed in Borenstein and Rose (1994). In other words, inflation is not fully observed and, as a consequence, the real asset prices are also incompletely observed.

As a benchmark case, we first consider fully observed inflation. In this case, the real asset market is complete, and the optimal policy can be obtained by solving

A. Bensoussan · S. P. Sethi (✉)
Naveen Jindal School of Management, University of Texas at Dallas,
Richardson, TX, USA
e-mail: sethi@utdallas.edu

A. Bensoussan
e-mail: axb046100@utdallas.edu

A. Bensoussan
City University of Hong Kong, Kowloon Tong, Hong Kong

H. Dawid and J. Arifovic (eds.), *Dynamic Analysis in Complex Economic Environments*,
Dynamic Modeling and Econometrics in Economics and Finance 26,
https://doi.org/10.1007/978-3-030-52970-3_4

the dynamic programming equation for the problem. The real optimal consumption process is the discrete-time equivalent of the optimal policy in the classical case considered in the continuous-time formulations of Karatzas et al. (1986), Merton (1971), and Sethi (1997). However, since the consumption basket price is also stochastic, its presence affects the optimal portfolio selection. Whereas the optimal portfolio in the classical case can be stated in terms of the risk-free fund and growth optimal risky fund, a result known as a Mutual Fund Theorem, and we show that the optimal portfolio with uncertain inflation can be characterized as a combination of three funds: the risk-free fund, the growth optimal fund (of the classical case), and a fund that arises from the correlation between the inflation uncertainty and the market risk. Every investor uses the first two funds, but the composition of the third fund may be different for different investors. However, if two investors have perfectly correlated consumption baskets, then they both will use the same third fund. Furthermore, in general, the amount invested in each of the three funds depends on their respective wealth, consumption basket prices, and utility functions. Henceforth, we will use the terms nominal consumption and consumption interchangeably. When we mean real consumption, it will be specified as such. The same convention will apply to the terms asset prices, wealth, savings, etc.

Following the analysis of the benchmark case, we study the situation when the investor receives noisy signals on inflation. Given the signal observations, the investor obtains the conditional probability distribution of the current basket price and, in turn, the conditional distribution of the current real asset prices. In general, the new risk due to the partial observability of the basket price affects the optimal policy. Interestingly enough, the characterization of the optimal portfolio in the partially observed case is the same as in the fully observed case. Thus, in both cases, the optimal portfolio is a linear combination of the risk-free fund, growth optimal fund, and the fund that arises from the correlation between the inflation uncertainty and the market risk. As before, the composition of the last fund for an investor depends on the nature of his consumption basket, and his allocation in the three funds depends on his wealth, utility function, and consumption basket price filter, which represents his best estimate given the observations.

There have been several studies on consumption measurement. Klenow (2003) discusses how the U.S. government measures consumption growth and how it considers the fact that the consumption basket changes over time. Inflation measurement and the problems with that are considered in Alchian and Klein (1973), Bradley (2001), and Shapiro and Wilcox (1997). Many of the social costs of inflation are caused by its unpredictability. The unpredictability is studied, e.g., by Ungar and Zilberhard (1993). The results of these studies are consistent with the present paper in the sense that our investor, due to noisy signals measurements, does not completely observe the consumption goods prices and, therefore, updates his belief about inflation from different consumption basket price signals.

The connection between inflation and asset prices is studied by Basak and Yan (2010), Campbell and Vuolteenaho (2004), and Cohen et al. (2005). According to them, the stock market suffers from money illusion, i.e., it incorrectly discounts real cash flows with nominal discount rates. Thus, when the inflation is high, the equity premium is also high and vice versa. In this paper, we do not consider money illusion. Optimal portfolio selection under inflation is studied, e.g., Brennan and Xia (2002), Chen and Moore (1985), Manaster (1979), Munk et al. (2004), and Solnik (1978). Brennan and Xia (2002) consider a more complicated inflation process but assume perfectly observed inflation. In our paper, we emphasize the fact that inflation signals are noisy and, therefore, the current consumption basket price is not completely observed. Portfolio selection with learning is also considered in Xia (2001) and Brennan (1998). In these papers, the investor learns about the stock returns, i.e., about the parameters of the price processes. As explained earlier, in the present paper the investor does not observe the consumption basket price directly, but infers it from the observed inflation signal. Thus, without the perfect information, the current real asset prices are also incompletely observed. In this way, our model differs from the above papers and also answers a different economic question: What is the effect of the noisy observations of inflation on the optimal portfolio selection?

Much more related to our paper is that of Bensoussan et al. (2009) that presents the continuous-time counterpart of our model. Also the results presented here are consistent with their continuous-time counterparts. However, the mathematical analysis of the discrete-time formulation, presented here for the first time, is different. More importantly, our discrete-time formulation paves the road for future researchers to perform related empirical studies since the data in practice can only be collected in discrete time.

The rest of the paper is organized as follows. Section 2 formulates the discrete-time model under considerations along with the underlying information sets and stochastic processes. The optimal policy under the fully observed inflation is derived in Sect. 3. Section 4 formulates the model in the partially observed case. Section 5 concludes the paper.

2 Discrete-Time Model

Let us consider a discrete-time model with the length of period h. Then the time period can be represented by

$$t \in \{0, h, 2h, \ldots, Nh = T\},$$

where N is the number of periods. We introduce notation:

$$\delta f(t) = f(t+h) - f(t).$$

2.1 Evolution of Prices of Stocks

Let us consider a probability space $(\Omega, \mathcal{A}, P)$. Let $\alpha_i(t)$ and $\sigma_{ij}(t)$ denote deterministic and bounded expected returns and volatility functions of time, respectively. Let $\delta w_j(t) = w_j(t+h) - w_j(t)$ denote independent Gaussian variables with 0 mean and variance h. Let $\mathcal{G}_t$ be the σ-algebra generated by $\delta w(s), s = 0, \ldots, t$, where $w(s)$ is an n-dimensional Gaussian random vector, i.e., $w(s) = (w_1(s), \ldots, w_n(s))^{\mathsf{T}}$. Then the evolution of the stock price of security i, $i = 1, 2, \ldots, n$, can be described by

$$Y_i(t+h) = Y_i(t) \exp\left[\left(\alpha_i(t) - \frac{1}{2}\sigma_{ii}(t)\right)h + \sum_{j=1}^{n} \sigma_{ij}(t) \cdot \delta w_j(t)\right]. \quad (1)$$

Let us introduce the following process

$$\theta(t) = \sigma^{-1}(t)\left(\alpha(t) - r\mathbf{1}\right), \quad (2)$$

known as the market price risk, where $\mathbf{1}$ denotes the unit column vector, and we assume that the market is complete so that the matrix $\sigma(t) = \left(\sigma_{ij}(t)\right)$ is invertible.

The dynamics of the nominal value of the risk-free asset is given by

$$Y_0(t+h) = Y_0(t)e^{rh}. \quad (3)$$

Let us define the process $Q(t)$ by

$$Q(t+h) = Q(t) \exp\left[-\theta(t) \cdot \delta w(t) - \frac{1}{2}h\left|\theta(t)\right|^2\right]; \quad Q(0) = 1. \quad (4)$$

The processes $Q(t)$ and $Q(t)Y_i(t)e^{-rt}$ are $(P, \mathcal{G}_t)$ martingales.

2.2 Risk-Neutral Probability

Define on $(\Omega, \mathcal{A})$ a probability $\hat{P}$ as follows

$$\left.\frac{d\hat{P}}{dP}\right|_{\mathcal{G}_t} = Q(t).$$

Now let us set

$$\delta\tilde{w}(t) = \delta w(t) + h\theta(t).$$

Then on $(\Omega, \mathcal{A}, \hat{P})$, the $\delta\tilde{w}(t)$ forms a sequence of independent Gaussian random variables with mean 0 and variance h.

We can also write (1) as

$$Y_i\left(t+h\right) = Y_i(t)\exp\left[\left(r - \frac{1}{2}\sigma_{ii}(t)\right)h + \sum_{j=1}^{n}\sigma_{ij}(t)\cdot\delta\tilde{w}_j(t)\right], \tag{5}$$

and $Y_i(t)e^{-rt}$ is a $\left(\hat{P}, \mathcal{G}_t\right)$ martingale.

2.3 Evolution of Basket Price

We consider another Wiener process $w_I(t)$, which is one-dimensional and correlated with $w(t)$. Then we have

$$E\left[\delta w_i(t)\delta w_I(t)\right] = \rho_i h,$$

for all $i \in \{1, \ldots, n\}$, and redefine $\mathcal{G}_t$ as the σ-algebra generated by $\delta w(s)$ and $\delta w_I(s), s = 0, \ldots, t$. Let $\rho^* = (\rho_1, \rho_2, \ldots, \rho_n)$ with $*$ denoting the transpose operation.

The dynamics of the basket price process $B(t)$ is given by

$$B\left(t+h\right) = B(t)\exp\left[\left(I - \frac{1}{2}\zeta^2\right)h + \zeta\cdot\delta w_I(t)\right]; \quad B\left(0\right) = B_0, \tag{6}$$

where $I > 0$ represents the expected periodic inflation and $\zeta > 0$ denotes the inflation volatility. The initial basket price B_0 is known when there is full observation, whereas it can be a random variable independent of $\mathcal{G}_t$ in the case of partial information.

Let us define the log basket price $L(t) = \log B(t)$, so that

$$L\left(t+h\right) = L(t) + \left(I - \frac{1}{2}\zeta^2\right)h + \zeta\cdot\delta w_I(t);\ L(0) = L_0 = \log B_0. \tag{7}$$

2.4 Self-financing Wealth Process

In the discrete-time setting, the nominal wealth at time t is defined by

$$X(t) = C(t)h + \varpi_0(t)e^{rt} + \varpi(t)Y(t), \tag{8}$$

where $\varpi_0(t)$ and $\varpi(t)$ denote the amount of riskless and risky assets owned by the investor, and $C(t)$ is the consumption process.

The self-financing condition implies

$$X(t+h) = \varpi_0(t)e^{rt}e^{rh} + \varpi(t)Y(t+h)$$

and, therefore, we have

$$\delta\left(X(t)e^{-rt}\right) = \varpi(t) \cdot \delta\left[Y(t)e^{-rt}\right] - C(t)h \cdot e^{-rt}, \tag{9}$$

where, by (5),

$$\delta\left[Y_i(t)e^{-rt}\right] = Y_i(t)e^{-rt}\left[\exp\left(-\frac{1}{2}\sigma_{ii}(t)h + \sum_{j=1}^{n}\sigma_{ij}(t)\cdot\delta\tilde{w}_j(t)\right) - 1\right].$$

Set

$$\delta\mu_i(t) = -\frac{1}{2}\sigma_{ii}(t)h + \sum_{j=1}^{n}\sigma_{ij}(t)\cdot\delta\tilde{w}_j(t); \quad \mu_i(0) = 0. \tag{10}$$

Then

$$\delta\left[Y_i(t)e^{-rt}\right] = Y_i(t)e^{-rt}\left[\exp\left(\delta\mu_i(t)\right) - 1\right]. \tag{11}$$

Let us define $\pi = (\pi_1, \pi_2, \ldots, \pi_n)$ with

$$\pi_i(t) = \frac{\varpi_i(t)Y_i(t)}{X(t)}, \tag{12}$$

representing the proportion of the wealth invested in security i. Then the evolution of wealth is given by

$$\delta\left[X(t)e^{-rt}\right] = X(t)e^{-rt}\sum_{i=1}^{n}\pi_i(t)\left[\exp\left(\delta\mu_i(t)\right) - 1\right] - C(t)h \cdot e^{-rt}. \tag{13}$$

3 Fully Observed Inflation Case

We consider a problem starting at t, with $X(t) = x$, $L(t) = L$, and dynamics

$$\delta\left[X(s)e^{-rs}\right] = X(s)e^{-rs}\sum_{i=1}^{n}\pi_i(s)\left[\exp\left(\delta\mu_i(s)\right) - 1\right] - C(s)h \cdot e^{-rs}, \tag{14}$$

$$\delta L(s) = \left(I - \frac{\zeta^2}{2}\right)h + \zeta\delta w_I(s). \tag{15}$$

With $U_1(\cdot)$ and $U_2(\cdot)$ denoting the utility of real consumption and real wealth, respectively, and $U_i'(0) = \infty$, $U_i'(\infty) = 0$, $i = 1, 2$, the performance is given by

$$J(\pi(\cdot), C(\cdot); x, L, t) = E\left[\sum_{s=t}^{T-h} h \cdot U_1\left(C(s)e^{-L(s)}\right) \cdot e^{-\beta(s-t)} + U_2\left(X(t)e^{-L(t)}\right) e^{-\beta(T-t)} | L(t) = L, X(t) = x\right]. \tag{16}$$

Here the wealth process $X(t)$ follows (13) and β as the utility discount rate. We define the *value function* as

$$V(x, L, t) = \sup_{C(\cdot),\pi(\cdot)} J(C(\cdot), \pi(\cdot); x, L, t). \tag{17}$$

3.1 Dynamic Programming

Now we have the following dynamic programming problem:

$$V(x, L, t) = \max_{\pi,C} h \cdot U_1\left(Ce^{-L}\right) + e^{-\beta h} E\left[V(X(t+h), L(t+h), t+h)\right], \tag{18}$$

where $V(x, L, T) = U_2\left(x \cdot e^{-L}\right)$. From (13) and (7), we have

$$\begin{aligned} X(t+h) &= x \cdot e^{rh}\left[1 + \sum_{i=1}^{n} \pi_i \cdot (\exp(\delta\mu_i(t)) - 1)\right] - C \cdot h \cdot e^{rh} \\ &= x \cdot e^{rh}\left[1 - \sum_{i=1}^{n} \pi_i + \sum \pi_i \exp\left(\alpha_i(t) - r - \frac{1}{2}\sigma_{ii}(t)\right)h \right. \\ &\quad \left. \cdot \exp\left(\sum_{j=1}^{n} \sigma_{ij}\delta w_j(t)\right)\right] - C \cdot h \cdot e^{rh} \end{aligned}$$

and

$$L(t+h) = L + \left(I - \frac{\zeta^2}{2}\right)h + \zeta\delta w_I(t).$$

We define

$$\delta\tilde{w}_I = \frac{\delta w_I - \rho^*\delta w}{\sqrt{1 - |\rho|^2}}.$$

Then $\delta\tilde{w}_I$ and δw are independent and the variance of $\delta\tilde{w}_I$ is h. Hence,

$$L(t+h) = L + \left(I - \frac{\zeta^2}{2}\right)h + \zeta\sqrt{1-|\rho|^2}\delta\tilde{w}_I + \zeta\rho^*\delta w$$

and

$$\begin{aligned}
&E\left[V\left(X(t+h), L(t+h), t+h\right)\right] \\
&= (2n)^{-\frac{n+1}{2}} \int \cdots \int V\left(xe^{rh}\left(1-\sum_{i=1}^{n}\pi_i\right) - C \cdot h \cdot e^{rh}\right. \\
&+ xe^{rh}\sum_{i=1}^{n}\pi_i \exp\left(\alpha_i(t) - r - \frac{1}{2}\sigma_{ii}(t)\right)h \exp\left(\sqrt{h}\sum_{j=1}^{n}\sigma_{ij}\xi_j\right), L + \left(I - \frac{\zeta^2}{2}\right)h \\
&\left. + \zeta\sqrt{h}\sum_{j=1}^{n}\rho_j\xi_j + \zeta\sqrt{h}\sqrt{1-|\rho|^2}\psi, t+h\right) \\
&\cdot \exp\left(-\frac{1}{2}\left(\sum_{j=1}^{n}\xi_j^2 + \psi^2\right)\right) d\xi_1 \cdots d\xi_n d\psi.
\end{aligned}$$

So, (18) becomes

$$\begin{aligned}
V(x, L, t) = \max_{\pi, C} hU_1\left(Ce^{-L}\right) + e^{-\beta h}\int \cdots \int \qquad (19) \\
V\left(xe^{rh}\left(1-\sum_{i=1}^{n}\pi_i\right) - C \cdot h \cdot e^{rh}\right. \\
+ xe^{rh}\sum_{i=1}^{n}\pi_i \cdot \exp\left(\left(\alpha_i(t) - r - \frac{1}{2}\sigma_{ii}(t)\right)h + \sqrt{h}\sum_{j=1}^{n}\sigma_{ij}\xi_j\right), \\
\left. L + \left(I - \frac{\zeta^2}{2}\right)h + \zeta\sqrt{h}\left(\sum_{j=1}^{n}\rho_j\xi_j + \sqrt{1-|\rho|^2}\psi\right), t+h\right) \\
\cdot \frac{\exp\left(-\frac{1}{2}\left(\sum_{j=1}^{n}\xi_j^2 + \psi^2\right)\right)}{(2n)^{\frac{n+1}{2}}} d\xi_1 \cdots d\xi_n d\psi.
\end{aligned}$$

3.2 Optimal Feedback Policy

Let $(\hat{C}(x, L, t), \hat{\pi}(x, L, t))$ be the optimal feedback consumption and investment policy corresponding to (19). It is convenient to introduce the notation:

$$\begin{aligned}\hat{X}_h(x, t; \xi) &= xe^{rh}\left(1 - \sum_{i=1}^{n} \hat{\pi}_i\right) - \hat{C} \cdot h \cdot e^{rh} \\ &\quad + xe^{rh} \sum_{i=1}^{n} \hat{\pi}_i \exp\left(\left(\alpha_i(t) - r - \frac{1}{2}\sigma_{ii}(t)\right) h + \sqrt{h}\,(\sigma\xi)_i\right)\end{aligned} \tag{20}$$

and

$$\hat{L}_h(L, \xi, \psi) = L + \left(I - \frac{\zeta^2}{2}\right) h + \zeta\sqrt{h} \cdot \left(\rho^*\xi + \sqrt{1 - |\rho|^2}\psi\right).$$

The necessary conditions of optimality are

$$\begin{aligned}&hU_1'\left(\hat{C}e^{-L}\right)e^{-L} + e^{-\beta h} \int \cdots \int \frac{\partial V}{\partial x}\left(\hat{X}_h(x, t; \xi), \hat{L}_h(L, \xi, \psi), t + h\right) \\ &\quad \cdot \frac{\exp\left(-\frac{1}{2}\left(|\xi|^2 + \psi^2\right)\right)}{(2n)^{\frac{n+1}{2}}} d\xi_1 \cdots d\xi_n d\psi \left(-he^{rh}\right) = 0\end{aligned} \tag{21}$$

and

$$\begin{aligned}&\int \cdots \int \frac{\partial V}{\partial x}\left(\hat{X}_h(x, t, \xi), \hat{L}_h(L, \xi, \psi), t + h\right)\Big[-xe^{rh} \\ &\quad + xe^{rh} \exp\left(\left(\alpha_i(t) - r - \frac{1}{2}\sigma_{ii}(t)\right) h + \sqrt{h}\,(\sigma\xi)_i\right)\Big] \frac{\exp\left(-\frac{1}{2}\left(|\xi|^2 + \psi^2\right)\right)}{(2n)^{\frac{n+1}{2}}} \\ &\quad d\xi_1 \cdots d\xi_n d\psi = 0, \quad i = 1, \ldots, n.\end{aligned} \tag{22}$$

We divide (21) by h and (22) by xe^{rh} to get

$$\begin{aligned}&U_1'\left(\hat{C}e^{-L}\right)e^{-L} = e^{-(\beta - r)h} \int \cdots \int \frac{\partial V}{\partial x}\left(\hat{X}_h(x, t, \xi), \hat{L}_h(L, \xi, \psi), t + h\right) \\ &\quad \cdot \frac{\exp\left(-\frac{1}{2}\left(|\xi|^2 + \psi^2\right)\right)}{(2n)^{\frac{n+1}{2}}} d\xi_1 \cdots d\xi_n d\psi\end{aligned} \tag{23}$$

and

$$\begin{aligned}&\int \cdots \int \frac{\partial V}{\partial x}\left(\hat{X}_h(x, t, \xi), \hat{L}_h(L, \xi, \psi), t + h\right) \\ &\quad \left[-1 + \exp\left(\left(\alpha_i(t) - r - \frac{1}{2}\sigma_{ii}(t)\right) h + \sqrt{h}\,(\sigma\xi)_i\right)\right]\end{aligned}$$

$$\cdot \frac{\exp\left(-\frac{1}{2}\left(|\xi|^2+\psi^2\right)\right)}{(2n)^{\frac{n+1}{2}}} d\xi_1 \cdots d\xi_n d\psi = 0, \quad i = 1, \ldots, n. \tag{24}$$

But, by (19), we also get by differentiating with respect to x:

$$\frac{\partial V}{\partial x}(x, L, t) = e^{-\beta h} \int \cdots \int \frac{\partial V}{\partial x}\left(\hat{X}_h(x, t, \xi), \hat{L}_h(L, \xi, \psi), t+h\right)$$
$$\left[e^{rh}\left(1-\sum_{i=1}^{n}\pi_i\right) + e^{rh}\sum_{i=1}^{n}\hat{\pi}_i \exp\left(\left(\alpha_i(t) - r - \frac{1}{2}\sigma_{ii}(t)\right)h + \sqrt{h}\sum_{j=1}^{n}\sigma_{ij}\xi_j\right)\right]$$
$$\cdot \frac{\exp\left(-\frac{1}{2}\left(|\xi|^2+\psi^2\right)\right)}{(2n)^{\frac{n+1}{2}}} d\xi_1 \cdots d\xi_n d\psi.$$

Multiplying (24) by $\hat{\pi}_i e^{rh}$ and summing up, we get from the above equation

$$\frac{\partial V}{\partial x} = e^{-(\beta-r)h} \int \cdots \int \frac{\partial V}{\partial x}\left(\hat{X}_h(x, t, \xi), \hat{L}_h(L, \xi, \psi), t+h\right) \tag{25}$$
$$\cdot \frac{\exp\left(-\frac{1}{2}\left(|\xi|^2+\psi^2\right)\right)}{(2n)^{\frac{n+1}{2}}} d\xi_1 \cdots d\xi_n d\psi.$$

Now comparing with (23), we have proven

$$U_1'\left(\hat{C}e^{-L}\right)e^{-L} = \frac{\partial V}{\partial x}(x, L, t), \tag{26}$$

which yields the optimal feedback $\hat{C}(x, L, t)$. It corresponds with the solution (3.3) obtained in the continuous-time model of Bensoussan et al. (2009).

To obtain $\hat{\pi}_i$, we must use relation (24), replacing $\hat{X}_h(x, t, \xi)$ and $\hat{L}_h(L, \xi, \psi)$ by formulas in (20). For convenience, we first write the integrand of the system (24), plug (20) into that integrand, and transform it by using the integration by substitution:

$$\frac{\partial V}{\partial x}\left(\hat{X}_h(x, t, \xi), \hat{L}_h(L, \xi, \psi), t+h\right)$$
$$= \frac{\partial V}{\partial x}\left(\left(x - \hat{C}h\right)e^{rh}, \hat{L}_h(L, \xi, \psi), t+h\right)$$
$$+ \int_0^1 \frac{\partial^2 V}{\partial x^2}\left(\left(x - \hat{C}h\right)e^{rh} + \theta x e^{rh}\sum_{k=1}^{n}\hat{\pi}_k\left(\exp\left(\left(\alpha_k(t) - r - \frac{1}{2}\sigma_{kk}(t)\right)h\right.\right.\right.$$
$$\left.\left.\left. + \sqrt{h}(\sigma\xi)_k\right) - 1\right), \hat{L}_h(L, \xi, \psi), t+h\right)$$
$$x e^{rh}\sum_{k=1}^{n}\hat{\pi}_k\left(\exp\left(\left(\alpha_k(t) - r - \frac{1}{2}\sigma_{kk}(t)\right)h + \sqrt{h}(\sigma\xi)_k\right) - 1\right)d\theta,$$

and write the system (24) as in (27) which gives $\hat{\pi}_i(x, L, t)$ with small h (see below).

$$
\begin{aligned}
0 = &\int \cdots \int \frac{\partial V}{\partial x}\left(\left(x - \hat{C}h\right)e^{rh}, \hat{L}_h(L, \xi, \psi), t + h\right)\left[\exp\left(\left(\alpha_i(t)\right.\right.\right. \\
&\left.\left.\left. - r - \frac{1}{2}\sigma_{ii}(t)\right)h + \sqrt{h}(\sigma\xi)_i\right) - 1\right]\frac{\exp\left(-\frac{1}{2}\left(|\xi|^2 + \psi^2\right)\right)}{(2n)^{\frac{n+1}{2}}}d\xi_1\cdots d\xi_n d\psi \\
&+ xe^{rh}\int \cdots \int \int_0^1 d\theta \frac{\partial^2 V}{\partial x^2}\left(\left(x - \hat{C}h\right)e^{rh} + \theta x e^{rh}\sum_k \hat{\pi}_k\left(\exp\left(\left(\right.\right.\right.\right. \\
&\left.\left.\left.\left.\alpha_k(t) - r - \frac{1}{2}\sigma_{kk}(t)\right)h + \sqrt{h}(\sigma\xi)_k\right) - 1\right), \hat{L}_h(L, \xi, \psi), t + h\right) \\
&\cdot \sum_{k=1}^{n}\hat{\pi}_k\left(\exp\left(\left(\alpha_k(t) - r - \frac{1}{2}\sigma_{kk}(t)\right)h + \sqrt{h}(\sigma\xi)_k\right) - 1\right)\left(\exp\left(\left(\alpha_i(t)\right.\right.\right. \\
&\left.\left.\left. - r - \frac{1}{2}\sigma_{ii}(t)\right)h + \sqrt{h}(\sigma\xi)_i\right) - 1\right)\frac{\exp\left(-\frac{1}{2}\left(|\xi|^2 + \psi^2\right)\right)}{(2n)^{\frac{n+1}{2}}}d\xi_1\cdots d\xi_n d\psi, \\
&\forall \quad i = 1, \ldots, n.
\end{aligned} \tag{27}
$$

3.3 Approximation for Small h

The system (27) is highly non-linear. We can simplify it for small h to obtain the same formulas as in the continuous time. We make the following three approximations by (20) and exponential function with small h:

$$
\begin{aligned}
&\left(x - \hat{C}h\right)e^{rh} \sim x, \\
&\hat{L}_h(L, \xi, \psi) \sim L + \zeta\sqrt{h}\left(\rho^*\xi + \sqrt{1 - |\rho|^2}\psi\right), \\
&\exp\left(\left(\alpha_i(t) - r - \frac{1}{2}\sigma_{ii}(t)\right)h + \sqrt{h}(\sigma\xi)_i\right) - 1 \sim \sqrt{h}(\sigma\xi)_i \\
&+ \left(\alpha_i(t) - r - \frac{1}{2}\sigma_{ii}(t) + \frac{1}{2}(\sigma\xi)_i^2\right)h.
\end{aligned}
$$

Then, by plugging the above approximations into (27), we obtain

$$
\begin{aligned}
0 = &\int \cdots \int \frac{\partial V}{\partial x}\left(x, L + \zeta\sqrt{h}\left(\rho^*\xi + \sqrt{1 - |\rho|^2}\psi\right), t + h\right)\left(\sqrt{h}(\sigma\xi)_i\right. \\
&\left. + \left(\alpha_i(t) - r - \frac{1}{2}\sigma_{ii}(t) + \frac{1}{2}(\sigma\xi)_i^2\right)h\right)\frac{\exp\left(-\frac{1}{2}\left(|\xi|^2 + \psi^2\right)\right)}{(2n)^{\frac{n+1}{2}}}d\xi_1\cdots d\xi_n d\psi
\end{aligned}
$$

$$+x\int_0^1\cdots\int\int_0^1 d\theta\frac{\partial^2 V}{\partial x^2}\left(x+\theta x\sum_k \hat{\pi}_k\left(\sqrt{h}\,(\sigma\xi)_k\right.\right.$$
$$\left.\left.\cdot\left(\alpha_k(t)-r-\frac{1}{2}\sigma_{kk}(t)\right)h\right),\hat{L}_h\left(L,\xi,\psi\right),t+h\right)$$
$$\cdot\sum_{k=1}^n \hat{\pi}_k\left(\left(\sqrt{h}\,(\sigma\xi)_k+\alpha_k(t)-r-\frac{1}{2}\sigma_{kk}(t)\right)h\right)\left(\left(\sqrt{h}\,(\sigma\xi)_i+\alpha_i(t)\right.\right.$$
$$\left.\left.-r-\frac{1}{2}\sigma_{ii}(t)\right)h\right)\frac{\exp\left(-\frac{1}{2}\left(|\xi|^2+\psi^2\right)\right)}{(2n)^{\frac{n+1}{2}}}d\xi_1\cdots d\xi_n d\psi,\ i=1,\ldots,n.$$

Next we apply Taylor's expansion to obtain

$$0\sim h\cdot\left(\alpha_i(t)-r\right)\frac{\partial V}{\partial x}\left(x,L,t\right)+\frac{\partial^2 V}{\partial x\partial L}\left(x,L,t\right)\zeta h$$
$$\cdot\int\cdots\int(\sigma\xi)_i\left(\rho^*\xi+\sqrt{1-|\rho|^2}\psi\right)\frac{\exp\left(-\frac{1}{2}\left(|\xi|^2+\psi^2\right)\right)}{(2n)^{\frac{n+1}{2}}}d\xi_1\cdots d\xi_n d\psi$$
$$+hx\frac{\partial^2 V}{\partial x^2}\left(x,L,t\right)\int\cdots\int\sum_k\hat{\pi}_k\left(\sigma\xi\right)_k\left(\sigma\xi\right)_i\frac{\exp\left(-\frac{1}{2}\left(|\xi|^2+\psi^2\right)\right)}{(2n)^{\frac{n+1}{2}}}$$
$$d\xi_1\cdots d\xi_n d\psi.$$

Hence, finally after dividing by h, we have

$$\left(\alpha_i(t)-r\right)\frac{\partial V}{\partial x}\left(x,L,t\right)+\frac{\partial^2 V}{\partial x\partial L}\left(x,L,t\right)\zeta\left(\sigma\rho\right)_i$$
$$+x\frac{\partial^2 V}{\partial x^2}\left(x,L,t\right)\left(\sigma\sigma^*\hat{\pi}\right)_i=0. \tag{28}$$

Recalling that

$$\alpha_i(t)-r=\left(\sigma\theta\right)_i,$$

we deduce

$$\theta\frac{\partial V}{\partial x}\left(x,L,t\right)+\zeta\rho\frac{\partial^2 V}{\partial x\partial L}\left(x,L,t\right)+x\frac{\partial^2 V}{\partial x^2}\left(x,L,t\right)\sigma^*\hat{\pi}=0. \tag{29}$$

Thus, we have

$$\hat{\pi}\left(x,L,t\right)=-\frac{\left(\sigma^*(t)\right)^{-1}\left[\theta\frac{\partial V}{\partial x}\left(x,L,t\right)+\zeta\rho\frac{\partial^2 V}{\partial x\partial L}\left(x,L,t\right)\right]}{x\frac{\partial^2 V}{\partial x^2}\left(x,L,t\right)}, \tag{30}$$

which can be compared with the formula (3.4) obtained in the continuous-time model of Bensoussan et al. (2009)

We can see that the first term on the right-hand side of (30) represents the risky mutual fund of classical Mutual Fund Theorem that states that the investor can limit his portfolio to investing simply in the risk-free fund and this risky mutual fund. The presence of the second term on the right-hand side of (30) requires the investor to consider a third fund due to the effect of uncertainty in inflation. Note that if the inflation is uncorrelated with all the risky assets, then the second term is zero. The inflation effect depends also on the inflation volatility $\varsigma > 0$ and on V_{Lx}, i.e., on the sensitivity of the marginal value V_x with respect to the ln-basket price. If the marginal value of nominal wealth rises (falls) in the basket price, then the higher the correlation, the more (less) funds the investor allocates to the stock market.

Now we state the following extension of the classical Mutual Fund Theorem.

Theorem 1 *With fully observed inflation, the optimal portfolio involves an allocation between the risk-free fund* F_1 *and two risky funds that consist only of risky assets:* $F_2(t) = (\sigma^*(t))^{-1}\theta(t)$ *and* $F_3(t) = (\sigma^*(t))^{-1}\rho$, *where the vector* $F_k(t)$ *represents the* k^{th} *portfolio's weights of the risky assets at time* $t, k = 2, 3$. *Furthermore, the optimal proportional allocations* $\mu_k(t)$ *of wealth in the fund* $F_k(t), k = 1, 2, 3$, *at time t are given by*

$$\mu_2(t) = \frac{-V_x(x, L, t)}{x(t)V_{xx}(X, L, t)},$$
$$\mu_3(t) = \frac{-\varsigma V_{Lx}(x, L, t)}{x(t)V_{xx}(X, L, t)},$$

and

$$\mu_1(t) = 1 - \mu_2(t) - \mu_3(t).$$

According to Theorem 1, the optimal portfolio can consist of investments in three funds, whereas the classical problem (without uncertain inflation) requires only two funds. The first fund is the risk-free asset and the second one is the growth optimum portfolio fund as in the classical problem. The third fund arises from the correlation between the inflation uncertainty and the market risk.

Three-fund theorems are not new. They arise, e.g., in the continuous-time portfolio models of Zhao (2007) and Brennan and Xia (2002). Zhao (2007) considers an optimal asset allocation policy for an investor concerned with the performance of his investment relative to a benchmark. In his case, one of the two risky funds replicates the benchmark portfolio. In the three-fund theorem obtained by Brennan and Xia (2002), one fund replicates real interest rate uncertainty, another one is the classical growth optimal fund, and the last one replicates the fully observed inflation uncertainty. They do not consider partially observed inflation as in the present paper.

Before we take up the case of partially observed inflation in Sect. 4, next, let us illustrate the special case of one period where we can obtain explicitly the optimal consumption and portfolio policies.

3.4 One-Period Problem

Now, let us take $T = h$ and $N = 1$. We call $V(x, L, 0) = V(x, L)$, $\alpha_i(0) = \alpha_i$, and $\sigma_i(0) = \sigma_{ij}$. Also, let $U_2(x, L) = U_2\left(xe^{-L}\right)$. Then, we get from (19)

$$V(x, L) = \max_{\pi, C}\left[hU_1\left(Ce^{-L}\right) + e^{-\beta h}\int\cdots\int U_2\left(xe^{rh}\left(1 - \sum_{i=1}^{n}\pi_i\right)\right.\right. \quad (31)$$

$$-C\cdot h\cdot e^{rh} + xe^{rh}\sum_{i=1}^{n}\pi_i\cdot\exp\left(\left(\alpha_i - r - \frac{1}{2}\sigma_{ii}\right)h + \sqrt{h}\sum_{j=1}^{n}\sigma_{ij}\xi_j\right),$$

$$L + \left(x - \frac{\varsigma^2}{2}\right)h + \varsigma\sqrt{h}\left(\rho^*\xi + \sqrt{1 - |\rho|^2\psi}\right)\Bigg)\frac{\exp\left(-\frac{1}{2}\left(|\xi|^2 + \psi^2\right)\right)}{(2n)^{\frac{n+1}{2}}}$$

$$\left. d\xi_1\cdots d\xi_n d\psi\right].$$

We still have (26). Now (22) becomes

$$0 = \int\cdots\int\frac{\partial U_2}{\partial x}\left(\left(x - \hat{C}h\right)e^{rh}, \hat{L}_h(x, \xi, \psi)\right)\Big[\exp\left(\left(\alpha_i - r\right.\right. \quad (32)$$

$$\left.\left.-\frac{1}{2}\sigma_{ii}\right)h + \sqrt{h}\left(\sigma\xi\right)_i\right) - 1\Big]\frac{\exp\left(-\frac{1}{2}\left(|\xi|^2 + \psi^2\right)\right)}{(2n)^{\frac{n+1}{2}}}d\xi_1\cdots d\xi_n d\psi$$

$$+xe^{rh}\int\cdots\int\int_0^1 d\theta\frac{\partial^2 U_2}{\partial x^2}\left(\left(x - \hat{C}h\right)e^{rh} + \theta xe^{rh}\right.$$

$$\cdot\sum_k\hat{\pi}_k\left(\exp\left(\left(\alpha_k(t) - r - \frac{1}{2}\sigma_{kk}(t)\right)h + \sqrt{h}\left(\sigma\xi\right)_k\right) - 1\right),$$

$$\left.\hat{L}_h(x, \xi, \psi)\right)\sum_k\hat{\pi}_k\left(\exp\left(\left(\alpha_k - r - \frac{1}{2}\sigma_{kk}\right)h + \sqrt{h}\left(\sigma\xi\right)_k\right) - 1\right)$$

$$\cdot\left(\exp\left(\left(\alpha_i - r - \frac{1}{2}\sigma_{ii}\right)h + \sqrt{h}\left(\sigma\xi\right)_i\right) - 1\right)\frac{\exp\left(-\frac{1}{2}\left(|\xi|^2 + \psi^2\right)\right)}{(2n)^{\frac{n+1}{2}}}$$

$$d\xi_1\cdots d\xi_n d\psi.$$

We use the small h approximation to solve the system (32). It amounts to using (30) with replacing

$$\frac{\partial V}{\partial x}(x, L, t) \quad \text{by} \quad U_2'\left(xe^{-L}\right)e^{-L},$$
$$\frac{\partial^2 V}{\partial x \partial L}(x, L, t) \quad \text{by} \quad -U_2''\left(xe^{-L}\right)\left(e^{-L}\right)^2 - U_2'\left(xe^{-L}\right)e^{-L},$$

and

$$\frac{\partial^2 V}{\partial x^2}(x, L, t) \quad \text{by} \quad U_2''\left(xe^{-L}\right)\left(e^{-L}\right)^2.$$

Therefore, we get from (30),

$$\hat{\pi}(x, L) = -\frac{(\sigma^*)^{-1}\left[(\theta - \zeta\rho)U_2'\left(xe^{-L}\right) - \zeta\rho U_2''\left(xe^{-L}\right)e^{-L}\right]}{xU_2''\left(xe^{-L}\right)e^{-L}}. \tag{33}$$

To obtain $\hat{C}(x, L)$, we use (26), which implies the calculation of $\frac{\partial V}{\partial x}(x, L)$. We use (25) to obtain

$$\frac{\partial V}{\partial x}(x, L) = e^{-(\beta - r)h}\int \cdots \int \frac{\partial U_2}{\partial x}\left(\hat{X}_h(x, \xi), \hat{L}_h(L, \xi, \psi)\right) \cdot \frac{\exp\left(-\frac{1}{2}\left(|\xi|^2 + \psi^2\right)\right)}{(2n)^{\frac{n+1}{2}}} d\xi_1 \cdots d\xi_n d\psi, \tag{34}$$

where

$$\hat{X}_h(x, \xi) = \left(x - \hat{C}h\right)e^{rh} + xe^{rh}\sum_{i=1}^{n}\hat{\pi}_i\left(\exp\left(\left(\alpha_i - r - \frac{1}{2}\sigma_{ii}\right)h + \sqrt{h}(\sigma\xi)_i\right) - 1\right)$$
$$\hat{L}_h(x, \xi, \psi) = L + \zeta\sqrt{h}\left(\rho^*\xi + \sqrt{1 - |\rho|^2}\psi\right) + \left(I - \frac{\zeta^2}{2}\right)h.$$

Using the small h approximation, we get

$$\frac{\partial V}{\partial x}(x, L) \sim \frac{\partial U_2}{\partial x}(x, L) = U_2'\left(xe^{-L}\right)e^{-L},$$

and thus we obtain $\hat{C}$ by solving

$$U_1'\left(\hat{C}e^{-L}\right) = U_2'\left(xe^{-L}\right). \tag{35}$$

So, if $U_1 = U_2$, we get $\hat{C}(x, L) = x$. Note that the real consumption on the period is $h\hat{C}(x, L)$, so we can consider it as negligible.

4 Partially Observed Inflation Case

We now consider that $L(t)$ is not observable, but we observe the signal

$$\delta Z(t) = L(t)h + m \cdot \delta w_Z(t); \quad Z(0) = 0, \tag{36}$$

where $w_Z(t)$ is independent from $w(t)$ and $w_I(t)$. In this case, we extend (7), by

$$\delta L(t) = \left(I - \frac{\zeta^2}{2}\right)h + \zeta \cdot \delta w_I(t); \quad L(0) = N(L_0, S_0). \tag{37}$$

where $L(0)$ is gaussian with mean L_0 and standard deviation S_0.

Let us define

$$\mathcal{G}^t = \sigma\left(\delta w(s), \delta Z(s), s = 0, \ldots, t-h\right).$$

We look for the Kalman filter

$$\hat{L}(t) = E\left[L(t)|\mathcal{G}^t\right]; \quad \hat{L}(0) = L_0.$$

Consider the mean $\bar{L}(t)$ evolving as

$$\delta\bar{L}(t) = \left(I - \frac{\zeta^2}{2}\right)h; \quad \bar{L}(0) = L_0.$$

On account of linearity, it is sufficient to consider

$$\hat{L}(t) = \bar{L}(t) + \sum_{s=0}^{t-h} K_1(s) \cdot \delta w(s) + \sum_{s=0}^{t-h} K_2(s)\left(\delta Z(s) - \bar{L}(s)h\right), \tag{38}$$

where $K_1(t)$ and $K_2(t)$ are deterministic functions.

Let $\hat{L}^-(t) = E\left[L(t)|\mathcal{G}^{t-h}\right]$. Then from (37), we get

$$\hat{L}^-(t+h) = \hat{L}(t) + \left(I - \frac{\zeta^2}{2}\right)h. \tag{39}$$

Now by (38), we have

$$\begin{aligned}\hat{L}^-(t) &= E\left[\hat{L}(t)|G^{t-h}\right] \\ &= \bar{L}(t) + \sum_{s=0}^{t-2h} K_1(s) \cdot \delta w(s) + \sum_{s=0}^{t-2h} K_2(s)\left(\delta Z(s) - \hat{L}(s)h\right) \\ &\quad + K_2(t-h)\left(\hat{L}(t-h) - \bar{L}(t-h)\right)h.\end{aligned}$$

Hence,

$$\hat{L}^{-}(t+h) = \bar{L}(t+h) + \sum_{s=0}^{t-h} K_1(s) \cdot \delta w(s) + \sum_{s=0}^{t-h} K_2(s)\left(\delta Z(s) - \bar{L}(s)h\right) + K_2(t)\left(\hat{L}(t) - \bar{L}(t)\right)h. \tag{40}$$

However, from (38) we get

$$\hat{L}(t+h) = \bar{L}(t+h) + \sum_{s=0}^{t-h} K_1(s) \cdot \delta w(s) + \sum_{s=0}^{t-h} K_2(s)\left(\delta Z(s) - \bar{L}(s)\right)h + K_1(t) \cdot \delta w(t) + K_2(t)\left(\delta Z(t) - \bar{L}(t)h\right),$$

and from (40)

$$\hat{L}(t+h) = \bar{L}^{-}(t+h) + K_1(t) \cdot \delta w(t) + K_2(t)\left(\delta Z(t) - \hat{L}(t)h\right).$$

Using (39), we deduce

$$\hat{L}(t+h) = \hat{L}(t) + \left(I - \frac{\zeta^2}{2}\right)h + K_1 \cdot \delta w(t) + K_2(t)\left(\delta Z(t) - \hat{L}(t)h\right). \tag{41}$$

Calling $\varepsilon(t) = L(t) - \hat{L}(t)$, we get

$$\varepsilon(t+h) = \varepsilon(t) + \zeta \cdot \delta w_I(t) - K_1(t) \cdot \delta w(t) - K_2(t)\left(\delta Z(t) - \hat{L}(t)h\right),$$

$$\varepsilon(t+h) = \varepsilon(t) + \zeta \cdot \delta w_I(t) - K_1(t) \cdot \delta w(t) - K_2(t)\left(\varepsilon(t)h + m \cdot \delta w_Z(t)\right). \tag{42}$$

Set $S(t) = E[\varepsilon(t)^2]$. Then we get

$$
\begin{aligned}
E\left[\varepsilon(t+h)^2\right] &= S(t)\left(1-hK_2(t)\right)^2 + m^2\left(K_2(t)\right)^2 h \\
&\quad + \zeta^2 h + |K_1(t)|^2 h - 2\zeta K_1(t)\rho h \\
&= S(t) + \zeta^2\left(1-|\rho|^2\right)h + h\left|K_1(t)-\zeta\rho\right|^2 \\
&\quad + \left(h^2 S(t) + m^2 h\right)\left(K_2(t) - \frac{S(t)}{hS(t)+m^2}\right)^2 - \frac{hS^2(t)}{hS(t)+m^2}.
\end{aligned}
$$

In order to minimize the error, the best choices are

$$
K_1(t) = \zeta\rho, \quad K_2(t) = \frac{S(t)}{hS(t)+m^2}, \tag{43}
$$

where $S(t)$ is the solution of

$$
S(t+h) = S(t) + \zeta^2\left(1-|\rho|^2\right)h - \frac{hS^2(t)}{hS(t)+m^2}; \quad S(0) = S_0. \tag{44}
$$

The Kalman filter is given by

$$
\begin{aligned}
\hat{L}(t+h) &= \hat{L}(t) + \left(I - \frac{\zeta^2}{2}\right)h + \zeta\rho\cdot\delta w(t) \\
&\quad + \frac{S(t)}{hS(t)+m^2}\left(\delta Z(t) - \hat{L}(t)h\right); \quad \hat{L}(0) = L_0.
\end{aligned} \tag{45}
$$

It is standard to check that the conditional probability of $L(t)$ given $\mathcal{G}^t$ is gaussian with mean $\hat{L}(t)$ and variance $S(t)$ (deterministic).

4.1 *Objective Function for Partially Observed Case*

Consider again the cost function (16). This time the consumption process $C(t)$ and the portfolio $\pi(t)$ are adapted to $\mathcal{G}^t$. Hence, the wealth process $X(t)$ is observable.

Introducing the function

$$
\begin{aligned}
\tilde{U}_1\left(C,\hat{L},s\right) &= \frac{1}{\sqrt{2n}}\int U_1\left(C\exp\left(-\left(\hat{L}+y\sqrt{S(s)}\right)\right)\right)e^{-\frac{1}{2}y^2}dy, \\
\tilde{U}_2\left(x,\hat{L},s\right) &= \frac{1}{\sqrt{2n}}\int U_2\left(x\exp\left(-\left(\hat{L}+y\sqrt{S(s)}\right)\right)\right)e^{-\frac{1}{2}y^2}dy,
\end{aligned}
$$

the cost function (16) can be written as

$$\tilde{J}_{x,\hat{L},t}\left(\pi\left(\cdot\right),C\left(\cdot\right)\right)=E\left[\sum_{s=t}^{T-h}h\tilde{U}_1\left(C(s),\hat{L}(s),s\right)e^{-\beta(s-t)}\right.$$
$$\left.+\tilde{U}_2\left(X(t),\hat{L}(t),T\right)e^{-\beta(T-t)}|X(t)=x,\hat{L}(t)=\hat{L}\right], \tag{46}$$

with evolution

$$\delta\hat{L}(s)=\left(I-\frac{\zeta^2}{2}\right)h+\zeta\rho\cdot\delta w(s)$$
$$+\frac{S(s)}{hS(s)+m^2}\left(\delta Z(s)-\hat{L}(s)h\right);\quad \hat{L}(t)=t, \tag{47}$$

$$\delta\left(X(s)e^{-rs}\right)=X(s)e^{-rs}\sum_{i=1}^{n}\pi_i(s)\left(e^{\delta\mu_h(s)}-1\right)$$
$$-C(s)he^{-rh};\qquad X(t)=x. \tag{48}$$

The innovation

$$\delta\tilde{w}_Z(t)=\frac{\delta Z(t)-\hat{L}(t)h}{m} \tag{49}$$

is independent from $\mathcal{G}^t$ and is gaussian with mean 0 and variance

$$E\left[\left(\delta\tilde{w}_Z(t)\right)^2\right]=E\left[\left(\frac{\varepsilon(t)h}{m}+\delta w_Z(t)\right)^2\right]$$
$$=\frac{h^2}{m^2}S(t)+h=h\frac{\left(m^2+hS(t)\right)}{m^2}.$$

Hence,

$$\frac{S(t)}{hS(t)+m^2}\left(\delta Z(t)-\hat{L}(t)h\right)=\frac{S(t)m}{hS(t)+m^2}\delta\tilde{w}_Z(t)$$

is gaussian with mean 0 and variance $\frac{hS^2(t)}{m^2+hS(t)}$.

Since

$$\delta\tilde{w}_Z(t)=\frac{\varepsilon(t)h}{m}+\delta w_Z(t),$$

we see that $\delta w(t)$ and $\delta\tilde{w}_Z(t)$ are independent.

So, we can write

$$\delta\hat{L}(s)=\left(I-\frac{\zeta^2}{2}\right)h+\zeta\rho*\cdot\delta w(s)+\delta\tilde{w}_I, \tag{50}$$

where

$$\delta \tilde{w}_I = \frac{S(t)m}{hS(t) + m^2} \delta \tilde{w}_Z(t)$$

is gaussian independent of $\delta w(t)$ and has a variance $\frac{hS^2(t)}{m^2+hS(t)}$.

4.2 Dynamic Programming

We write the analog of (19):

$$\tilde{V}\left(x, \hat{L}, t\right) = \max_{\pi, C}\left[h\tilde{U}_1\left(C, \hat{L}, t\right) + e^{-\beta h}\int \cdots \int \tilde{V}\left(xe^{rh}\left(1 - \sum_{i=1}^{n}\pi_i\right) - C \cdot h \cdot e^{rh} + xe^{rh}\sum_{i=1}^{n}\pi_i \cdot \exp\left(\left(\alpha_i(t) - r - \frac{1}{2}\sigma_{ii}(t)\right)h + \sqrt{h}\sum_{j=1}^{n}\sigma_{ij}\xi_j\right), \hat{L} + \left(I - \frac{\zeta^2}{2}\right)h + \zeta\rho^*\xi\sqrt{h} + \frac{\sqrt{h}S(t)}{\sqrt{m^2 + hS(t)}}\psi, t + h\right) \frac{\exp\left(-\frac{1}{2}\left(|\xi|^2 + \psi^2\right)\right)}{(2n)^{\frac{n+1}{2}}} d\xi_1 \cdots d\xi_n d\psi\right], \tag{51}$$

$$\tilde{V}\left(x, \hat{L}, T\right) = \tilde{U}_2\left(x, \hat{L}, T\right).$$

The optimal feedback $\hat{C}(x, \hat{L}, t)$ is the solution of

$$\frac{\partial \tilde{U}_1}{\partial C}\left(c, \hat{L}, t\right) = \frac{\partial \tilde{V}}{\partial x}(x, t), \tag{52}$$

and we will have for $\hat{\pi}$ a system analogous to (27).

For small h, we have the result

$$\hat{\pi}\left(x, \hat{L}, t\right) = -\frac{(\sigma^*(t))^{-1}\left[\theta\frac{\partial \tilde{V}}{\partial x}\left(x, \hat{L}, t\right) + \zeta\rho\frac{\partial^2 \tilde{V}}{\partial x \partial \hat{L}}\left(x, \hat{L}, t\right)\right]}{x\frac{\partial^2 \tilde{V}}{\partial x^2}\left(x, \hat{L}, t\right)},$$

which is similar to (30); the difference is that here we have $\hat{L}$ and $\tilde{V}$ instead of L and V in (30).

We can now state the following three-fund theorem in the case of partially observed inflation.

Theorem 2 *Under the partially observed inflation, Theorem 1 holds with a modified proportional allocations of wealth between the funds:*

$$\tilde{\mu}_2(t) = \frac{-\tilde{V}_x\left(X, \hat{L}, t\right)}{X(t)\tilde{V}_{xx}\left(X, \hat{L}, t\right)},$$

$$\tilde{\mu}_3(t) = \frac{-\varsigma \tilde{V}_{Lx}\left(X, \hat{L}, t\right)}{X(t)\tilde{V}_{xx}\left(X, \hat{L}, t\right)},$$

and

$$\tilde{\mu}_1(t) = 1 - \tilde{\mu}_2(t) - \tilde{\mu}_3(t).$$

where $\tilde{\mu}_k(t)$ *is the proportional wealth invested in the* k^{th} *fund at time t.*

Theorems 1 and 2 imply that the components of the funds are arrived in the same manner under the fully observed and partially observed inflation; only the relative allocations of the wealth invested in these funds are different. Thus, in both cases the optimal portfolio is a linear combination of the risk-free fund, the growth optimum fund, and the fund that arises from the correlation between the inflation uncertainty and the market risk. The proportions of the wealth invested in these funds are different because the investor's belief on the consumption basket price is not the same under different information sets, i.e., because $\hat{L}$ is not the same as L. Thus, the noisy signals affect the optimal solution through the value function derivatives.

5 Concluding Remarks

We have formulated a discrete-time version of the optimal portfolio and consumption decision model under partially observed inflation, for the first time to our knowledge. The investor observes noisy signals on the consumption basket price over time. Based on these signals, he updates his estimates of the consumption basket and the real asset prices in any given period, and then decides on his investment portfolios and his consumption rate in that period. We show that a modified Mutual Fund Theorem consisting of three funds holds. The funds are a risk-free fund, a growth optimum fund, and a fund that arises from the correlation between the inflation uncertainty and the market risk. In general, the wealth invested in these funds depends on the investor's utility function and on his beliefs about the consumption basket price. However, the funds are robust over different information sets on the consumption basket price. That is, the investor uses the same three funds regardless of the noise in observing the consumption basket price. We show the results obtained are consistent with those obtained in the continuous-time version of the problem. Moreover, since in practice, the decisions are made in discrete time and therefore the data available on potential empirical explorations of the problem require a discrete-time formulation; this paper fills an important gap in the literature.

References

Alchian, A. A., & Klein, B. (1973). On a correct measure of inflation. *Journal of Money, Credit and Banking*, *5*, 173–191.
Basak, S., & Yan, H. (2010). Equilibrium asset prices and investor behaviour in the presence of money illusion. *The Review of Economic Studies*, *77*(3), 914–936.
Bensoussan, A., Keppo, J., & Sethi, S. P. (2009). Optimal consumption and portfolio decisions with partially observed real prices. *Mathematical Finance*, *19*(2), 215–236.
Borenstein, S., & Rose, N. L. (1994). Competition and price dispersion in the U.S. airline industry. *Journal of Political Economy*, *102*, 653–683.
Bradley, R. (2001). Finite sample effects in the estimation of substitution bias in the consumer price index. *Journal of Official Statistics*, *17*, 369–390.
Brennan, M. J. (1998). The role of learning in dynamic portfolio decisions. *European Economic Review*, *1*, 295–306.
Brennan, M. J., & Xia, Y. (2002). Dynamic asset allocation under inflation. *Journal of Finance*, *57*, 1201–1238.
Campbell, J., & Vuolteenaho, T. (2004). Inflation Illusion and stock prices. *American Economic Review Papers Proceedings*, *94*, 19–23.
Chen, S-N., & Moore, W. T. (1985). Uncertain inflation and optimal portfolio selection: A simplified approach. *The Financial Review*, *20*, 343–352.
Cohen, R., Polk, C., & Vuolteenaho, T. (2005). Money illusion in the stock market: The Modigliani-Cohn hypothesis. *Quarterly Journal of Economics*, *120*, 639–668.
Karatzas, I., Lehoczky, J. P., Sethi, S. P., & Shreve, S. E. (1986). Explicit solution of a general consumption/investment problem. *Mathematics of Operations Research*, *11*(2), 261–294.
Klenow, P. J. (2003). Measuring consumption growth: The impact of new and better products. *Federal Reserve Bank Minneapolis Quarterly Review*, *27*, 10–23.
Manaster, S. (1979). Real and nominal efficient sets. *Journal of Finance*, *34*, 93–102.
Merton, R. (1971). Optimum consumption and portfolio rules in a continuous time model. *Journal of Economic Theory*, *3*, 373–413.
Munk, C., Sorensen, C., & Nygaard Vinther, T. (2004). Dynamic asset allocation under mean-reverting returns, stochastic interest rates and inflation uncertainty. *International Review of Economics & Finance*, *13*, 141–166.
Sethi, S. P. (1997). *Optimal consumption and investment with bankruptcy*. Norwell, MA: Kluwer Academic Publishers.
Shapiro, M. D., & Wilcox, D. W. (1997). Alternative strategies for aggregating prices in the CPI. *Federal Reserve Bank St. Louis Review*, *79*, 113–125.
Solnik, B. H. (1978). Inflation and optimal portfolio choice. *Journal of Financial and Quantitative Analysis*, *13*, 903–925.
Ungar, M., & Zilberhard, B.-Z. (1993). Inflation and its unpredictability-theory and empirical evidence. *Journal of Money, Credit and Banking*, *25*, 709–720.
Xia, L. (2001). Learning about predictability: The effects of parameter uncertainty on dynamic asset allocation. *Journal of Finance*, *56*, 205–246.
Zhao, Y. (2007). A dynamic model of active portfolio management with benchmark orientation. *Journal of Banking and Finance*, *31*, 3336–3356.

Dynamic Games of Common-Property Resource Exploitation When Self-image Matters

Ngo Van Long

Abstract The purpose of this paper is to model the influence of Kantian moral scruples in a dynamic environment. Our objectives are twofold. Firstly, we investigate how a Nash equilibrium among agents who have moral scruples may ensure that the exploitation of a common-property renewable resource is Pareto efficient at every point of time. Secondly, we outline a prototype model that shows, in an overlapping generation framework, how a community's sense of morality may evolve over time and identifies conditions under which the community may reach a steady-state level of morality in which everyone is perfectly Kantian.

Keywords Tragedy of the commons · Dynamic games · Nash equilibrium · Self-image · Categorical imperative

JEL-Classifications C71 · D62 · D71

1 Introduction

Many economic ills can be attributed to the lack of incentives for agents to cooperate. For example, it is well recognized that contributions to public goods tend to be under-supplied and exploitation of public-owned assets tend to be excessive (Gordon 1954; Hardin 1968). A most serious challenge facing the world is the danger of climate change, which is difficult to combat because the quality of global environmental resources is a public good. The prevailing incentives to free-ride render fruitless the United Nations' efforts of implementing the Kyoto Protocol. (For dynamic games of climate change, see, among others, Wirl (1995, 2011), Wirl and Dockner (1995), Yang (2003), Deissenberg and Leitmann (2004), Grafton et al. (2017); see Long (2010) for a survey.)

N. Van Long (✉)
Department of Economics, McGill University, Montreal, Canada
e-mail: ngo.long@mcgill.ca

H. Dawid and J. Arifovic (eds.), *Dynamic Analysis in Complex Economic Environments*, Dynamic Modeling and Econometrics in Economics and Finance 26,
https://doi.org/10.1007/978-3-030-52970-3_5

However, there are instances where common-property resources are properly managed, as well documented by Ostrom (1990). A mechanism which ensures reasonable cooperation by private agents is the enforcement of social norms. Economic models of the working of social norms typically include a group of agents that punish violators (Sethi and Somanathan 1996; Breton et al. 2010).[1] Recently, there are models in which norms are respected without an explicit punishment mechanism (Brekke et al. 2003; Roemer 2010, 2015; Wirl 2011; Long 2016, 2017). These authors, following the footsteps of Laffont (1975), emphasize the fact that many economic agents, being motivated by moral scruples, feel the need to act in accordance with moral principles such as the categorical imperative Kant (1785).[2] The modeling of the influence of morality on economic behavior differs among economists. Following the tradition of Arrow (1973), Sen (1977), and Laffont (1975), the recent papers by Roemer (2010, 2015), Long (2016, 2017), Grafton et al. (2017) rely on the concept of Kantian equilibrium originated from Laffont (1975). This equilibrium concept departs from the Nash equilibrium concept by supposing that agents do not behave in the Nashian way: they do not take the actions of others as given.[3] Using an alternative approach, the papers by Brekke et al. (2003) and Wirl (2011), following earlier works by Fehr and Schmidt (1999), Bolton and Ockenfels (2000), and Charness and Rabin (2002), keep the Nashian framework but endow agents with a sense of morality, such that deviations from the Kantian ideal imposes a quadratic loss of one's self-respect.[4]

Most of the Kant-based models mentioned in the preceding paragraph (with the exception of Wirl (2011)) restrict attention to a static framework, i.e., there is no stock dynamics. The purpose of this paper is to model explicitly the influence of Kantian moral scruples in a dynamic environment. Our objectives are twofold. Firstly, we investigate how a Nash equilibrium among agents who have moral scruples may ensure that the exploitation of a common-property renewable resource is Pareto efficient at every point of time. Secondly, we outline a prototype model that shows, in an overlapping generation framework, how a community's sense of morality may evolve over time and identifies conditions under which the community may reach a steady-state level of morality in which everyone is perfectly Kantian.[5]

[1]There is a large literature on social norms in a market environment. For some recent contributions, see Deissenberg and Peguin-Feissole (2006), Dasgupta et al. (2016), Ulph and Ulph (2017).

[2]Kant (1785) wrote that "There is only one categorical imperative and it is this: Act only on the maxim by which you can at the same time will that it should become a universal law." Translated by Hill and Zweig (2002, p. 222).

[3]Binmore (2005) argued against the Kantian approach. A counter-argument was offered in Grafton et al. (2017).

[4]Wirl (2011) assumes the co-existence of green consumers and brown consumers, who behave in a Nashian fashion in a dynamic game of global warming.

[5]For an alternative approach without overlapping generations, see Alger and Weibull (2016).

2 Related Literature

Many generations of economics students have been told that a central result of economic theory is that if all agents are self-interested maximizers of their own material wellbeing, the outcome of a competitive equilibrium is Pareto efficient. This result is of course subject to a number of qualifications, but these are quite often relegated to footnotes. Many authors have attributed to Adam Smith the vision of a miraculous achievement of the price mechanism, ignoring the fact that Smith himself held a much more nuanced view. In fact, in *The Wealth of Nations*, Smith (1776) pointed out that there are cases where the pursuit of self-interest ought to be severely restrained.[6] Moreover, Adam Smith never said that economic agents are solely interested in personal gains. In *The Theory of Moral Sentiments*, Smith (1790) emphasized the crucial importance of the respect for social norms and moral duties. He wrote

> Upon the tolerable observance of these duties, depends the very existence of human society, which would crumble into nothing if mankind were not generally impressed with a reverence for those important rules of conduct.[7]

Smith (1790) discussed at length the role of natural sympathies in human activities and the human urge to be accepted as a respectable moral being. According to Smith, humans desire to merit the approval of other members of their community: we judge our actions as we think others would judge them. Through interaction with those around us, we learn "*general rules concerning what is fit and proper either to be done or to be avoided.*"[8] Moreover, humans desire not only to be praised, but to be truly deserving of praise. They feel happiness by acting in a way which merits the self-approval which comes from knowing that they have acted according to the standard of "*the impartial and well-informed spectator ... within the breast.*"[9]

In the last few decades, Smith's views have been vindicated by research in experimental economics; see, e.g., Dawes and Thaler (1988), Bolle and Ockenfels (1990), Fehr and Schmidt (1999), Bolton and Ockenfels (2000), Charness and Rabin (2002), Camerer (2003), Camerer and Fehr (2006), Andreoni et al. (2008). Referring to Adam Smith's *The Theory of Moral Sentiments*, Smith (2003, p. 466) elaborates on

[6]On banking regulation, Smith (1776, p. 308) wrote that "Such regulations may, no doubt, be considered as in some respect a violation of natural liberty. But those exertions of natural liberty of a few individuals, which might endanger the security of the whole society are, and ought to be, restrained by the laws of all governments." On moral hazard, he noted that the interest of agents are not aligned with that of the principals: "The directors of such companies, however, being the managers rather of other's money than of their own, it cannot be well expected, that they should watch over it with the same anxious vigilance with which the partners in a private copartnery frequently watch over their own ... Negligence and profusion, therefore, must always prevail, more or less, in the management of the affairs of such a company." (Smith, 1776, Book 5, Chap. 1, p. 700). See Muller (1993) for a review of Adam Smith's fundamental works.

[7]Smith, *The Theory of Moral Sentiments*, 1790, Part III, Chap. V, p. 190.

[8]The Theory of Moral Sentiments, edited by Macfie and Raphael (1976), The Glasgow Edition of the Works and Correspondence of Adam Smith, Oxford University Press. Book III, Chap. 4, Part 7, p. 159.

[9]The Theory of Moral Sentiments, Book III, Chap. 2, p. 130.

the important message of the eighteenth century Scottish philosophers such as Smith and Hume:

"Research in economic psychology has prominently reported examples where 'fairness' considerations are said to contradict the rationality assumptions of the standard socioeconomic science model (SSSM). But experimental economics have reported mixed results on rationality: people are often better (e.g., in two-person anonymous interactions), in agreement with (e.g., in flow supply and demand markets), or worse (e.g., in asset trading), in achieving gains for themselves and others than is predicted by rational analysis. Patterns of these contradictions and confirmations provide important clues to the implicit rules or norms that people may follow, and can motivate new theoretical hypotheses for examination in both the field and the laboratory. The pattern of results greatly modifies the prevailing, and I believe misguided, rational SSSM, and richly modernizes the unadultered message of the Scottish philosophers."

The importance of self-image has been emphasized in the economic literature. Recent contributions to this stream of literature include Brekke et al. (2003), Akerlof and Kranton (2005), and Elster (2017). Outside of economics, self-image has been a key theme in moral philosophy and in psychology. Indeed, Rabbi Hillel, a first century sage, posed the following questions:

> If I am not for myself, then who is for me? And if I am not for others, then who am I? If not now, when?[10]

While the concern for self-image can be a source of good, the failure of not being seen as having lived up to one's ideal can be a source of misery. In Jean-Paul Sartre's 1947 play, titled Huis Clos, the main character, Garcin, finally reached a devastating awareness:

> Tous ces regards qui me mangent … Alors, c'est ça l'enfer. Je n'aurais jamais cru … Vous vous rappelez: le soufre, le bûcher, le gril … Ah! quelle plaisanterie. Pas besoin de gril: l'enfer, c'est les Autres.[11]

However, the self-image (as reflected in the eyes of others) that Garcin was obsessed with should be only a first rung in the moral ladder. According to Adam Smith, a higher rung is reached when the eyes of others no longer matter. One then applies the standard of "*the impartial and well-informed spectator … within the breast.*" Smith's view echoes Confucius' doctrine of shame as a guiding principle for moral behavior, as recorded in the Analects:

> Guide them with government orders, regulate them with penalties, and the people will seek to evade the law and be without shame. Guide them with virtue, regulate them with ritual, and they will have a sense of shame and become upright.[12]

---

[10]Cited in Arrow (1974), *The Limits of Organization*. New York: W.W. Norton.

[11]"All those looks that eat me … So that is hell. I never thought … You remember: the sulfur, the stake, the grill … Ah! what a joke. No need for a grill: Hell is the Others." Scene 5, Huis Clos, by Sartre (1947).

[12]Cited in Bowles (2016, p. 11).

Complementing the growing literature on the need to modify the standard model of economic behavior to account for humans' concern for morality, this paper constructs a model of a dynamic game of common-property resource exploitation in which agents care not only about their material wellbeing, but also about their self-image. I show that, despite the well-known incentives to free ride when agents exploit a common asset, a social optimum may be within reach provided that agents have a precise idea of what actions would be prescribed by Kantian ethics, and they feel bad if their own actions do not match the moral ideal.

3 Modeling Individual Tradeoff Between Self-image and Material Wellbeing

For exposition, this section restricts attention to a static framework. We assume that individuals care about their material wellbeing, denoted by M_i, while at the same time, they attach a value v_i to their self-image. Their self-image suffers if they under-contribute to a public good, or if they overexploit a common-property asset.

3.1 Specification of the Self-image Function and the Material Wellbeing Function

In the case of exploitation of a common-property resource, such as a pasture, the economic literature typically supposes that individuals have a tendency to overexploit, i.e., their demands are excessive. Let $e_i \geq 0$ denote the individual's actual level of exploitation, and e_i^K the level of exploitation that the Kantian social norms would dictate. Then $e_i - e_i^K$ is the individual's extent of excessive demand (excessive exploitation). We assume that exploitation in excess of the social norms causes a loss of self-image equal to $\theta_i \times \left(e_i - e_i^K\right) \times \sigma$, where $\sigma > 0$ is a scale parameter that reflects the (objective) severity of the effect of the overexploitation, and $\theta_i > 0$ is the individual's coefficient of the (subjective) loss of self-esteem associated with excessive exploitation.

For tractability, we assume that an individual's self-image function, denoted by v_i, takes the following simple form

$$v_i = A_i - \theta_i^u \times \max\left\{0, (e - e_i^K)\sigma\right\} \tag{1}$$

where A_i is a positive constant.

Turning to the material payoff M_i of an individual i we assume that it consists his "harvest" q_i from the common-property resource, net of the effort cost of harvesting $g_i(e_i)$.

The size of his harvest may depend not only on his exploitation level e_i but also on the aggregate level of exploitation, because of overcrowding externalities. We write

$$q_i = f_i(e_i, E),$$

with $\partial f_i/\partial e_i > 0$ and $\partial f_i/\partial E < 0$, where

$$E \equiv \sum_{i=1}^{n} e_i.$$

Let us define

$$E_{-i} = E - e_i.$$

The material wellbeing of individual i is

$$M_i = f_i(e_i, E_{-i} + e_i) - g_i(e_i). \tag{2}$$

Individual i chooses $e_i \geq 0$ to maximize his payoff, defined as the sum of his material wellbeing and his self-image:

$$U_i = M_i + v_i. \tag{3}$$

In this maximization problem, he takes E_{-i} as given. In other words, here we use the concept of Nash equilibrium.

3.2 A Digression: Specification of the Individual-Specific Kantian Ideals

If all individuals have identical characteristics and circumstances, as is assumed in the model formulated in Laffont (1975), one may suppose that $e_i^K = e^K$ for all i, and that e^K is the value of e that would maximize the material wellbeing of a representative individual. In the case of homogeneous individuals, clearly there are no differences between the Kantian levels and the optimum that a Benthamite utilitarian social planner would want to achieve. Let us turn now to the case where individuals are heterogeneous. What would be a plausible specification of individual-specific duties?

Due to space limitation, it is not possible to offer here a detailed discussion of this important issue. Let me simply mention two important approaches that have been proposed to address this subject. The first approach is that of Bilodeau and Gravel (2004). They argue that "to treat everyone similarly, a maxim must prescribe to everyone actions that are in some sense equivalent" (p. 647). They propose the concept of morally equivalent actions by introducing a system of universalization, i.e., a binary relation that compares any two actions (possibly undertaken by two persons with different characteristics) and determines whether they are morally equivalent. They insist that a Kantian maxim, if obeyed by all, must "yield everyone's most preferred outcome if everyone else is constrained to play a morally equivalent strategy" (p. 647). Bilodeau and Gravel (2004) show that, in the setting of voluntary contributions to a public good, if a system of universalization satisfies certain axioms, any Kantian maxim that is consistent with it is necessarily Pareto efficient.[13]

The second approach is more operational and is due to Roemer (2010, 2015). Roemer (2010) defines a Kantian equilibrium for a class of games where each individual can only take a single action, for which he can contemplate alternative outcomes that would result from scaling his action level up or down. We can shed light on Roemer's approach by considering the following example.

Consider a game of exploitation of a common-property resource (such as a common pasture). Consider a small community in which there are n households. Let e_i be the number of goats that household i keeps. Assume that the final output, say goat milk, is obtained by letting the goats (an input) graze on the common pasture (a second input). The community's aggregate output of milk is $Q = \xi F(E)$, where $E = \sum e_i$, and $\xi > 0$ is the quality of the pasture. Assume that $F(0) = 0$, $F'(0) > 0$, and $F''(E) < 0$. The output of milk per goat is Q/E, and therefore the quantity of milk collected by household i is $e_i Q/E$. Assume that, due to different levels of skills among households, the effort cost incurred by household i in keeping e_i goats is given by

$$g_i(e_i) = \beta_i g(e_i),$$

where $g(.)$ is a strictly convex and increasing function defined for all $e_i \geq 0$, with $g(0) = 0 = g'(0)$. Without loss of generality, assume $1 = \beta_1 \leq \beta_2 \leq \beta_3 \cdots \leq \beta_n$. What is the Kantian number of goats that household i should keep? Following Roemer (2010), let us define a Kantian allocation of input levels as a strictly positive vector $(e_1^K, e_2^K, e_3^K, \ldots, e_n^K)$ such that for each household i, if it were to modify e_i^K by applying a scaling factor $\lambda > 0$ (so that its exploitation would be changed to λe_i^K), it would find that, for all λ such that $0 < \lambda \neq 1$, its material wellbeing would fall, on the assumption that all other households would change their e_j^K by the same factor λ. This thought experiment reflects the Kantian dictum that when one contemplates doing something, one should ask oneself: how would I like it if everyone else behaved in the same way?

Formally then, in our common pasture example, an allocation $(e_1^K, e_2^K, e_3^K, \ldots, e_n^K)$ is a Kantian equilibrium (in thought) if and only if

$$1 = \arg\max_{\lambda > 0} \frac{\lambda e_i^K \xi F(\lambda e_i^K + \lambda E_{-i}^K)}{\lambda e_i^K + \lambda E_{-i}^K} - \beta_i g(\lambda e_i^K).$$

[13]Technically, the axioms involve two requirements on a system of universalization: tightness and differentiability (p. 648).

Let the material payoff of household i be denote by M_i. Let

$$M_i(\lambda) \equiv \frac{\lambda e_i^K \xi F(\lambda e_i^K + \lambda E_{-i}^K)}{\lambda e_i^K + \lambda E_{-i}^K} - \beta_i g(\lambda e_i^K).$$

Differentiating M_i with respect to λ, we get the first-order equation

$$\frac{e_i^K}{E^K}\xi F'(\lambda E^K)E^K - \beta_i g'(\lambda e_i^K)e_i^K = 0 \text{ for } i = 1, 2, \ldots, n.$$

Evaluated at $\lambda = 1$, we get the condition that characterizes the Kantian allocation:

$$\xi F'(E^K) = \beta_i g'(e_i^K). \tag{4}$$

Remark Equation (4) implies that the Kantian input allocation is efficient: the marginal social product of the total input is equated to the marginal cost for each agent. Condition (4) that characterizes the Kantian equilibrium allocation in this model (where utility is *linear* in consumption) is also the condition that characterizes the optimal allocation under the standard utilitarian objective of maximizing the *non-weighted* sum of individuals' utilities. (However, this is not always the case; as shown in the Appendix, the Kantian equilibrium allocation in a public good model (where utility is *non-linear* in the public good) can be obtained only by maximizing a *weighted* sum of individuals' utilities.)

We can next compute e_i^K and E^K as follows

$$e_i^K = g^{'-1}\left(\frac{\xi F'(E^K)}{\beta_i}\right). \tag{5}$$

Summing (5) over $i = 1, 2, \ldots, n$, we get

$$E^K = \sum_i g^{'-1}\left(\frac{\xi F'(E^K)}{\beta_i}\right). \tag{6}$$

Since F' is decreasing and g'^{-1} is increasing, the right-hand side of Eq. (6) is decreasing E. The left-hand side is linear and increasing in E. Therefore there exists a unique $E^K > 0$. Next, we can calculate e_i^K using (5). It can be shown that at the Kantian equilibrium, weaker households (those with a high value β_i) keep fewer goats than stronger households and enjoy a lower level of material wellbeing.

4 Renewable Resource Exploitation by Image-Conscious Agents

In this section, we show how the tragedy of the commons can be avoided if agents are endowed with a sufficiently strong desire to maintain a good self-image. For simplicity, let us assume that individuals are homogeneous. To fix ideas, we use a model of common access fishery. The "common access fishery model" has been interpreted more broadly to mean a model of rivalrous exploitation of any kind of renewable resource.

Let $R(t)$ denote the resource stock, and $x_i(t)$ denote agent i's rate of exploitation. Assume that

$$\dot{R}(t) = G(R_t) - \sum_{i=1}^{n} x_i(t),$$

where $G(R)$ is the natural growth function, with $G(0) = 0$, $G'(0) > 0$, and $G''(R) \leq 0$.

Let us assume that agent i's instantaneous material wellbeing is simply an increasing and concave function of his rate of exploitation. We denote this function by $M_i(x_i(t))$. Agents live for ever and discount their future utility at the rate $\rho > 0$. The life-time payoff of agent i, starting from any time $\tau \geq 0$ is

$$P_i(\tau) = \int_{\tau}^{\infty} e^{-\rho(t-\tau)} M_i(x_i(t))dt.$$

4.1 Cooperative Solution When Individuals Are Homogeneous

When individuals are homogeneous, the cooperative solution is straightforward. It is as if there were a social planner who would maximize the life-time utility of an infinitety lived representative individual. (One can think of this agent as a family line.) The planner solves the following optimal control problem: choose the extraction rate per capita to maximize the discounted life-time material wellbeing of the representative agent:

$$\max_{x(t) \geq 0} \int_{0}^{\infty} e^{-\rho t} M(x(t))dt,$$

subject to

$$\dot{R}(t) = G(R(t)) - nx(t),$$

with

$$\lim_{t \to \infty} R(t) \geq 0.$$

The above optimal control problem can also be solved using the Hamilton–Jacobi–Bellman equation. Let $V_P(.)$ denote the value function of the planner (here, the subscript P denote the planner). The Hamilton–Jacobi–Bellman (HJB) equation is

$$\rho V_P(R_t) = \max_{x \geq 0} \left[M(x_t) + (G(R_t) - nx_t) V_P'(R_t) \right]. \tag{7}$$

The first-order condition is

$$M'(x_t) - nV_P'(R_t) = 0.$$

This yields x_t as a function of R_t

$$x_t = \phi \left(nV_P'(R_t) \right),$$

where

$$\phi(.) = (M')^{-1}.$$

Thus we obtain the following first-order differential equation[14]

$$\rho V_P(R) = M \left(\phi \left(nV_P'(R) \right) \right) + \left[G(R) - n\phi \left(nV_P'(R) \right) \right] V_P'(R).$$

Define

$$x^K(R) \equiv \phi \left(nV_P'(R) \right). \tag{8}$$

Then we obtain a first-order differential equation relating V_P to V_p' :

$$\rho V_P(R) = M(x^K(R)) + \left[G(R) - nx^K(R) \right] V_P'(R).$$

Using the usual transversality condition, this equation can be solved to yield the value function and hence the optimal harvest rule.

Example 1 Assume that the growth function of the biomass is

$$G(R) = R^\gamma - \delta R, 0 < \gamma < 1,$$

and the material wellbeing function is unbounded above

$$M(x) = \frac{x^{1-\gamma}}{1-\gamma}, \text{ where } \gamma \in (0, 1).$$

---

[14]We seek a solution $V_P(R)$ such that an appropriate transversality condition is met, e.g., $\lim_{t\to\infty} e^{-\rho t} V_P(R(t)) = 0$. See Dockner et al. (2000).

Denote by $V_P(R)$ the social planner's value function. The HJB equation is

$$\rho V_P(R) = \max_{x \geq 0} \left\{ \frac{x^{1-\gamma}}{1-\gamma} + V_P'(R) \left[R^\gamma - \delta R - nx \right] \right\}.$$

The first-order condition is

$$x^{-\gamma} = n V_P'(R).$$

Try the value function

$$V_P(R) = A + B \frac{R^{1-\gamma}}{1-\gamma},$$

where A and B are to be determined. Then

$$V_P' = B R^{-\gamma}.$$

The first-order condition then gives

$$x^{-\gamma} = n B R^{-\gamma},$$

i.e., the harvesting rule is linear:

$$x = (nB)^{-1/\gamma} R.$$

Substituting this into the HJB equation to get

$$\rho A + \rho B \frac{R^{1-\gamma}}{1-\gamma} = \frac{(nB)^{\frac{(\gamma-1)}{\gamma}} R^{1-\gamma}}{1-\gamma} + B - \delta R^{1-\gamma} - (nB)^{\frac{(\gamma-1)}{\gamma}} R^{1-\gamma}.$$

Then, since the above equation must hold for all $R > 0$, the coefficients of the terms involving $R^{1-\gamma}$ must add up to zero, i.e.,

$$(nB)^{-1/\gamma} = \frac{\rho + \delta(1-\gamma)}{n\gamma} > 0.$$

Thus the Kantian rate of exploitation is

$$x^K(R) \equiv \frac{\rho + \delta(1-\gamma)}{n\gamma} R.$$

Example 2 Let

$$G(R) = \kappa R - R^\eta \text{ where } \eta > 1 \text{ and } \kappa > 0,$$

and assume the utility function is bounded above:

$$M(x) = \frac{x^{1-\eta}}{1-\eta} \text{ where } \eta > 1.$$

The planner's HJB equation is

$$\rho V_P(R) = \max_{x \geq 0} \left\{ \frac{x^{1-\eta}}{1-\eta} + V_P'(R)\left[\kappa R - R^\eta - nx\right] \right\}.$$

Assume that $\rho > \kappa - 1$. The first-order condition is

$$x^{-\eta} = nV_P'(R).$$

We conjecture the following value function

$$V_P(R) = A + \frac{DR^{1-\eta}}{1-\eta},$$

where A and D are to be determined. Then

$$V_P'(R) = DR^{-\eta},$$

$$x = (nD)^{-\frac{1}{\eta}} R.$$

Plugging this exploitation rule into the HJB equation, we obtain

$$\rho A + \rho \frac{DR^{1-\eta}}{1-\eta} = \frac{(nD)^{(\eta-1)/\eta} R^{1-\eta}}{1-\eta} + \kappa DR^{1-\eta} - D - (nD)^{(\eta-1)/\eta} R^{1-\eta},$$

which yields

$$(nD)^{-1/\eta} = \frac{\rho + \kappa(\eta - 1)}{n\eta} > 0.$$

Thus the Kantian rate of exploitation is

$$x^K = \frac{\rho + \kappa(\eta - 1)}{n\eta} R.$$

4.2 *Non-cooperative Exploitation by Agents with Moral Scruples*

Does the central planner's solution co-incide with Nash behavior by agents who have concerns for self-image? We assume that self-image is related to the difference between one's action level and the Kantian action, $x^K(R)$, as specified by

Eq. (8) above. Assume that an individual's utility function is the sum of two functions: (i) the material wellbeing function, $M_i(x)$, and (ii) the self-esteem function, $v_i(R, x_i, x^K(R))$ defined by

$$v_i(R, x_i, x^K(R)) = A_i - \theta_i \max\left[0, \sigma_i(R)(x_i - x^K(R))\right],$$

where A_i is a constant (let us call A_i "agent i's intrinsic level of self-esteem"), $\theta_i \in [0, 1]$ is a parameter called agent i's "degree of moral scruple," $\sigma_i(R)$ is agent i's perception of the harm that he would inflict on other individuals if he were to overexploit the resource stock, and $x_i - x^K(R)$ is a measure of his deviation from the Kantian ideal action. This formulation says that if $x_i > x^K(R)$, then agent i feels bad because he overextracts, violating the Kantian norm. Note that if $x_i < x^K(R)$, then his self-esteem is not affected.

Each individual chooses $x_i(t)$ to maximize

$$W_i = \int_0^\infty e^{-\rho t}\left\{M(x_{it}) + A_i - \theta_i \max\left[0, \sigma_i(R_t)(x_{it} - x^K(R_t))\right]\right\} dt,$$

subject to

$$\dot{R}_t = G(R_t) - x_{it} - \sum_{j \neq i} x_{jt},$$

and $\lim_{t\to\infty} R(t) \geq 0$.

We now state and prove Proposition 1.

Proposition 1 *Suppose that the agent's "perception of harm function" $\sigma_i(R)$ is equal to $(n-1)V_P'(R)$, where $V_P(R)$ is the value function of the social planner's problem, as defined in Eq. (7). If agent i expects that all other agents use the extraction strategy $x_j = x^K(R)$ as given by (8) then, provided that $\theta_i = 1$, he will himself use the same extraction strategy, $x_i = x^K(R)$, resulting in a equilibrium that is socially optimal at every point of time. At the Markov-perfect Nash equilibrium, the value function of agent i turns out to be equal to the social planner's value function, $V_P(R)$, plus the constant term A_i/ρ.*

$$W_i(R) = \frac{A_i}{\rho} + V_P(R). \tag{9}$$

Proof We only need to verify that the candidate value function $W_i(R)$ as specified by Eq. (9) does indeed satisfy agent i's HJB equation and leads to the exploitation strategy $x_i = x^K(R)$. Given that $\sigma_i(R) = (n-1)V_P'(R)$, the HJB equation for agent i is

$$\rho W_i(R) = \max_{x_i}\left\{M(x_i) + A_i - \theta_i \max\left[0, (n-1)V_P'(R)(x_i - x^K(R))\right]\right.$$
$$\left. + \left[G(R) - (n-1)x^K(R) - x_i\right] W_i'(R)\right\}.$$

Using our candidate value function, the first-order condition is

$$M_i'(x_i) - [\theta_i(n-1)+1]\, V_P'(R) = 0.$$

With $\theta_i = 1$, we get

$$x_i = M'^{-1}\left(nV_P'(R)\right) \equiv x^K(R).$$

Substituting this into the HJB equation of agent i, we get

$$\rho W_i(R) = M(x^K(R)) + A_i - 0 + \left[G(R) - x^K(R)\right] V_P'(R).$$

By plugging (9) to the left-hand side of the above equation, we can verify that the claim that (9) is agent i's value function is indeed valid. ■

5 A Discrete-Time Model of Renewable Resource Exploitation By Image-Conscious Agents

Let us see how our result for the continuous-time model can be adapted for the case of discrete time. Again we first solve the social planner's problem. After that, we show how the socially optimal outcome can be implemented as a Nash equilibrium among agents with a sufficiently strong concern for self-image. As expected, the basic result of the continuous-time model carries over to the discrete-time model, provided that the "perception of harm" function $\sigma_i(R)$ is suitably modified, as discussed after the statement of Proposition 2 below. This shows the robustness of our conclusion concerning achieving the social optimum by means of Nash behavior of agents who have a sufficiently strong concern for self-image.

5.1 The Social Planner's Problem in Discrete Time

Let X_t be the agregate harvest, i.e.,

$$X_t = \sum_{i=1}^{n} x_{it}.$$

We assume that the law governing the dynamics of the stock is

$$R_{t+t} = g(R_t, X_t),$$

where $g_R > 0$ and $g_X < 0$.

Let β be the discount factor, where $0 < \beta < 1$. The social planner's Bellman equation is

$$\begin{aligned} V_P(R_t) &= \max_{x_t \geq 0} \{M(x_t) + \beta V_P(R_{t+1})\} \\ &= \max_{x_t \geq 0} \{M(x_t) + \beta V_P(g(R_t, nx_t)\} . \end{aligned}$$

The first-order condition is

$$M'(x_t) + \beta V_P'(g(R_t, nx_t))ng_X(R_t, nx_t) = 0.$$

(Note that $V_P' > 0$ and $g_X < 0$). From the first-order condition, we obtain x_t as a function of R_t. We denote this solution by

$$x_t = x^K(R_t, V_P'). \tag{10}$$

Then, substituting (10) into the Bellman equation, we get a first-order differential equation that relate V_P to V_P' :

$$V_P(R_t) = M(x^K(R_t, V_P')) + \beta V_P(g\left[R_t, nx^K(R_t)\right])ng_X\left[R_t, nx^K(R_t)\right].$$

Imposing the transversality condition, this first-order differential equation in V_P can be solved to yield the value function V_P and hence the Kantian level of exploitation.

Example 3 This example is drawn from the fish war model of Levhari and Mirman (1980). Assume

$$G(R, X) = (R - X)^\alpha \text{ where } 0 < \alpha < 1,$$

and

$$M(x_i) = \ln x_i.$$

Then the Bellman equation is

$$V(R) = \max_x \{\ln x + \beta V((R - X)^\alpha)\}.$$

The first-order condition is

$$\frac{1}{x} = \alpha n(R - nx)^{\alpha-1}\beta V'((R - nx)^\alpha).$$

Try the value function

$$V(R) = D + B\ln R.$$

where B and D are to be determined. Then

$$V'(R_{t+1}) = \frac{B}{R_{t+1}} = \frac{B}{(R_t - nx_t)^{\alpha}}.$$

This allows us to solve for the optimal harvesting rule:

$$x_t = \frac{R_t}{n(1+\alpha\beta B)}$$

By the standard method, we find that

$$B = \frac{1}{(1-\alpha\beta)} > 0.$$

5.2 The Individual's Optimization Problem in Discrete Time

Assume that agent i has a utility function that is the sum of two functions: (i) the material wellbeing function, $M(x)$ and (ii) the self-esteem function, $v_i(R, x_i, x^K(R))$ defined by

$$v_i(R, x_i, x^K(R)) = A_i - \theta_i \max\left[0, \sigma_i(R)(x_i - x^K(R))\right].$$

where A_i is a constant and $\theta_i \in [0, 1]$. We may think of A_i as agent i's intrinsic level of self-esteem.

Proposition 2 *Suppose the agent's "perception of harm function" $\sigma_i(R)$ is equal to $-(n-1)\beta V_P'(g[R_t, nx^K(R_t)])g_{X_t} > 0$, where g_x is evaluated at $X_t = nx^K(R_t)$. If agent i expects that all other agents use the extraction strategy $x_j = x^K(R)$, then, provided that $\theta_i = 1$, he will himself use the same extraction strategy, $x_i = x^K(R)$, resulting in a equilibrium that is socially optimal. At the Markov-perfect Nash equilibrium, the value function of agent i turns out to be equal to the social planner's value function, $V_P(R)$, plus the constant term A_i/ρ,*

$$W_i(R) = \frac{A_i}{\rho} + V_P(R), \tag{11}$$

where

$$\frac{1}{1+\rho} \equiv \beta.$$

Discussion: Comparing Proposition 2 (for the discrete-time model) with Proposition 1 (for the continuous-time model), we see the "perception of harm" function $\sigma_i(R)$ must be suitably modified to get the desired result. In the continuous-time case, we required that $\sigma_i(R_t) = (n-1)V_P'(R_t)$, where $V_P(R)$ is the value function of the social planner's problem, and thus $V_P'(R_t)$ is the marginal value of the *concurrent* stock of resource. In the discrete-time case, we required that $\sigma_i(R_t) = -(n-1)\beta V_P'((gR_t, nx^K(R_t)))g_{X_t}$, i.e.,

$$\sigma_i(R_t) = (n-1)\beta V_P'(g(R_t, nx^K(R_t)))|g_{X_t}|,$$

i.e.,

$$\sigma_i(R_t) = (n-1)\beta V_P'(R_{t+1})|g_{X_t}|, \tag{12}$$

where, of course, $R_{t+1} = g(R_t, nx^K(R_t))$. Here, we note two differences between the "perception of harm" functions for the discrete-time case and for the continuous-time case. First, in the Eq. (12), V_P' is valued at R_{t+1}, not at R_t: it is the shadow price of the next period's stock, not of the concurrent stock, that matters. Second, the discount factor β appears in the Eq. (12) because an agent's extraction at date t reduces the stock at a later date, $t+1$.

Proof of Proposition 2 We only need to verify that the value function $W_i(R)$ specified by Eq. (11) satisfies agent i's Bellman equation and leads to the exploitation strategy $x_i = x^K(R)$. The Bellman equation is

$$\begin{aligned} W_i(R_t) = \max_{x_i} \{ &M(x_{it}) + A_i - \theta_i \max\left[0, -(n-1)\beta V_P'(g\left[R_t, nx^K(R_t)\right])\right. \\ &\left.\times g_X(x_{it} - x^K(R_t))\right] + \beta W_i'\left(g\left[R_t, (n-1)x^K(R_t) + x_{it}\right]\right)\}. \end{aligned}$$

The first-order condition is

$$\begin{aligned} &M'(x_{it}) + (n-1)\beta V_P'(g\left[R_t, nx^K(R_t)\right])g_X \\ &= -\beta W_i'(g\left[R_t, (n-1)x^K(R_t) + x_{it}\right])g_X. \end{aligned}$$

Given that all agents $j \neq i$ use the strategy $x_j = x^K(R)$, and the above First-order condition is identical to the social planner's first-order equation,

$$M'(x_{it}) + \beta V_P'(g\left[R_t, x^K(R_t)\right])g_X = 0.$$

This completes the proof. ■

6 A Model of the Evolution of the Concern for Self-image

In the preceding model, the parameter θ_i may be called the degree of pro-socialness of agent i. So far, we assume that θ_i is time-independent. Now, we open a new window, and ask: what if agent i actually is a sequence of overlapping generations? How would θ_i change from one generation to the next?

Let us consider a simple model that addresses this issue. For simplicity, we abstract from the dynamics of the resource stock. To compensate for this over-simplification, we add a feature that reflects overcrowding externalities.

Think of a village populated by n famillies. Each family consists of a parent and a child. Time is discrete. In period t, the parent works to feed the family and contributes a fraction of her income to the village's education of the young generation. We assume that moral attitude is formed in an individual when he is a child. Once the child becomes an adult in period t, he cannot change his θ_{it} (which was formed in period $t-1$).

Assume that in period t, each parent i chooses the number of goats e_{it} to maximize his utility function, which is the sum of the material payoff and of his self-image. His material payoff is

$$M_{it} = M(e_{it}, E_{-it}) = \frac{e_{it}\xi F(e_{it} + E_{-it})}{e_{it} + E_{-it}} - \beta_i g(e_{it}),$$

where ξ is the productivity parameter of the pasture. His self-image function is

$$v_{it} = A - \theta_{it} \max\left\{0, (e_{it} - e^K)\sigma\right\},$$

where σ is an objective measure of the degree of damage that his overexploitation inflicts on other members of the community. The individual takes θ_{it} as given. We assume that e^K is the exploitation level that a social planner would ask each agent to carry out, assuming that the social planner's objective is to maximize Ω_t, defined as the sum of the material payoffs:

$$\Omega_t = \sum_{i=1}^{n} M_{it}.$$

Consider the case where all members of generation t are homogeneous, in the sense that $\theta_{it} = \theta_t$ and $\beta_i = \beta_j = \beta$. We can then solve for the Kantian level e^K (which is of course independent of σ and θ_t) and Nash equilibrium e_t^N of this game. Let $s \equiv 1/n$. Clearly $e^K = sE^K$, where E^K is the solution of $\xi F'(E^K) = \beta g'(E^K/n)$.

Let $E_t^N = ne_t^N$. The symmetric Nash equilibrium can be shown to satisfy the Kuhn–Tucker condition

$$\left[(1-s)\frac{\xi F(E_t^N)}{E_t^N} + s\xi F'(E_t^N) - \beta g'\left(\frac{E_t^N}{n}\right)\right] - \theta_t\sigma \leq 0,$$

with equality holding if $e_t^N = e^K$. We can state the following result:

Lemma 1 *There is a threshold level $\widetilde{\theta}$ such that if $\theta_t \geq \widetilde{\theta}$ then $e_t^N = e^K$. The threshold $\widetilde{\theta}$ is given by*

$$\widetilde{\theta} \equiv \frac{1-s}{\sigma}\left[\frac{\xi F(E^K)}{E^K} - \beta g'(sE^K)\right] > 0.$$

Proof This follows from the above Kuhn–Tucker condition. ■

Corollary 1 *If the agents perceive that σ is equal to σ^*, where*

$$\sigma^* \equiv (n-1)\left[\left(\frac{1}{n}\right)\left(\frac{\xi F(E^K)}{E^K} - \xi F'(E^K)\right)\right] > 0,$$

then $\widetilde{\theta} = 1$. Under these conditions, as long as $\theta_t < 1$, the Nash equilibrium exploitation E_t^N will exceed E^K.

Proof This follows immediately from Lemma 1 and from the fact that $\xi F'(E^K) = \beta g'(sE^K)$. ■

Remark The value σ^* as defined in Corollary 1 has an intuitive economic interpretation. The term inside the square brackets is the excess of average product over marginal product, divided by the number of agents in the community. It is, therefore, an indicator of the marginal loss imposed on the representative agent if an agent deviates by increasing e_{it} above the Kantian level e^K. When this term is multiplied by $n-1$, the result is a measure of harm that a deviating agent inflicts on the other $n-1$ agents. If $\sigma = \sigma^*$ then when $\theta_t = 1$, each agent's concern for self-image fully internalizes the cost that his deviation would impose on others. The resulting Nash equilibrium is then Pareto efficient.

In what follows, we assume $\sigma = \sigma^*$ and consider the realistic scenario where $\theta_t \leq 1$.

Proposition 3 *Assume $\theta_t < 1$. Then the Nash equilibrium exploitation E_t^N is a function of θ_t and of ξ. An increase in θ_t will reduce E_t^N, and an increase in ξ will increase E_t^N.*

Proof Apply the implicit function theorem to the equation

$$\left[(1-s)\frac{\xi F(E_t^N)}{E_t^N} + s\xi F'(E_t^N) - \beta g'\left(\frac{E_t^N}{n}\right)\right] - \theta_t\sigma^* = 0.$$

■

Example 4 Assume that

$$\beta g(e) = \gamma e, \tag{13}$$

where $\gamma > 0$ and

$$\xi F(E) = \xi E - \frac{\xi E^2}{2} \text{where } \xi > \gamma. \tag{14}$$

Then

$$E^K = 1 - (\gamma/\xi) > 0.$$

In this case, $\sigma^* = (1-s)(\xi - \gamma)/2$. Then, for all $\theta_t \in (0, 1)$,

$$E_t^N = \frac{(2 - \theta_t(1-s))E^K}{1+s} < E^K.$$

And the Nash equilibrium material wellbeing of the representative adult in period t is

$$\widehat{M}(\theta_t) = \frac{1}{n}\left[(\xi - \gamma)E_t^N(\theta_t) - \frac{\xi\left(E_t^N(\theta_t)\right)^2}{2}\right]. \tag{15}$$

Proposition 4 *For all $\theta_t \in (0, 1)$, a marginal increase in θ_t leads to an improvement in the community's material wellbeing in period t.*

Proof The Nash equilibrium material wellbeing of the community in period t is

$$\frac{e_t^N(\theta_t)\xi F(E_t^N(\theta_t))}{E_t^N(\theta_t)} - \beta g(e_t^N(\theta_t)) = \frac{1}{n}\xi F(E_t^N(\theta_t)) - \beta g\left(\frac{E_t^N(\theta_t)}{n}\right) \equiv \widehat{M}_t(\theta_t).$$

Then

$$\frac{d\widehat{M}_t}{d\theta_t} = \frac{dM_t}{dE_t}\frac{dE_t^N(\theta_t)}{d\theta_t} = \left[\frac{1}{n}\xi F'(E_t^N) - \frac{1}{n}g'\left(\frac{E_t^N}{n}\right)\right]\frac{dE_t^N}{d\theta_t} > 0.$$

This completes the proof. ■

We assume that parents care about the future material wellbeing of their children when they reach their adulthood. Parents in period t know that if every member of the future generation has a higher value θ_{it+1}, then everyone will be having a higher level of material wellbeing. For this reason, they collectively have an incentive to provide a moral education for their children. Let us consider a simple model of the cost of providing moral education and show how θ evolves over time.

Let $\kappa > 0$ be the discount factor. The representative adult in period t wants to choose e_{it} and aggregate education expenditure Z_t to maximize

$$W_{it} \equiv \left[\frac{e_{it}\xi F(e_{it} + E_{-it})}{e_{it} + E_{-it}} - \beta_i g(e_{it}) - \frac{1}{n}Z_t\right] + A - \theta_{it}\max\left\{0, (e_{it} - e^K)\sigma^*\right\} + \kappa\widehat{M}_{t+1}(\theta_{t+1}), \tag{16}$$

where $\kappa \widehat{M}_{t+1}(\theta_{t+1})$ is the value that the parent attaches to the material wellbeing of the child in the latter's adult phase. In this formulation, each parent pays (e.g., through taxation) a fraction $1/n$ of the aggregate education expenditure Z_t.

While the parent chooses e_{it} non-cooperatively, taking E_{-it} as given, we assume that all parents make a collective choice (e.g., by voting) when it comes to choosing the common level Z_t. Thus Z_t is determined as an outcome of a collective deliberation on the community's educational budget. Once Z_t has been voted on, everyone has to pay his share, Z_t/n.

We must model how θ_{t+1} is influenced by Z_t.

Let $I_t \geq 0$ denote the gross investment in the stock θ_t, such that

$$\theta_{t+1} = (1 - \delta)\theta_t + I_t,$$

where $\delta \geq 0$ is the rate of depreciation of θ_t. We assume that for any target I_t, the required expenditure in terms of the numeraire good is

$$Z_t = \eta I_t + \frac{1}{2} I_t^2,$$

where η is a positive constant.

The community chooses $I_t \geq 0$ that maximizes

$$\kappa \widehat{M}_{t+1}(\theta_{t+1}) - \frac{1}{n}\left(\eta I_t + \frac{1}{2} I_t^2\right), \tag{17}$$

subject to $\theta_{t+1} = (1 - \delta)\theta_t + I_t$.

Proposition 5 *Assume (13) and (14). Let*

$$\omega \equiv \frac{\kappa(1 - s)^2(\xi - \gamma)(1 - \gamma/\xi)}{(1 + s)^2}.$$

Moreover, assume $\omega > \eta$. Then problem (17) gives rise to a dynamic path of θ_t that converges to a positive steady-state θ^* given by

$$\theta^* = \frac{\omega - \eta}{\omega + \delta} \leq 1.$$

If both $\eta = 0$ and $\delta = 0$, then $\theta^* = 1$, which implies that at the steady state, all agents will achieve the Kantian level of exploitation, i.e., $e_i^* = e^K$.

Proof Omitted. ■

7 Conclusion

We have shown that the problem of excessive exploitation of the commons can be avoided if agents who choose their exploitation level non-cooperatively in the manner described by Nash are at the same time sufficiently concerned about their self-image as a person imbued with Kantian morality.[15] Moreover, we argue that in each generation, parents have an interest in the collective provision of moral education for their children. This can give rise to an evolution of pro-social attitude in the population. Darwin himself has written on the evolution of moral qualities. In *The Descent of Man*, Darwin (1874) wrote that "Selfish and contentious people will not cohere, and without coherence, nothing can be affected. A tribe possessing a greater number of courageous, sympathetic and faithful members, who were always ready to warn each other of danger, to aid and to defend each other would spread and be victorious over other tribes. Thus, the social and moral qualities would tend slowly to advance and be diffused throughout the world." (Darwin 1874, Chap. 5, p. 134–5.)[16]

While Darwin did not explicitly mention moral education as a factor that reinforces the cultural selection process, it should be obvious that tribal leaders do provide moral education to children in the form of morality tales, so that they would grow up as cooperative adults and benefit from the material gains brought about by social cooperation. The transmission of pro-social values across generations is in fact a co-evolutionary process, both by conscious decisions and by natural selection.[17]

Acknowledgements I thank two anonymous reviewers for their helpful comments.

Appendix

Kantian Equilibrium with Heterogeneous Contributors to a Public Good

In Sect. 3.2, we found that the condition characterizing the Kantian equilibrium allocation in the common-property resource model (where utility is *linear* in consumption) is also the condition that characterizes the optimal allocation under the standard utilitarian objective of maximizing the *non-weighted* sum of individuals' utilities. This appendix shows that this equivalence between the Kantian equilibrium (with heterogeneous agents) and the Benthamite utilitarian maximization does not carry over

[15]As pointed out by a reviewer, if there are both "green" and "brown" agents, as in Wirl (2011), the effect of "green" agents is weakened because the incentive to free ride increases for the "browns".

[16]Darwin's argument was the basis for the theory evolution employing group selection. Admittedly, this theory is not without its critics. Whether group selection is a good hypothesis or not is a matter of debate. For interesting discussions of these issues, see Gould (1980, 1993).

[17]For a discussion of co-evolution, see e.g. Binmore (2005).

to a public good model (where utility is *non-linear* in the public good). Indeed, we prove below that the Kantian equilibrium in a public good model with heterogeneous consumers is equivalent to maximizing a *weighted* sum of individuals' utilities.

Consider the following simple model of private contributions to a public good. Let s_i denote the contribution of agent i. Assume that the benefit that each agent derives from the public good S is $B(S)$ where $B(S)$ is increasing and strictly concave, with $\lim_{S\to\infty} B'(S) = 0$. The cost to agent i is

$$\psi_i(s_i) = \frac{1}{\alpha_i} c(s_i),$$

where $1 = \alpha_1 \le \alpha_2 \le \alpha_3 \le \cdots \le \alpha_n$, and $c(s)$ is strictly convex and increasing function, with $c'(0) = 0 = c(0)$. Agent 1 is the highest cost agent. Define a Kantian equilibrium of contributions as a strictly positive vector $(s_1^K, s_2^K, s_3^K, \ldots, s_n^K)$ such that for each household i, if it changes s_i^K to λs_i^K, it will find that, for all λ such that $0 < \lambda \ne 1$, its material wellbeing will fall, assuming that all other households would change their s_j^K by the same factor λ.

Formally, a vector $(s_1^K, s_2^K, s_3^K, \ldots, s_n^K)$ is a Kantian equilibrium (in thought) if and only if

$$1 = \arg\max_{\lambda > 0} B(\lambda S^K) - \frac{1}{\alpha_i} c(\lambda s_i^K).$$

Again, let M_i denote the material payoff of household i:

$$M_i(\lambda) = B(\lambda S) - \frac{1}{\alpha_i} c(\lambda s_i^K).$$

Differentiating M_i with respect to λ, we get the first-order equation

$$B'(\lambda S) S^K - \frac{1}{\alpha_i} c'(\lambda s_i^K) s_i^K = 0 \text{ for } i = 1, 2, \ldots, n.$$

Evaluated at $\lambda = 1$, we get

$$B'(S^K) S^K = \frac{1}{\alpha_i} c'(s_i^K) s_i^K = \frac{1}{\alpha_1} c'(s_1^K) s_1^K. \tag{18}$$

Take the special case where

$$c(s) = \frac{s^{1+\varepsilon}}{1+\varepsilon} \text{ with } \varepsilon > 0.$$

Then

$$B'(S^K) S^K = \frac{1}{\alpha_i} \left(s_i^K\right)^{1+\varepsilon},$$

and

$$\frac{s_j^K}{s_1^K} = \left(\frac{\alpha_j}{\alpha_1}\right)^{\frac{1}{1+\varepsilon}} \equiv \gamma_j \geq 1.$$

It follows that

$$S^K = s_1^K \sum_{j=1}^{n} \gamma_j \equiv s_1^K \Gamma,$$

and

$$s_1^K = \frac{S^K}{\Gamma} \text{ and } s_j^K = \gamma_j s_1^K = \frac{\gamma_j}{\Gamma} S^K.$$

Then

$$B'(S^K)S^K = \left(s_1^K\right)^{1+\varepsilon} = \left(\frac{S^K}{\Gamma}\right)^{1+\varepsilon},$$

and

$$B'(S^K) = \frac{1}{\Gamma^{1+\varepsilon}} \left(S^K\right)^{\varepsilon}.$$

Since the left-hand side is decreasing in S and the right-hand side is increasing in S, there exists a unique $S^K > 0$, given that we have assumed that $\lim_{S\to\infty} B'(S) = 0$. Thus we can compute s_1^K and $s_j^K = \gamma_k s_1^K$, for all $j = 2, 3, \ldots, n$.

It is easy to see that the Kantian solution $(s_1^K, s_2^K, s_3^K, \ldots, s_n^K)$ maximizes M, a weighted sum of material payoffs,

$$M \equiv \sum_{i=1}^{n} \omega_i M_i,$$

where the weights ω_i are given by

$$\omega_i \equiv \frac{\gamma_i}{\Gamma}.$$

It can also be verified that

$$\frac{s_i^K}{S^K} = \frac{\gamma_i}{\Gamma} = \omega_i.$$

The Kantian solution is Pareto efficient. Indeed, the Samuelsonian efficiency condition is satisfied: the sum of individuals' marginal rate of substitution (MRS) of the private good for the public good is equal to the marginal rate of transformation (MRT) between the private good and the public good. At the Kantian allocation, the Lindhal price for individual i is

$$P_i = \frac{B'(S^K)}{c'(s_i^K)/\alpha_i} = \frac{\frac{s_i^K}{S^K} B'(S^K)}{\frac{s_1^K}{S^K} c'(s_1^K)/\alpha_1}.$$

Thus the sum of these Lindhal prices are equal to 1 (using Eq. (18)):

$$\sum P_i = \frac{B'(S^K)}{\frac{s_1^K}{S^K} c'(s_1)/\alpha_1} = 1,$$

i.e., the sum of MRS equals MRT.

References

Akerlof, G. A., & Kranton, R. E. (2005). Identity and the economics of organizations. *Journal of Economic Perspectives*, *19*, 9–32.

Alger, I., & Weibull, J. W. (2016). Evolution and Kantian morality. *Games and Economic Behavior*, *98*, 56–67.

Andreoni, J., Harbaugh, W. T., & Vesterlund, L. (2008). Altruism in experiments. In S. N. Durlauf & L. E. Blume (Eds.), *The new Palgrave dictionary in economics* (2nd ed.). New York: Palgrave Macmillan.

Arrow, K. J. (1973). Social responsibility and economic efficiency. *Public Policy*, *21*, 303–317.

Arrow, K. J. (1974). *The limits of organization*. New York: W.W. Norton.

Binmore, K. (2005). *Natural justice*. Oxford University Press.

Breton, M., Sbragia, L., & Zaccour, G. (2010). A dynamic model of international environmental agreements. *Environmental and Resource Economics*, *45*, 25–48.

Bilodeau, M., & Gravel, N. (2004). Voluntary provision of a public good and individual morality. *Journal of Public Economics*, *88*, 645–666.

Bolle, F., & Ockenfels, A. (1990). Prisoners' Dilemma as a game with incomplete information. *Journal of Economic Psychology*, *11*, 69–84.

Bolton, G. E., & Ockenfels, A. (2000). ERC: A theory of equity, reciprocity, and competition. *American Economic Review*, *90*(1), 166–192.

Bowles, S. (2016). *The moral economy: Why good incentives are no substitute for good citizens*. Yale University Press.

Brekke, K. A., Kverndokk, S., & Nyborg, K. (2003). An economic model of moral motivation. *Journal of Public Economics*, *87*, 1967–1983.

Camerer, C. (2003). *Behavioral game theory: Experiments in strategic interaction*. Princeton University Press.

Camerer, C., & Fehr, E. (2006). When does "Economic Man" dominate social behavior? *Science*, *331*(5757), 47–52.

Charness, G., & Rabin, M. (2002). Understanding social preferences with simple tests. *Quarterly Journal of Economics*, *117*, 817–869.

Darwin, C. (1874). *The descent of man*. New York: Caldwell.

Dasgupta, P., Southerton, D., Ulph, A., & Ulph, D. (2016). Consumer behavior with environmental and social externalities: Implications for analysis and policy. *Environmental and Resource Economics*, *65*(1), 191–226.

Dawes, R., & Thaler, R. (1988). Anomalies: Cooperation. *Journal of Economic Perspectives*, *2*, 187–197.

Deissenberg, C., & Leitmann, G. (2004). An algorithmic solution to the interval Kyoto game. In *Computing in economics and finance 2004*. Society for Computational Economics, Vol. 312.
Deissenberg, C., & Peguin-Feissole, A. (2006). Beliefs, norms, and markets. Editorial. *European Journal of Economic and Social Systems* (Lavoisier), *19*(2), 167–669.
Dockner, E., Jorgensen, S., Long, N. V., & Sorger, G. (2000). *Differential games in economics and management science*. Cambridge, U.K.: Cambridge University Press.
Elster, J. (2017). On seeing and being seen. *Social Choice and Welfare*, *49*(3/4), 721–734.
Fehr, E., & Schmidt, K. M. (1999). A theory of fairness, competition, and cooperation. *Quarterly Journal of Economics*, *114*(3), 817–868.
Gordon, S. (1954). The economic theory of a common property resource: The fishery. *Journal of Political Economy*, *62*(2), 124–142.
Gould, S. J. (1980). *The Panda's thumb: More reflections on natural history*. N.Y.: W.W. Norton.
Gould, S. J. (1993). *Eight little piggies: Reflections on natural history*. N.Y.: W.W. Norton.
Grafton, R. Q., Kompas, T., & Long, N. V. (2017). A brave new world? Kantian-Nashian interactions and the dynamics of global climate change mitigation. *European Economic Review*, *99*, 31–42.
Hardin, G. (1968). The tragedy of the commons. *Science*, *162*, 1243–1248.
Hill, T. E, Jr., & Zweig, A. (2002). *Groundwork for the metaphysics of morals*. Oxford: Oxford University Press.
Kant, I. (1785). Grundlegung zur Metaphysik der Sitten. Translated by Gregor, M. J. (1998). *Groundwork of the metaphysics of morals*. Cambridge, U.K.: Cambridge University Press.
Laffont, J.-J. (1975). Macroeconomic constraints, economic efficiency and ethics: An introduction to Kantian economics. *Economica*, *42*, 430–437.
Levhari, D., & Mirman, L. (1980). The great fish wars: An example of using a dynamic Nash-Cournot solution. *Bell Journal of Economics*, *11*, 322–334.
Long, N. V. (2010). *A survey of dynamic games in economics*. Singapore and London: World Scientific.
Long, N. V. (2016). Kant-Nash equilibrium in a quantity-setting oligopoly. In P. von Mouche & F. Quartieri (Eds.), *Equilibrium theory for cournot oligopolies and related games: Essays in Honour of Koji Okuguchi* (pp. 179–202). New York: Springer.
Long, N. V. (2017). Mixed-strategy Kant-Nash equilibrium in games of voluntary contributions to a public good. In W. Buchholz & D. Ruebbelke (Eds.), *The theory of externalities and public goods* (pp. 107–126). New York: Springer.
Muller, J. Z. (1993). *Adam Smith in his time and ours: Designing the decent society*. New York, N.Y.: The Free Press.
Ostrom, E. (1990). *Governing the commons: The evolution of institutions for collective actions*. Cambridge: Cambridge University Press.
Roemer, J. E. (2010). Kantian equilibrium. *Scandinavian Journal of Economics*, *112*(1), 1–24.
Roemer, J. E. (2015). Kantian optimization: A microfoundation for cooperation. *Journal of Public Economics*, *127*, 45–57.
Sartre, J.-P. (1947). *Huis Clos*. Paris: Editions Gallimard.
Sen, A. (1977). Rational fools: A critique of the behavioral foundation of utility. *Philosophy and Public Affairs*, *6*(4), 317–344.
Sethi, R., & Somanathan, E. (1996). The evolution of social norms in common property resource use. *American Economic Review*, *86*(4), 766–788.
Smith, A. (1790 [2002]). *The theory of moral sentiments* (revised edition, 1790). T. Creech, and J. Bell & Co., Edinburg. (1790). Republished in the series Cambridge Texts in the History of Philosophy, edited by Knud Haakonssen. Cambridge University Press.
Smith, A. (1776). *An Inquiry into the Nature and Causes of the Wealth of Nations*. London: W. Strahan.
Smith, V. L. (2003). Constructivist and ecological rationality in economics. *American Economic Review*, *93*(3), 456–508.
Ulph, A., & Ulph, D. (2017). *A theory of consumption norms and implications for environmental policy*. Typescript: University of Manchester.

Wirl, F. (1995). The exploitation of fossil fuels under the threat of global warming and carbon taxes: A dynamic game approach. *Environmental and Resource Economics*, *5*, 333–352.
Wirl, F. (2011). Global warming and heterogeneous (green and brown) consumers. *Scandinavian Journal of Economics*, *113*, 866–884.
Wirl, F., & Dockner, E. (1995). Leviathan governments and carbon taxes: Costs and potential benefits. *European Economic Review*, *39*, 1215–1236.
Yang, Z. (2003). Reevaluation and renegotiation of climate change coalitions: A sequential closed-loop game approach. *Journal of Economic Dynamics and Control*, *27*, 1563–1594.

The Effects of Political Short-Termism on Transitions Induced by Pollution Regulations

Giovanni Di Bartolomeo, Enrico Saltari, and Willi Semmler

Abstract We study the dynamic problem of pollution control enacted by some policy of regulation and mitigation. The dynamics of the transition from one level of regulation and mitigation to another usually involves inter-temporal trade-offs. We focus on how different policymaker's time horizons affect these trade-offs. We refer to shorter lengths in policymaker's time horizons as political short-termism or inattention, which is associated with political economy or information constraints. Formally, inattention is modeled using Non linear Model Predictive Control. Therefore, it is a dynamic concept: our policymakers solve an inter-temporal decision problem with finite horizon that involves the repetitive solution of an optimal control problem at each sampling instant in a receding horizon fashion. We find that political short-termism substantially affects the transition dynamics. It leads to quicker, but costlier, transitions. It also leads to an under-evaluation of the environmental costs that may accelerate climate change.

G. Di Bartolomeo · E. Saltari (✉)
Facoltà di Economia, Sapienza University of Rome, Rome, Italy
e-mail: enrico.saltari@uniroma1.it

G. Di Bartolomeo
e-mail: giovanni.dibartolomeo@uniroma1.it

W. Semmler
New School for Social Research, New York, NY, USA
e-mail: semmlerw@newschool.edu

University of Bielefeld, Bielefeld, Germany

H. Dawid and J. Arifovic (eds.), *Dynamic Analysis in Complex Economic Environments*, Dynamic Modeling and Econometrics in Economics and Finance 26,
https://doi.org/10.1007/978-3-030-52970-3_6

1 Introduction

As widely stated now, anthropogenic pollution resulting from economic activity has been observed for a long time.[1] The pollution is a by-product of economic activity and has negative effects on welfare. In the short run, the negative effects on welfare are mitigation costs—costs of controlling pollution—and in the long run there is cost arising from social, ecological, and economic damages resulting from the greater pollution. Yet, in the long run there are likely to be also welfare gains. Nordhaus (1992, 2014), and Bonen et al. (2016), Orlov et al. (2018) provide an explicit treatment of both mitigation and adaptation costs.[2]

Although an equilibrium between long-run cost and benefits can be achieved, regulation standards need to change across time. Some technologies become obsolete and then policymakers find it optimal to disincentive their use. By contrast, new technologies substitute the old one and need to impose new regulation standards. Moreover, regulation standards can be used in a strategic way to incentive innovation to more efficient production techniques.[3]

In both cases, the regulator faces the transition from one type of regulation to another one. Moving from a standard to another one is, in fact, a dynamic process that can have large transition costs.

In this paper, we are dealing with dynamic transitions involved by changes in regulation standards. Therefore, we mainly deal with mitigation rather than adaptation costs. In the shorter run, however, policymakers are always subjected to a trade-off in emission regulations. Specifically, we look at trade-offs in the well-known problem of pollution control in the transition from one level of regulation and mitigation to another. We focus on how different policymaker's time horizons affect these transitions. We refer to shorter lengths in policymaker's time horizons as political short-termism or policy inattention.

The determination of the optimal path of emissions requires the solution of an optimal control problem (Nordhaus 1992, 2014). In our setup, political short-termism is modeled using Nonlinear Model Predictive Control (NMPC). Differently from the traditional optimal control, NMPC does not involve a maximization over the entire planning horizon. It instead involves the repetitive solution of a dynamic decision problem at each sampling instant in a receding horizon fashion (Grüne et al. 2015). We interpret a shorter horizon as measuring inattention.

Along the above lines, we consider two polar scenarios. In the first one, somewhat resembling emerging markets, we assume that the policymaker aims to regulate pollution through a technology, placing new standards of regulation, not to allow a

[1]See Spengler and Sexton (1983) and Gallegati et al. (2017) for the nexus of economic growth, CO_2 emission, and global temperature rise. For the nexus of CO_2 emission, climate disasters, and adaptation policies, see Mittnik et al. (2020).

[2]Orlov et al. (2018) show that indeed the agents in the short run, the current generation, might face some welfare losses, as compared to business-as-usual, but in the long run, for future generations, there can also be some gains, since increases in temperature and damages are avoided.

[3]See, e.g., Porter (1991), Gore (1992), and Porter and van der Linde (1995).

pollution to go above a certain level. In the second one, the regulator is supposed to bring down the pollution level to a lower level by moving from a high level of pollution to a lower one. It mimics the case of an obsolete technology to be replaced by a new technology, a case one might observe in the advanced countries.[4]

Our main finding is that policy inattention substantially affects the transition dynamics. Present-centric policy thinking matters, it affects the transition dynamics, leading to quicker, but more expensive, transitions in both the case of growing emerging market economies and the case of advanced countries. Independently of the case considered, in fact, inattention always leads to an under-evaluation of the environmental costs. This means that inattention allows, in either of our two cases above, for a larger buildup of a pollution stock that is likely to threaten the threshold—the carbon budget—below which the current Paris agreement on the upper bound of temperature rises, namely, 1.5–2 °C is not ensured.

Other recent researches use NMPC to study environmental economic problems. Greiner et al. (2014) study the transition of an economy from non-renewable to renewable energy. They study the conditions when a transition to renewable energy can take place, and whether it takes place before non-renewable energy is exhausted. A socially optimal solution is considered that takes into account the negative externality from the non-renewable energy in the longer run. They also study how tax rates and subsidies can be used to mimic the optimal solution in a market economy.

Nyambuu and Semmler (2014) consider optimal extraction and production of non-renewable resources that are finite in quantity. They show an inverted hump-shaped path for the price and a hump-shaped path for the extraction rate, in the case of modest initial stock of proved reserves.

Weller et al. (2015) and Kellett et al. (2019) develop a receding horizon implementation of the Integrated Assessment Model (IAM) of climate economics (Nordhaus 1992, 2014) and compute the social cost of carbon in the presence of uncertainty of future damages. Their receding horizon approach provides a decision-making framework to deal with key geophysical and economic uncertainties arising from the long-run pollution effects.

We use a similar approach as the above researches, but in a different perspective. Greiner et al. (2014), Nyambuu and Semmler (2014), Weller et al. (2015) and Kellett et al. (2019) use NMPC to mimic the dynamic programming solution and to obtain global solution without linear approximations. We instead use the NMPC approach to model policymaker's inattention. From this point of view, our paper is related to the pioneering studies of Buchanan and Tullock (1962: Chap. 4), Nordhaus (1975), and Simon (1995: 90), who emphasizes the question of time horizon and how policymaker's choices would be affected by it. For instance, when a government is almost

[4]Note that the Paris agreement allows in principle for the emerging markets a different path to a low carbon economy than for advanced economies (see Task Force on Climate-related Financial Disclosures 2017).

certain to lose the coming election, it may leave a legacy of policies that ties the hands of its opponents.[5]

Recently, the idea of political short-termism has been introduced by Di Bartolomeo et al. (2018) to study public debt dynamics in differential games. They find that shortsightedness induces policymakers to be initially more aggressive in stabilizing the debt, but it finally leads to excessive public debt in the long run. These initially too aggressive policies inertially trap policymakers along a dynamic path consistent with high long-run debt. Others have investigated further effects of impatience and discount factor shocks on policymakers' behavior (Niemann and von Hagen 2008; Adam 2011; Niemann 2011; and Niemann et al. 2013).

Alternatively, one can interpret the policymakers' different time perspectives in terms of limited capabilities of forecasting the effects of their policies. Policymakers as the other economic agents often make decisions under limited information, they respond imprecisely to the continuously available information, face uncertainties of the future, or they have a limited information processing capacity (Simon 1957, 1995).[6]

A prominent theory is rational inattention proposed by Sims (1998). As long processing information is costly, the agents may find it unreasonable to use all available sources of information. They would rather focus on selected sources, and they may rationally take their choices on incomplete information.[7]

The rest of the paper is organized as follows. Section 2 describes our framework and formally introduces the idea of the inattentive policymaker. Section 3 presents our results, i.e., the interaction effects of inattention and environmental policies. Both cases of new- and old-technology regulation are introduced. Section 4 concludes the chapter.

2 A Model of Pollution Control

Next, we present a more general model that allows to study the two cases above of an emerging market economy with higher growth rates and an advanced matured economy with lower growth rates, having a long history of pollution.

---

[5]Some examples are provided by Persson and Svensson (1989), Alesina and Tabellini (1990), and Chari and Cole (1993).

[6]See also Deissenberg and Cellarier (1999), Dawid et al. (2005), Arifovic et al. (2010), and Hebert and Woodford (2017).

[7]See among others, Sims (2003, 2006, 2010) and Woodford (2009). A complete survey on this issue is outside the scope of the present paper. Alternative interpretations could be based on the existence of externalities, troubles, or even corruption (bribery). See, e.g., Accinelli et al. (2014), who formalize joint dynamics of corruption and pollution in a model of evolutionary game theory.

2.1 The Economic Framework

Our general pollution control model is borrowed from Saltari and Travaglini (2016).[8] The model is based on a cost–benefit analysis of pollution.[9] Pollution is a by-product of economic activity and emissions from economic activity negatively affect welfare. Therefore, a certain level of emission is unavoidable, and thus producing goods and services may not be possible without generating some pollution.

Denoting the stock of pollution at time t by $p(t)$, the equation of motion that describes pollution dynamics can be written as the difference between the emissions ($z(t)$) and the ecological decay of the pollution stock ($\delta p(t)$):

$$\dot{p}(t) = z(t) - \delta p(t) \tag{1}$$

where pollution decay is assumed to be a linear function of the pollution stock level. We can refer to (1) as the emission equation.

The aim of the policymakers is to choose the level of emissions to maximize net social benefits that can be written in a compact form as follows:

$$W(0) = \int_0^T e^{-\rho t}(B(t) - C(t))dt \tag{2}$$

where ρ indicates the discount rate, the interval $[0, T]$ represents the planning horizon, $B(t) = [\alpha p(t)]^\theta$ are the gross benefits, and $C(t) = z(t) + \omega z(t)^2/2$ are the gross costs.

Pollution is related to production and we can write the benefit, $B(t)$, as related to capital via pollution, $\alpha p(t)$. The specification used is consistent with a standard production function, where pollution is a by-product of the use of capital. The parameter $\alpha > 0$ increases in the effect of natural abatement and falls in the marginal propensity to pollute of the community; $\theta \in (0, 1)$ increases in output elasticities of the production factor and falls in the elasticity of pollution.[10]

The damages of emissions, $C(t)$, are nonlinear as they include an increasing quadratic term. Thus, the marginal adjustment cost is increasing in the size of emissions. The specification, $C(t)$, captures the idea that additional units of emissions increase more than proportionally the disutility endured by society. An acceleration of the rate of emissions then increases the social costs of any incremental unit of pollution released.

---

[8]We refer to them for derivation details. See also, e.g., Fisher et al. (1972), Kamien and Schwartz (1991), Dockner and van Long (1993), Kolstad and Krautkraemer (1993), Tahvonen (1995), Jorgensen et al. (2010), and Athanassoglou and Xepapadeas (2012).

[9]Cost–benefit analysis raises several methodological and theoretical challenges that are far beyond the scope of our paper. Palmer et al. (1995) and Pearce et al. (2006) provide a comprehensive discussion of cost–benefit analysis and policy applications.

[10]For a formal derivation, we refer to Saltari and Travaglini (2016). It is worth mentioning that we need to use discrete controls to introduce NMPC techniques in the setup developed by Saltari and Travaglini (2016). By contrast, for the sake of comparison, we assume the state variables evolving in continuous time.

2.2 The Policymakers' Problem and Inattention

We first characterize the standard problem, and then we introduce inattention. In both cases, denoting p_0 the stock of pollution at the beginning of the planning horizon, we assume that the policymakers aim to implement a different level of pollution, p_T, for example, defined by an agreed upon carbon budget. During the transition from p_0 to p_T, constrained by the emission Eq. (1), the policymakers would choose a sequence of emissions, which maximizes net benefits (2).

In a full information context, the behavior of the rational policymaker can be found using the standard tools of control theory to solve the net benefit maximization problem. Formally, our policymaker solves

$$
\begin{aligned}
\max_{z(t)} W(0) &= \int_0^T e^{-\rho t}([\alpha p(t)]^\theta - z(t) - \frac{\omega}{2} z(t)^2)dt \\
\text{s.}t. & \\
\dot{p}(t) &= z(t) - \delta p(t) \\
p(0) &= p_0 \\
p(T) &= p_T
\end{aligned}
\tag{3}
$$

The Hamiltonian for the problem (3) can be easily derived and solved. We denote the (rational expectations) corresponding solution by $\{z^{RE}(t)\}_0^T$.

The solution of (3) using control theory is consistent with the idea that the length of the policy horizon is the result of myopia or limited rationality. Different lengths capture different policymakers' perspectives or constraints, for instance, the chances of survival in office by the government or some constitutional constraints. Following Di Bartolomeo et al. (2018), we can interpret a time preference for the short run against the long run as a measure of political instability, i.e., the frequency of government turnover, which depends on voter preferences, political institutions, and salient events and issues. Alternatively, we can assume that people often make decisions under limited information, they respond imprecisely to the continuously available information, or they have a limited information processing capacity (Simon 1990; Sims 1998).

A way to model the above concept of rational inattention in a dynamic setting is to use NMPC (Grüne et al. 2015). NMPC does not involve a maximization over the entire planning horizon, but it involves the repetitive solution of an optimal control problem at each sampling instant in a receding horizon fashion. Then a shorter horizon can be interpreted as measuring stronger inattention.

We denote the choices of the policymaker operate under rational inattention by $\{z_N^{RI}(t)\}_0^T$, where $N < T$ is the degree of inattention. Formally, the emission at each time $\tau \in [0, T]$ is determined to optimize a performance index with a receding horizon. At each time τ, the optimal emission $z(\tau)$ is determined over the horizon $[\tau, \tau + N]$, solving

$$\max_{z(t)} W(0) = \int_{\tau}^{\tau+N} e^{-\rho t}([\alpha p(t)]^{\theta} - z(t) - \frac{\omega}{2}z(t)^2)dt$$
$$\text{s.}t.$$
$$\dot{p}(t) = z(t) - \delta p(t)$$
$$p(\tau) = \left(\int_0^{\tau} z_N^{RI}(k)e^{-\delta k}dk + p_0\right)e^{\delta\tau}$$
$$p(\tau + N) = p_F \tag{4}$$

Then the optimal value at time τ ($z(\tau)$) is used as the actual input to the controlled system. Note that the initial condition ($p(\tau)$) of the problem (4) is obtained from the previous horizon solution. See the Appendix for details.

Summing up, the NMPC solution consists of the first optimal inputs of series of control problems, each over a given (moving) horizon of length N.

3 Inattention and Environmental Policies

Environmental policies are driven by specific-country considerations, desired targets and trade-off may, in fact, differ across different economies. For instance, relevant differences arise between low-income countries and high-income countries. Stern and Stiglitz (2017: 19) emphasize how the imperative of development and poverty reduction may justify slower and more moderate emission reductions over the short term. Low-income countries thus could do less to reduce their emissions in the short term to ensure poverty reduction. Specifically, Stern and Stiglitz (2017) underline that low-income countries tend to have less ambitious objectives for emission reductions and/or to require a lower carbon price to achieve a given level of emission reductions.

Along the above lines, we consider two simple scenarios. In the first one, we look at the problem of the policymaker who faces the transition from a low level of pollution to a higher, targeted, level, consistent with the society desired production. The scenario is consistent with a regulation policy of emerging economies or the regulation of new-introduced technologies that substitutes some old obsolete ones. Formally, in this scenario, we assume $p_0 < p_T$.

The second case describes the problem of a policymaker in a mature economy. Now, the policymaker should manage the transition from a high level of pollution to a lower one for an obsolete technology that is going to be substituted by a new, more efficient one. For a long time, both technologies can coexist. Thus, the policymaker could aim to regulate the old (inefficient) technology to be used less, reducing the associated level of pollution.[11]

The second scenario is characterized by $p_0 > p_T$.

[11] We focus on the regulation of the old obsolete technology. Clearly, the case of the new efficient one is already described by the first scenario.

We refer to the first scenario as the case of "growth and pollution regulation," while we refer to the second as the case of "obsolete technology and pollution abatement." In both scenarios, the model is solved by numerical simulations.[12]

We calibrate the model by using a reasonable set of parameter values. The annual discount factor ρ is set at 0.04 (corresponding to a 4% rate). The ecological decay of the pollution stock is 5% per year (i.e., $\delta = 0.05$). The other parameters are $\omega = 1$, $\theta = 0.3$, and $\alpha^{\theta} = 0.5$. These values are consistent with an elasticity ranging from about 0.3 to 3.3. Moreover, we assume that $p_0 = 3$ and $p_T = 14$ in the first scenario, whereas $p_0 = 45$ and $p_T = 14$ in the second one.[13]

We compare the optimal regulation designed by a rational policymaker (i.e., problem (3)) to inattention (i.e., problem (4)), which is captured by different values for the policymaker's (moving) horizon of length N. Specifically, we consider three different cases: strong inattention, inattention, and weak inattention (respectively, time length equal to 90, 110, and 130). The value for T is set at 160; therefore, the planning horizon for the rational policymaker is [0, 160].

3.1 Growth and Pollution Regulation

New technologies substitute the old ones and one needs to impose regulation standards. Therefore, the policymaker faces a transition from one level of regulation to another one. Specifically, the regulator faces the problem to move from an initial low level of pollution and production to an upper bound standard compatible with a desired growth rate. Our results are illustrated in Fig. 1. The path depends on the regulator's inattention. The solid line represents the case of an attentive policymaker.

During the transition dynamics, optimal emission regulation requires to achieve gradually the desired standard. In the absence of inattention, the optimal control solution requires an "overshooting policy" that results in reversed-hump-shaped dynamics for emission (Saltari and Travaglini 2016). The emissions are initially reduced and only at about the mid-planning horizon these start to converge to the desired standard. The rationale of the dynamics is due to the high social cost of pollution. Similar optimal dynamics hold for extraction and production of non-renewable resources (e.g., Nyambuu and Semmler 2014).

How does inattention affect the policymaker decisions? As the degree of inattention increases, the regulator tends to reach the desired standard faster, while underestimating the impact on the environment during the transition.

The average effects of inattention during the transition dynamics can be quantified. Table 1 reports them. The table also reports percent deviations from the rational

---

[12]NMPC is implemented following Grüne et al. (2015) and using the Matlab routines developed by Grüne and Pannek (2017).

[13]For the sake of comparison, we use the same parameters proposed by Saltari and Travaglini (2016). However, our findings are qualitatively robust to changes in the parameterization. Results are available upon request.

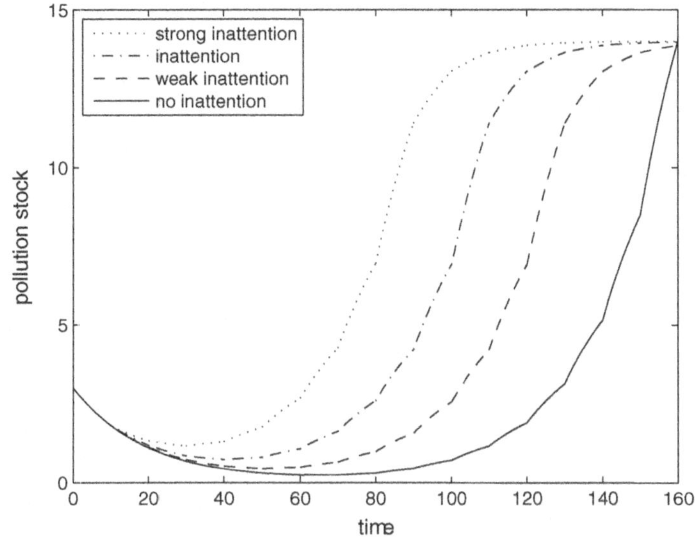

Fig. 1 Emission regulation path for a new technology

Table 1 Effects of inattention (new technology)

	Pollution (stock) average	%	Emission (flow) average	%
Strong inattention	8.37	167	0.46	172
Inattention	6.76	115	0.37	121
Weak inattention	5.13	63	0.28	69
No inattention	3.14	–	0.17	–

expectation benchmark. Compared to the optimal control policy, strong inattention implies a pollution stock and average emissions about two times larger. Notable differences emerge for all cases of inattention.

Thus overall, inattention and shortsightedness allow for a larger buildup of a pollution stock that is likely to threaten the threshold, adjusted for developing economies, below which the carbon budget, and the current Paris agreement on the upper bound of temperature rise, is not ensured.

3.2 *Obsolete Technologies and Pollution Abatement*

The effects of introducing a new technology that makes the old one (more polluting) obsolete are illustrated in Fig. 2. This is more the case of advanced countries that have been using for a long time fossil fuel energy. Such old technology is assumed to be regulated to bring pollution down to a lower level. Figure 2 describes the transition

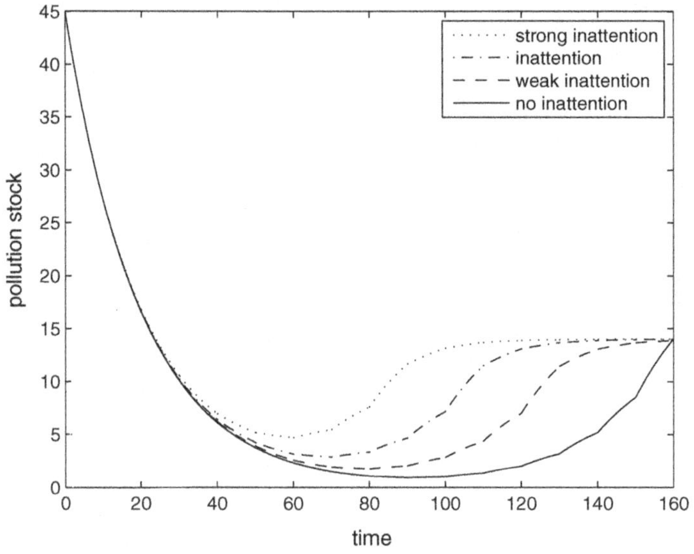

Fig. 2 Emission regulation path for an obsolete technology

from a soft standard (which is associated to a high level of pollution) to a hard standard. The path depends on the regulator's inattention. The solid line represents again the case of an attentive policymaker.

During the transition dynamics, optimal policies require to quickly abate the pollution level to converge to lower levels, to the new desired standard. As the degree of inattention increases, the policymaker will again tend to reach the desired standard faster, but at a higher cost. The regulator again under-evaluates the environmental impacts of the transition to the new desired standard.

The average effects of inattention during the transition dynamics of the regulation of an obsolete technology are described in Table 2. The table reports the average pollution and emission and percent deviations from the rational expectation benchmark.

Here too, inattention and shortsightedness allow for a larger buildup of a pollution stock that is likely to threaten the threshold for advanced economies, below which the

Table 2 Effects of inattention (obsolete technology)

	Pollution (stock) average	%	Emission (flow) average	%
Strong inattention	13.98	58	0.45	170
Inattention	12.41	41	0.37	120
Weak inattention	10.80	22	0.28	68
No inattention	8.81	–	0.17	–

carbon budget, and the current Paris agreement on the upper bound of temperature rise, is not ensured.

4 Conclusions

We studied the effects regulator's inattention in the transition from two different levels of environmental regulation. We can refer to political short-termism or policy inattention as shorter lengths in policymaker's time horizons. The rationale of different time perspectives can be found in policy uncertainty, institutional constraints, or limited rationality due to limited information or rational inattention.

Independently of its rationale, policy inattention was modeled using NMPC. In each instant of time, the regulator can solve an optimization problem considering the effects of the policy for a limited horizon. A shorter horizon is interpreted as a measure of inattention. Of course, as time passes, the regulator revises the plan forward. The NMPC approach provides a principled decision-making framework in which to deal with policymaker's inattention, which complements the existing models based on optimal control methods.

Our main result is that no matter whether the regulator designs a plan to achieve a lower (fast growing emerging market economies) or higher level of emission standard (advanced countries with old energy technology), political short-termism leads to quicker, but more expensive, transitions associated to an under-evaluation of the environmental risk. Hereby the targeted upper limits of emissions and temperature are threatened not to be ensured.

Acknowledgements The authors are grateful to an anonymous referee, Bas van Aarle, Marco Di Pietro, Francesco Forte, Behnaz Minooei Fard, and Joseph Plasmans for comments. They also acknowledge financial support by Sapienza University of Rome. An earlier version of this paper has been circulated under the title "Inattention, and pollution regulation policies."

Appendix

Both problems (3) and (4) are solved by maximizing one or more Hamiltonians of the following kind:

$$H(k) = e^{-\rho t}\Big([\alpha p(k)]^{\theta} - z(k) - \frac{\omega}{2}z(k)^2 + \mu(k)[z(k) - \delta p(k)]\Big) \tag{5}$$

with $k \in [k_L, k_U]$, $p(k_L) = p_{k_L}$, and $p(k_U) = p_{k_U}$, which requires

$$\frac{\partial H(k)}{\partial z(k)} = 0 \Rightarrow -1 - \omega z(k) + \mu(k) = 0 \tag{6}$$

$$\dot{p}(k) = \frac{\partial H(k)}{\partial \mu(k)} \Rightarrow \dot{p}(k) = z(k) - \delta p(k) \tag{7}$$

$$\dot{\mu}(k) = \rho\mu(k) - \frac{\partial H(k)}{\partial p(k)} \Rightarrow \alpha^{\theta}\theta p(k)^{\theta-1} = (\rho + \delta)\mu(k) - \dot{\mu}(k) \tag{8}$$

The optimal policy plan stemming from (3) needs to solve (6)–(7) imposing $p(k_L) = p_0$ and $p(k_U) = p_T$. By contrast, the solution of (4) is obtained by solving a series of Eqs. (6)–(7), at each instant of time $k \in [0, T]$, while $z_N^{RI}(k)$ is obtained by solving (6)–(7) imposing $p(k_L) = (\int_0^{k_L} z_N^{RI}(i)e^{-\delta k_L}di + p_0)e^{\delta k_L}$ and $p(k_L + N) = p_T$.[14]

References

Accinelli, E., Policardo, L., & Sanchez Carrera, E. (2014). On the dynamics and effects of corruption on environmental protection. In A. Pinto Adrego & D. Zilberman (Eds.), *Modeling, dynamics, optimization and bioeconomics I* (Vol. 73, pp. 23–41). Springer Proceedings in Mathematics & Statistics.

Adam, K. (2011). Government debt and optimal monetary and fiscal policy. *European Economic Review, 55*, 57–74.

Alesina, A., & Tabellini, G. (1990). A positive theory of fiscal deficits and government debt. *Review of Economic Studies, 57*, 403–414.

Arifovic, J., Dawid, H., Deissenberg, C., & Kostyshyna, O. (2010). Learning benevolent leadership in a heterogeneous agents economy. *Journal of Economic Dynamics and Control, 34*, 1768–1790.

Athanassoglou, S., & Xepapadeas, A. (2012). Pollution control with uncertain stock dynamics: When, and how, to be precaution. *Journal of Environmental Economics and Management, 63*, 304–320.

Bonen, T., Loungani, P., Semmler, W., & Koch, S. (2016). *Investing to mitigate and adapt to climate change: A framework model*. IMF Working Paper No 164.

Buchanan, J. M., & Tullock, G. (1962). *The calculus of consent. Logical foundations of constitutional democracy*. Ann Arbor, USA: University of Michigan Press.

Chari, V., & Cole, H. (1993). *Why are representative democracies fiscally irresponsible*. Federal Reserve Bank of Minneapolis Staff report No. 163.

Dawid, H., Deissenberg, C., & Ševčík, P. (2005). Cheap talk, gullibility, and welfare in an environmental taxation game. In A. Haurie & G. Zaccour (Eds.), *Dynamics games: Theory and applications*. Berlin, Germany: Springer.

Deissenberg, C., & Cellarier, L. (1999). The influence of clean up capital subsidies in environmental optimal control models with complex dynamics. In *Computing in economics and finance*. Society for Computational Economics (Vol. 323).

Di Bartolomeo, G., Di Pietro, M., Saltari, E., & Semmler, W. (2018). Public debt stabilization: The relevance of policymakers' time horizons. *Public Choice, 177*, 287–299.

Dockner, E. J., & van Long, N. (1993). International pollution control: Cooperative versus noncooperative strategies. *Journal of Environmental Economics and Management, 25*, 13–29.

[14]The representation of NMPC in continuous-time models is not intuitive. From a practical point of view, NMPC requires to convert these models into a discrete time by sampling (for details, see Grüne and Pannek 2017: 16–28).

Fisher, A. C., Kutrilla, I. V., & Cicchetti, J. (1972). The economics of environmental preservation: A theoretical and empirical analysis. *American Economic Review, 62,* 605–619.

Gallegati, M., Gallegati, M., Ramsey, J., & Semmler, W. (2017). Global CO_2 emissions, global temperature and World GDP growth rates. Manuscript, New School for Social Research.

Gore, A. (1992). *Earth in the balance.* London, United Kingdom: Earthscan.

Greiner, A., Gruene, L., & Semmler, W. (2014). Economic growth and the transition from non-renewable to renewable energy. *Environment and Development Economics, 19,* 417–439.

Grüne, L., & Pannek, J. (2017). *Nonlinear model predictive control* (2nd ed.). Berlin, Germany: Springer.

Grüne, L., Semmler, W., & Stieler, M. (2015). Using nonlinear model predictive control for dynamic decision problems in economics. *Journal of Economic Dynamics and Control, 60,* 112–133.

Hebert, B., & Woodford, M. (2017). *Rational inattention and sequential information sampling.* NBER Working paper No 23787.

Jorgensen, S., Martin-Herran, G., & Zaccour, G. (2010). Dynamic games in the economics and management of pollution. *Environmental Modeling & Assessment, 15,* 433–467.

Kamien, M. I., & Schwartz, N. L. (1991). *The calculus of variations and optimal control in economics and management.* New York, USA: Elsevier.

Kellett, C., Weller, S., Faulwasser, T., Grüne, L., & Semmler, W. (2019). Feedback, dynamics, and optimal control in climate economics. *Annual Reviews of Control.*

Kolstad, C. D., & Krautkraemer, J. A. (1993). Natural resource use and the environment. In A. Kneese & J. Sweeney (Eds.), *Handbook of natural resource and energy economics* (Vol. 3). Amsterdam, The Netherlands: Elsevier.

Mittnik, S., Semmler, W., & Haider, A. (2020). Climate disaster risks —Empirics and a Multi-Phase Dynamic Model. Econometrics, 8(3), 33; https://doi.org/10.3390/econometrics8030033.

Niemann, S. (2011). Dynamic monetary-fiscal interactions and the role of monetary conversatism. *Journal of Monetary Economics, 58,* 234–247.

Niemann, S., Pichler, P., & Sorger, G. (2013). Central bank independence and the monetary instrument problem. *International Economic Review, 54,* 1031–1055.

Niemann, S., & von Hagen, J. (2008). Coordination of monetary and fiscal policies: A fresh look at the issue. *Swedish Economic Policy Review, 15,* 89–124.

Nordhaus, W. D. (1975). The political business cycle. *Review of Economic Studies, 42,* 169–190.

Nordhaus, W. D. (1992). An optimal transition path for controlling greenhouse gases. *Science, 258,* 1315–1319.

Nordhaus, W. (2014). Estimates of the social cost of carbon: Concepts and results from the DICE-2013R model and alternative approaches. *Journal of Association Environmental Resource Economics, 1,* 273–312.

Nyambuu, U., & Semmler, W. (2014). Trends in the extraction of non-renewable resources: The case of fossil energy. *Economic Modelling, 37,* 271–279.

Orlov, S., Rovenskaya, E., Puaschunder, J., & Semmler, W. (2018). *Green bonds, transition to a low-carbon economy, and intergenerational fairness: Evidence from an extended DICE model.* IIASA Working Paper No 1, Laxenburg, Austria.

Palmer, K., Oates, W., & Portney, P. (1995). Tightening environmental standards: The benefit-cost or the no-cost paradigm? *Journal of Economic Perspectives, 9,* 119–132.

Pearce, D., Atkinson, G., & Mourato, S. (2006). *Cost-benefit analysis and the environment: Recent developments.* Paris, France: OECD.

Persson, T., & Svensson, L. E. O. (1989). Why a stubborn conservative would run a deficit: Policy with time-inconsistent preferences. *The Quarterly Journal of Economics, 104,* 325–345.

Porter, M. (1991). America's green strategy. *Scientific American, 264,* 168.

Porter, M., & van der Linde, C. (1995). Toward a new conception of the environment competitiveness relationship. *Journal of Economic Perspectives, 9,* 97–118.

Saltari, E., & Travaglini, G. (2016). Pollution control under emission constraints: Switching between regimes. *Energy Economics, 53,* 212–219.

Simon, H. A. (1957). *Models of man: Social and rational. Mathematical essays on rational human behavior in society setting*. New York, USA: Wiley.

Simon, H. A. (1995). A behavioral model of rational choice. *Quarterly Journal of Economics, 69,* 99–118.

Sims, C. A. (1998). Stickiness. *Carnegie-Rochester Conference Series on Public Policy, 49,* 317–356.

Sims, C. A. (2003). Implications of rational inattention. *Journal of Monetary Economics, 50,* 665–690.

Sims, C. A. (2006). Rational inattention: Beyond the linear-quadratic case. *American Economic Review, 96,* 158–163.

Sims, C. A. (2010). Rational inattention and monetary economics. *Handbook of Monetary Economics, 3,* 155–181.

Simon, H. A. (1990). Bounded rationality. In: Eatwell J., Milgate M., Newman P. (Eds.), *Utility and Probability*. London: The New Palgrave. Palgrave Macmillan.

Spengler, J. D., & Sexton, K. A. (1983). Indoor air pollution: A public health perspective. *Science, 221,* 9–17.

Stern, N., & Stiglitz, J. E. (2017). *Report of the high-level commission on carbon prices*. Washington, USA: The World Bank.

Tahvonen, O. (1995). Dynamics of pollution control when damage is sensitive to the rate of pollution accumulation. *Environmental and Resource Economics, 5,* 9–27.

Task Force on Climate-related Financial Disclosures (2017). Recommendations of the task force on climate-related financial disclosures. Final report. G-20 Financial Stability Board, Basel, Switzerland.

Weller, S. R., Hafeez, S., & Kellett, C. M. (2015). A receding horizon control approach to estimating the social cost of carbon in the presence of emissions and temperature uncertainty. In *IEEE 54th Annual Conference on Decision and Control*. December 15–18. Osaka, Japan.

Woodford, M. (2009). Information-constrained state-dependent pricing. *Journal of Monetary Economics, 56,* 100–124.

Capital Control, Exchange Rate Regime, and Monetary Policy: Indeterminacy and Bifurcation

William A. Barnett and Jingxian Hu

Abstract Will capital controls enhance macroeconomic stability? How will the results be influenced by the exchange rate regime and monetary policy reaction? Are the consequences of policy decisions involving capital controls easily predictable, or more complicated than may have been anticipated? We will answer the above questions by investigating the macroeconomic dynamics of a small open economy. In recent years, these matters have become particularly important to emerging market economies, which have often adopted capital controls. We especially investigate two dynamical characteristics: indeterminacy and bifurcation. Four cases are explored, based on different exchange rate regimes and monetary policy rules. With capital controls in place, we find that indeterminacy depends upon how the central bank's response to inflation and its response to the output gap coordinate with each other in the Taylor rule. When forward-looking, both passive and active monetary policy can lead to indeterminacy. Compared with flexible exchange rates, fixed exchange rate regimes produce more complex indeterminacy conditions, depending upon the stickiness of prices and the elasticity of substitution between labor and consumption. We show the existence of Hopf bifurcation under capital control with fixed exchange rates and current-looking monetary policy. To determine empirical relevance, we test indeterminacy empirically using Bayesian estimation. Fixed exchange rate regimes with capital controls produce larger posterior probability of the indeterminate region than a flexible exchange rate regime. Fixed exchange rate regimes with current-looking monetary policy lead to several kinds of bifurcation under capital

Forthcoming in Herbert Dawid and Jasmina Arifovic (eds.), *Dynamic Analysis in Complex Economic Environments—Essays in Honor of Christophe Deissenberg*, Springer.

W. A. Barnett (✉)
University of Kansas, Lawrence, USA
e-mail: williamabarnett@gmail.com

Center for Financial Stability, NY City, USA

ICEMR Institute for Nonlinear Dynamical Inference, Moscow, Russia

J. Hu
Boise State University, Boise, USA
e-mail: jingxianhu@boisestate.edu

H. Dawid and J. Arifovic (eds.), *Dynamic Analysis in Complex Economic Environments*, Dynamic Modeling and Econometrics in Economics and Finance 26,
https://doi.org/10.1007/978-3-030-52970-3_7

controls. We provide monetary policy suggestions on achieving macroeconomic stability through financial regulation.

Keywords Capital controls · Open economy monetary policy · Exchange rate regimes · Bayesian methods · Bifurcation · Indeterminacy

JEL Code F41 · F31 · F38 · E52 · C11 · C62

1 Introduction

Since the Great Recession following the 2008 financial crisis, the potential problems caused by free capital movements among countries have drawn attention to the relationship between financial regulation, capital controls, and macroeconomic stability. Some researchers support capital controls with prudential macroeconomic policy. According to that view, capital controls can mitigate systemic risk, reduce business cycle volatility, and increase macroeconomic stability. Related research includes Farhi and Werning (2012, 2014), Korinek (2011, 2014), Ostry et al. (2012), and Magud et al. (2012).

According to Mundell's (1963), "impossible trinity" in international economics, an open economy cannot simultaneously have independent monetary policy, fixed exchange rates, and free capital movement.[1] Under prudential macroeconomic policy with control of capital flows, we investigate combinations of exchange rate regimes and monetary policies that could stabilize the economy. Is it possible that the choices of exchange rate regime and monetary policy could generate instability and increased volatility, even though capital flows are controlled? How to make such policy decisions and to what extent the policy should be adjusted are challenging questions relevant to all monetary authorities.

In this paper, we explore the dynamics of an economic system with capital controls. We investigate the possible instability or nonuniqueness of equilibria and their relevancy to the policy under capital controls. In contrast, Farhi and Werning (2012, 2014) and Korinek (2011, 2014), study welfare implications of capital controls from a theoretic perspective, while Ostry et al. (2012) and Magud et al. (2012), investigate the relationship of capital controls to macroeconomic stability using empirical methods. Our contribution is to investigate dynamical characteristics with emphasis on indeterminacy and bifurcation.

Indeterminacy occurs if the equilibrium of an economic system is not unique, resulting in the existence of multiple equilibria. Under those circumstances, consumers' and firms' forecasts of macroeconomic variables, such as output and inflation rates, can lead to the phenomenon of "self-fulfilling prophecy." The economy can move from one equilibrium to another. A new equilibrium, driven by economic agents' beliefs, could be a better one or a worse one. If capital controls

[1]Mundell's (1963), "impossible trinity" is alternatively often called the "Mundell-Fleming trilemma" to recognize the relevancy of Fleming (1962).

signal to people that they are protected from the risk of international financial market volatility, then the beliefs-driven equilibrium may be better than without those controls. Alternatively, if imposition of capital controls produces panic and induces evasion of the controls, the equilibrium can be worse than equilibrium without capital controls. As a result, we investigate the existence of multiple equilibria in an open economy with different exchange rate regimes and monetary policies. We empirically examine indeterminacy using Bayesian methods to estimate the probability of the indeterminacy region. We also acquire the posterior estimates of parameters and the impulse responses under both fundamental shocks and sunspot shocks.

We find that the existence of indeterminacy depends upon how inflation and output gap coordinate with each other in their feedback to interest rate setting in the Taylor rule. Our results expand the conclusions of previous literature on indeterminacy and monetary policy to the case of capital controls. See, e.g., Cochrane (2011) and Benhabib et al. (2001). When monetary policy is forward-looking with capital controls, we find that both passive feedback and active feedback can generate indeterminacy.[2] Chatelain and Ralf (2018a, b) find that the determinacy theory of fiscal, macro-prudential or Taylor rules only relies on the assumption that the policy instruments are forward-looking variables when policy targets are forward-looking.

The exchange rate regime can alter the conditions for indeterminacy. Compared with flexible exchange rates, a fixed exchange regime produces more complex conditions, depending on the stickiness of price setting and the elasticity of substitution between labor and consumption. Interestingly, the degree of openness does not play a large role in our results. This difference from previous literature evidently is associated with the control of international capital mobility.

We introduce into our model incompleteness of international capital markets and staggered price setting, in contrast with Airaudo and Zanna (2012), who analyze global equilibrium determinacy in a flexible price open economy with active interest rate rules on inflation. Benhabib and Farmer (1999) find that staggered price setting can cause indeterminacy to arise. We find that when the price is close to flexible with capital controls, indeterminacy is possible.

The other primary objective of our paper is to investigate the existence of bifurcation phenomena in an open economy with capital controls. Bifurcation is defined to occur, if a qualitative change in dynamics occurs, when the bifurcation boundary is crossed by the deep parameters of the economy's structure. Such deep parameters are not only those of private tastes and technology, but also of monetary policy rules. Such qualitative change can be between instability and stability. But the change can also be between different kinds of instability or between different kinds of stability, such as monotonic stability and periodic damped stability, or multiperiodic damped stabilitiy. Existence of bifurcation boundaries can motivate policy intervention. A slight change to the parameters of private tastes or technology or to the parameters of central bank feedbacks to output and inflation as policy instruments can induce a fundamental change in the nature of the economy's dynamics.

---

[2]With passive monetary policy, the parameter multiplied by inflation or output gap in Taylor rule is defined to be between 0 and 1. With an active monetary policy, the parameter is larger than 1.

The previous literature investigating bifurcation without capital controls includes Barnett and Duzhak (2008, 2010, 2014), Barnett and Eryilmaz (2013, 2014), and the survey paper Barnett and Chen (2015). In contrast, we introduce capital controls and an exchange rate peg. Without capital controls, Woodford (1986, 1989) and Franke (1992), find that capital market imperfections can lead to more complex dynamics than perfect capital markets. Chatelain and Ralf (2018a, b) find that the inflation auto-correlation parameter crosses a saddle-node bifurcation when shifting from near-zero to zero probability of not reneging commitment of optimal monetary policy. We find that there can exist Hopf bifurcation under capital controls, fixed exchange rates, and current-looking monetary policy. We determine the conditions under which the monetary policy rule or private deep parameters will generate instability. We encounter several kinds of bifurcation when the model's parameters are estimated by Bayesian methods.

This paper is structured as follows. We illustrate the model in Sect. 2 and derive the equilibria in Sect. 3. The dynamical systems under different exchange rate regimes and monetary policies are discussed in Sect. 4. In Sects. 5 and 6, we analyze the conditions for indeterminacy and bifurcation and their economic implications. In Sects. 7 and 8, we test indeterminacy empirically and locate bifurcation boundaries numerically. Section 9 is the conclusion.

2 Model

In light of Gali and Monacelli (2005) and Farhi and Werning (2012, 2014), our model is an open economy New Keynesian model consisting of a small open economy that imposes capital controls and chooses between flexible exchange rates and fixed exchange rates. Compared with the Mundell-Fleming IS-LM-BP model, the New Keynesian model has solid micro-foundation on both the demand side and the supply side. As a result, we are able to analyze the influence of the deep structural parameters on the economy's dynamics.

We choose the discrete time version of the linear rational expectations model to facilitate analyzing the indeterminacy and bifurcation conditions. For analyzing indeterminacy, the linear rational expectations model automatically fixes the list of predetermined variables, thereby eliminating the need to differentiate between predetermined variables and jump variables.[3] Discrete time also permits location of bifurcation boundaries in a linear system, as in Barnett and Duzhak (2008, 2010, 2014) and Barnett and Eryilmaz (2013, 2014). In addition, rational expectations allow us to differentiate between fundamental shocks and non-fundamental forecasting errors. Farmer et al. (2015) and Beyer and Farmer (2004) find methods to change the system from indeterminate to determinate by moving the non-fundamental forecasting errors. The number of those errors equals the degree of indeterminacy to the fundamental shocks set. In the rational expectations model, it is possible for beliefs

[3] See Sims (2002).

to drive the economy to another path that converges to a steady state, producing a self-fulfilling prophecy. In principle, it is possible to regulate or influence those beliefs. This phenomenon is different from "animal spirit."

There is a continuum of small open economies, indexed along the unit interval. Different economies share identical preferences, technology, and market structure. Following the conventions in this literature, we use variables without i-index to refer to the small open economy being modeled. Variables with i-index refer to variables in economy i, among the continuum of economies making up the world economy. Variables with a star correspond to the world economy as a whole, while j denotes a particular good within an economy.

2.1 Households

A representative household seeks to maximize

$$E_0 \sum_{t=0}^{\infty} \beta^t \left[\frac{C_t^{1-\sigma}}{1-\sigma} - \frac{N_t^{1+\varphi}}{1+\varphi} \right], \tag{1}$$

where N_t denotes hours of labor, C_t is a composite consumption index defined by

$$C_t \equiv \left[(1-\alpha)^{\frac{1}{\eta}} \left(C_{H,t}\right)^{\frac{\eta-1}{\eta}} + \alpha^{\frac{1}{\eta}} \left(C_{F,t}\right)^{\frac{\eta-1}{\eta}} \right]^{\frac{\eta}{\eta-1}},$$

with $C_{H,t} \equiv \left(\int_0^1 C_{H,t}(j)^{\frac{\varepsilon-1}{\varepsilon}} dj \right)^{\frac{\varepsilon}{\varepsilon-1}}$, $C_{F,t} \equiv \left(\int_0^1 (C_{i,t})^{\frac{\gamma-1}{\gamma}} di \right)^{\frac{\gamma}{\gamma-1}}$, $C_{i,t} \equiv \left(\int_0^1 C_{i,t}(j)^{\frac{\varepsilon-1}{\varepsilon}} dj \right)^{\frac{\varepsilon}{\varepsilon-1}}$.

The parameter $\varepsilon > 1$ denotes the elasticity of substitution among goods within any given country. The parameter $\alpha \in [0, 1]$ denotes the degree of home bias in preferences and is an index of openness, while $\eta > 0$ measures the elasticity of substitution between domestic and foreign goods, and γ measures the elasticity of substitution among goods produced in different countries.

The household's budget constraint takes the form

$$\int_0^1 P_{H,t}(j) C_{H,t}(j) dj + \int_0^1 \int_0^1 P_{i,t}(j) C_{i,t}(j) dj di + E_t\{Q_{t,t+1} D_{t+1}\}$$
$$+ \int_0^1 E_t\{\mathcal{E}_{i,t} Q_{t,t+1}^i D_{t+1}^i\} di \le W_t N_t + T_t + D_t + \int_0^1 \left(\frac{1+\tau_t}{1+\tau_t^i} \right) \mathcal{E}_{i,t} D_t^i di, \tag{2}$$

where D_{t+1} is holding of the home portfolio, consisting of shares in firms. Holding of country i's portfolio is D_{t+1}^i, while $Q_{t,t+1}$ is the price of the home portfolio, and $Q_{t,t+1}^i$ is the price of country i's portfolio. The nominal wage is W_t. The lump sum transfer/tax at t is T_t. We model the capital control, following Farhi and Werning (2014), with τ_t denoting the subsidy on capital outflows (tax on capital inflows) in home country and τ_t^i denoting the subsidy on capital outflows (tax on capital inflows) in country i. We assume that country i does not impose capital control, so that $\tau_t^i = 0$. Taxes on capital inflows are rebated as a lump sum to households. We introduce Δ and Θ to be the variables that capture the dynamics of capital control, τ_t, where $1 + \tau_{t+1} \equiv \frac{\Delta_{t+1}}{\Delta_t} \equiv \frac{\Theta_{t+1}^{\sigma}}{\Theta_t^{\sigma}}$, following Farhi and Werning (2012, 2014).

After the derivation that is shown in Appendix 1, the budget constraint can be rewritten as

$$P_t C_t + E_t\{Q_{t,t+1} D_{t+1}\} + E_t\{\mathcal{E}_t Q_{t,t+1}^* D_{t+1}^*\} \leq W_t N_t + T_t + D_t + (1+\tau_t)\mathcal{E}_t D_t^*. \quad (3)$$

Maximizing utility of a household subject to its budget constraint yields two Euler equations

$$\beta E_t\left\{\left(\frac{C_{t+1}}{C_t}\right)^{-\sigma}\left(\frac{P_t}{P_{t+1}}\right)\left(\frac{1}{Q_{t,t+1}}\right)\right\} = 1,$$
$$\beta E_t\left\{\left(\frac{C_{t+1}}{C_t}\right)^{-\sigma}\left(\frac{P_t}{P_{t+1}}\right)\left(\frac{\mathcal{E}_{t+1}}{\mathcal{E}_t}\right)(1+\tau_{t+1})\left(\frac{1}{Q_{t,t+1}^*}\right)\right\} = 1. \quad (4)$$

The log-linearized form is

$$c_t = E_t\{c_{t+1}\} - \frac{1}{\sigma}(r_t - E_t\{\pi_{t+1}\} - \rho),$$
$$c_t = E_t\{c_{t+1}\} - \frac{1}{\sigma}\left(r_t^* + \left[E_t\{e_{t+1}\} - e_t\right] + E_t\{\tau_{t+1}\} - E_t\{\pi_{t+1}\} - \rho\right), \quad (5)$$

For the representative household in country i, the problem is to maximize

$$E_0 \sum_{t=0}^{\infty} \beta^t \left[\frac{C_t^{i1-\sigma}}{1-\sigma} - \frac{N_t^{i1+\varphi}}{1+\varphi}\right], \quad (6)$$

subject to the budget constraint

$$P_t^i C_t^i + E_t\{Q_{t,t+1}^i D_{t+1}^i\} + E_t\left\{\frac{Q_{t,t+1}^{i*} D_{t+1}^{i*}}{\mathcal{E}_{i,t}}\right\} \leq W_t^i N_t^i + T_t^i + D_t^i + \frac{D_t^{i*}}{\mathcal{E}_{i,t}}. \quad (7)$$

Notice that there is no capital control in the country i.

The first order conditions also provides us with two Euler equations

$$\beta E_t\left\{\left(\frac{C^i_{t+1}}{C^i_t}\right)^{-\sigma}\left(\frac{P^i_t}{P^i_{t+1}}\right)\left(\frac{1}{Q^i_{t,t+1}}\right)\right\}=1,$$

$$\beta E_t\left\{\left(\frac{C^i_{t+1}}{C^i_t}\right)^{-\sigma}\left(\frac{P^i_t}{P^i_{t+1}}\right)\left(\frac{\mathcal{E}_{i,t}}{\mathcal{E}_{i,t+1}}\right)\left(\frac{1}{Q^{i*}_{t,t+1}}\right)\right\}=1, \tag{8}$$

where $\mathcal{Q}_{i,t} \equiv \frac{\mathcal{E}_{i,t}P^i_t}{P_t}$ is the real exchange rate.

Combined with the two Euler equations for the home country, we get the Backus-Smith condition,

$$C_t = \Theta_t C^i_t \mathcal{Q}^{\frac{1}{\sigma}}_{i,t}. \tag{9}$$

Taking logs on both sides and integrating over i, we get

$$c_t = c^*_t + \frac{1}{\sigma}q_t + \theta_t \tag{10}$$

2.2 Uncovered Interest Parity

The pricing equation for foreign bonds and domestic bonds are, respectively

$$\left(R^*_t\right)^{-1} = E_t\left\{Q^*_{t,t+1}\right\},$$

$$\left(R_t\right)^{-1} = E_t\left\{Q_{t,t+1}\right\}. \tag{11}$$

We combine them to get the Uncovered Interest Parity conditions

$$R_t = (1+\tau_{t+1})R^*_t\frac{\mathcal{E}_{t+1}}{\mathcal{E}_t}$$

Taking logs on both sides, we get

$$r_t - r^*_t = E_t\{\tau_{t+1}\} + E_t\{e_{t+1}\} - e_t, \tag{12}$$

The effective terms of trade are $S_t \equiv \frac{P_{F,t}}{P_{H,t}} = \left(\int_0^1 S^{1-\gamma}_{i,t}\,di\right)^{\frac{1}{1-\gamma}}$.

Following Gali and Monacelli (2005), under the purchasing power parity condition, $P_{H,t} = P_{F,t}$.

The bilateral nominal exchange rate is defined by the law of one price, $P_{i,t}(j) = \mathcal{E}_{i,t}P^i_{i,t}(j)$, where $P^i_{i,t}(j)$ is the price of country i's good j, expressed in country

i's currency. It follows that $P_{i,t} = \mathcal{E}_{i,t} P^i_{i,t}$. The nominal effective exchange rate is defined as $\mathcal{E}_t \equiv \left(\int_0^1 \mathcal{E}_{i,t}^{1-\gamma} di\right)^{\frac{1}{1-\gamma}}$.

The real exchange rate is defined as $\mathcal{Q}_{i,t} \equiv \frac{\mathcal{E}_{i,t} P^i_t}{P_t}$.

We can rewrite the uncovered interest parity condition as

$$r_t - r_t^* = \sigma\left[E_t\{\theta_{t+1}\} - \theta_t\right] + \left[E_t\{s_{t+1}\} - s_t\right] + E_t\left\{\pi_{H,t+1}\right\} - E_t\left\{\pi^*_{t+1}\right\}. \quad (13)$$

2.3 Firms

The supply side in this paper is the same as in Gali and Monacelli (2005). Details of the derivation can be found in their paper.

A representative firm in the home country has a linear technology,

$$Y_t(j) = A_t N_t(j), \quad (14)$$

$$Y_t \equiv \left[\int_0^1 Y_t(j)^{1-\frac{1}{\varepsilon}} dj\right]^{\frac{\varepsilon}{\varepsilon-1}},$$

$$Z_t \equiv \int_0^1 \frac{Y_t(j)}{Y_t} dj,$$

$$N_t \equiv \int_0^1 N_t(j) dj = \frac{Y_t Z_t}{A_t}.$$

The firm follows staggered price setting, as in Calvo's (1983) model. Each period, $1 - \omega$ of firms set new prices. The pricing decision is forward-looking. Firms set the price as a mark-up over a weighted average of expected future marginal costs. As $\omega \to 0$, the price approaches flexibility.

The dynamics of domestic inflation are given by

$$\pi_{H,t} = \beta E_t\left\{\pi_{H,t+1}\right\} + \lambda \widehat{mc}_t, \quad (15)$$

where

$$\lambda \equiv \frac{(1 - \beta\omega)(1 - \omega)}{\omega}.$$

3 Equilibrium

In this section, we assume that $\sigma = \eta = \gamma = 1$ (Cole-Obstfeld case).

3.1 Demand Side

The market clearing condition in the representative small open economy is

$$\begin{aligned} Y_t(j) &= C_{H,t}(j) + \int_0^1 C^i_{H,t}(j)di \\ &= \left(\frac{P_{H,t}(j)}{P_{H,t}}\right)^{-\varepsilon}\left[(1-\alpha)\left(\frac{P_{H,t}}{P_t}\right)^{-\eta} C_t + \alpha\int_0^1 \left(\frac{P_{H,t}}{\mathcal{E}_{i,t}P^i_{F,t}}\right)^{-\gamma}\left(\frac{P^i_{F,t}}{P^i_t}\right)^{-\eta} C^i_t di\right]. \end{aligned} \quad (16)$$

After the derivation in Appendix, we get

$$y_t = E_t\{y_{t+1}\} - (r_t - E_t\{\pi_{t+1}\} - \rho) - \alpha\left[E_t\{s_{t+1}\} - s_t\right] + \left[E_t\{\theta_{t+1}\} - \theta_t\right]. \quad (17)$$

3.2 Supply Side

At the steady state of the economy, we have

$$y_t = a_t + n_t. \quad (18)$$

The deviation of real marginal cost from its steady state is

$$\widehat{mc_t} \equiv mc_t - mc = \mu - \nu + c_t + \varphi n_t + \alpha s_t - a_t = \mu - \nu + (\varphi + 1)(y_t - a_t) + \theta_t.$$

Thus at equilibrium, the dynamic equation for inflation is

$$\begin{aligned} \pi_{H,t} &= \beta E_t\left\{\pi_{H,t+1}\right\} + \lambda\widehat{mc_t} \\ &= \beta E_t\left\{\pi_{H,t+1}\right\} + \lambda(\mu - \nu) + \lambda(\varphi + 1)y_t - \lambda(\varphi + 1)a_t + \lambda\theta_t. \end{aligned} \quad (19)$$

3.3 Equilibrium Dynamics in Output Gap

The output gap is defined to be the following deviation of output from its natural level:

$$x_t \equiv y_t - \bar{y}_t.$$

The dynamics of the economy with capital controls and flexible exchange rates, but without monetary policy, can be written as

$$x_t = E_t\{x_{t+1}\} - [r_t - E_t\{\pi_{H,t+1}\} - \rho] + [E_t\{a_{t+1}\} - a_t] + \frac{\varphi}{\varphi+1}[E_t\{\theta_{t+1}\} - \theta_t], \quad (20)$$

$$\pi_{H,t} = \beta E_t\{\pi_{H,t+1}\} + \lambda(\varphi+1)x_t, \quad (21)$$

$$r_t - r_t^* = [E_t\{\theta_{t+1}\} - \theta_t] + [E_t\{s_{t+1}\} - s_t] + E_t\{\pi_{H,t+1}\} - E_t\{\pi_{t+1}^*\}.$$

If the exchange rate is fixed, then $e_{t+1} = e_t$,

$$r_t - r_t^* = [E_t\{\theta_{t+1}\} - \theta_t].$$

In the following sections of this paper, we assume that purchasing power parity holds, so that $S_t = 1$ and $[E_t\{s_{t+1}\} - s_t] = 0$.

4 Capital Control, Exchange Rate Regime, and Monetary Policy: Four Cases

In this section, we summarize four cases of the dynamical system, such that the exchange rate regime can be flexible or fixed and monetary policy can be current-looking or forward-looking.

4.1 Capital Control, Flexible Exchange Rate, Current-Looking Monetary Policy

This case is characterized by the following equations:

$$x_t = E_t(x_{t+1}) - [r_t - E_t(\pi_{H,t+1}) - \rho] + [E_t(a_{t+1}) - a_t] + \frac{\varphi}{\varphi+1}[E_t(\theta_{t+1}) - \theta_t],$$

$$
\begin{aligned}
\pi_{H,t} &= \beta E_t(\pi_{H,t+1}) + \lambda(\varphi + 1)x_t, \\
r_t - r_t^* &= [E_t(\theta_{t+1}) - \theta_t] + E_t(\pi_{H,t+1}) - E_t(\pi_{t+1}^*), \\
r_t &= a_\pi \pi_{H,t} + a_x x_t.
\end{aligned} \tag{22}
$$

4.2 *Capital Control, Fixed Exchange Rate, Current-Looking Monetary Policy*

This case is characterized by the following equations:

$$
\begin{aligned}
x_t &= E_t(x_{t+1}) - [r_t - E_t(\pi_{H,t+1}) - \rho] + [E_t(a_{t+1}) - a_t] \\
&\quad + \frac{\varphi}{\varphi + 1}[E_t(\theta_{t+1}) - \theta_t], \\
\pi_{H,t} &= \beta E_t(\pi_{H,t+1}) + \lambda(\varphi + 1)x_t, \\
r_t - r_t^* &= [E_t(\theta_{t+1}) - \theta_t], \\
r_t &= a_\pi \pi_{H,t} + a_x x_t.
\end{aligned} \tag{23}
$$

4.3 *Capital Control, Flexible Exchange Rate, Forward-Looking Monetary Policy*

This case is characterized by the following equations:

$$
\begin{aligned}
x_t &= E_t(x_{t+1}) - [r_t - E_t(\pi_{H,t+1}) - \rho] + [E_t(a_{t+1}) - a_t] \\
&\quad + \frac{\varphi}{\varphi + 1}[E_t(\theta_{t+1}) - \theta_t], \\
\pi_{H,t} &= \beta E_t(\pi_{H,t+1}) + \lambda(\varphi + 1)x_t, \\
r_t - r_t^* &= [E_t(\theta_{t+1}) - \theta_t] + E_t(\pi_{H,t+1}) - E_t(\pi_{t+1}^*), \\
r_t &= a_\pi E_t(\pi_{H,t+1}) + a_x E_t(x_{t+1}).
\end{aligned} \tag{24}
$$

4.4 *Capital Control, Fixed Exchange Rate, Forward-Looking Monetary Policy*

This case is characterized by the following equations:

$$\begin{aligned}
x_t &= E_t(x_{t+1}) - [r_t - E_t(\pi_{H,t+1}) - \rho] + [E_t(a_{t+1}) - a_t] \\
&\quad + \frac{\varphi}{\varphi+1}[E_t(\theta_{t+1}) - \theta_t], \\
\pi_{H,t} &= \beta E_t(\pi_{H,t+1}) + \lambda(\varphi+1)x_t, \\
r_t - r_t^* &= [E_t(\theta_{t+1}) - \theta_t], \\
r_t &= a_\pi E_t(\pi_{H,t+1}) + a_x E_t(x_{t+1}).
\end{aligned} \tag{25}$$

The four cases have the same IS curve and Phillips curve. The differences lie in the uncovered interest parity conditions between flexible exchange rates and fixed exchange rates, and in the interest rate feedback rule between current-looking monetary policy and forward-looking monetary policy.

It should be observed that our uncovered interest parity (UIP) condition is somewhat unusual. The usual UIP condition mainly describes the relationship between exchange rates and nominal interest rates. In our UIP condition, the nominal interest rate depends upon capital controls and upon how large the expectation of future domestic inflation will deviate from world inflation.

If the capital flow is free, so that $\tau_{t+1} = \sigma(\theta_{t+1} - \theta_t) = 0$, then under fixed exchange rates, the domestic nominal interest rate should equal the world nominal interest rate. As a result, the monetary authority loses its autonomy, in accordance with Mundell's trilemma. Second, under flexible exchange rates, the expectation of future world inflation plays a role in the dynamical system. Even though the domestic government stops targeting exchange rates and allows the exchange rate to float freely, the system is still influenced by the expectations of the world inflation.

We also investigate how expectations about future domestic inflation and output gap change the results of our analysis, compared with the current-looking monetary policy with the central bank setting the nominal interest rate.

5 Indeterminacy Conditions

In this section, we investigate the indeterminacy conditions for the four cases of policy combinations. We follow the method for linear rational expectations models by Lubik and Schorfheide (2003, 2004), Lubik and Marzo (2007), Sims (2002), Farmer et al. (2015), Beyer and Farmer (2004, 2006). The resulting conditions are summarized in Table 1.

In Lubik and Schorfheide (2003), the indeterminacy condition is provided as follows. First, the system can be written as

$$\boldsymbol{\Gamma}_0 \mathbf{X}_t = \boldsymbol{\Gamma}_1 \mathbf{X}_{t-1} + \boldsymbol{\Psi} \boldsymbol{\varepsilon}_t + \boldsymbol{\Pi} \boldsymbol{\eta}_t, \tag{26}$$

Table 1 Indeterminacy conditions

Policies	Indeterminacy conditions
Capital control Flexible exchange rates Current-looking monetary policy	$\lambda(\varphi+1)(1-a_\pi)+a_x(\beta-1)>0$
Capital control Fixed exchange rates Current-looking monetary policy	$(\varphi+1)^2(\beta+\lambda-1)+\beta[a_x(\beta-1)-\lambda a_\pi]>0$
Capital control Flexible exchange rates Forward-looking monetary policy	$\begin{cases} a_x<\varphi+1 \\ \lambda(\varphi+1)(1-a_\pi)+a_x(\beta-1)>0 \end{cases}$ or $\begin{cases} a_x>\varphi+1 \\ \lambda(\varphi+1)(1-a_\pi)+a_x(\beta-1)<0 \end{cases}$
Capital control Fixed exchange rates Forward-looking monetary policy	$\begin{cases} a_x<\varphi+1 \\ \lambda(\varphi+1)(\varphi+1-a_\pi)+a_x(\beta-1)>0 \end{cases}$ or $\begin{cases} a_x>\varphi+1 \\ \lambda(\varphi+1)(\varphi+1-a_\pi)+a_x(\beta-1)<0 \end{cases}$

where $\mathbf{X}_t$ is the $n \times 1$ vector of endogenous variables and their expectations, while $\boldsymbol{\varepsilon}_t$ is the $l \times 1$ vector of exogenous variables, and $\boldsymbol{\eta}_t$ is the $k \times 1$ vector of non-fundamental forecasting errors. Those forecast errors represent beliefs and permit self-fulfilling equilibria.

The reduced form of the above system is

$$\mathbf{X}_t = \boldsymbol{\Gamma}_0^{-1}\boldsymbol{\Gamma}_1\mathbf{X}_{t-1} + \boldsymbol{\Gamma}_0^{-1}\boldsymbol{\Psi}\boldsymbol{\varepsilon}_t + \boldsymbol{\Gamma}_0^{-1}\boldsymbol{\Pi}\boldsymbol{\eta}_t. \tag{27}$$

Applying generalized Schur decomposition (also called QZ decomposition) and letting $\mathbf{w}_t = \mathbf{Z}'\mathbf{X}_t$, the equation above can be written as

$$\begin{bmatrix} \boldsymbol{\Lambda}_{11} & \boldsymbol{\Lambda}_{12} \\ 0 & \boldsymbol{\Lambda}_{22} \end{bmatrix}\begin{bmatrix} \mathbf{w}_{1,t} \\ \mathbf{w}_{2,t} \end{bmatrix} = \begin{bmatrix} \boldsymbol{\Omega}_{11} & \boldsymbol{\Omega}_{12} \\ 0 & \boldsymbol{\Omega}_{22} \end{bmatrix}\begin{bmatrix} \mathbf{w}_{1,t-1} \\ \mathbf{w}_{2,t-1} \end{bmatrix} + \begin{bmatrix} \mathbf{Q}_{1.} \\ \mathbf{Q}_{2.} \end{bmatrix}(\boldsymbol{\Psi}\boldsymbol{\varepsilon}_t + \boldsymbol{\Pi}\boldsymbol{\eta}_t). \tag{28}$$

It is assumed that the following $m \times 1$ vector, $\mathbf{w}_{2,t}$, is purely explosive, where $0 \leq m \leq n$:

$$\mathbf{w}_{2,t} = \boldsymbol{\Lambda}_{22}^{-1}\boldsymbol{\Omega}_{22}\mathbf{w}_{2,t-1} + \boldsymbol{\Lambda}_{22}^{-1}\mathbf{Q}_{2.}(\boldsymbol{\Psi}\boldsymbol{\varepsilon}_t + \boldsymbol{\Pi}\boldsymbol{\eta}_t).$$

A nonexplosive solution of the linear rational expectation model for $\mathbf{X}_t$ exists, if $\mathbf{w}_{2,0} = \mathbf{0}$ and $\mathbf{Q}_{2.}\boldsymbol{\Psi}\boldsymbol{\varepsilon}_t + \mathbf{Q}_{2.}\boldsymbol{\Pi}\boldsymbol{\eta}_t = 0$.

By singular value decomposition of $\mathbf{Q}_{2.}\boldsymbol{\Pi}$, we find

$$\mathbf{Q}_{2.}\mathbf{\Pi} = \mathbf{UDV}' = \begin{bmatrix} \mathbf{U}_{.1} & \mathbf{U}_{.2} \end{bmatrix} \begin{bmatrix} \mathbf{D}_{11} & \mathbf{0} \\ \mathbf{0} & \mathbf{0} \end{bmatrix} \begin{bmatrix} \mathbf{V}'_{.1} \\ \mathbf{V}'_{.2} \end{bmatrix} = \mathbf{U}_{.1}\mathbf{D}_{11}\mathbf{V}'_{.1}. \tag{29}$$

The m explosive components of $\mathbf{X}_t$ generate $r \leq m$ restrictions for the expectation errors. The stability condition can be rewritten as

$$\mathbf{U}_{.1}\mathbf{D}_{11}(\mathbf{V}'_{.1}\boldsymbol{\lambda}\boldsymbol{\varepsilon}_t + \mathbf{V}'_{.1}\boldsymbol{\eta}_t) = 0. \tag{30}$$

Let $\boldsymbol{\eta}_t = \mathbf{A}_1\boldsymbol{\varepsilon}_t + \mathbf{A}_2\boldsymbol{\zeta}_t$, where $\boldsymbol{\zeta}_t$ is a $p \times 1$ vector of sunspot shocks. The solution for the forecast errors is

$$\boldsymbol{\eta}_t = (-\mathbf{V}_{.1}\mathbf{D}_{11}^{-1}\mathbf{U}'_{.1}\mathbf{Q}_{2.}\boldsymbol{\Psi} + \mathbf{V}_{.2}\mathbf{M}_1)\boldsymbol{\varepsilon}_t + \mathbf{V}_{.2}\mathbf{M}_2\boldsymbol{\zeta}_t. \tag{31}$$

When the dimension of the vector of forecast errors, k, equals the number of stability restrictions, r, the linear rational expectations model has a unique solution. When $k > r$, there is indeterminacy (multiple stable solutions), and $k - r$ is the degree of indeterminacy.

5.1 Capital Control, Flexible Exchange Rate, Current-Looking Monetary Policy

Proposition 1 *Under capital control, flexible exchange rate and current-looking monetary policy, there exists one degree of indeterminacy, when* $\lambda(\varphi + 1)(1 - a_\pi) + a_x(\beta - 1) > 0$.

Proof See Appendix 7.

This condition can be rewritten as

$$a_\pi + \frac{(1-\beta)}{\lambda(\varphi + 1)} a_x < 1. \tag{32}$$

Indeterminacy is mainly determined by the values of a_π, a_x and λ. To satisfy this inequality, a_π must be between zero and one. If λ is large, then a_x can be large or small, so long as λ is sufficiently larger than a_x. If λ is small, a_x has to be small to generate indeterminacy.

Thus, indeterminacy is most likely to happen under passive interest rate feedback on inflation and flexible price. If the price is sticky, the passive interest rate feedback on the output gap in addition to inflation will also produce multiple equilibria.

As has been analyzed by Bullard and Schaling (2006), when a_π is between zero and one, the Taylor principle is violated. In this situation, nominal interest rates rise by less than the increase in the inflation, leading a decrease in the real interest rate. This drop in real interest rate makes the output gap larger through the IS curve equation. A rise in the output gap will increase the inflation through the Phillips curve equation.

Thus, a passive monetary policy response on inflation will enlarge the inflation level, making the economy move further away from the unique equilibrium.

5.2 Capital Control, Fixed Exchange Rate, Current-Looking Monetary Policy

Proposition 2 *Under capital control, fixed exchange rates, and current-looking monetary policy, there exists one degree of indeterminacy, when*

$$(\varphi + 1)^2(\beta + \lambda - 1) + \beta[a_x(\beta - 1) - \lambda a_\pi] > 0.$$

Proof See Appendix 8.

This condition can be rewritten as

$$a_x(1 - \beta) + \lambda a_\pi < \frac{(\varphi + 1)^2(\beta + \lambda - 1)}{\beta}. \tag{33}$$

Since $1-\beta > 0$, to satisfy this inequality, we must have $\beta+\lambda-1 > 0$. In addition, a_π and a_x cannot be too large. The economic intuition behind these conditions is that the price has to be flexible and central banks' response to inflation and output gap has to be passive to generate indeterminacy.

5.3 Capital Control, Flexible Exchange Rate, Forward-Looking Monetary Policy

Proposition 3 *Under capital control, flexible exchange rates, and forward-looking monetary policy, there exists one degree of indeterminacy, when*

$$\begin{cases} a_x < \varphi + 1 \\ \lambda(\varphi + 1)(1 - a_\pi) + a_x(\beta - 1) > 0 \end{cases} \text{or} \begin{cases} a_x > \varphi + 1 \\ \lambda(\varphi + 1)(1 - a_\pi) + a_x(\beta - 1) < 0 \end{cases}.$$

Proof See Appendix 9.

This condition can be rewritten as

$$\begin{cases} a_x < \varphi + 1 \\ a_\pi + \frac{(1-\beta)}{\lambda(\varphi+1)} a_x < 1 \end{cases} \text{or} \begin{cases} a_x > \varphi + 1 \\ a_\pi + \frac{(1-\beta)}{\lambda(\varphi+1)} a_x > 1 \end{cases}. \tag{34}$$

Compared with Case 1, Case 3 must consider a_x first. When a_x is small, only if a_π is between zero and one, there may exist indeterminacy. When a_x is large, there are two possibilities for indeterminacy to appear. One is that a_π is also large. The other is when λ is small.

Thus, under the forward-looking monetary policy, the central bank's response to the output gap matters more than its response to the inflation. Both passive and active monetary policy is possible to generate indeterminacy, depending on the cooperation of these two feedback.

5.4 Capital Control, Fixed Exchange Rate, Forward-Looking Monetary Policy

Proposition 4 *Under capital control, fixed exchange rates, and forward-looking monetary policy, there exists one degree of indeterminacy, when*

$$\begin{cases} a_x < \varphi + 1 \\ \lambda(\varphi+1)(\varphi+1-a_\pi) + a_x(\beta-1) > 0 \end{cases} \text{or} \begin{cases} a_x > \varphi + 1 \\ \lambda(\varphi+1)(\varphi+1-a_\pi) + a_x(\beta-1) < 0 \end{cases}.$$

Proof See Appendix 10.

This condition can be rewritten as

$$\begin{cases} a_x < \varphi + 1 \\ a_\pi + \frac{(1-\beta)}{\lambda(\varphi+1)} a_x < \varphi + 1 \end{cases} \text{or} \begin{cases} a_x > \varphi + 1 \\ a_\pi + \frac{(1-\beta)}{\lambda(\varphi+1)} a_x > \varphi + 1 \end{cases}. \tag{35}$$

This case is similar to Case 3. When a_x is small, only if a_π is between zero and one, indeterminacy is possible to exist. When a_x is large, either a large a_π or a small λ will produce multiple equilibria.

Different from Case 3, the restrictions that are put on the central bank's response to inflation and output gap are looser. This indicates that in the monetary policy parameter space, the chance to generate indeterminacy is higher under the fixed exchange rate regime.

6 Bifurcation Conditions

In this section, we investigate the existence of bifurcation in the system under the four policy cases. The results are summarized in Table 2. With Hopf bifurcation, the economy can converge to a stable limit cycle or diverge from an unstable limit cycle. We use the following theorem from Gandolfo (2010), to determine conditions for the existence of Hopf bifurcation.

Theorem *Consider the system,* $y_{t+1} = \varphi(y_t, \alpha)$. *Suppose that for each* α *in the relevant interval, the system has a smooth family of equilibrium points,* $y_e = y_e(\alpha)$,

Table 2 Bifurcation conditions

Policies	Bifurcation conditions	Possible
Case 1	$[(\varphi+1)(\beta+\lambda-1)+a_x\beta]^2+4\lambda(\varphi+1)^2(1-a_\pi\beta)<0$ $(\varphi+1)(1-\beta+\lambda a_\pi)+a_x=0$	No
Case 2	$[(\varphi+1)(\beta+\varphi)+a_x\beta]^2+4\lambda(\varphi+1)^2(\varphi+1-a_\pi\beta)<0$ $(1-\lambda)(\varphi+1)^2+\beta(1-\beta)(\varphi+1)+\lambda a_\pi\beta(\varphi+1)+a_x\beta=0$	Yes
Case 3	$[(\beta-1)(\varphi+1)-\lambda(a_\pi-1)(\varphi+1)+a_x]^2+4\lambda(\varphi+1)(1-a_\pi)(\varphi+1-a_x)<0$ $(1-\beta)(\varphi+1)+a_x\beta=0$	No
Case 4	$[(\beta+\lambda(\varphi+1-a_\pi)-1)(\varphi+1)+a_x]^2+4\lambda(\varphi+1)(\varphi+1-a_\pi)(\varphi+1-a_x)<0$ $(1-\beta)(\varphi+1)+a_x\beta=0$	No

at which the eigenvalues are complex conjugates, $\lambda_{1,2} = \theta(\alpha) \pm i\omega(\alpha)$*. If there is a critical value,* α_0*, of the parameter* α *such that*

(1) *the eigenvalues' modulus becomes unity at* α_0*, but the eigenvalues are not roots of unity (from the first up to the fourth), namely*

$$\left|\lambda_{1,2}(\alpha_0)\right| = +\sqrt{\theta^2 + \omega^2} = 1,\ \lambda_{1,2}^{j}(\alpha_0) \neq 1 \text{ for j} = 1, 2, 3, 4,$$

(2) $$\left.\frac{d\left|\lambda_{1,2}(\alpha)\right|}{d\alpha}\right|_{\alpha=\alpha_0} \neq 0,$$

then there is an invariant closed curve bifurcating from α_0.

6.1 Capital Control, Flexible Exchange Rate, Current-Looking Monetary Policy

Proposition 5 *Under capital control, flexible exchange rates, and current-looking monetary policy, there would exist Hopf bifurcation, if* $[(\varphi+1)(\beta+\lambda-1)+a_x\beta]^2 + 4\lambda(\varphi+1)^2(1-a_\pi\beta) < 0$ and $(\varphi+1)(1-\beta+\lambda a_\pi) + a_x = 0$.

However, according to the meaning of the parameters, the second equation cannot be satisfied.

Proof See Appendix 11.

6.2 Capital Control, Fixed Exchange Rate, Current-Looking Monetary Policy

Proposition 6 *Under capital control, fixed exchange rates, and current-looking monetary policy, there exists Hopf bifurcation, when* $[(\varphi+1)(\beta+\varphi)+a_x\beta]^2+4\lambda(\varphi+1)^2(\varphi+1-a_\pi\beta) < 0$ and $(1-\lambda)(\varphi+1)^2+\beta(1-\beta)(\varphi+1)+\lambda a_\pi\beta(\varphi+1)+a_x\beta = 0$.

Since $\lambda = \frac{(1-\beta\omega)(1-\omega)}{\omega}$ *with* $0<\beta<1$*, and* $0<\omega<1$*, it follows that* λ *goes to* $+\infty$*, when* ω *approaches* 0. *In this case, it is possible for the second equality to hold.*

Proof See Appendix 11.

The condition will be satisfied when λ is larger than one, which happens when the price is flexible.

6.3 Capital Control, Flexible Exchange Rate, Forward-Looking Monetary Policy

Proposition 7 *Under capital control, flexible exchange rates, and forward-looking monetary policy, there could exist Hopf bifurcation, if* $[(\beta - 1)(\varphi + 1) - \lambda(a_\pi - 1)(\varphi+1)+a_x]^2+4\lambda(\varphi+1)(1-a_\pi)(\varphi+1-a_x) < 0$ *and* $(1-\beta)(\varphi+1)+a_x\beta = 0$. *However, according to the economic meaning of the parameters, the second equation cannot be satisfied with parameter values within their feasible range.*

Proof See Appendix 11.

6.4 Capital Control, Fixed Exchange Rate, Forward-Looking Monetary Policy

Proposition 8 *Under capital control, fixed exchange rates, and forward-looking monetary policy, there could exist Hopf bifurcation, if* $[(\beta + \lambda(\varphi+1-a_\pi) - 1)(\varphi+1) + a_x]^2 + 4\lambda(\varphi+1)(\varphi+1-a_\pi)(\varphi+1-a_x) < 0$ *and* $(1-\beta)(\varphi+1)+a_x\beta = 0$. *However, according to the meaning of the parameters, the second equation cannot be satisfied.*

Proof See Appendix 11.

7 Empirical Test for Indeterminacy

In this section, we test indeterminacy using Bayesian likelihood estimation, following Lubik and Schorfheide (2004, 2005). We compute the posterior probability of the determinate and the indeterminate regions of the parameter space. Then we estimate the parameters' posterior means and 90% probability intervals. We also study impulse responses of the fundamental and sunspot shocks. Last, we compute variance decompositions to study the importance of individual shocks. We use GAUSS for computations.

7.1 Model for Testing Indeterminacy: Four Cases

Case 1: Capital Control, Flexible Exchange Rate, Current-looking Monetary Policy

In this case, the model is

$$\begin{aligned}
x_t &= E_{t-1}[x_t] + \eta_{1,t}, \\
\pi_{H,t} &= E_{t-1}\left[\pi_{H,t}\right] + \eta_{2,t}, \\
x_t &= E_t[x_{t+1}] - \frac{1}{\varphi+1} r_t + \frac{1}{\varphi+1} E_t[\pi_{H,t+1}] + z_t - \frac{\varphi}{\varphi+1} r_t^* + \frac{\varphi}{\varphi+1} \pi_{t+1}^* + \rho, \\
\pi_{H,t} &= \beta E_t[\pi_{H,t+1}] + \lambda(\varphi+1)x_t, \\
r_t &= a_\pi \pi_{H,t} + a_x x_t + \varepsilon_{r,t}, \\
z_t &= \rho_z z_{t-1} + \varepsilon_{z,t}, \\
r_t^* &= \rho_R r_{t-1}^* + \varepsilon_{R,t}, \\
\pi_t^* &= \rho_\pi \pi_{t-1}^* + \varepsilon_{\pi,t},
\end{aligned} \tag{36}$$

which can be written as

$$\begin{aligned}
\boldsymbol{\Gamma}_0(\boldsymbol{\theta})\mathbf{s}_t &= \boldsymbol{\Gamma}_1(\boldsymbol{\theta})\mathbf{s}_{t-1} + \boldsymbol{\Psi}(\boldsymbol{\theta})\boldsymbol{\varepsilon}_t + \boldsymbol{\Pi}(\boldsymbol{\theta})\boldsymbol{\eta}_t, \\
\boldsymbol{\eta}_t &= \mathbf{A}_1\boldsymbol{\varepsilon}_t + \mathbf{A}_2\boldsymbol{\zeta}_t,
\end{aligned} \tag{37}$$

with

$$\begin{aligned}
\mathbf{s}_t &= \left[x_t, \pi_{H,t}, r_t, E_t\left[x_{t+1}\right], E_t\left[\pi_{H,t+1}\right], z_t, r_t^*, \pi_t^*\right]', \\
\boldsymbol{\varepsilon}_t &= \left[\varepsilon_{r,t}, \varepsilon_{z,t}, \varepsilon_{R,t}, \varepsilon_{\pi,t}\right]', \\
\boldsymbol{\eta}_t &= \left[(x_t - E_{t-1}[x_t]), \left(\pi_{H,t} - E_{t-1}\left[\pi_{H,t}\right]\right)\right]'.
\end{aligned}$$

The law of motion for $\mathbf{s}_t$ can be written as:

$$\mathbf{s}_t = \boldsymbol{\Gamma}_1^*(\boldsymbol{\theta})\mathbf{s}_{t-1} + \mathrm{B}_1(\boldsymbol{\theta})\boldsymbol{\varepsilon}_t + \mathrm{B}_2(\boldsymbol{\theta})\boldsymbol{\varepsilon}_t + \boldsymbol{\Pi}^*(\boldsymbol{\theta})\mathbf{V}_{.2}(\boldsymbol{\theta})\mathrm{M}_\zeta\boldsymbol{\zeta}_t. \tag{38}$$

Details about the above matrices can be found in Lubik and Schorfheide (2004).

Case 2: Capital Control, Fixed Exchange Rate, Current-looking Monetary Policy

In this case, the model is

$$\begin{aligned}
x_t &= E_{t-1}[x_t] + \eta_{1,t}, \\
\pi_{H,t} &= E_{t-1}\left[\pi_{H,t}\right] + \eta_{2,t}, \\
x_t &= E_t[x_{t+1}] - \frac{1}{\varphi+1} r_t + E_t[\pi_{H,t+1}] + z_t - \frac{\varphi}{\varphi+1} r_t^* + \rho, \\
\pi_{H,t} &= \beta E_t[\pi_{H,t+1}] + \lambda(\varphi+1)x_t, \\
r_t &= a_\pi \pi_{H,t} + a_x x_t + \varepsilon_{r,t}, \\
z_t &= \rho_z z_{t-1} + \varepsilon_{z,t}, \\
r_t^* &= \rho_R r_{t-1}^* + \varepsilon_{R,t},
\end{aligned} \tag{39}$$

which can be written as (37) with

$$\mathbf{s}_t = \left[x_t, \pi_{H,t}, r_t, E_t\left[x_{t+1}\right], E_t\left[\pi_{H,t+1}\right], z_t, r_t^*\right]',$$
$$\boldsymbol{\varepsilon}_t = \left[\varepsilon_{r,t}, \varepsilon_{z,t}, \varepsilon_{R,t}\right]',$$
$$\boldsymbol{\eta}_t = \left[(x_t - E_{t-1}[x_t]), \left(\pi_{H,t} - E_{t-1}\left[\pi_{H,t}\right]\right)\right]'.$$

Case 3: Capital Control, Flexible Exchange Rate, Forward-looking Monetary Policy

In this case, the model is:

$$\begin{aligned}
x_t &= E_{t-1}[x_t] + \eta_{1,t},\\
\pi_{H,t} &= E_{t-1}\left[\pi_{H,t}\right] + \eta_{2,t},\\
x_t &= E_t[x_{t+1}] - \frac{1}{\varphi+1} r_t + \frac{1}{\varphi+1} E_t[\pi_{H,t+1}] + z_t - \frac{\varphi}{\varphi+1} r_t^* + \frac{\varphi}{\varphi+1} \pi_{t+1}^* + \rho,\\
\pi_{H,t} &= \beta E_t[\pi_{H,t+1}] + \lambda(\varphi+1)x_t,\\
r_t &= a_\pi E_t[\pi_{H,t+1}] + a_x E_t[x_{t+1}] + \varepsilon_{r,t},\\
z_t &= \rho_z z_{t-1} + \varepsilon_{z,t},\\
r_t^* &= \rho_R r_{t-1}^* + \varepsilon_{R,t},\\
\pi_t^* &= \rho_\pi \pi_{t-1}^* + \varepsilon_{\pi,t},
\end{aligned} \tag{40}$$

which can be written as (37) with

$$\mathbf{s}_t = \left[x_t, \pi_{H,t}, r_t, E_t\left[x_{t+1}\right], E_t\left[\pi_{H,t+1}\right], z_t, r_t^*, \pi_t^*\right]',$$
$$\boldsymbol{\varepsilon}_t = \left[\varepsilon_{r,t}, \varepsilon_{z,t}, \varepsilon_{R,t}, \varepsilon_{\pi,t}\right]',$$
$$\boldsymbol{\eta}_t = \left[(x_t - E_{t-1}[x_t]), \left(\pi_{H,t} - E_{t-1}\left[\pi_{H,t}\right]\right)\right]'.$$

Case 4: Capital Control, Fixed Exchange Rate, Forward-looking Monetary Policy

In this case, the model is

$$\begin{aligned}
x_t &= E_{t-1}[x_t] + \eta_{1,t},\\
\pi_{H,t} &= E_{t-1}\left[\pi_{H,t}\right] + \eta_{2,t},\\
x_t &= E_t[x_{t+1}] - \frac{1}{\varphi+1} r_t + E_t[\pi_{H,t+1}] + z_t - \frac{\varphi}{\varphi+1} r_t^* + \rho,\\
\pi_{H,t} &= \beta E_t[\pi_{H,t+1}] + \lambda(\varphi+1)x_t,\\
r_t &= a_\pi E_t[\pi_{H,t+1}] + a_x E_t[x_{t+1}] + \varepsilon_{r,t},\\
z_t &= \rho_z z_{t-1} + \varepsilon_{z,t},\\
r_t^* &= \rho_R r_{t-1}^* + \varepsilon_{R,t},
\end{aligned} \tag{41}$$

which can be written as (37) with

$$\mathbf{s}_t = \left[x_t, \pi_{H,t}, r_t, E_t\left[x_{t+1}\right], E_t\left[\pi_{H,t+1}\right], z_t, r_t^*\right]',$$
$$\boldsymbol{\varepsilon}_t = \left[\varepsilon_{r,t}, \varepsilon_{z,t}, \varepsilon_{R,t}\right]',$$
$$\boldsymbol{\eta}_t = \left[(x_t - E_{t-1}[x_t]), \left(\pi_{H,t} - E_{t-1}\left[\pi_{H,t}\right]\right)\right]'.$$

7.2 *Data Description: China 1999(1) to 2004(4) and 2011(4) to 2017(3)*

We choose China as the example of a small open economy which imposes capital control and has the time periods of two exchange rate regimes. There are several reasons for this choice. First, for the common examples of small open economies, such as Australia, Canada, New Zealand, and the UK, they have seldom imposed controls on capital flows in history. Second, among the major emerging market economies which impose capital control, not many of them have experienced both flexible exchange rate regimes and fixed exchange rate regimes during the periods of capital controls. From the data of China/U.S. Foreign Exchange Rate shown in Fig. 1, we take the period of 1999(1) to 2004(4), as the time of fixed exchange rate regime. Even though China is not a perfect example for the pure floating exchange rate regime during the current financial market transition, we select the time period from 2011(4) to 2017(3), as a proxy for the flexible exchange rate regime, considering the trend and the volitility of exchange rate (Chinese Yuan/U.S. Dollar) reflected in the data. See Fig. 1, for more details. From consideration of the sample size, we extend the sample before the year of 2015, when China switched from the crawling peg relative to the U.S. dollar to the peg relative to the basket of currencies. The models of Case 1 and Case 3 are fitted to the data of 2011(4) to 2017(3). Case 2 and Case 4 are fitted to the data of 1999(1) to 2004(4).

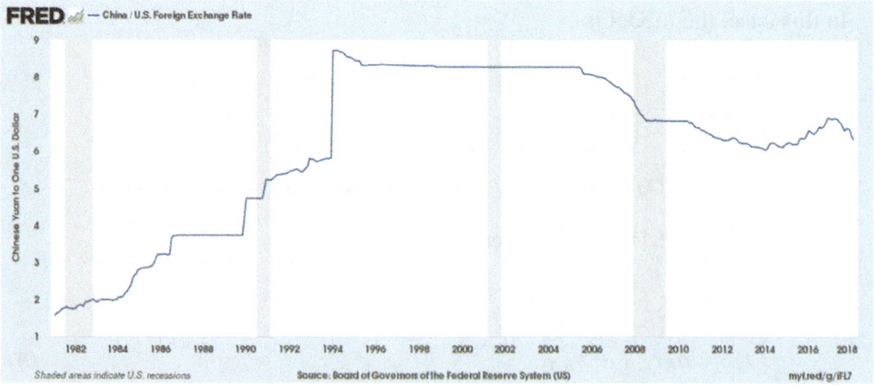

Fig. 1 China/U.S. foreign exchange rate

We use quarterly data from the database, FRED, of the Federal Reserve Bank of St. Louis. The output level is measured as the real Gross Domestic Product (GDP). We take the HP trend of real GDP as the potential output level of China. The output gap is calculated as the log of real GDP minus the log of HP trend. Inflation is measured as the log of Consumer Prive Index (CPI). The nominal interest rate is the central bank rates for China.

The prior means and densities are chosen based on previous research, such as Lubik and Schorfheide (2004, 2005), Lubik and Marzo (2007) and Zheng and Guo (2013). Notice that the period of 1999(1) to 2004(4), in China, is the time under passive monetary policy response to inflation, so we set the prior mean of a_π to be 0.8. While during 2011(4) to 2017(3), in China, the central bank's response to inflation is active. We set the prior mean of a_π to be 1.1.

Following previous literature, the monetary policy parameters follow Gamma distribution.[4] The parameter for price stickiness follows Beta distribution. The correlations between shocks follow Normal distribution. The exogenous shocks follow Inverse Gamma distribution. The prior distributions are reported in Tables 3, 4, 5 and 6.

7.3 Parameter Estimation

Under the flexible exchange rate regime and current-looking monetary policy in China (see Table 7), the posterior mean of the central bank's response to inflation a_π is 2.33. The policy response to output gap a_x is 0.46. If inflation increases by 1%, the nominal interest rate raises by 233 base points. If the real output is 1% higher than its potential level, the nominal interest rate responses by increasing 46 base points. There exist correlations between fundamental shocks. Indeterminacy can influence the transmission of structural shocks related to monetary policy, technology, foreign interest rate and foreign inflation. ω equals to 0.99, reflecting that the price is very sticky.

Under the fixed exchange rate regime and current-looking monetary policy in China (see Table 8), the posterior mean of policy response to inflation a_π is 0.22. The policy response to output gap a_x is 0.22. Unlike the standard calibration results of a New Keynesian model, the central bank's response to inflation and output gap has similar weight in the monetary policy function.

Under the flexible exchange rate regime and forward-looking monetary policy in China (see Table 9), the posterior mean of policy response to inflation a_π is 0.59. The policy response to output gap a_x is 0.42. These two feedbacks have similar weights in the monetary policy response function. The correlations between fundamental

---

[4] We would like to thank the referee for the suggestion of testing the robustness of the estimates with respect to the prior distribution. Considering the limited space, readers who have further interests could find more details of the robustness test in Hu (2018). We find that in a DSGE model with indeterminacy, the estimation is highly sensitive to the prior distribution and the data set.

Table 3 Prior distributions-flexible exchange rate, current-looking monetary policy, China

Parameter	Density	Prior mean	Prior standard deviation
a_π	Gamma	1.1000	0.5000
a_x	Gamma	0.2500	0.1500
ω	Beta	0.8000	0.1000
π^*	Gamma	4.0000	2.0000
r^*	Gamma	2.0000	1.0000
φ	Gamma	2.0000	0.7500
ρ_z	Beta	0.9000	0.1000
ρ_R	Beta	0.5000	0.2000
ρ_π	Beta	0.7000	0.1000
ρ_{zR}	Normal	0.0000	0.4000
$\rho_{z\pi}$	Normal	0.0000	0.4000
$\rho_{R\pi}$	Normal	0.0000	0.4000
$M_{r\zeta}$	Normal	0.0000	1.0000
$M_{z\zeta}$	Normal	0.0000	1.0000
$M_{R\zeta}$	Normal	0.0000	1.0000
$M_{\pi\zeta}$	Normal	0.0000	1.0000
σ_r	Inverse Gamma	0.2500	4.0000
σ_z	Inverse Gamma	0.8000	4.0000
σ_R	Inverse Gamma	0.3000	4.0000
σ_π	Inverse Gamma	0.3000	4.0000
σ_ζ	Inverse Gamma	0.2000	4.0000

Table 4 Prior distributions-fixed exchange rate, current-looking monetary policy, China

Parameter	Density	Prior mean	Prior standard deviation
a_π	Gamma	0.8000	0.5000
a_x	Gamma	0.2500	0.1500
ω	Beta	0.8000	0.1000
π^*	Gamma	4.0000	2.0000
r^*	Gamma	2.0000	1.0000
φ	Gamma	2.0000	0.7500
ρ_z	Beta	0.9000	0.1000
ρ_R	Beta	0.5000	0.2000

(continued)

Table 4 (continued)

Parameter	Density	Prior mean	Prior standard deviation
ρ_{zR}	Normal	0.0000	0.4000
$M_{r\zeta}$	Normal	0.0000	1.0000
$M_{z\zeta}$	Normal	0.0000	1.0000
$M_{R\zeta}$	Normal	0.0000	1.0000
σ_r	Inverse Gamma	0.2500	4.0000
σ_z	Inverse Gamma	0.8000	4.0000
σ_R	Inverse Gamma	0.3000	4.0000
σ_ζ	Inverse Gamma	0.2000	4.0000

Table 5 Prior distributions-flexible exchange rate, forward-looking monetary policy, China

Parameter	Density	Prior mean	Prior standard deviation
a_π	Gamma	1.1000	0.5000
a_x	Gamma	0.2500	0.1500
ω	Beta	0.8500	0.1000
π^*	Gamma	4.0000	2.0000
r^*	Gamma	2.0000	1.0000
φ	Gamma	2.0000	0.7500
ρ_z	Beta	0.9000	0.1000
ρ_R	Beta	0.5000	0.2000
ρ_π	Beta	0.7000	0.1000
ρ_{zR}	Normal	0.0000	0.4000
$\rho_{z\pi}$	Normal	0.0000	0.4000
$\rho_{R\pi}$	Normal	0.0000	0.4000
$M_{r\zeta}$	Normal	0.0000	1.0000
$M_{z\zeta}$	Normal	0.0000	1.0000
$M_{R\zeta}$	Normal	0.0000	1.0000
$M_{\pi\zeta}$	Normal	0.0000	1.0000
σ_r	Inverse Gamma	0.2500	4.0000
σ_z	Inverse Gamma	0.8000	4.0000
σ_R	Inverse Gamma	0.3000	4.0000
σ_π	Inverse Gamma	0.3000	4.0000
σ_ζ	Inverse Gamma	0.2000	4.0000

Table 6 Prior distributions-fixed exchange rate, forward-looking monetary policy, China

Parameter	Density	Prior mean	Prior standard deviation
a_π	Gamma	0.8000	0.5000
a_x	Gamma	0.2500	0.1500
ω	Beta	0.8000	0.1000
π^*	Gamma	4.0000	2.0000
r^*	Gamma	2.0000	1.0000
φ	Gamma	2.0000	0.7500
ρ_z	Beta	0.9000	0.1000
ρ_R	Beta	0.5000	0.2000
ρ_{zR}	Normal	0.0000	0.4000
$M_{r\zeta}$	Normal	0.0000	1.0000
$M_{z\zeta}$	Normal	0.0000	1.0000
$M_{R\zeta}$	Normal	0.0000	1.0000
σ_r	Inverse Gamma	0.2500	4.0000
σ_z	Inverse Gamma	0.8000	4.0000
σ_R	Inverse Gamma	0.3000	4.0000
σ_ζ	Inverse Gamma	0.2000	4.0000

shocks exist. The transmission of these fundamental shocks is also influenced by the indeterminacy. Price is very sticky.

Under the fixed exchange rate regime and forward-looking monetary policy in China (see Table 10), the posterior mean of policy response to inflation a_π is 0.31. The policy response to output gap a_x is 0.29. These two feedbacks have similar weights in the monetary policy response function.

7.4 *Posterior Probability of the Determinate and the Indeterminate Regions*

The posterior probabilities of the determinate and indeterminate regions indicate that indeterminacy is a greater risk under fixed exchange rate regimes than under flexible exchange rate regimes. The forward-looking monetary policy reduces the probability of indeterminate region under flexible exchange rate regimes. However, under fixed exchange rate regimes, a forward-looking monetary policy increases the probability of indeterminacy. Tables 11, 12, 13 and 14 show the estimation results of the posterior probabilities of the determinate and indeterminate regions.

Table 7 Parameter estimation results-flexible exchange rate, current-looking monetary policy, China

Parameter	Mean	Standard deviation	90% posterior interval lower bound	90% posterior interval upper bound
a_π	2.3296	0.0775	2.2824	2.4474
a_x	0.4600	0.0274	0.4109	0.4776
ω	0.9888	0.0002	0.9886	0.9891
π^*	4.7341	0.0011	4.7328	4.7348
r^*	0.2246	0.0573	0.1762	0.2697
φ	0.7383	0.1432	0.6542	0.9976
ρ_z	0.9778	0.0057	0.9653	0.9804
ρ_R	0.9707	0.0095	0.9683	0.9876
ρ_π	0.6387	0.0174	0.6317	0.6653
ρ_{zR}	0.9596	0.0181	0.9434	0.9740
$\rho_{z\pi}$	−0.6645	0.0419	−0.7095	−0.6481
$\rho_{R\pi}$	−0.4416	0.0556	−0.5323	−0.4128
$M_{r\zeta}$	−0.2613	0.1750	−0.6390	−0.1439
$M_{z\zeta}$	−0.6844	0.1165	−0.7770	−0.4905
$M_{R\zeta}$	−0.6962	0.1780	−0.8476	−0.3938
$M_{\pi\zeta}$	0.3297	0.1516	0.2239	0.5487
σ_r	0.6276	0.0171	0.5985	0.6384
σ_z	0.2537	0.0210	0.2359	0.2996
σ_R	0.5105	0.0256	0.4827	0.5256
σ_π	0.3867	0.0146	0.3853	0.3955
σ_ζ	0.2579	0.0232	0.2604	0.2687

Notes The posterior summary statistics are calculated by the Metropolis-Hastings algorithm

7.5 *Impulse Responses*

Under flexible exchange rate regime and current-looking monetary policy (see Fig. 2), an unanticipated tightening of monetary policy reduces output and inflation. Interest rate increases immediately. One unit positive technology shock increases output, inflation, and interest rate permanently. In response to foreign interest rate shock, output, inflation, and interest rate increase permanently. This increase of domestic interest rate in response to foreign interest shock shows the dependence of monetary policy, even under the controlled capital flows and flexible exchange rates. Foreign inflation shock only takes effect under flexible exchange rate regimes. Under foreign inflation shock, output, inflation, and interest rate decrease permanently. In response to sunspot driven inflationary expectation, output firstly decreases and then increases permanently. Interest rate also increases permanently. It firstly jumps up and then drops to a lower positive level.

Table 8 Parameter estimation results-fixed exchange rate, current-looking monetary policy, China

Parameter	Mean	Standard deviation	90% posterior interval lower bound	90% posterior interval upper bound
a_π	0.2233	0.1079	0.0490	0.3929
a_x	0.2228	0.1304	0.0307	0.4100
ω	0.5238	0.0403	0.4569	0.5904
π^*	1.6333	0.4921	0.8176	2.4383
r^*	0.8588	0.3797	0.2562	1.4656
φ	3.5772	0.8794	2.1815	4.9473
ρ_z	0.9271	0.0464	0.8631	0.9991
ρ_R	0.6162	0.1577	0.3973	0.9181
ρ_{zR}	0.7459	0.0000	0.7459	0.7459
$M_{r\zeta}$	−0.4526	0.0000	−0.4526	−0.4526
$M_{z\zeta}$	0.3725	0.0000	0.3725	0.3725
$M_{R\zeta}$	−0.2618	0.0000	−0.2618	−0.2618
σ_r	0.1456	0.0211	0.1123	0.1787
σ_z	0.3814	0.0463	0.3074	0.4582
σ_R	0.3775	0.0722	0.2559	0.4898
σ_ζ	0.0986	0.0145	0.0751	0.1210

Notes The posterior summary statistics are calculated by the Metropolis-Hastings algorithm

Under the same exchange rate regime, there are some differences in the impulse responses when monetary policy is forward-looking (see Fig. 3). First, all the responses of output, inflation, and interest rate go back to their steady states in the long run. Second, under a positive technology shock, output and interest rate firstly increase and then decrease. Third, inflation decreases in response to both technology shock and foreign interest rate shock. This response of inflation to foreign interest rate shock is different from that under current-looking monetary policy. Last, under foreign inflation shock, output, inflation, and interest rate increase, rather than decrease. This is different from their responses under current-looking monetary policy.

Under fixed exchange rate regime and current-looking monetary policy (see Fig. 4), output, inflation, and interest rate increase in response to an unanticipated tightening of monetary policy. Under technology shock and foreign interest rate shock, output increases permanently. Inflation and interest rate decrease permanently. This response of domestic interest rate in the opposite direction of foreign interest rate shows the monetary policy independence under capital controls and fixed exchange rate regimes, in line with the Mundell-Fleming trilemma. The sunspot driven inflationary expectation increases output, inflation, and interest rate. This reflects the fact of self-fulfilling prophecy.

When the monetary policy is forward-looking under fixed exchange rate regime (see Fig. 5), technology shock increases output and decreases inflation and interest

Table 9 Parameter estimation-flexible exchange rate, forward-looking monetary policy, China

Parameter	Mean	Standard deviation	90% posterior interval lower bound	90% posterior interval upper bound
a_π	0.5865	0.0828	0.5391	0.6395
a_x	0.4208	0.0202	0.4063	0.4515
ω	1.0336	0.0021	1.0322	1.0362
π^*	4.7384	0.0081	4.7321	4.7513
r^*	0.4026	0.1295	0.2939	0.5384
φ	1.2647	0.0715	1.2209	1.3865
ρ_z	0.8178	0.0082	0.8017	0.8187
ρ_R	0.2214	0.0186	0.2061	0.2289
ρ_π	0.8800	0.0118	0.8645	0.8847
ρ_{zR}	0.5536	0.0555	0.4776	0.5935
$\rho_{z\pi}$	−0.9811	0.0207	−0.9883	−0.9745
$\rho_{R\pi}$	−0.3931	0.0507	−0.4219	−0.3351
$M_{r\zeta}$	−0.2957	0.1272	−0.3137	−0.0037
$M_{z\zeta}$	0.4469	0.1332	0.2856	0.5151
$M_{R\zeta}$	0.0437	0.1892	−0.1567	0.2854
$M_{\pi\zeta}$	−0.4836	0.1460	−0.5804	−0.3983
σ_r	0.4161	0.0154	0.4003	0.4249
σ_z	0.3233	0.0104	0.3213	0.3364
σ_R	0.2343	0.0141	0.2170	0.2439
σ_π	0.4184	0.0122	0.4020	0.4257
σ_ζ	0.1672	0.0093	0.1572	0.1745

Notes The posterior summary statistics are calculated by the Metropolis-Hastings algorithm

rate. Inflation and interest rate first increase and then decrease in response to foreign interest rate shock. These are different from their responses under current-looking monetary policy. It also shows that the monetary policy is not completely independent when it is forward-looking, which slightly deviates from the Mundell-Fleming trilemma.

7.6 *Variance Decomposition*

The variance decomposition results provide the contributions of each shock to the fluctuations in output gap, inflation, and interest rate.

Under the flexible exchange rate regime and current-looking monetary policy in China (see Table 15), foreign interest rate shock contributes to most of the fluctuations in output gap (45.51%), inflation (56.84%), and interest rate (32.28%). Foreign

Table 10 Parameter estimation results-fixed exchange rate, forward-looking monetary policy, China

Parameter	Mean	Standard deviation	90% posterior interval lower bound	90% posterior interval upper bound
a_π	0.3053	0.1138	0.1186	0.4917
a_x	0.2931	0.1478	0.0563	0.5139
ω	0.6624	0.0291	0.6152	0.7109
π^*	1.5837	0.5183	0.7034	2.3970
r^*	0.7854	0.3560	0.2126	1.3447
φ	2.6055	0.7281	1.4279	3.7583
ρ_z	0.9423	0.0406	0.8882	0.9996
ρ_R	0.5040	0.1079	0.3299	0.6768
ρ_{zR}	0.2947	0.0000	0.2947	0.2947
$M_{r\zeta}$	−0.9480	0.0000	−0.9480	−0.9480
$M_{z\zeta}$	0.0991	0.0000	0.0991	0.0991
$M_{R\zeta}$	−0.2598	0.0000	−0.2598	−0.2598
σ_r	0.2272	0.0306	0.1781	0.2759
σ_z	0.3278	0.0452	0.2567	0.3984
σ_R	0.2148	0.0403	0.1499	0.2759
σ_ζ	0.1049	0.0145	0.0815	0.1277

Notes The posterior summary statistics are calculated by the Metropolis-Hastings algorithm

Table 11 Determinacy versus indeterminacy-flexible exchange rate, current-looking monetary policy, China

Probability	
Determinacy	Indeterminacy
0.5709	0.4291

Notes The posterior probabilities are calculated by the Metropolis-Hastings algorithm

Table 12 Determinacy versus indeterminacy-fixed exchange rate, current-looking monetary policy, China

Probability	
Determinacy	Indeterminacy
0.0327	0.9673

Notes The posterior probabilities are calculated by the Metropolis-Hastings algorithm

Table 13 Determinacy versus indeterminacy-flexible exchange rate, forward-looking monetary policy, China

Probability	
Determinacy	Indeterminacy
0.6071	0.3929

Notes The posterior probabilities are calculated by the Metropolis-Hastings algorithm

Table 14 Determinacy versus indeterminacy-fixed exchange rate, forward-looking monetary policy, China

Probability	
Determinacy	Indeterminacy
0.0322	0.9678

Notes The posterior probabilities are calculated by the Metropolis-Hastings algorithm

inflation shock also makes important contribution. It explains the fluctuations in output gap (30.16%), inflation (21.38%), and interest rate (20.81%).

When monetary policy is forward-looking under the flexible exchange rate regime (see Table 16), foreign inflation shock contributes to most of the fluctuations in output gap (51.1%) and inflation (63.15%). Monetary policy shock contributes to 79.61% of fluctuation in interest rate.

Under the fixed exchange rate regime and current-looking monetary policy (see Table 17), technology shock contributes to most of the fluctuations in output gap (45.53%), inflation (69.06%), and interest rate (58.23%). Foreign interest rate shock explains the fluctuations in output gap (46.61%), inflation (28.55%), and interest rate (24.79%).

When monetary policy is forward-looking under the fixed exchange rate regime (see Table 18), technology shock still contributes to most of the fluctuations in output gap (61.76%), inflation (91.8%), and interest rate (62.68%).

8 Numerical Bifurcation Analysis

In this section, we detect bifurcation numerically. In line with our former analysis, we find numerically that bifurcation exists under fixed exchange rate regimes and current-looking monetary policy. We used MatContM, following Kuznetsov (2013), and Mathematica to perform the computations. We find that at certain values of the deep parameters, the dynamical system becomes unstable. Several kinds of bifurcation appear at those values, both when computed forward and backward at those values. Notice that a_x and a_π are the central bank's response in the Taylor rule to the output gap and inflation, respectively. We find that when capital controls are imposed, policymakers should be cautious when adjusting the nominal interest rate under fixed exchange rate regimes with current-looking monetary policy.

To explore bifurcation phenomena, we define a and b such that

$$a = 1 + \frac{a_x}{\varphi + 1} + \frac{\varphi + 2}{\beta}, \tag{42}$$

$$b = \frac{1 + a_\pi \lambda}{\beta} + \frac{(\varphi + 1)(1 - \lambda)}{\beta^2} + \frac{a_x}{\beta(\varphi + 1)}. \tag{43}$$

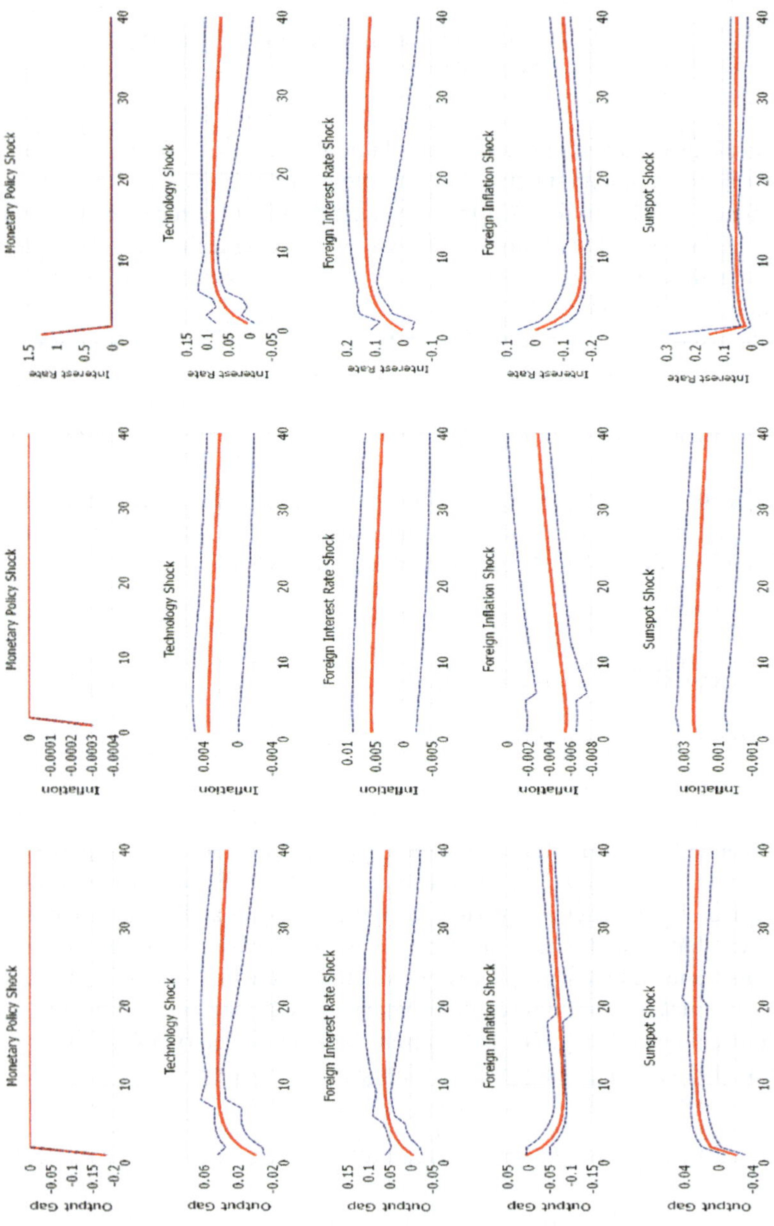

Fig. 2 Impulse responses-flexible exchange rate, current-looking monetary policy, China

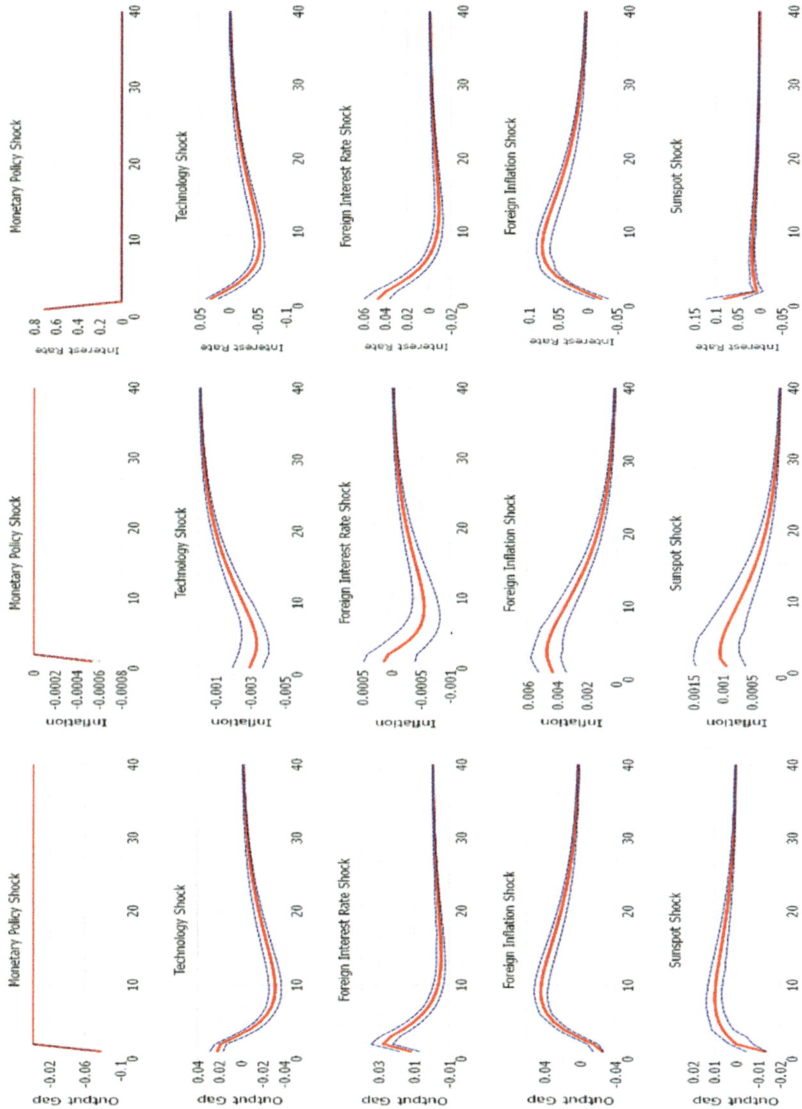

Fig. 3 Impulse responses-flexible exchange rate, forward-looking monetary policy, China

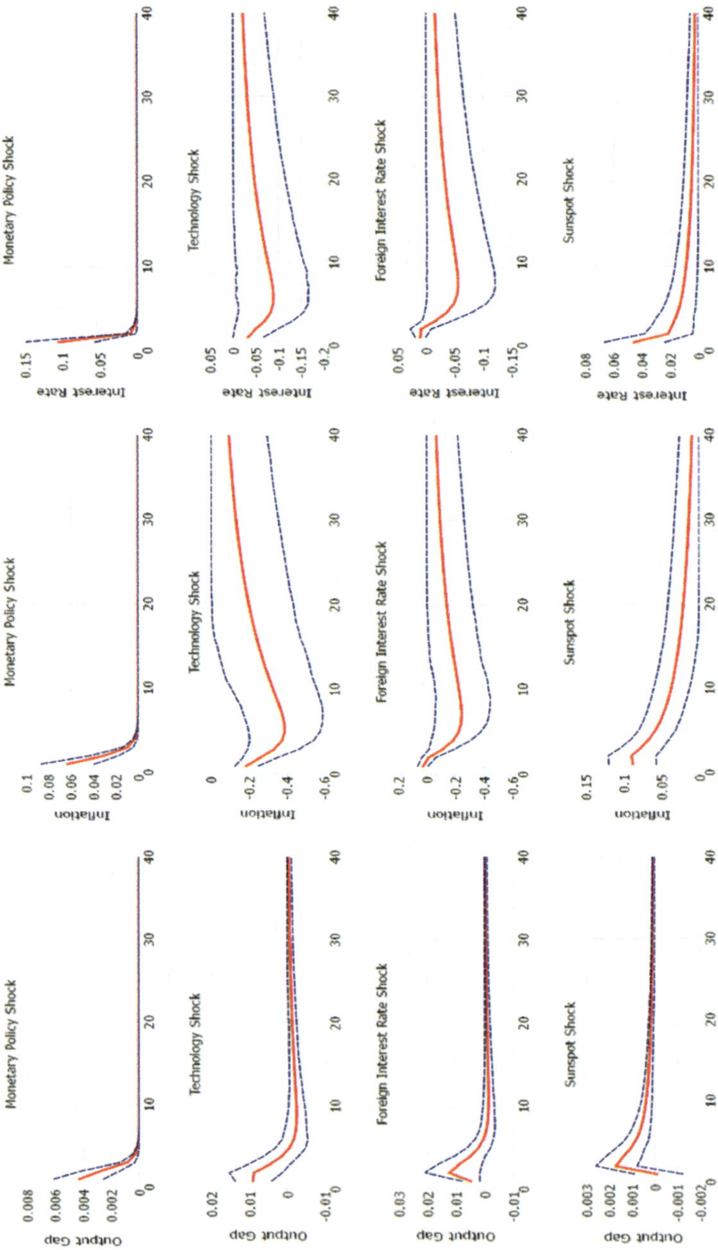

Fig. 4 Impulse responses-fixed exchange rate, current-looking monetary policy, China

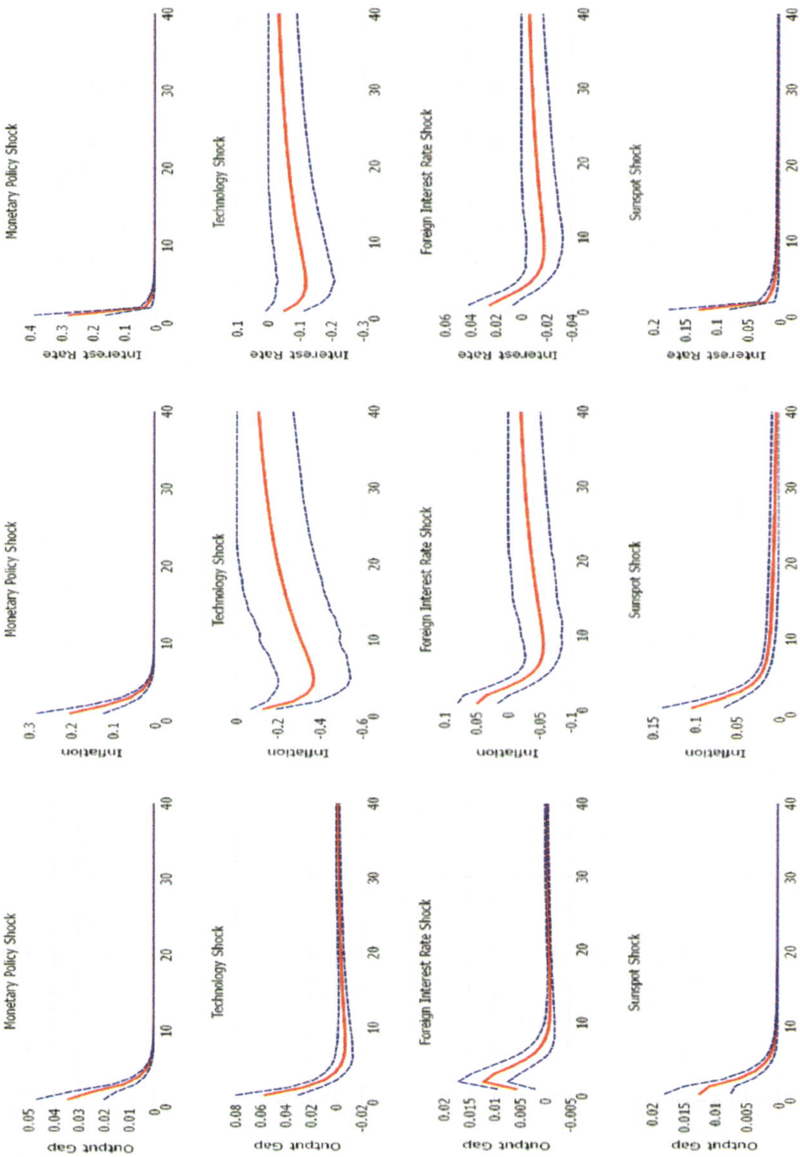

Fig. 5 Impulse responses-fixed exchange rate, forward-looking monetary policy, China

Table 15 Variance decomposition-flexible exchange rate, current-looking monetary policy, China

	Output gap	Inflation	Interest rate
Monetary policy shock	0.0418 [0.0273, 0.0496]	0.0001 [0.0000, 0.0002]	0.3205 [0.1657, 0.3458]
Technology shock	0.1405 [0.1251, 0.1444]	0.1536 [0.1353, 0.1988]	0.0984 [0.0881, 0.1342]
Foreign interest rate shock	0.4551 [0.4060, 0.4901]	0.5684 [0.4904, 0.7671]	0.3228 [0.2879, 0.3898]
Foreign inflation shock	0.3016 [0.2204, 0.3642]	0.2138 [0.0597, 0.2939]	0.2081 [0.1578, 0.2586]
Sunspot shock	0.0610 [0.0402, 0.0681]	0.0641 [0.0183, 0.0803]	0.0502 [0.0457, 0.0658]

Notes This table reports the posterior mean and 90% probability intervals

Table 16 Variance decomposition-flexible exchange rate, forward-looking monetary policy, China

	Output gap	Inflation	Interest rate
Monetary policy shock	0.1318 [0.1057, 0.1696]	0.0008 [0.0005, 0.0013]	0.7961 [0.7484, 0.8720]
Technology shock	0.2698 [0.2500, 0.2907]	0.3268 [0.3111, 0.3327]	0.0600 [0.0387, 0.0746]
Foreign interest rate shock	0.0569 [0.0229, 0.0850]	0.0111 [0.0066, 0.0150]	0.0106 [0.0068, 0.0144]
Foreign inflation shock	0.5110 [0.4641, 0.5476]	0.6315 [0.6138, 0.6439]	0.1153 [0.0734, 0.1502]
Sunspot shock	0.0304 [0.0133, 0.0404]	0.0297 [0.0149, 0.0383]	0.0180 [0.0025, 0.0224]

Notes This table reports the posterior mean and 90% probability intervals

As the results summarized in Table 19, at $a = 4.88$ and $b = 3.88$, we find a branch point, and it is an unstable improper node. Selecting this branch point as the initial point and computing backward, we get a bifurcation where another branch point shows up. At $a = 4.85$, $b = 3.85$, we find the same types of bifurcation as above. At $a = 4.85$, $b = 1$, we detect a neutral saddle and it is unstable improper node. At $a = 4.85$, $b = -5.85$, we find a period doubling point and it is a saddle point. These results are also indicated by Figs. 6, 7, 8, 9 and 10.

Table 17 Variance decomposition-fixed exchange rate, current-looking monetary policy, China

	Output gap	Inflation	Interest rate
Monetary policy shock	0.0592 [0.0047, 0.1398]	0.0025 [0.0000, 0.0056]	0.1339 [0.0000, 0.3496]
Technology shock	0.4553 [0.3316, 0.5970]	0.6906 [0.6003, 0.8085]	0.5823 [0.3808, 0.7581]
Foreign interest rate shock	0.4661 [0.2271, 0.6335]	0.2855 [0.1562, 0.4023]	0.2479 [0.0965, 0.3856]
Sunspot shock	0.0195 [0.0024, 0.0419]	0.0214 [0.0036, 0.0416]	0.0359 [0.0043, 0.0723]

Notes This table reports the posterior mean and 90% probability intervals

Table 18 Variance decomposition-fixed exchange rate, forward-looking monetary policy, China

	Output gap	Inflation	Interest rate
Monetary policy shock	0.2795 [0.0740, 0.4802]	0.0403 [0.0000, 0.0917]	0.2900 [0.0006, 0.6070]
Technology shock	0.6176 [0.3737, 0.8654]	0.9180 [0.8408, 0.9804]	0.6268 [0.2484, 0.9672]
Foreign interest rate shock	0.0540 [0.0162, 0.0877]	0.0281 [0.0096, 0.0452]	0.0206 [0.0039, 0.0368]
Sunspot shock	0.0490 [0.0113, 0.0858]	0.0137 [0.0005, 0.0303]	0.0626 [0.0012, 0.1226]

Notes This table reports the posterior mean and 90% probability intervals

Since the values of a and b are also functions of the monetary policy parameters and deep structural parameters, we find that certain values of monetary policy, a_x and a_π, will lead the economy into instability. These values should be avoided by the policymakers.

9 Conclusion

We investigated the dynamical properties and stability of the macroeconomy under capital controls. Conditional on different exchange rate regimes and monetary policies, we classified our analysis into four different cases. We show that under certain conditions of the deep parameters and monetary policy parameters, the macro economy will have multiple equilibria and can be unstable, especially under fixed exchange rate regimes and current-looking monetary policy. Monetary authorities

Table 19 Numerical bifurcation results

Variable parameter	Fixed point continuation	Eigenvalues	Origin	Bifurcation continuation	
Vary a	(1) Branch point a = 4.88, b = 3.88	Real and positive	Unstable improper node	Backward	Branch point
	(2) Period doubling a = −4.88, b = 3.88	Real and negative	Asymptotically stable improper node	Forward	Resonance 1–2 LPPD
Vary b	(3) Branch point a = 4.85, b = 3.85	Real and positive	Unstable improper node	Backward	Branch point
	(4) Neutral saddle a = 4.85, b = 1	Real and positive	Unstable improper node		
	(5) Period doubling a = 4.85, b = −5.85	Real with opposite signs	Saddle point	Backward	LPPD Resonance 1–2

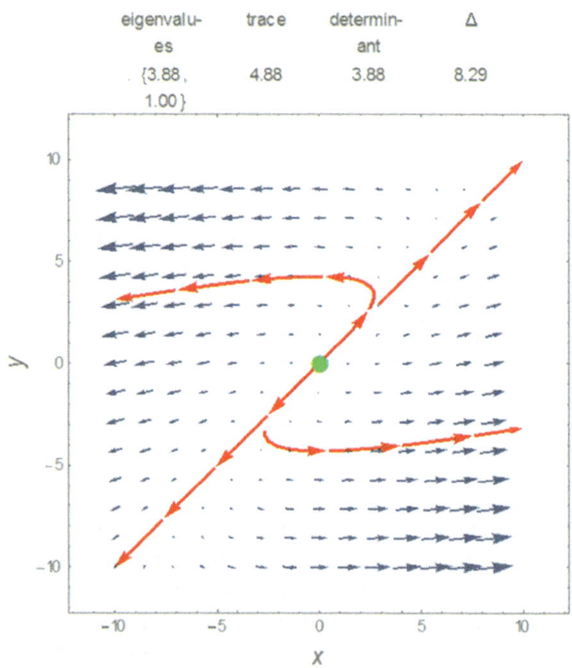

Fig. 6 Branch point (a = 4.88, b = 3.88)

Fig. 7 Period doubling (a = −4.88, b = 3.88)

eigenvalues	trace	determinant	Δ
{−3.88, −1.00}	−4.88	3.88	8.29

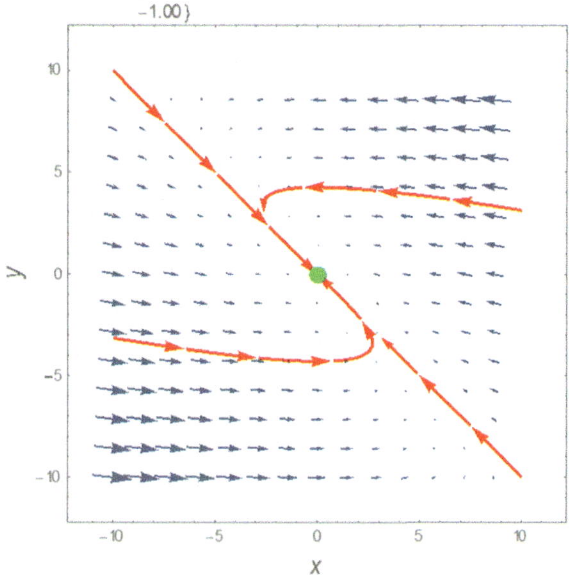

Fig. 8 Branch point (a = 4.85, b = 3.85)

eigenvalues	trace	determinant	Δ
{3.85, 1.00}	4.85	3.85	8.12

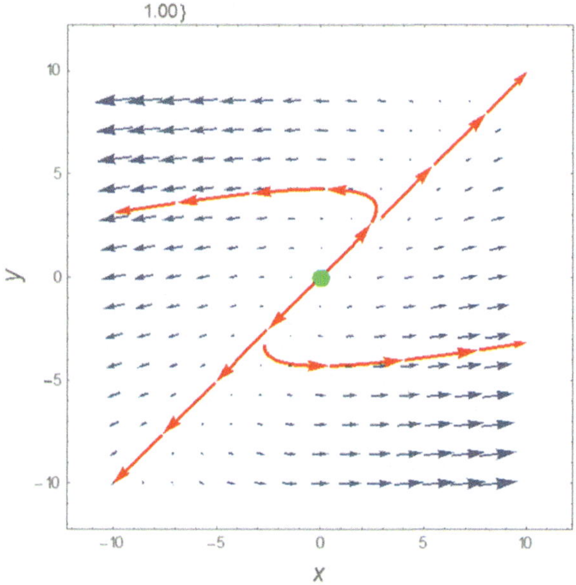

Fig. 9 Neutral saddle (a = 4.85, b = 1)

eigenvalues	trace	determinant	Δ
{4.63, 0.22}	4.85	1.00	19.52

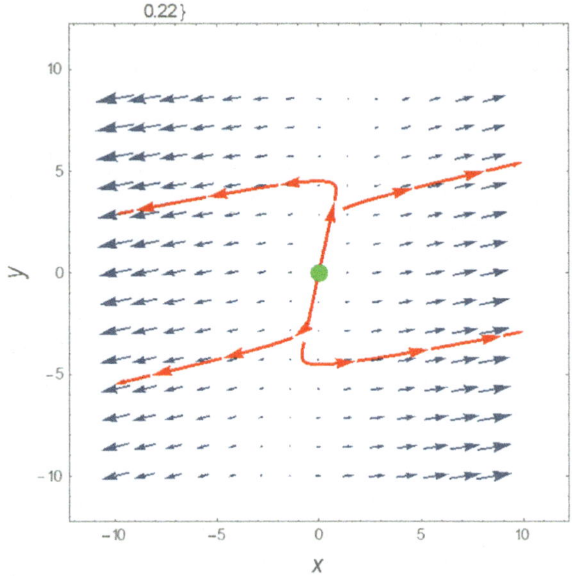

eigenvalues	trace	determinant	Δ
{5.85, -1.00}	4.85	-5.85	46.92

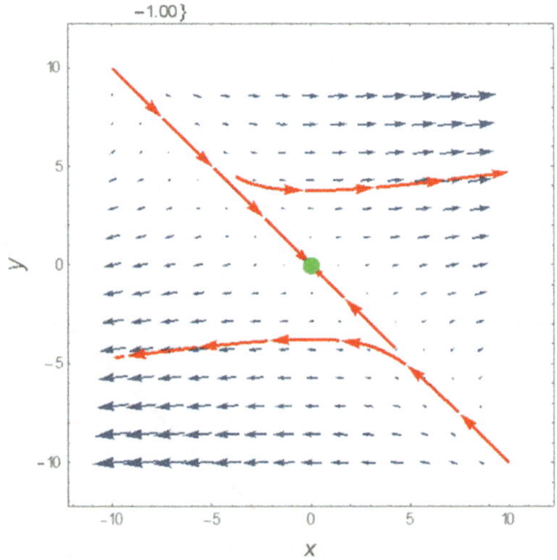

Fig. 10 Period doubling (a = 4.85, b = −5.85)

need to be cautious when they make policy decisions with capital controls. Only when taking these complexities into consideration, can macro-prudential policy with capital controls play its role in stabilizing the macro economy. The common view that capital controls can provide a simple solution to difficult problems can be seriously misguided, producing unanticipated risk. The economy could become trapped in a worse equilibrium or in an instability region, leading the economy onto a volatile path.

Under capital control, policymakers could move the economic system from indeterminate equilibria to determinate equilibrium by adjusting non-fundamental forecasting error to the set of fundamental shocks. One method would be by influencing people's belief. An alternative method, more directly under government control, would be by changing the value of policy parameters to move the system from an instability region to a stability region.

We assume purchasing power parity, thereby removing the dynamics of terms of trade and exchange rates from the dynamical systems. Extensions of our model could permit solving for the dynamics of exchange rates and terms of trade. In addition, some of our results produce indeterminacy, and some produce deterministic business cycles without stochastic shocks. Extensions to explore stability in a stochastic economic system is a future research goal.

Appendix 1: Households Problem

A representative household seeks to maximize

$$E_0 \sum_{t=0}^{\infty} \beta^t \left[\frac{C_t^{1-\sigma}}{1-\sigma} - \frac{N_t^{1+\varphi}}{1+\varphi} \right],$$

where N_t denotes hours of labor, C_t is a composite consumption index defined by

$$C_t \equiv \left[(1-\alpha)^{\frac{1}{\eta}} \left(C_{H,t}\right)^{\frac{\eta-1}{\eta}} + \alpha^{\frac{1}{\eta}} \left(C_{F,t}\right)^{\frac{\eta-1}{\eta}} \right]^{\frac{\eta}{\eta-1}},$$

with $C_{H,t} \equiv \left(\int_0^1 C_{H,t}(j)^{\frac{\varepsilon-1}{\varepsilon}} dj \right)^{\frac{\varepsilon}{\varepsilon-1}}$, $C_{F,t} \equiv \left(\int_0^1 (C_{i,t})^{\frac{\gamma-1}{\gamma}} di \right)^{\frac{\gamma}{\gamma-1}}$, $C_{i,t} \equiv \left(\int_0^1 C_{i,t}(j)^{\frac{\varepsilon-1}{\varepsilon}} dj \right)^{\frac{\varepsilon}{\varepsilon-1}}$.

The household's budget constraint takes the form

$$\int_0^1 P_{H,t}(j) C_{H,t}(j) dj + \int_0^1 \int_0^1 P_{i,t}(j) C_{i,t}(j) dj di + E_t\left\{ Q_{t,t+1} D_{t+1} \right\}$$
$$+ \int_0^1 E_t\left\{ \mathcal{E}_{i,t} Q^i_{t,t+1} D^i_{t+1} \right\} di \le W_t N_t + T_t + D_t + \int_0^1 \left(\frac{1+\tau_t}{1+\tau^i_t} \right) \mathcal{E}_{i,t} D^i_t di.$$

The optimal allocation of any given expenditure within each category of goods yields the demand functions, $C_{H,t}(j) = \left(\frac{P_{H,t}(j)}{P_{H,t}}\right)^{-\varepsilon} C_{H,t}$ and $C_{i,t}(j) = \left(\frac{P_{i,t}(j)}{P_{i,t}}\right)^{-\varepsilon} C_{i,t}$, where $P_{H,t} \equiv \left(\int_0^1 P_{H,t}(j)^{1-\varepsilon} dj\right)^{\frac{1}{1-\varepsilon}}$ and $P_{i,t} \equiv \left(\int_0^1 P_{i,t}(j)^{1-\varepsilon} dj\right)^{\frac{1}{1-\varepsilon}}$.

So $\int_0^1 P_{H,t}(j)C_{H,t}(j)dj = P_{H,t}C_{H,t}$ and $\int_0^1 P_{i,t}(j)C_{i,t}(j)dj = P_{i,t}C_{i,t}$.

The optimal allocation of expenditures on imported goods by country of origin implies $C_{i,t} = \left(\frac{P_{i,t}}{P_{F,t}}\right)^{-\gamma} C_{F,t}$, where $P_{F,t} \equiv \left(\int_0^1 P_{i,t}^{1-\gamma} di\right)^{\frac{1}{1-\gamma}}$, so that

$$\int_0^1 P_{i,t}C_{i,t}di = P_{F,t}C_{F,t}.$$

The optimal allocation of expenditures between domestic and imported goods is given by $C_{H,t} = (1-\alpha)\left(\frac{P_{H,t}}{P_t}\right)^{-\eta} C_t$ and $C_{F,t} = \alpha\left(\frac{P_{F,t}}{P_t}\right)^{-\eta} C_t$, where $P_t \equiv \left[(1-\alpha)\left(P_{H,t}\right)^{1-\eta} + \alpha\left(P_{F,t}\right)^{1-\eta}\right]^{\frac{1}{1-\eta}}$, so that

$$P_{H,t}C_{H,t} + P_{F,t}C_{F,t} = P_tC_t.$$

The effective nominal exchange rate is defined by $\mathcal{E}_t = \frac{\int_0^1 \mathcal{E}_{i,t} D_t^i di}{\int_0^1 D_t^i di}$. Hence, we have $\int_0^1 \mathcal{E}_{i,t} D_t^i di = \mathcal{E}_t \int_0^1 D_t^i di = \mathcal{E}_t D_t^*$ and $\int_0^1 \mathcal{E}_{i,t} Q_{t,t+1}^i D_{t+1}^i di = \int_0^1 \mathcal{E}_t Q_{t,t+1}^i D_{t+1}^* di = \mathcal{E}_t D_{t+1}^* \int_0^1 Q_{t,t+1}^i di = \mathcal{E}_t D_{t+1}^* Q_{t,t+1}^*$.

Thus, the budget constraint can be rewritten as

$$P_tC_t + E_t\{Q_{t,t+1}D_{t+1}\} + E_t\{\mathcal{E}_t Q_{t,t+1}^* D_{t+1}^*\} \leq W_tN_t + T_t + D_t + (1+\tau_t)\mathcal{E}_t D_t^*.$$

Maximizing utility of a household subject to its budget constraint yields two Euler equations

$$\beta E_t\left\{\left(\frac{C_{t+1}}{C_t}\right)^{-\sigma}\left(\frac{P_t}{P_{t+1}}\right)\left(\frac{1}{Q_{t,t+1}}\right)\right\} = 1,$$

$$\beta E_t\left\{\left(\frac{C_{t+1}}{C_t}\right)^{-\sigma}\left(\frac{P_t}{P_{t+1}}\right)\left(\frac{\mathcal{E}_{t+1}}{\mathcal{E}_t}\right)(1+\tau_{t+1})\left(\frac{1}{Q_{t,t+1}^*}\right)\right\} = 1.$$

The log-linearized form is

$$c_t = E_t\{c_{t+1}\} - \frac{1}{\sigma}(r_t - E_t\{\pi_{t+1}\} - \rho),$$

$$c_t = E_t\{c_{t+1}\} - \frac{1}{\sigma}\left(r_t^* + \left[E_t\{e_{t+1}\} - e_t\right] + E_t\{\tau_{t+1}\} - E_t\{\pi_{t+1}\} - \rho\right),$$

where $(R_t)^{-1} = E_t\{Q_{t,t+1}\}$ and $(R_t^*)^{-1} = E_t\{Q_{t,t+1}^*\}$ and

$$\pi_{t+1} \equiv p_{t+1} - p_t \equiv \log P_{t+1} - \log P_t.$$

Appendix 2: Backus-Smith Condition

Combined the Euler equations for the home country and country i, we get

$$\frac{Q_{t,t+1}^*}{Q_{t,t+1}} = \frac{\mathcal{E}_{t+1}}{\mathcal{E}_t}(1+\tau_{t+1}),$$

$$\frac{Q_{t,t+1}^{i*}}{Q_{t,t+1}^i} = \frac{\mathcal{E}_{i,t}}{\mathcal{E}_{i,t+1}},$$

$$\left(\frac{C_{t+1}}{C_t}\right) = \left(\frac{C_{t+1}^i}{C_t^i}\right)\left[\frac{\mathcal{Q}_{i,t+1}(1+\tau_{t+1})}{\mathcal{Q}_{i,t}}\right]^{\frac{1}{\sigma}} = \left(\frac{C_{t+1}^i}{C_t^i}\right)\left[\frac{\mathcal{Q}_{i,t+1}\Delta_{t+1}}{\mathcal{Q}_{i,t}\Delta_t}\right]^{\frac{1}{\sigma}},$$

where we define Δ and Θ to be the variables that captures the dynamics of τ_t, such that

$$1+\tau_{t+1} \equiv \frac{\Delta_{t+1}}{\Delta_t} \equiv \frac{\Theta_{t+1}^{\sigma}}{\Theta_t^{\sigma}}.$$

Taking the log, we get $\tau_{t+1} = \sigma(\theta_{t+1} - \theta_t)$, resulting in the Backus-Smith condition,

$$C_t = \Theta_t C_t^i \mathcal{Q}_{i,t}^{\frac{1}{\sigma}}.$$

Taking logs on both sides and integrating over i, we get

$$c_t = c_t^* + \frac{1}{\sigma}q_t + \theta_t$$

Appendix 3: Uncovered Interest Parity

The pricing equation for foreign bonds and domestic bonds are, respectively

$$(R_t^*)^{-1} = E_t\{Q_{t,t+1}^*\},$$

$$(R_t)^{-1} = E_t\{Q_{t,t+1}\}.$$

We combine them to get the Uncovered Interest Parity conditions,

$$E_t\{Q_{t,t+1}R_t - Q^*_{t,t+1}R^*_t\} = 0,$$

$$R_t = (1+\tau_{t+1})R^*_t\frac{\mathcal{E}_{t+1}}{\mathcal{E}_t}.$$

Taking logs on both sides, we get

$$r_t - r^*_t = E_t\{\tau_{t+1}\} + E_t\{e_{t+1}\} - e_t,$$

where $e_t \equiv \int_0^1 e^i_t di$ is the log nominal effective exchange rate.

The bilateral terms of trade between the domestic country and country i are

$$S_{i,t} \equiv \frac{P_{i,t}}{P_{H,t}}.$$

The effective terms of trade are

$$S_t \equiv \frac{P_{F,t}}{P_{H,t}} = \left(\int_0^1 S^{1-\gamma}_{i,t}di\right)^{\frac{1}{1-\gamma}}.$$

Taking logs, we get

$$s_t \equiv p_{F,t} - p_{H,t},$$

$$s_t = \int_0^1 s_{i,t}di(\text{when } \gamma = 1).$$

Under the purchasing power parity condition, $P_{H,t} = P_{F,t}$, so that $S_t = 1$.

Log linearizing, $P_t \equiv \left[(1-\alpha)\left(P_{H,t}\right)^{1-\eta} + \alpha\left(P_{F,t}\right)^{1-\eta}\right]^{\frac{1}{1-\eta}}$ becomes $p_t \equiv (1-\alpha)p_{H,t} + \alpha p_{F,t} = p_{H,t} + \alpha s_t$, when $\eta = 1$.

It follows that

$$\pi_t = \pi_{H,t} + \alpha(s_t - s_{t-1})$$

and

$$E_t\{\pi_{t+1}\} = E_t\left\{\pi_{H,t+1}\right\} + \alpha\left[E_t\{s_{t+1}\} - s_t\right].$$

The bilateral nominal exchange rate is defined by the law of one price,

$$P_{i,t}(j) = \mathcal{E}_{i,t}P^i_{i,t}(j),$$

where $P^i_{i,t}(j)$ is the price of country i's good j, expressed in country i's currency.

It follows that $P_{i,t} = \mathcal{E}_{i,t} P^i_{i,t}$. The nominal effective exchange rate is defined as

$$\mathcal{E}_t \equiv \left(\int_0^1 \mathcal{E}_{i,t}^{1-\gamma} di \right)^{\frac{1}{1-\gamma}}.$$

Log linearizing $P_{F,t} \equiv \left(\int_0^1 P_{i,t}^{1-\gamma} di \right)^{\frac{1}{1-\gamma}}$ and substituting $P_{i,t}$ into $P_{F,t}$, we get

$$p_{F,t} = \int_0^1 (e_{i,t} + p^i_{i,t}) di = e_t + p^*_t,$$

where $p^*_t \equiv \int_0^1 p^i_{i,t} di$ is the log world price index. Combining the previous result with terms of trade, we get

$$s_t = e_t + p^*_t - p_{H,t}.$$

The real exchange rate is defined as $\mathcal{Q}_{i,t} \equiv \frac{\mathcal{E}_{i,t} P^i_t}{P_t}$.

We can rewrite the uncovered interest parity condition as

$$r_t - r^*_t = E_t\{\tau_{t+1}\} + E_t\{e_{t+1}\} - e_t.$$

Since $\tau_{t+1} = \sigma(\theta_{t+1} - \theta_t)$ and $e_t = s_t + p_{H,t} - p^*_t$, it follows that

$$r_t - r^*_t = \sigma\left[E_t\{\theta_{t+1}\} - \theta_t\right] + \left[E_t\{s_{t+1}\} - s_t\right] + E_t\left\{\pi_{H,t+1}\right\} - E_t\left\{\pi^*_{t+1}\right\}.$$

Appendix 4: Equilibrium of Demand Side

The market clearing condition in the representative small open economy is

$$\begin{aligned} Y_t(j) &= C_{H,t}(j) + \int_0^1 C^i_{H,t}(j) di \\ &= \left(\frac{P_{H,t}(j)}{P_{H,t}}\right)^{-\varepsilon} \left[(1-\alpha)\left(\frac{P_{H,t}}{P_t}\right)^{-\eta} C_t + \alpha \int_0^1 \left(\frac{P_{H,t}}{\mathcal{E}_{i,t} P^i_{F,t}}\right)^{-\gamma} \left(\frac{P^i_{F,t}}{P^i_t}\right)^{-\eta} C^i_t di \right], \end{aligned}$$

where the assumption of symmetric preferences across countries produces

$$C^i_{H,t}(j) = \alpha \left(\frac{P_{H,t}(j)}{P_{H,t}}\right)^{-\varepsilon} \left(\frac{P_{H,t}}{\mathcal{E}_{i,t} P^i_{F,t}}\right)^{-\gamma} \left(\frac{P^i_{F,t}}{P^i_t}\right)^{-\eta} C^i_t.$$

Substituting into $Y_t \equiv \left[\int_0^1 Y_t(j)^{1-\frac{1}{\varepsilon}} dj\right]^{\frac{\varepsilon}{\varepsilon-1}}$, we get

$$Y_t = \left(\frac{P_{H,t}}{P_t}\right)^{-\eta} \left[(1-\alpha)C_t + \alpha \int_0^1 \left(\frac{\mathcal{E}_{i,t} P^i_{F,t}}{P_{H,t}}\right)^{\gamma-\eta} \mathcal{Q}^{\eta}_{i,t} C^i_t di\right],$$

$$Y_t = S_t^{\alpha} C_t\big[(1-\alpha) + \alpha\Theta_t^{-1}\big].$$

The first order log linear approximation is

$$y_t = \alpha s_t + c_t - \theta_t.$$

Substituting this into $c_t = E_t\{c_{t+1}\} - \frac{1}{\sigma}(r_t - E_t\{\pi_{t+1}\} - \rho)$, we get

$$y_t = E_t\{y_{t+1}\} - (r_t - E_t\{\pi_{t+1}\} - \rho) - \alpha\big[E_t\{s_{t+1}\} - s_t\big] + \big[E_t\{\theta_{t+1}\} - \theta_t\big].$$

Appendix 5: Equilibrium of Supply Side

At the steady state of the economy, we have

$$y_t = a_t + n_t.$$

The real marginal cost is

$$mc_t = -\nu + c_t + \varphi n_t + \alpha s_t - a_t,$$

while the steady state real marginal cost is

$$mc \equiv -\mu.$$

The deviation of real marginal cost from its steady state is

$$\widehat{mc_t} \equiv mc_t - mc = \mu - \nu + c_t + \varphi n_t + \alpha s_t - a_t = \mu - \nu + (\varphi + 1)(y_t - a_t) + \theta_t.$$

Thus at equilibrium, the dynamic equation for inflation is

$$\begin{aligned}\pi_{H,t} &= \beta E_t\{\pi_{H,t+1}\} + \lambda\widehat{mc_t} \\ &= \beta E_t\{\pi_{H,t+1}\} + \lambda(\mu - \nu) + \lambda(\varphi + 1)y_t - \lambda(\varphi + 1)a_t + \lambda\theta_t.\end{aligned}$$

Appendix 6: Equilibrium Dynamics in Output Gap

The natural level of output is defined to be the equilibrium output in the absence of nominal rigidities, where the deviation of real marginal cost from its steady state equals 0, as follows:

$$\widehat{mc_t} = 0 \Rightarrow \bar{y}_t = a_t - \frac{1}{\varphi + 1}\theta_t + \frac{\nu - \mu}{\varphi + 1}.$$

The output gap is defined to be the following deviation of output from its natural level: $x_t \equiv y_t - \bar{y}_t$, so that

$$y_t = x_t + \bar{y}_t = x_t + \left(a_t - \frac{1}{\varphi + 1}\theta_t + \frac{\nu - \mu}{\varphi + 1}\right).$$

We substitute that equation into the dynamics of output and inflation and also substitute π_{t+1} into the expression of $\pi_{H,t+1}$ to acquire

$$x_t = E_t\{x_{t+1}\} - [r_t - E_t\{\pi_{H,t+1}\} - \rho] + [E_t\{a_{t+1}\} - a_t] + \frac{\varphi}{\varphi + 1}[E_t\{\theta_{t+1}\} - \theta_t],$$

$$\pi_{H,t} = \beta E_t\{\pi_{H,t+1}\} + \lambda(\varphi + 1)x_t,$$

together with the uncovered interest parity condition

$$r_t - r_t^* = [E_t\{\theta_{t+1}\} - \theta_t] + [E_t\{s_{t+1}\} - s_t] + E_t\{\pi_{H,t+1}\} - E_t\{\pi_{t+1}^*\}.$$

The above three equations constitute the dynamics of the economy with capital controls and flexible exchange rates, but without monetary policy.

If the exchange rate is fixed, then $e_{t+1} = e_t$, so that

$$E_t\{\pi_{H,t+1}\} = E_t\{\pi_{t+1}^*\} - [E_t\{s_{t+1}\} - s_t],$$

$$r_t - r_t^* = [E_t\{\theta_{t+1}\} - \theta_t].$$

When purchasing power parity holds, $S_t = 1$ and $[E_t\{s_{t+1}\} - s_t] = 0$.

Appendix 7: Proof of Proposition 1

Under capital control, flexible exchange rates, and current-looking monetary policy, the system can be rewritten as

$$
\begin{aligned}
E_t(x_{t+1}) &= \left(1 + \frac{a_x}{\varphi+1} + \frac{\lambda}{\beta}\right)x_t - \frac{(1-a_\pi\beta)}{\beta(\varphi+1)}\pi_{H,t} - [E_t(a_{t+1}) - a_t] \\
&\quad + \frac{\varphi}{\varphi+1}r_t^* - \frac{\varphi}{\varphi+1}E_t(\pi_{t+1}^*) - \rho, \\
E_t(\pi_{H,t+1}) &= \frac{1}{\beta}\pi_{H,t} - \frac{\lambda(\varphi+1)}{\beta}x_t.
\end{aligned}
$$

The two-dimensional subsystem for the conditional expectations, $\boldsymbol{\xi}_t = \left[\xi_t^x \; \xi_t^{\pi_H}\right]'$, where $\xi_t^x = E_t(x_{t+1})$ and $\xi_t^{\pi_H} = E_t(\pi_{H,t+1})$ can be written as

$$
\boldsymbol{\xi}_t = \boldsymbol{\Gamma}_1^* \boldsymbol{\xi}_{t-1} + \boldsymbol{\Psi}^* \boldsymbol{\varepsilon}_t + \boldsymbol{\Pi}^* \boldsymbol{\eta}_t.
$$

The eigenvalues for $\boldsymbol{\Gamma}_1^*$ are

$$
\mu_1, \mu_2 = \frac{A + \frac{1}{\beta} \pm \sqrt{\left(A + \frac{1}{\beta}\right)^2 - \frac{4(A-EB)}{\beta}}}{2},
$$

where

$$
\begin{aligned}
A &= 1 + \frac{a_x}{\varphi+1} + \frac{\lambda}{\beta}, \\
B &= \frac{(1-a_\pi\beta)}{\beta(\varphi+1)}, \\
E &= \lambda(\varphi+1).
\end{aligned}
$$

Since the number of non-fundamental errors $k = 2$, when $r = m = 1$, there will be one degree of indeterminacy. This requires that only one of the roots, μ_1 and μ_2, be unstable, resulting in this conclusion.

Appendix 8: Proof of Proposition 2

Under capital control, fixed exchange rates, and current-looking monetary policy, the system can be rewritten as

$$
\begin{aligned}
E_t(x_{t+1}) &= \left(1 + \frac{a_x}{\varphi+1} + \frac{\varphi+1}{\beta}\right)x_t \\
&\quad - \left(\frac{1}{\beta} - \frac{a_\pi}{\varphi+1}\right)\pi_{H,t} - [E_t(a_{t+1}) - a_t] + \frac{\varphi}{\varphi+1}r_t^* - \rho, \\
E_t(\pi_{H,t+1}) &= \frac{1}{\beta}\pi_{H,t} - \frac{\lambda(\varphi+1)}{\beta}x_t.
\end{aligned}
$$

The eigenvalues of matrix $\mathbf{\Gamma}_1^*$ are

$$\mu_1, \mu_2 = \frac{A + \frac{1}{\beta} \pm \sqrt{\left(A + \frac{1}{\beta}\right)^2 - \frac{4(A-EB)}{\beta}}}{2},$$

where

$$\begin{aligned} A &= 1 + \frac{a_x}{\varphi + 1} + \frac{\varphi + 1}{\beta}, \\ B &= \frac{1}{\beta} - \frac{a_\pi}{\varphi + 1}, \\ E &= \lambda(\varphi + 1). \end{aligned}$$

This result follows.

Appendix 9: Proof of Proposition 3

Under capital control, flexible exchange rates, and forward-looking monetary policy, the system can be rewritten as

$$\begin{aligned} \left(1 - \frac{a_x}{\varphi + 1}\right) E_t(x_{t+1}) &= \left[1 - \frac{\lambda(a_\pi - 1)}{\beta}\right] x_t - \frac{(1 - a_\pi)}{\beta(\varphi + 1)} \pi_{H,t} - [E_t(a_{t+1}) - a_t] \\ &\quad + \frac{\varphi}{\varphi + 1} r_t^* - \frac{\varphi}{\varphi + 1} E_t(\pi_{t+1}^*) - \rho, \\ E_t(\pi_{H,t+1}) &= \frac{1}{\beta} \pi_{H,t} - \frac{\lambda(\varphi + 1)}{\beta} x_t. \end{aligned}$$

The eigenvalues of matrix $\mathbf{\Gamma}_1^*$ are

$$\mu_1, \mu_2 = \frac{\frac{A}{F} + \frac{1}{\beta} \pm \sqrt{\left(\frac{A}{F} + \frac{1}{\beta}\right)^2 - \frac{4(A-EB)}{F\beta}}}{2},$$

where

$$\begin{aligned} A &= 1 - \frac{\lambda(a_\pi - 1)}{\beta}, \\ B &= \frac{1 - a_\pi}{\beta(\varphi + 1)}, \\ E &= \lambda(\varphi + 1), \end{aligned}$$

$$F = 1 - \frac{a_x}{\varphi + 1}.$$

This result follows.

Appendix 10: Proof of Proposition 4

Under capital control, fixed exchange rates, and forward-looking monetary policy, the system can be rewritten as

$$\begin{aligned}\left(1 - \frac{a_x}{\varphi + 1}\right) E_t(x_{t+1}) &= \left[1 + \frac{\lambda(\varphi + 1 - a_\pi)}{\beta}\right] x_t \\ &\quad - \left[\frac{1}{\beta} - \frac{a_\pi}{\beta(\varphi + 1)}\right] \pi_{H,t} - [E_t(a_{t+1}) - a_t] + \frac{\varphi}{\varphi + 1} r_t^* - \rho, \\ E_t(\pi_{H,t+1}) &= \frac{1}{\beta} \pi_{H,t} - \frac{\lambda(\varphi + 1)}{\beta} x_t.\end{aligned}$$

The eigenvalues of matrix $\boldsymbol{\Gamma}_1^*$ are

$$\mu_1, \mu_2 = \frac{\frac{A}{F} + \frac{1}{\beta} \pm \sqrt{\left(\frac{A}{F} + \frac{1}{\beta}\right)^2 - \frac{4(A-EB)}{F\beta}}}{2},$$

where

$$\begin{aligned} A &= 1 + \frac{\lambda(\varphi + 1 - a_\pi)}{\beta}, \\ B &= \frac{1}{\beta} - \frac{a_\pi}{\beta(\varphi + 1)}, \\ E &= \lambda(\varphi + 1), \\ F &= 1 - \frac{a_x}{\varphi + 1}. \end{aligned}$$

This result follows.

Appendix 11: Proof of Propositions 5–8

1. Case 1

We rewrite the system in 2×2 form as

$$\begin{bmatrix} E_t(x_{t+1}) \\ E_t(\pi_{H,t+1}) \end{bmatrix} = \begin{bmatrix} A & -B \\ -\frac{E}{\beta} & \frac{1}{\beta} \end{bmatrix} \begin{bmatrix} x_t \\ \pi_{H,t} \end{bmatrix} + \mathbf{\Psi Z}_t + \mathbf{C}, \tag{A.1}$$

where A, B, E, and $\mathbf{Z}_t$ are defined the same as in Case 1 for indeterminacy. The characteristic equation is

$$\mu^2 - \left(A + \frac{1}{\beta}\right)\mu + \frac{A - EB}{\beta} = 0.$$

For bifurcation to exist, the following conditions must be satisfied:

$$D = \left(A + \frac{1}{\beta}\right)^2 - 4\frac{A - EB}{\beta} < 0,$$

$$|\mu_{1,2}| = \sqrt{\theta^2 + \omega^2} = \sqrt{\mu_1 \mu_2} = \sqrt{\frac{A - EB}{\beta}} = 1.$$

This result follows.

2. Case 2

We again rewrite the system in 2×2 form as Eq. (A.1), but with A, B, E, and $\mathbf{Z}_t$ defined as in Case 2 for indeterminacy. The characteristic equation and the bifurcation condition equations are the same as in Case 1, but with the different settings of A, B, E, and $\mathbf{Z}_t$.

This result follows.

3. Case 3

We rewrite the system in 2×2 form as Eq. (A.2), but with A, B, E, F and $\mathbf{Z}_t$ defined as in Case 3 for indeterminacy. The system in 2×2 form

$$\begin{bmatrix} E_t(x_{t+1}) \\ E_t(\pi_{H,t+1}) \end{bmatrix} = \begin{bmatrix} \frac{A}{F} & -\frac{B}{F} \\ -\frac{E}{\beta} & \frac{1}{\beta} \end{bmatrix} \begin{bmatrix} x_t \\ \pi_{H,t} \end{bmatrix} + \Psi \mathbf{Z}_t + \mathbf{C} \tag{A.2}$$

is The characteristic equation is

$$\mu^2 - \left(\frac{A}{F} + \frac{1}{\beta}\right)\mu + \frac{A - EB}{F\beta} = 0.$$

For bifurcation to exist, the following conditions must be satisfied.

$$D = \left(\frac{A}{F} + \frac{1}{\beta}\right)^2 - 4\frac{A - EB}{F\beta} < 0,$$

$$\left|\mu_{1,2}\right| = \sqrt{\theta^2 + \omega^2} = \sqrt{\mu_1 \mu_2} = \sqrt{\frac{A - EB}{F\beta}} = 1.$$

This result follows.

4. Case 4

We again rewrite the system in 2×2 form as Eqs. (A.2), but with A, B, E, F and $\mathbf{Z}_t$ defined the same as in Case 4 for indeterminacy. The characteristic equation and the bifurcation condition equations are the same as in Case 3, but with different settings of A, B, E, F and $\mathbf{Z}_t$.

This result follows.

References

Airaudo, M., & Zanna, L.-F. (2012). Interest Rate rules, endogenous cycles, and chaotic dynamics in open economies. *Journal of Economic Dynamic & Control, 36*, 1566–1584.

Barnett, W. A., & Chen, G. (2015). Bifurcation of macroeconometric models and robustness of dynamical inferences. *Foundations and Trends in Econometrics, 8*(1–2), 1–144.

Barnett, W. A., & Duzhak, E. A. (2008). Non-robust dynamic inferences from macroeconometric models: Bifurcation stratification of confidence regions. *Physica A, 387*, 3817–3825.

Barnett, W. A., & Duzhak, E. A. (2010). Empirical assessment of bifurcation regions within new Keynesian models. *Economic Theory, 45*, 99–128.

Barnett, W. A., & Duzhak, E. A. (2014). Structural stability of the generalized Taylor rule. *Macroeconomic Dynamics*, (forthcoming).

Barnett, W. A., & Eryilmaz, U. (2013). Hopf Bifurcation in the Clarida, Gali, and Gertler model. *Economic Modelling, 31*, 401–404.

Barnett, W. A., & Eryilmaz, U. (2014). An analytical and numerical search for bifurcations in open economy new Keynesian models. *Macroeconomic Dynamics*, 1–22.

Benhabib, J., & Farmer, R. E. A. (1999). Indeterminacy and sunspots in macroeconomics. In J. Taylor & M. Woodford (Eds.), *Handbook of macroeconomics* (Vol. 1, Part A, Chapter 6, pp. 387–448).

Benhabib, J., Schmitt-Grohé, S., & Uribe, M. (2001). Monetary policy and multiple equilibria. *American Economic Review, 91*(1), 167–186.

Beyer, A., & Farmer, R. E. A. (2004). *On the indeterminacy of New-Keynesian economics*. European Central Bank Working Paper No. 323.

Beyer, A., & Farmer, R. E. A. (2006). *A method to generate structural impulse-responses for measuring the effects of shocks in structural macro models*. European Central Bank Working Paper No. 586.

Bullard, J., & Schaling, E. (2006). *Monetary policy, determinacy, and learnability in the open economy*. European Central Bank Working Paper No. 611.

Calvo, G. A. (1983). Staggered prices in a utility-maximizing framework. *Journal of Monetary Economics, 12*, 383–396.

Chatelain, J.-B., & Ralf, K. (2018a). *Imperfect credibility versus no credibility of optimal monetary policy*. PSE Working papers n° 2018-39.

Chatelain, J.-B., & Ralf, K. (2018b). *The indeterminacy of determinacy with fiscal, macro-prudential or Taylor rules*. https://ssrn.com/abstract=3239610 or http://dx.doi.org/10.2139/ssrn.3239610.

Cochrane, J. H. (2011). Determinacy and identification with Taylor rules. *Journal of Political Economy, 119*(3), 565–615.

Farhi, E., & Werning, I. (2014). Dilemma not Trilemma? Capital controls and exchange rate with volatile capital flows. *IMF Economics Review, 62*, 569–605.
Farhi, E., & Werning, I. (2012). *Dealing with the Trilemma: Optimal capital controls with fixed exchange rates*. NBER Working Paper No. 18199.
Farmer, R. E. A., Khramov, V., & Nicolò, G. (2015). Solving and estimation indeterminate DSGE models. *Journal of Economic Dynamic and Control, 54*, 17–36.
Fleming, J. M. (1962). *Domestic financial policies under fixed and floating exchange rates*. IMF Staff Papers (Vol. 9, pp. 369–379). Reprinted in Cooper, R. N. (Ed.). (1969). *International finance*. New York: Penguin Books.
Franke, R. (1992). Stable, unstable, and persistent cyclical behavior in a Keynes-Wicksell monetary growth model. *Oxford Economic Papers, New Series, 44*(2), 242–256.
Galí, J., & Monacelli, T. (2005). Monetary policy and exchange rate volatility in a small open economy. *Review of Economic Studies, 72*, 707–734.
Gandolfo, G. (2010). *Economic dynamics*, 4th ed. Springer.
Hu, J. (2018). *Essays in open macroeconomic dynamics*. ProQuest Dissertations & Theses Global, Order No. 10808068.
Korinek, A. (2011). *The new economics of capital controls imposed for prudential reasons*. IMF Working Paper, WP/11/298.
Korinek, A. (2014). *Regulating capital flows to emerging markets: An externality view*. Johns Hopkins University and NBER, working paper.
Kuznetsov, Y. A. (2013). A tutorial for MatcontM GUI
Lubik, T. A., & Schorfheide, F. (2003). Computing sunspot equilibria in linear rational expectations models. *Journal of Economic Dynamics and Control, 28*(2), 273–285.
Lubik, T. A., & Schorfheide, F. (2004). Testing for indeterminacy: An application to U.S. monetary policy. *American Economic Review, 94*(1), 190–217.
Lubik, T. A., & Schorfheide, F. (2005). A Bayesian look at the new open economy macroeconomics. *NBER Macroeconomics Annual, 20*, 313–366.
Lubik, T. A., & Marzo, M. (2007). An inventory of simple monetary policy rules in a new Keynesian macroeconomic model. *International Review of Economics and Finance, 16*, 15–36.
Magud, N. E., Reinhart, C. M., & Vesperoni, E. R. (2012). *Capital inflows, exchange rate flexibility, and credit booms*. IMF Working Paper, WP/12/41.
Mundell, R. A. (1963). Capital mobility and stabilization policy under fixed and flexible exchange rates. *Canadian Journal of Economic and Political Science, 29*(4), 475–485. Reprinted in Mundell, R. A. (1968). *International economics*. New York: Macmillan.
Ostry, J. D., Ghosh, A. R., Chamon, M., & Qureshi, M. S. (2012). Tools for managing financial-stability risks from capital inflows. *Journal of International Economics, 88*, 407–421.
Sims, C. A. (2002). Solving linear rational expectations models. *Computational Economics, 20*(1), 1–20.
Woodford, M. (1986). Stationary sunspot equilibria in a finance constrained economy. *Journal of Economic Theory, 40*, 128–137.
Woodford, M. (1989). Imperfect financial intermediation and complex dynamics. In W. A. Barnett, J. Geweke & K. Shell (Eds.), *Economic complexity: Chaos, sunspots, bubbles and nonlinearity* (Chap. 13, pp. 309–334). Cambridge, UK: Cambridge U. Press.
Zheng, T., & Guo, H. (2013). Estimating a small open economy DSGE model with indeterminacy: Evidence from China. *Economic Modelling, 31*, 642–652.

A Multi-agent Methodology to Assess the Effectiveness of Systemic Risk-Adjusted Capital Requirements

Andrea Gurgone and Giulia Iori

Abstract We propose a multi-agent approach to compare the effectiveness of macroprudential capital requirements, where banks are embedded in an artificial macroeconomy. Capital requirements are derived from alternative systemic risk metrics that reflect both the vulnerability and impact of financial institutions. Our objective is to explore how systemic risk measures could be translated into capital requirements and test them in a comprehensive framework. Based on our counterfactual scenarios, we find that macroprudential capital requirements derived from vulnerability measures of systemic risk can improve financial stability without jeopardizing output and credit supply. Moreover, macroprudential regulation applied to systemic important banks might be counterproductive for systemic groups of banks.

1 Introduction

The concept of *systemic risk* (SR) is relatively recent in economic and financial literature. The first appearance in scientific articles dates back to the early 90s, even if citations reveal that most of these contributions have been revived after 2008 when the term regained strength with the crisis. ECB (2009, p. 134) provides a general definition: "*it refers to the risk that financial instability becomes so widespread that it impairs the functioning of a financial system to the point where economic growth and welfare suffer materially.*" The European Systemic Risk Board (ESRB) was established by the EU on 16 December 2009, based on the recommendation of the "*de Larosière report*" of bringing the European Union forward. The ESRB has a macroprudential mandate whose objective is to prevent and mitigate systemic risk in the EU. The recommendation of ESRB has shaped the conduct of macroprudential

A. Gurgone (✉)
Economics Department, Bamberg University, Bamberg, Germany
e-mail: andrea.gurgone@uni-bamberg.de

G. Iori
Department of Economics, City, University of London, London, UK
e-mail: G.Iori@city.ac.uk

H. Dawid and J. Arifovic (eds.), *Dynamic Analysis in Complex Economic Environments*, Dynamic Modeling and Econometrics in Economics and Finance 26,
https://doi.org/10.1007/978-3-030-52970-3_8

policies in EU countries and provided guidance for its implementation through a set of macroprudential policy tools (ESRB 2014a, b). Within this framework, the systemic risk buffer (SRB) is designed to prevent and mitigate structural systemic risks of a long-term, non-cyclical nature that are not covered by the Capital Requirements, including excessive leverage. The SRB is an additional capital requirement imposed on credit institutions, proportional to their total risk exposure, to cover unexpected losses and keep themselves solvent in a crisis. The introduction of a capital buffer applies to all systemically important institutions, at both the global (G-SIIs) and national (O-SIIs) levels. While for some instruments authorities have recommended prescriptive measures (such as the credit-to-gdp gap for the countercyclical capital buffer), considerable differences across countries exist regarding the level, range, and calculation basis of the SRB. There is no maximum limit for the SRB, but authorization from the European Commission is required for buffer rates higher than 3%. Caps on the SRB have been under the spotlight as often perceived as being too low to mitigate the risk some institutions pose to the financial system. Furthermore, SRBs are hard to implement, *inter alia* because they need to be computed from a reliable measure of systemic risk: it is, however, unclear which metric performs better and under what circumstances. The task is more intricate given that systemic events are observed infrequently, as a banking crisis is observed on average every 35 years for OECD countries (Danielsson et al. 2018).

In this article, we propose a methodology to explore the effectiveness of capital surcharges implemented in the form of a systemic risk buffer derived from different systemic risk measures. Banks are required to maintain a level of common equity tier 1 adequate to meet a systemic risk-weighted share of their assets. By assuming that banks adopt different capital rules within a multi-agent macroeconomic model, we quantify the impact of such policies in a stress test scenario-based analysis. Many techniques have been proposed so far to measure systemic risk, but there is no consensus among scholars on which is most appropriate. We consider two alternative classes, namely, *market-based* and *network* approaches. Each one can measure systemic risk in terms of both vulnerability and impact. Vulnerability focuses on the effect of a systemic event on the capital of a given bank, while impact captures the losses produced by the distress of one, or few, institutions on the rest of the financial system.

We conduct counterfactual policy experiments in an agent-based model (ABM) of the economy based on Gurgone et al. (2018). The original model is expanded to allow banks to employ systemic risk measures to determine their capital requirements.[1] In the first set of experiments, we assume that capital requirements are set on the basis of vulnerability metrics, so that fragile banks are required to hold more equity capital than sound banks. However, this might not be satisfactory, as it does not operate on the systemic impact of banks. Hence, in the second set of experiments, capital requirements depend on the impact of banks on the system, or the extent of externalities they produce in case of default.

[1]Note that we do not consider in our model the full range of capital buffers typically used by macroprudential authorities, e.g. countercyclical capital buffers, liquidity buffer ratio, etc.

We find that systemic-capital requirements based on vulnerability can stabilize the economy. Having them in place is preferable to a standard rule that determines regulatory equity as a fixed fraction of assets. On the other hand, systemic-capital requirements based on impact may lead to suboptimal outcomes and produce detrimental effects on financial stability. This is relevant when systemic risk is not concentrated in a few superspreaders but is diluted in groups of banks with similar behaviour and exposures to risk. Moreover, both market and network policies turn out to be procyclical. They also differ in some aspects: the formers exhibit a regime switch during the first period of a crisis, while the latters can better capture the evolution of systemic risk but are highly correlated with the exposures to equity ratio prevailing in the financial system.

This paper is the first attempt to: (i) compare systemic risk measures recently proposed in the literature from both the perspectives of the vulnerability of single institutions to system-wide shocks and the individual impacts of institution distress on the financial system overall; (ii) suggest how to incorporate heterogeneous systemic risk metrics into banks' capital requirements; (iii) analyse the impact of the SRB macroprudential tool by means of simulated data generated by a multi-agents model, rather than empirically observed data that, given the rare occurrence of systemic crisis, are scant. Our simulated economy produces data on returns on equities of banks and at the same time includes a network structure of interlocked balance sheets, and thus it allows for a double comparison.

The usage of an ABM allows us to apply both network- and market-based techniques to measure systemic risk. Financial networks between banks and firms and within the interbank sector arise endogenously as a consequence of interaction in ABMs. This feature can be employed to run network-based algorithms as DebtRank. This would not be feasible in an aggregate macroeconomic model. Moreover, working with a model rather than a dataset permits to design how to make comparisons and explore counterfactual scenarios that generate artificial data.

The paper is organized as follows: Sect. 2 presents the related literature. Section 3 describes the modelling framework, distress dynamics, systemic risk measures, and macroprudential policies. Section 4 goes through the results of the simulations and policy experiments. Conclusions are in Sect. 5.

2 Related Literature

Our paper contributes to a vast, post-crisis, literature that focusses on empirical testing and comparison of systemic risk methodologies. The most common measures of systemic risk used in the literature are Marginal Expected Shortfall (MES), defined as the expected daily percentage decrease in the equity value of a financial institution when the aggregate stock market declines by at least 2% on a single day; Long Run Marginal Expected Shortfall (LRMES) defined as the expected equity loss, over a given time horizon, conditional on a sufficiently extreme phenomenon (such as a hypothetical 40% market index decline over a 6-month period); SRISK introduced by

Acharya et al. (2012) and Brownlees and Engle (2016) which measures the expected capital shortfall, or the capital a firm is expected to have, conditional on a prolonged market decline (SRISK can be expressed in terms of LRMES). The sum of SRISK across all firms provides the total systemic risk of the system and can be thought of as the capital required by the system in the case of a bailout; CoVaR Adrian and Brunnermeier (2016) and Chun et al. (2012) which is defined as the risk (VaR) of the financial system conditional on an institution being in distress, i.e. at its own VaR level; Delta conditional value at risk ($\Delta CoVaR$) which measures the risk materializing at the system level if an institution is in distress relative to a situation where the same institution is at its median; Codependence risk (Co-Risk) (Giudici and Parisi 2018) the change in the survival probability of an institution when potential contagion deriving from all other institutions is included; Lower Tail Dependence (LTD) introduced by Zhou (2010) is estimated from the joint probability return distributions of individual financial institutions and the industry index, and aims to measure the probability of a simultaneous extreme, lower tail event in the financial sector as a whole and the equity values of individual financial institutions. A large part of the empirical literature has focussed on empirical testing and comparison of alternative systemic risk methodologies by means of econometric methods. Benoit et al. (2013) provide a theoretical and empirical comparison of three market-based measures of systemic risk, namely MES, SRISK, and $\Delta CoVaR$. They find that there is no measure able to fully account for multiple aspects of systemic risk, but SRISK is better than $\Delta CoVaR$ for describing both the too-big-to-fail and too-interconnected-to-fail dimensions. This may be possible because SRISK is a combination of market and balance sheet metrics and as such not purely a market-based measure given the inclusion of leverage. Kleinow et al. (2017) empirically compare four widespread measures of systemic risk, namely MES, Co-Risk, $\Delta CoVaR$, and LTD using data on US financial institutions. Their estimates point out that the four metrics are not consistent with each other over time; hence, it is not possible to fully rely on a single measure. Rodríguez-Moreno and Peña (2013) consider six measures of systemic risk using data from stock, credit, and derivative markets. They quantitatively evaluate such metrics through a "horse race", exploiting a sample composed of the biggest European and US banks. Their results favour systemic risk measures based on simple indicators obtained from credit derivatives and interbank rates, rather than more complex metrics whose performance is not as satisfactory. Similarly, Pankoke (2014) opposes sophisticated to simple measures of systemic risk and concludes that simple measures have more explanatory power. Overall these papers find that different systemic risk measures focus on different characteristics of systemic risk and do not appear to capture its complex multidimensional nature, resulting in different rankings. Nucera et al. (2016) and Giglio et al. (2016) both apply principal component analysis to a range of systemic risk measures in the attempt to capture the multiple aspects of systemic risk. A useful discussion on the difficulty in finding a measure that can capture all aspects of systemic risk can be found in Hansen (2013).

Other studies assume that the regulator is disposed to tolerate a systemic-wide risk level and aims to reach the most parsimonious feasible capitalization at the aggregate level. Such an objective is formally translated into a constrained optimization problem, whose solution includes both the unique level of capital in the banking system and its distribution across banks. Tarashev et al. (2010) find that if capital surcharges are set in order to equalize individual contributions to systemic risk, then a lower level of aggregate capital is needed to reach the system-wide risk objective. Webber and Willison (2011) find that optimal systemic-capital requirements increase in balance sheet size and in the value of interbank obligations. However, they are also found to be strongly procyclical.

Another set of contributions presents network approaches to quantify systemic risk. Battiston et al. (2016) propose a network-based stress test building on the DebtRank algorithm. The framework is flexible enough to account for impact and vulnerability of banks, as well as to decompose the transmission of financial distress in various rounds of contagion and to estimate the distribution of losses. They perform a stress test on a panel of European banks. The outcome indicates the importance of including contagion effects (or indirect effects) in future stress tests of the financial system, so as not to underestimate systemic risk. Alter et al. (2014) study a reallocation mechanism of capital in a model of interbank contagion. They compare systemic risk mitigation approaches based on risk portfolio models with reallocation rules based on network centrality metrics and show that allocation rules based on centrality measures outperform credit risk measures. Gauthier et al. (2012) compare capital allocation rules derived from five different measures of systemic risk by means of a network-based model of interbank relations applied to a dataset including the six greatest banks of Canada. They also employ an iterative optimization process to solve the optimal allocation of capital surcharges that minimizes total risk, while keeping constant the total amount of capital to be kept aside. The adopted framework leads to a reduction of the probability of systemic crises of about 25%; however, results are sensitive to including derivatives and cross-shareholdings in the data. Poledna et al. (2017) propose to introduce a tax on individual transactions that may lead to an increase in systemic risk. The amount of the tax is determined by the marginal contribution of each transaction to systemic risk, as quantified by the DebtRank methodology. This approach reduces the probability of a large-scale cascading event by re-shaping the topology of the interbank networks. While the tax deters banks from borrowing from systemically important institutions, it does not alter the efficiency of the financial network, measured by the overall volume of interbank loans. The scheme is implemented in a macro-financial agent-based model, and the authors show that capital surcharges for G-SIBs could reduce systemic risk, but they would have to be substantially larger than those specified in the current Basel III proposal in order to have a measurable impact.

Finally, our paper provides a contribution to the literature that estimates macroprudential capital requirements using systemic risk measures. Brownlees and Engle (2016) and Acharya et al. (2012) have estimated the capital shortfall of an institution given a shock in the system. Gauthier et al. (2012) compare five approaches to assigning systemic-capital requirements to individual Canadian banks based on each bank's contribution to systemic risk, while van Oordt (2018) applies market-based measures to calculate the countercyclical capital buffer.

3 The Model

3.1 Macroeconomic Model

The macroeconomy is based on an amended version of the agent-based model (ABM) in Gurgone et al. (2018). The economy is composed of several types of agents: households, firms, banks, a government, a central bank, and a special agency. The (discrete) numbers of households, firms and banks are N^H, N^F, and N^B, respectively. Interactions take place in different markets: firms and households meet on markets for goods and for labour, while firms borrow from banks on the credit market and banks exchange liquidity on the interbank market. The CB buys government-issued bills on the bond market. The role of the government is to make transfer payments to the household sector. The governmental budget is balanced, namely the transfers are funded by taxes while the level of the public debt is maintained at a steady level. The CB generates liquidity by buying government bills and providing advances to those banks that require them; it furthermore holds banks' reserve deposits in its reserve account. Households work and buy consumption goods by spending their disposable income.[2] It is made up of wage and asset incomes after taxes and transfers. In the labour market, households are represented by unions in their wage negotiations with firms, while on the capital market, they own firms and banks, receiving a share of profits as part of their asset income. Firms borrow from banks in order to pay their wage bills in advance, hire workers, produce and sell their output on the goods market. The banking sector provides credit to firms, subject to regulatory constraints. In each period, every bank tries to anticipate its liquidity needs and accesses the interbank market as a lender or a borrower. If a bank is short of liquidity, it seeks an advance from the CB.

The special agency was not present in Gurgone et al. (2018). It has been introduced as a convenient way to model the secondary market for loans. It acts as a liquidator when banks default or when banks exceed the regulatory constraint and thus must deleverage. The assets in its portfolio are then put on the market and can be purchased by those banks that have a positive credit supply. Further details about the working of the special agency are described in the section below.

3.2 Distress Dynamics

Banks and firms default if their equity turns negative. Distress propagates through defaults in the credit and interbank markets and banks' deposits. The transmission begins when firms cannot repay loans due to a negative outcome in the goods market. Shocks propagate from firms to banks, within the interbank market, and from banks

[2]The reference model (Gurgone et al. 2018) does not include households' borrowing since it is mainly focused on credit to firms and on the interbank market.

to firms.[3] The process is illustrated in Fig. 1 and terminates only when there are no new losses. The balance sheets of firms and banks are illustrated in Table 1.

Liquidation of assets The contagion dynamic is enhanced by the forced liquidation of assets sold by defaulted banks in order to repay creditors. The role of liquidator is operated by a special agency that buys the assets of bank i at price p:

$$p_\tau = p_{\tau-1}\left(1 - \frac{\Delta q_{i,\tau}}{q_t}\frac{1}{\epsilon}\right) \quad (1)$$

where $\Delta q_{i,\tau}$ is the quantity of loans that bank i needs to liquidate,[4] ϵ is the asset price elasticity, and q_t is the total quantity of loans in period t. Banks that need liquidity enter the market in a random order represented by the subscript τ; we assume that at the end of each period of the simulation, the initial asset price is set again at $p_0 = 1$. The assets purchased by the agency are then put on sale before the credit market opens (lending to firms). Banks with positive net worth and complying with the regulatory leverage rate can buy them at their net present value.

Recovery rates The effective loss on a generic asset A_{ij} owed by j to i is $A_{ij}(0)(1 - \varphi_{ij}(t))$, where φ is the recovery rate. Each of j's creditors can recover $\varphi_{ij} = \frac{\mathcal{A}_j}{\mathcal{L}_j}$, i.e. the ratio of borrower's assets ($\mathcal{A}$) to liabilities ($\mathcal{L}$). However, the nominal value of illiquid assets is not immediately convertible in cash and must be first liquidated to compensate creditors. We denote the liquidation value of the assets of bank j with $\mathcal{A}^{liq}_{j,t}$, with $\mathcal{A}^{liq}_{j,t} \leq \mathcal{A}_{j,t}$. The actual recovery rate can be written as

$$\varphi_{ij} \equiv \frac{\mathcal{A}^{liq}_j}{\mathcal{L}_j}$$

Furthermore, we assume that there is a pecking order of creditors, so that they are not equal from the viewpoint of bankruptcy law: the most guaranteed is the central bank, then depositors and, finally banks with interbank loans. For instance, those creditors who claim interbank loans towards the defaulted bank j recover the part of

---

[3]If the net worth of a bank is negative, it defaults on its liabilities including the deposits of firms and households. A deposit guarantee scheme is not implemented.

[4]Banks first determine their liquidity need, then compute the fair value of their portfolio loan by loan. Next, they determine Δq taking into account Eq. (1). Lastly, they choose which loans should be liquidated to reach their objective.

The loans for sale are evaluated at their fair market value by discounting cash flows:

$$L^{fv}_{ij} = \frac{L_{ij}(1 + Sr^f)(1 - \rho^f_j)}{\underline{r}^S}$$

where $L_{i,j}$ is the book value of the loan of bank i to firm j, S is the residual maturity, r^f is the interest rate on the loan, ρ^f is the default probability of firm j, and $\underline{r}$ is the risk-free rate.

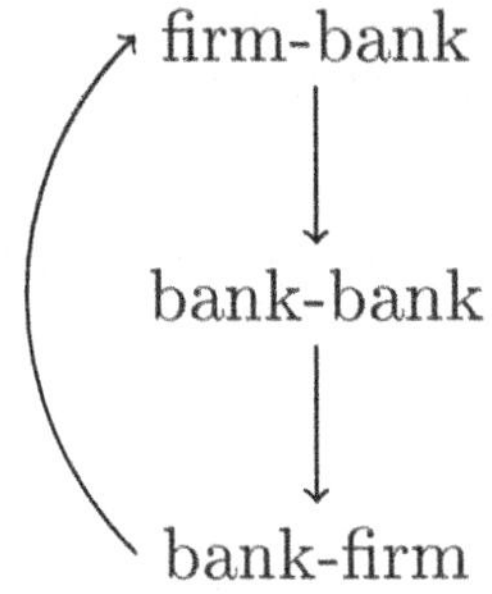

Fig. 1 Diagram of the distress transmission. The distress is transmitted through the credit market (firm–bank), the interbank market (bank–bank) and banks' deposits (bank–firms)

Table 1 Balance sheets of banks (left) and firms (right). Loans to firms (L), interbank lending (I^l), liquidity (R), deposits (Dep), interbank borrowing (I^b), advances from the central bank (Adv)

Banks	
Assets	Liabilities
L	Dep
I^l	I^b
R	Adv
	nw^B
Firms	
Assets	Liabilities
Dep	L
	nw^F

j's assets left after the other creditors have been compensated. The recovery rate on an interbank loan can be expressed as

$$\varphi_{ij} = \max\left(0, \frac{\mathcal{A}_j^{liq} - A_j^{CB} - D_j}{\mathcal{L}_j - A_j^{CB} - D_j}\right) \tag{2}$$

where A^{CB} are central bank's loans to j and D are j's deposits. It is worth noticing that *loss given default* is $LGD \equiv 1 - \varphi$, so that the net worth of creditor i updates as $nw_{i,t}^B = nw_{i,t-1}^B - LGD_{ij,t} I_{i,t}^l$.

3.3 Measuring Systemic Risk

Before defining *systemic risk-adjusted capital requirements* (SCR) we clarify how we measure SR. We do it along two dimensions, that is, vulnerability and impact. Vulnerability should be understood as the sensitivity of banks to a system-wide shock in terms of reduction in their equity. Conversely, impact measures the equity losses of the financial system originated from the distress of a chosen bank. Two distinct techniques are adopted to quantify vulnerability and impact, that is, network- and market-based approaches.

3.3.1 Network Approach: DebtRank

DebtRank is a systemic risk measure and an algorithm introduced by Battiston et al. (2012). It is conceived as a network measure inspired by feedback centrality with financial institutions representing nodes. Distress propagates recursively from one (or more) node to the other, potentially giving rise to more than one round of contagion. Despite DebtRank is a measure of impact in a strict sense, the algorithm can provide both measures of vulnerability and impact (see section "DebtRank" for details) that we denote, respectively, by DR^{vul} and DR^{imp}.

When accounting for vulnerability, we impose a common shock on the balance sheets of all banks and let that the algorithm computes how the equities were affected after the shock had died out. Individual vulnerabilities produced by the stress test are expressed in terms of the relative equity loss of each bank (h) at the last step of the algorithm ($\tau = T$) after we impose a shock on assets.

$$h_{i,T} \equiv \frac{nw_{i,T}^{B} - nw_{i,0}^{B}}{nw_{i,0}^{B}} \tag{3}$$

If impact is considered, we impose the default of one bank at a time and observe the effects on equities of all the other. The impact of each bank on the rest of the system is the overall loss into capital produced by the default of bank i. The value for each institution (g) is obtained by imposing its default at the beginning of the algorithm.

$$g_i = \sum_{j=1}^{N^b} h_{j,T}\, nw_{i,0}^{B} \tag{4}$$

Each measure is computed by repeating DebtRank 1000 times for vulnerability and 500 for impact.[5] In each run, recovery rates are randomly distributed between 0 and 1. In the end, the value of SR indexes is determined by an expected shortfall, that is, by computing the average over the observations exceeding the 99th percentile. Finally, the items on the balance sheets of firms and banks that are the input of the algorithm are entered as weighted averages over the last 30 periods. This avoids excessive time volatility of SR measures which would occur if DebtRank were computed with period-by-period inputs. Further details and the calibration procedure are detailed in sections "Calibration of DebtRank" and "DebtRank".

3.3.2 Market-Based Approach: LRMES and ΔCoVaR

Long Run Marginal Shortfall or $LRMES$ (Brownlees and Engle 2012) describes the expected loss of equity conditional on a prolonged market decline. The last represents

[5]The number of repetitions is lower in DR-imp to contain its computational time: by imposing the default bank-by-bank we end up with $500 \times N^B$ runs of DebtRank for each period in the simulation.

a systemic event which is defined as a drop of 40% of the market index over a period of 6 months. Considering this, we interpret $LRMES$ as a measure of vulnerability. Following Acharya et al. (2012), $LRMES$ is computed as an approximated function of Marginal Expected Shortfall (MES)

$$LRMES_{i,t} = 1 - \exp\{-18MES^{Sys}_{i,t+h|t}\} \tag{5}$$

where $MES^{Sys}_{i,t+h|t} = E_t\left(r_{i,t+h|t}|r < \Omega\right)$ is the tail expectation of the firm equity returns conditional on a systemic event, which happens when i's equity returns r from $t-h$ to t are less than a threshold value Ω. Further details can be found in section "SRISK". Banks compute their $LRMES$ based on the last 200 observations starting from 50 periods prior to the external shock. The required information is individual and market monthly returns. The first is computed as returns on equity (ROE) of bank i that correspond to the relative change in i's net worth during each step of the simulation.[6] The same logic is applied to obtain market returns, which are weighted by the net worth of each bank. Being $LRMES$ a function of the individual and market cross-correlation, $LRMES$ accounts somehow the interconnectedness of banks in the financial system.

Another well-known measure of systemic risk is $\Delta CoVaR$, which quantifies the systemic distress conditional to the distress of a specific financial firm, namely it accounts for the impact of a bank on the financial system.

CoVaR is implicitly defined as the VaR of the financial system (sys) conditional on an event $C(r_{i,t})$ of institution i:

$$Pr\left[r_{sys,t} \leq CoVaR^{sys|C(r_i)} \mid C(r_{i,t})\right] = \alpha \tag{6}$$

where r represents ROE and the conditioning event $C(r_i)$ corresponds to a loss of i equal or above to its Var^i_α level.

$\Delta CoVaR$ is a statistical measure of tail dependency between market returns and individual returns, which is able to capture co-movements of variables in the tails and account for both spillovers and common exposures. $\Delta CoVaR$ is the part of systemic risk that can be attributed to i: it measures the change in value at risk of the financial system at α level when the institution i shifts from its normal state (measured with losses equal to its median Var) to a distressed state (losses greater or equal to its Var).

$$\Delta CoVaR^{sys|i}_\alpha = CoVaR^{sys|r_i=VaR_{i,\alpha}}_\alpha - CoVaR^{sys|r_i=VaR_{i,0.5}}_\alpha \tag{7}$$

A flaw of $\Delta CoVaR$ is its (at best) contemporaneity with systemic risk: it fails to capture the build-up of risk over time and suffers from procyclicality. Furthermore, contemporaneous measures lead to the "*volatility paradox*" (Brunnermeier and Sannikov 2014), inducing banks to increase the leverage target when contemporaneously measured volatility is low. A workaround would be to substitute contemporaneous

[6] We account the final value of the net worth before a bank is recapitalized; otherwise, returns would be upward biased by shareholders' capital.

with a forward-looking version of $\Delta CoVaR$ (Adrian and Brunnermeier 2016, p. 1725). The latter is obtained by projecting on the regressors of $\Delta CoVaR$ their estimated coefficients, where the independent variables include individual banks' characteristics and macro-state variables. Nevertheless, our model lacks the wide range of variables that can be employed in empirical works, and as a result our measure of forward $\Delta CoVaR$ turns out to be strongly proportional to the VaR of banks, thus failing to capture the build-up of systemic risk.

3.4 Adjusted Capital Requirements

In the benchmark case, i.e. without employing any SR measures, banks comply with standard regulatory capital requirements. The net worth must be greater or equal than a fraction $\frac{1}{\lambda} = 4.5\%$ of their risk-weighted assets (RWA).[7]

$$nw_{i,t}^{B} \geq \frac{1}{\lambda} RWA_{i,t} \tag{8}$$

Differently, Systemic Risk-Adjusted Capital Requirements (SCR) are derived from measures of SR. These metrics are then mapped into a coefficient that can be interpreted as weighting the total assets by systemic risk.[8] In other words, banks must hold a minimum net worth equal to a fraction of their assets given by the risk-weighted coefficient ψ.

$$nw_{i,t}^{B} \geq \psi_{i,t} \mathcal{A}_{i,t} \tag{9}$$

where $\psi_{i,t} \equiv \frac{\frac{1}{\lambda}}{1-(1-\frac{1}{\lambda})sr_{i,t}}$ and sr is a generic SR index.[9]

If a $sr = 0$, then $\psi = \frac{1}{\lambda}$ and a bank must have a capital greater or equal than a standard regulatory threshold. When $sr = 1$, then $\psi = 1$ and capital requirements are as strict as possible, so that equity should equal assets, $nw^{B} = \mathcal{A}$.

Banks manage their balance sheet to meet capital requirements by setting their lending to firms and banks (which is limited upward by (8) or (9)) and passively raising new capital by the cumulation of profits.

Equation (9) can be obtained starting from the approach of Acharya et al. (2012) and setting the expected capital shortfall (CS) equal to zero.[10] CS is the capital

---

[7] We assign a weight $\omega_1 = 100\%$ to loans to firms and $\omega_2 = 30\%$ to interbank lending. Liquidity is assumed to be riskless; hence, its weight is $\omega_3 = 0$. Risk-weighted assets of bank i can be expressed as $RWA_{it} = \omega_1 L_{it}^{F} + \omega_2 I_{it}^{l} + \omega_3 R_{it} = L_{it}^{F} + \omega_2 I_{it}^{l}$.

[8] We do not define an objective in terms of macroprudential policy, but each bank is subject to capital requirements as a function of its measured systemic risk.

[9] SR metrics (sr) are normalized in the interval $[0, 1]$.

[10] We consider the nominal value of equity rather than its market value to accommodate the characteristics of the macroeconomic model. If the market values are considered, CS corresponds to $SRISK$.

needed to restore capital adequacy ratio to the value set by the regulator: it is the difference between minimum regulatory capital expressed as a fraction $\frac{1}{\lambda}$ of assets and the value of equity in case of a crisis. Following Acharya et al. (2012), to obtain (10) we assume that debt and liquidity are unchanged in case of a systemic crisis, hence $E_t\left[\mathcal{L}_{i,t+\tau}|\, crisis_{t+\tau}\right] = \mathcal{L}_{i,t}$.

$$\begin{aligned} CS_{i,t+\tau|t} &= E_t\left[\frac{1}{\lambda}\mathcal{A}_{i,t+\tau} - nw^B_{i,t+\tau}|\, crisis_{t+\tau}\right] \\ &= E_t\left[\frac{1}{\lambda}\mathcal{L}_{i,t+\tau}|\, crisis_{t+\tau}\right] - E_t\left[\left(1-\frac{1}{\lambda}\right)nw^B_{i,t+\tau}|\, crisis_{t+\tau}\right] \\ &= \frac{1}{\lambda}\mathcal{L}_{i,t+\tau} - E_t\left[\left(1-\frac{1}{\lambda}\right)nw^B_{i,t+\tau}|\, crisis_{t+\tau}\right] \end{aligned} \tag{10}$$

In other words, (9) determines the minimum level of capital that a bank should hold in order that its expected capital shortfall conditional to a systemic event equals zero.

3.4.1 Vulnerability Adjusted Capital Requirements

Adjusted capital requirement based on vulnerability are obtained under the assumption that the conditional value of net worth is determined by a vulnerability measure:

$$E_t\left[nw^B_{i,t+\tau}|\, crisis_{t+\tau}\right] = (1 - vul^j_{i,t})nw^B_{i,t} \tag{11}$$

where $j = \{LRMES,\ DR^{vul}\}$. Capital requirements for bank i are then obtained in (12) by imposing $CS = 0$, so that it should always maintain a capital buffer great enough to avoid recapitalization during periods of distress.

$$nw^B_{i,t} \geq \frac{\frac{1}{\lambda}}{1-(1-\frac{1}{\lambda})LRMES_{i,t}}\mathcal{A}_{i,t} \tag{12}$$

3.4.2 Impact-Adjusted Capital Requirements

We adopt a top-down approach to ensure consistency with the previous rule. Otherwise stated, capital requirements are determined to zero expected capital shortfall, which is computed top-down proportionally to the impact of each agent. Adjusted capital requirements are defined by deriving the equity values that each bank must satisfy to offset the aggregate capital shortage. The idea is that banks contribute to the aggregate CS in proportion to their systemic impact. To this end, we rewrite CS in aggregate terms as the sum of the individual capital shortages. To keep internal consistency and to avoid aggregation issues we also assume that the individual capital shortages values are computed with the same procedure in Sect. 3.4.1 (respectively, by $LRMES$ and DR^{vul}).

Each bank should contribute to the expected capital shortage in proportion to its systemic importance. We follow the approach in Gauthier et al. (2012), but rather than determining the equity capital that should be reallocated to bank i from the total capitalization of the system, the left-hand side of (13) states the extra amount of CET1 capital as a fraction of the aggregate CS. This means that the additional capital required for each bank is

$$nw^{+}_{i,t} = \frac{imp^{j}_{i,t}}{\sum_{i=1}^{N^b} imp^{j}_{i,t}} \sum_{i=1}^{N^b} CS_{i,t+\tau|t} \tag{13}$$

where $j = \{\Delta CoVaR,\ DR^{imp}\}$.

$$imp_{i,t} = \begin{cases} \frac{\Delta CoVaR^{sys|i}_{t}}{CoVaR^{sys|r_i=VaR_{i,\alpha}}} & if\ j = \Delta CoVaR \\ \frac{DR^{imp}_{t,i}}{\sum_i nw^{B}_{i,t}+\sum_k nw^{F}_{k,t}} & if\ j = DR^{imp} \end{cases}$$

Hence, the target level of capital for bank i is given by the minimum regulatory level of capital plus the additional capital,

$$nw^{tag}_{i,t} = \frac{1}{\lambda}\mathcal{A}_{i,t} + nw^{+}_{i,t} \tag{14}$$

We can write adjusted capital requirement in the same form of (12).

$$nw^{tag}_{i,t} \geq \frac{\frac{1}{\lambda}}{1-(1-\frac{1}{\lambda})\zeta_i}\mathcal{A}_{i,t} \tag{15}$$

with $\zeta_i = \frac{nw^{+}_{i,t}}{(1-\frac{1}{\lambda})(\frac{1}{\lambda}\mathcal{A}_{i,t}+nw^{+}_{i,t})}$.

4 Results

This section presents the results of simulations and policy experiments. We compare the benchmark scenario, where all banks are subject to the same fixed regulatory ratio of RWA, to those where SCRs are derived from measures of vulnerability or impact of financial institutions, as described in Sect. 3.4. We run a set of 100 Monte Carlo simulations for each scenario under different seeds of the pseudo-random number generator.

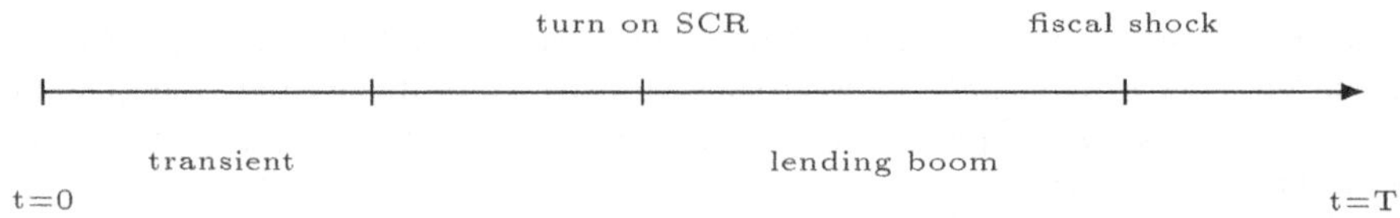

Fig. 2 Timeline of the simulations

The simulations are based on a variant of the macroeconomic model in Gurgone et al. (2018) in which the wage-price dynamics is dampened by setting the wage rate constant, so that business-cycle fluctuations are eliminated and the model converges to a quasi-steady-state after a transient period. Moreover, we supply to the lack of fluctuations of credit by simulating a lending boom, that is, increasing the credit demand of firms in the periods before an external shock. It increases the exposures of banks and contributes to the build-up of the risk. Note that despite the elimination of business cycles, the baseline dynamics produces a series of defaults and bankruptcies of firms and banks. These have a very lower extent before the shock than after. The presence of such financial distress helps systemic risk measures to better capture the characteristics of banks. We turn on systemic-capital requirements at the beginning of the lending boom, so that macroprudential regulation becomes binding. We finally impose a fiscal shock of 10 periods that consists in a progressive reduction of transfers to the household sector. The purpose of the shock is to reduce the disposable income of households, which in turn affects consumption and firms' profits. Firms with negative equity then cannot repay their debts to the banking sector, and thus the initial shock triggers a series of losses through the interlocked balance sheets of agents. At the time of the shock, transfers are reduced by 20% and then by an additional 1% per period with respect to the period before the shock. Figure 2 summarizes what happens during each simulation.

The behaviour of SR measures over time is shown in Sect. 4.1. Autocorrelation is analysed in Sect. 4.2, and the effects of SCR are presented in Sect. 4.3.

4.1 SR Measures Over Time

In the next lines, we conduct a qualitative analysis of the behaviour of SR metrics over the shock. For this purpose SCRs are not active; rather, the results show the evolution of risk measures to understand their differences.

Figure 3 shows a comprehensive representation of the time pattern of SR metrics. The evolution of impact and vulnerability presents a parallel trend within market- and network-based measures. This reflects their construction: for market-based measures, conditional volatility of returns, which is estimated by a TGARCH model, is employed to construct $LRMES$ and $\Delta CoVaR$ (see Appendix). Market-based measures exhibit a regime switch during the initial phase of the shock, persistently shifting from lower to higher values and exceeding the network-based counterparts

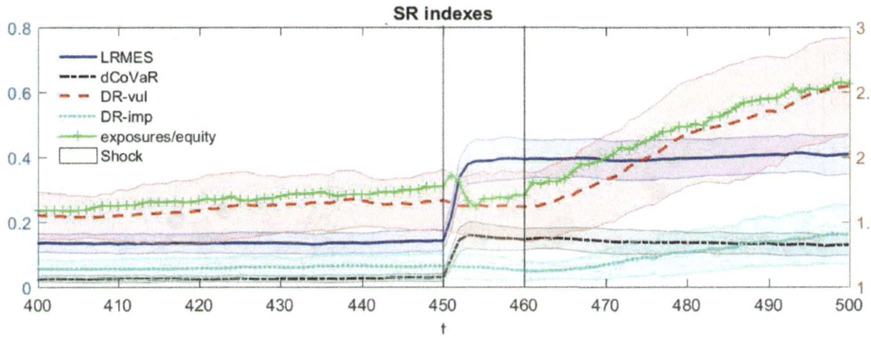

Fig. 3 Time average and standard deviation of SR indexes

in the immediate aftermath of the crisis. On the other side, network-based measures reflect the leverage dynamics of banks' balance sheets, that is, the increase in credit demand prior to the shock and reduced equity after it. Their trend is approximated by the exposure to equity ratio of the economy.

Some observations can be inferred with the help of Fig. 3. First, all measures are procyclical. SR metrics are not able to anticipate the forthcoming crisis before the shock; hence, they cannot be used as early warning signals. This could partially depend on the exogenous nature of the shock imposed in our simplified framework, whereas alternatively a crisis might arise from the endogenous developments in the system. Moreover, measured systemic risk adjusts only after the beginning of the shock. Of course, this descends from the construction of our variables. In particular, the behaviour of network-based measures is sensitive to the length of the time windows considered to input the past values of balance sheet items, as there is a trade-off between shortening the windows and the volatility of network-based indexes. Second, network metrics have a smooth adjustment process, while market indicators show an "off-on" pattern. Therefore, the first should be preferred because it would be more desirable to conduct macroprudential policy smoothly than suddenly imposing restrictions on banks' capital requirements, even more so if the change cannot be easily anticipated. Third, a stylized behaviour of SR indexes can be characterized despite the time series are computed for the average. Vulnerability and impact of network-based measures are higher before the shock and lower after compared to market-based. This is clear looking at $t \in [450, 460]$ in Fig. 3, or at the individual breakdown represented in Fig. 4. The latter is also useful to point out the limits of our approach: capital requirements are determined separately for vulnerability and impact. Instead, they could be considered jointly, because otherwise low-vulnerability but high-impact banks would be penalized by capital requirements built on impact and vice versa.

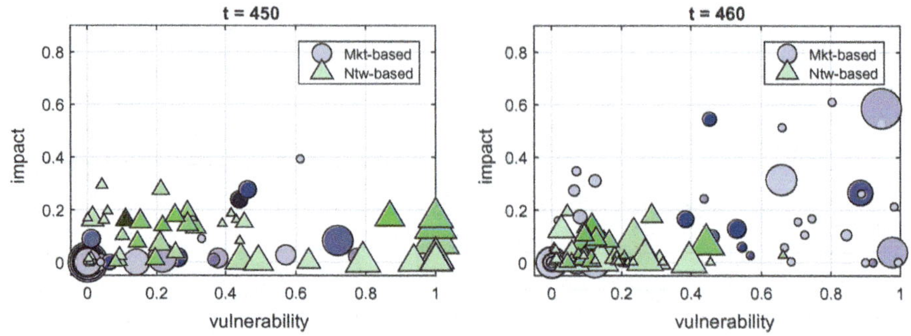

Fig. 4 Market- and network-based SR measures over the shock. Sizes represent assets, colour is total equity, with dark (light) corresponding to the highest (lowest) value

4.2 Rank Correlation

Banks behaviour could be consistent with the objective of macroprudential regulation if such policies are based on stable values of the variables measuring SR. Therefore, a desirable property of SR measures is stability over time, that is, the ranking of systemically important financial institutions has no high variability and identifies the same set of subjects in a given time span absent substantial changes in the financial environment. We study the autocorrelation of SR metrics to understand how stable they are.

We consider a measure of rank correlation, Kendall's tau (τ^k), which is a non-parametric measure of the correlation between pairs of ranked variables with values between -1 and 1. If two variables are perfectly correlated $\tau^k = 1$, otherwise if there is no correlation at all $\tau^k = 0$.

$$\tau^k = \frac{C - D}{n(n-1)/2}$$

where C and D are the total number of concordant and discordant pairs and n is the sample size. Moreover, when two variables are statistically independent, a z statistics built on τ^k tends to distribute as a standard normal; therefore, it can be tested the null of no correlation versus the alternative of non-zero correlation. We compute τ^k between the rank of SR measures of each bank and its lagged values. Results are reported in Table 2. When market-based measures are considered, the ranking has a high and persistent autocorrelation. On the other hand, network-based measures are autocorrelated to a lower extent. The difference could be explained in terms of construction, as market-based measures are obtained from conditional variances (or conditional VaR), which in turn are estimated through a TGARCH model, where conditional variances are assumed to follow an autoregressive process (see section "SRISK"). Conversely, network-based measures do not assume any

Table 2 Kendall's correlation coefficients. Reported statistics refers to the average of τ^k computed for each bank. Permutations p-values are reported in parenthesis, that is, $p = 1 - \frac{\#successes}{\#experiments}$, where $successes$ is the number of times when $p < 0.01$

SR metric	Lags			
	+1	+5	+10	+15
LRMES	0.834	0.616	0.465	0.340
	(0.000)	(0.000)	(0.020)	(0.160)
$\Delta CoVaR$	0.807	0.618	0.457	0.334
	(0.000)	(0.000)	(0.020)	(0.140)
DR-vul	0.784	0.598	0.423	0.286
	(0.000)	(0.000)	(0.080)	(0.300)
DR-imp	0.875	0.681	0.493	0.343
	(0.000)	(0.000)	(0.040)	(0.180)

dependence on past values, rather they depend on the network structure and credit–debt relationships, so that the outcome of the DebtRank algorithm might change as a result of small variations in the configuration of the network.

4.3 Policy Experiments

We present here the results of the policy experiments obtained under the four scenarios with active SCR and the benchmark case. Results for each policy are elaborated out of 100 Monte Carlo runs. We cleaned the data to remove the outliers by trimming the observations above (below) the third (first) quartile plus (minus) 3 times the interquartile range.

We start by focusing on the macroeconomic performance under SRC in Figs. 5 and 6. Within the vulnerability-based rules, market and network measures have approximately the same behaviour for credit and output. They produce dynamics similar to the benchmark prior to the shock and yield a deterioration after. Most certainly the procyclicality of SR measures leads to a restriction in the credit supplied to the real economy after $t = 450$ and consequently to the lowered output. Looking at impact-based measures, they do worse than the benchmark even before the shock. In this case, *DR-imp* produces a slightly better performance than $\Delta CoVaR$ on average, but in both cases with remarkable volatility. We have hypothesized several reasons at the roots of the pattern for impact-based rules. The first is that the map from SR measures to SCR might non-achieve an optimal distribution of capital: for instance, demanding to hold extra capital in proportion to impact only does not account for the actual default probabilities, so that financially sound banks might be required to further increase their capital. This results in hindering the lending activity. Another reason is that the model dynamics might be defective of the emergence of high-impact systemic important banks: impact-based capital requirements would work better if

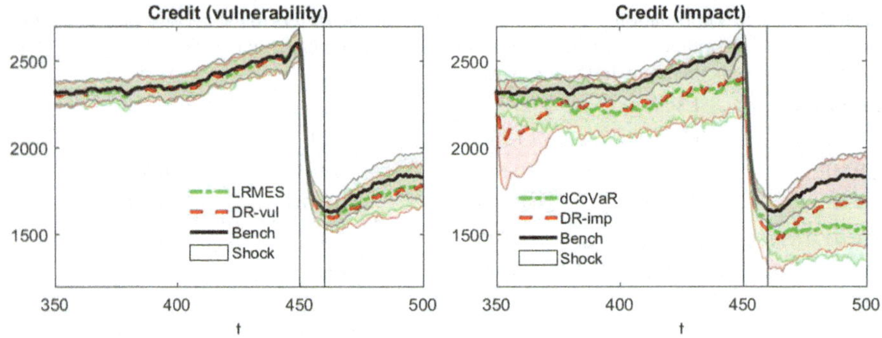

Fig. 5 Time average and standard deviation of credit. (*Left*) Measures of vulnerability. (*Right*) Measures of impact

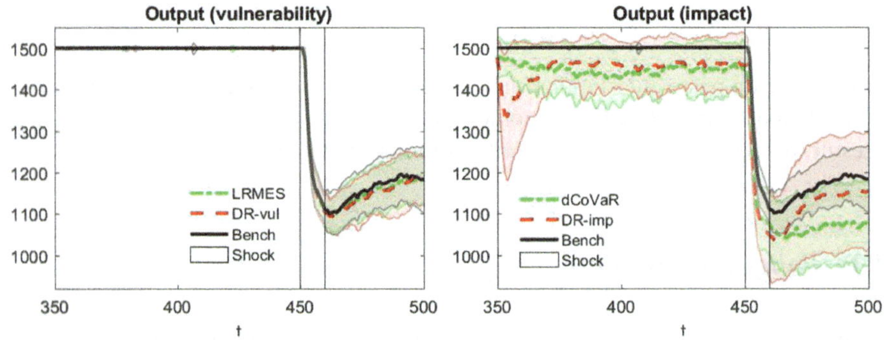

Fig. 6 Time average and standard deviation of output. (*Left*) Measures of vulnerability. (*Right*) Measures of impact

applied to few highly systemic banks than to many banks that are systemic to a lower degree. SCR would allow isolating the first group without impairing too much lending. The second group of banks, which seems prevailing in our simulations, can be defined as "*systemic as a herd*" (Adrian and Brunnermeier 2016) because its members show moderate values of impact but present similar behaviours and exposures to risk. Thus, SCR can be counterproductive because they limit the lending capacity of a part of the financial system. Following this line of thinking, SCR based on impact lead to an increase in the variance of the distribution of equity (Fig. 9), as they affect the profitability of some banks but allow others for high exposures. As a result, under impact-SCR the capitalization of the financial system as a whole is worse-off (Fig. 8). In light of this, the probability of contagion is greater under rules based on impact, as in Fig. 7. The greater financial fragility of the banking sector makes it more likely that at least 10% of all banks (or firms) are simultaneously in bankruptcy. Conversely, vulnerability-based policies decrease the likelihood of contagion.

Figures 9 and 10 illustrate the feasibility of SCR. Demanded capital requirements cannot be attained by a part of those banks with lower values of equity, which are

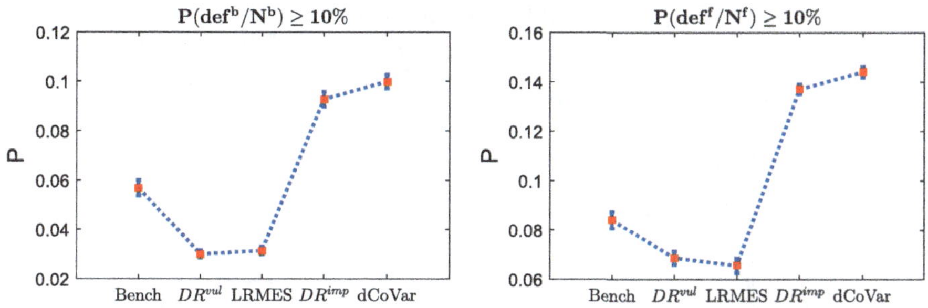

Fig. 7 Probability that at least 10% of all banks *(left)* or firms *(right)* are in bankruptcy

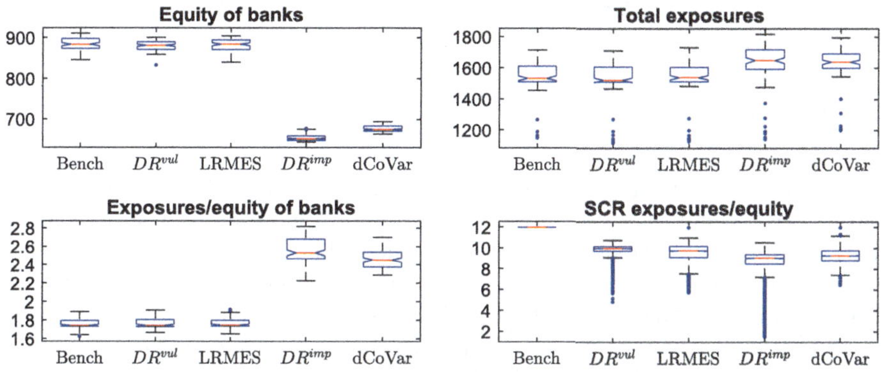

Fig. 8 (*Top-left*) Aggregate equity of banks. (*Top-right*) Aggregate exposures of banks. (*Bottom-left*) Aggregate exposures/equity ratio of banks. (*Bottom-right*) Maximum aggregate exposures/equity ratio allowed under SCR

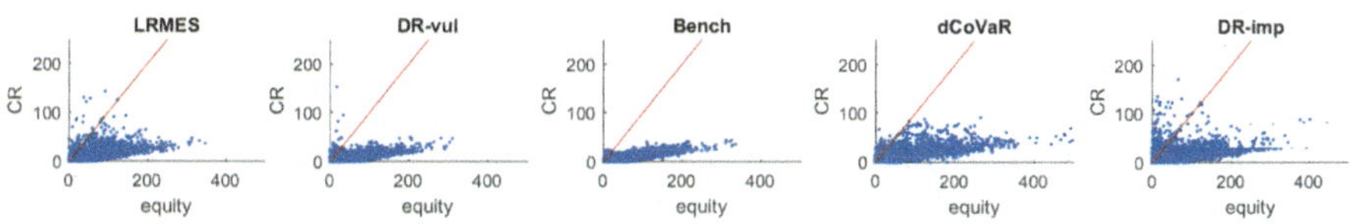

Fig. 9 Capital Requirements (CR) versus equity of banks under different rules. The x- and y-axes represent, respectively, the left- and right-hand sides of Eq. (9)

represented above the 45° line in Fig. 9. This is more marked in the case of *DR-imp*. However, the scatter plots do not provide an adequate representation of density, so we compare the feasibility of SCR by means of a CDF in Fig. 10. About 92% of observations have a $CR/equity < 1$ in the benchmark case, around 88% under $LRMES$ and $DR\text{-}vul$, 79% under $\Delta CoVar$ and 76% under *DR-imp*. So, it is less likely that banks comply with rules based on impact compared to rules based on vulnerability.

We conclude that SCR built on vulnerability minimize the probability of a contagion and achieve a macroeconomic performance comparable to the benchmark case

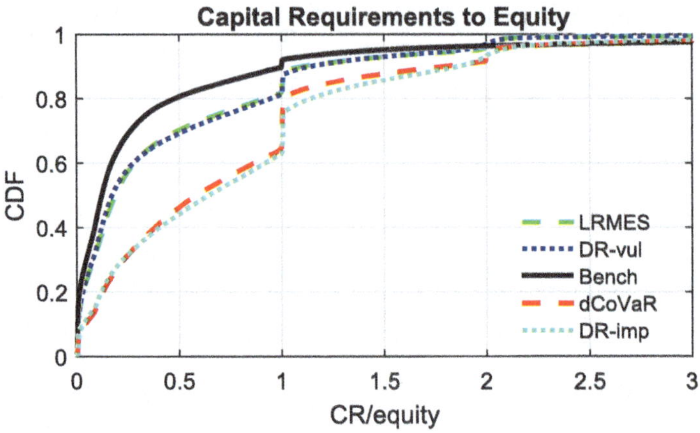

Fig. 10 CDF of capital requirements to equity ratio

before the shock. Due to their procyclicality, all SCR bring about credit rationing and reduced output after the crisis. This calls for a relaxation of macroprudential rules after the shock. Despite capital requirements based on impact should reduce the damages caused by systemic banks, we do not observe an improvement with respect to the benchmark case. This could descend from the construction of impact-based SCR, or because the model dynamics rarely let arise "*too-big-to-fail*" or "*too-interconnected-to-fail*" banks, but rather financial institutions are "*systemic as a herd*". Hence, imposing restrictions based on impact affects the lending ability of a number of banks and in turn their net worth, reducing financial soundness and paving the way to instability.

5 Concluding Remarks

We presented a methodology to compare a set of lender-targeted macroprudential rules in which banks are subject to capital requirements built on systemic risk measures. Four metrics are considered: the first set is composed of two market-based measures (*LRMES* and $\Delta CoVaR$), while the second one includes network-based measures (*DR-vul* and *DR-imp*). Each set contains a metric for vulnerability, which states how much a financial institution is systemically vulnerable to an adverse shock, and one measure for impact, which accounts for the effects of the distress of single banks on the financial system. Capital requirements are derived in Sect. 3 so that required capital is proportional to each bank's expected (or induced) capital shortage, which in turn depends on the SR measures. The construction and the calibration of SCRs aim to ease the comparison within each set of market- and network-based measures.

In Sect. 4 we employ an agent-based macroeconomic model to analyse and compare qualitatively and quantitatively macroprudential rules. We find that all systemic risk measures are procyclical to some degree. While market-based metrics display a regime switch after the exogenous shock, the network-based ones smoothly adjust with the exposures to equity ratio of the banking sector. This suggests that they lack predictive power and thus cannot be used to build early warning systems. In particular, the performance of market-based measures is sensitive to the past values of return-to-equity of financial institutions. If the time series of each bank is volatile enough, the SR measures can capture the dependency between individual and market changes and reflect the true systemic risk. Otherwise, systemic risk is underestimated. On the other hand, network-based measures exhibit a trade-off between procyclicality and variance: the longer the time windows of past input balance sheet data, the lower the variance. Using alternative calibrations, network-based measures could capture better the build-up of systemic risk but the ranking of individual institutions would show lower autocorrelation. This translates into less reliable measures and more difficult implementation of macroprudential policy.

Another key result is that SCRs based on vulnerability can reduce contagion and to achieve a macroeconomic performance similar to the benchmark case before the aggregate shock. After it, they should be relaxed to accommodate credit demand from firms. Despite procyclicality, the map from vulnerability to capital requirement provides an improvement with respect to the benchmark case. This can be interpreted as evidence that the individual measured values reflect the actual vulnerability of banks in case of a systemic event.

Differently, SCRs based on impact cannot beat the benchmark. This result is specific to our model and has several interpretations: while SCRs based on vulnerability are derived assuming that banks must be recapitalized depending on their expected losses conditional to a systemic event, this is not true using a measure of impact. In this case, the capital requirement depends on the individual contribution to the expected aggregate shortfall, which is not directly connected to the equity of banks. Even though it is widely accepted that systemic banks can be identified and regulated conditional to the impact on the financial system, this logic does not work well in our framework. One explanation is that raising additional capital to comply with regulation is easier for banks with high equity than for small ones, being equal their impact. This puts small banks at a disadvantage by impairing their lending ability and creates a less equal equity distribution, and a lower aggregate capitalization of the banking system than in the other scenarios. Moreover, results suggest that macroprudential policy should treat differently "*too-big*" or "*too-interconnected-to-fail*" and "*systemic as a herd*" institutions. In the first case, the impact of one bank has critical effects on the financial system; hence, it is rational to impose capital surcharges. In the latter case—as emerges in our model—banks are part of a homogeneous group in terms of individual impacts, behaviour, and risk exposures. When hit by a common shock, the herd might produce systemic effects. However, imposing capital requirements based on individual impacts may not be efficient at the macroeconomic level because it affects lending of a relevant part of the financial system, reduces profits and equity, and makes the financial system more fragile.

This work can be extended in several ways. The regulation of systemic groups of banks, as opposite to SIFIs, can be studied in-depth; macroprudential rules could be built to combine indicators of both impact and vulnerability to derive SCRs; the analysis of systemic risk can be repeated in a model capable to generate endogenous crisis without any exogenous shocks; finally, the model can be feed with real data for an empirical comparison.

Appendix

Calibration of DebtRank

In general, our approach is similar to that adopted in Battiston et al. (2016), but we have adapted the algorithm to account for the structure of the underlying macro-model, as described in greater detail in section "DebtRank". Given that the macro-environment includes firms, we first impose the shock on firms' assets to compute the systemic vulnerability index DR^{vul}. Next, the induced distress transmits linearly to the assets of creditors (i.e. banks). This allows capturing the specific dynamics of the distress process.

Our calibration strategy aims to compare market- and network-based measures on a common ground. To do so, we apply to DebtRank the definition of systemic crisis employed in the SRISK framework. SRISK is computed by LRMES, which represents the expected equity loss of a bank in case of a systemic event. This is represented by a decline of market returns of 40% over the next 6 months. We run 100 Monte Carlo simulations of the macro-model, record the market ROE and the firms' losses to equity ratio. Then, we compute the change in market ROE over the past 180 periods (approximately 6 months). Finally, we construct a vector of the losses of firms to their equities in those periods where the ROE declined at least by −40%.

To compute vulnerabilities by DebtRank, we randomly sample from the vector of the empirical distribution of losses/equity at each repetition of the algorithm. Finally, we obtain DR^{vul} for each bank as an average of the realized values, after removing the $1st$ and the $99th$ percentiles (Fig. 11).

DebtRank

We employ a differential version of the DebtRank algorithm in order to provide a network measure of systemic risk. Differential DebtRank (Bardoscia et al. 2015) is a generalization of the original DebtRank (Battiston et al. 2012) which improves the latter by allowing agents to transmit distress more than once. Moreover, our formulation has similarities with Battiston et al. (2016), where it is assumed a sequential

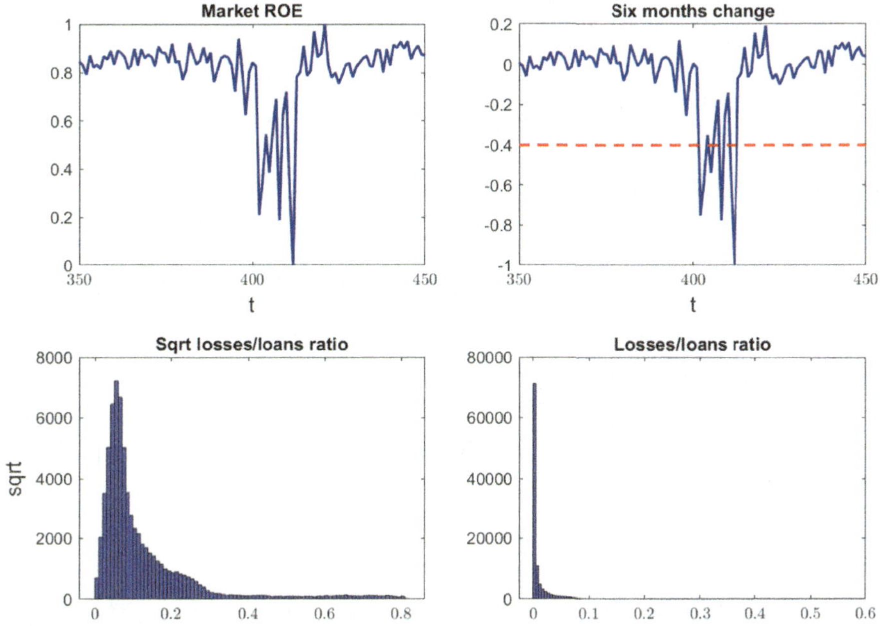

Fig. 11 (*Top-left*) rescaled market ROE from a random Monte Carlo run. (*Top-right*) 6-month chance of market ROE. The red dashed line represents the threshold of −40%. (*Bottom-left*) Histogram of the square root of the losses/loans ratio of firms, where values equal to zero are ignored. (*Bottom-right*) Histogram of the losses/loans ratio of firms

process of distress propagation. In our case, we first impose an external shock on firms' assets, and then we sequentially account for the propagation to the banking sector through insolvencies on loans, to the interbank network, and to firms' deposits.

The relative equity loss for banks (h) and firms (f) is defined as the change in their net worth (respectively, nw^B, and nw^F) from $\tau = 0$ to τ with respect to their initial net worth. In particular, the initial relative equity loss of firms happens at $\tau = 1$ due to an external shock on deposits:

$$h_i(\tau) = \min\left[\frac{nw_i^B(0) - nw_i^B(\tau)}{nw_i^B(0)}\right]$$
$$f_j(\tau) = \min\left[\frac{nw_j^F(0) - nw_j^F(\tau)}{nw_j^F(0)}\right]$$

The dynamics of the relative equity loss in firms and banks sectors is described by the sequence:

- Shock on deposits in the firms sector:

$$f_j(1) = \min\left[1,\ \frac{D_j^F(0) - D_j^F(1)}{nw_j^F(0)}\right] = \min\left[1,\ \frac{loss_j(1)}{nw_j^F(0)}\right]$$

- Banks' losses on firms' loans:

$$h_i(\tau+1) = \min\left[1,\ h_i(\tau) + \sum_{j\in J} \Lambda_{ij}^{fb}(1-\varphi_j^{loan})(p_j(\tau) - p_j(\tau-1))\right]$$

- Banks' losses on interbank loans:

$$h_i(\tau+1) = \min\left[1,\ h_i(\tau) + \sum_{k\in K} \Lambda_{ik}^{bb}(1-\varphi_k^{ib})(p_k(\tau) - p_k(\tau-1))\right]$$

- Firms' losses on deposits:

$$f_j(\tau+1) = \min\left[1,\ f_j(\tau) + \Lambda_{jk}^{fb}(1-\varphi_k^{dep})(p_k(\tau) - p_k(\tau-1))\right]$$

where p_j is the default probability of debtor j and φ^i, $i = \{loan, ib, dep\}$ is the recovery rate on loans, interbank loans, and deposits. Recovery rates on each kind of asset are randomly extracted from a vector of observations generated by the benchmark model.

For the sake of simplicity, we can define it as linear in f_j (h_k for banks), so that $p_j(\tau) = h(\tau)$.[11] Λ is the exposure matrix that represents credit/debt relationships in the firms–banks network. It is written as a block matrix, where Λ^{bb} refers to the interbank market, Λ^{bf} refers to deposits, Λ^{fb} refers to firm loans and Λ^{ff} is a matrix of zeros.

$$\Lambda = \begin{bmatrix} \Lambda^{bb} & \Lambda^{bf} \\ \Lambda^{fb} & \Lambda^{ff} \end{bmatrix}$$

[11] In a more realistic setting the default probability could be written as

$$p_j(\tau) = f_j(\tau)\exp(\alpha(h_j(\tau)) - 1)$$

where if $\alpha = 0$ it corresponds to the linear DebtRank, while if $\alpha \to \infty$ it is the Furfine algorithm (Bardoscia et al. 2016). Moreover, we can assume that deposits are not marked-to-market, but they respond to the Furfine algorithm; in other words, the distress propagates only in case of default of the debtor. For deposits, it might be reasonable to assume

$$p_j^D(\tau-1) = \begin{cases} 1 & \text{if } h_k(\tau-1) = 1 \\ 0 & \text{otherwise} \end{cases}.$$

The exposure matrix Λ represents potential losses over equity related to each asset at the beginning of the cycle, where each element has the value of assets at the numerator and the denominator is the net worth of the related creditor in our specification firms have no intra-sector links, hence $\Lambda^{ff} = 0$. In case there are $N^b = 2$ banks and $N^f = 3$ firms, the matrix Λ looks like

$$\Lambda = \begin{bmatrix} 0 & \frac{Ib_{12}}{nw_2^B} & \frac{D_{13}}{nw_1^F} & \frac{D_{12}}{nw_2^F} & \frac{D_{15}}{nw_3^F} \\ \frac{Ib_{21}}{nw_1^B} & 0 & \frac{D_{23}}{nw_1^F} & \frac{D_{24}}{nw_2^F} & \frac{D_{25}}{nw_3^F} \\ \frac{L_{31}^f}{nw_1^B} & \frac{L_{32}^f}{nw_2^B} & 0 & 0 & 0 \\ \frac{L_{41}^f}{nw_1^B} & \frac{L_{42}^f}{nw_2^B} & 0 & 0 & 0 \\ \frac{L_{51}^f}{nw_1^B} & \frac{L_{52}^f}{nw_2^B} & 0 & 0 & 0 \end{bmatrix}$$

SRISK

SRISK (Brownlees and Engle 2012) is a widespread measure of systemic risk based on the idea that the latter arises when the financial system as a whole is undercapitalized, leading to externalities for the real sector. To apply the measure to our model, we follow the approach of Brownlees and Engle (2012). The SRISK of a financial firm i is defined as the quantity of capital needed to re-capitalize a bank conditional to a systemic crisis

$$SRISK_{i,t} = \min\left[0,\ \frac{1}{\lambda}\mathcal{L}_i - \left(1 - \frac{1}{\lambda}\right) nw_{i,t}^B (1 - MES_{i,t+h|t}^{Sys})\right]$$

where $MES_{i,t+h|t}^{Sys} = E\left(r_{i,t+h|t} | r < \Omega\right)$ is the tail expectation of the firm equity returns conditional on a systemic event, which happens when i's equity returns r from $t - h$ to t are less than a threshold value Ω.

Acharya et al. (2012) propose to approximate MES^{Sys} with its *Long Run Marginal Expected Shortfall* (LRMES), defined as a

$$LRMES_{i,t} = 1 - \exp\{-18MES_{i,t}^{2\%}\}$$

LRMES represents the expected loss on equity value in case the market return drops by 40% over the next 6 months. Such approximation is obtained through extreme value theory, by means of the value of MES that would be if the daily market return drops by -2%.

The bivariate process driving firms' (r_i) and market (r_m) returns is

$$r_{m,t} = \sigma_{m,t}\epsilon_{m,t}$$
$$r_{i,t} = \sigma_{i,t}\rho_{i,t}\epsilon_{m,t} + \sigma_{i,t}\sqrt{1-\rho_{i,t}^2}\xi i, t$$
$$(\xi_{i,t}, \epsilon_{m,t}) \sim F$$

where $\sigma_{m,t}$ is the conditional standard deviation of market returns, $\sigma_{i,t}$ is the conditional standard deviation of firms' returns, $\rho_{i,t}$ is the conditional market/firm correlation and ϵ and ξ are i.i.d. shocks with unit variance and zero covariance.

$MES^{2\%}$ is expressed setting $\Omega = -2\%$:

$$MES_{i,t-1}^{\Omega} = \sigma_{i,t}\rho_{i,t}E_{t-1}\left(\epsilon_{m,t}|\epsilon_{m,t} < \frac{\Omega}{\sigma_{m,t}}\right) + \sigma_{it}\sqrt{1-\rho_{i,t}^2}E_{t-1}\left(\xi_{i,t}|\epsilon_{m,t} < \frac{\Omega}{\sigma_{m,t}}\right)$$

Conditional variances $\sigma_{m,t}^2$, $\sigma_{i,t}^2$ are modelled with a TGARCH model from the GARCH family (Rabemananjara and Zakoian 1993). Such specification captures the tendency of volatility to increase more when there are bad news:

$$\sigma_{m,t}^2 = \omega_m + \alpha_m r_{m,t-1}^2 + \gamma_m r_{m,t-1}^2 I_{m,t-1}^- + \beta_m \sigma_{m,t-1}^2$$
$$\sigma_{i,t}^2 = \omega_i + \alpha_i r_{i,t-1}^2 + \gamma_i r_{i,t-1}^2 I_{i,t-1}^- + \beta_i \sigma_{i,t-1}^2$$

$I_{m,t}^- = 1$ if $r_{m,t} < 0$ and $I_{i,t}^- = 1$ when $r_{i,t} < 0$, 0 otherwise.

Conditional correlation ρ is estimated by means of a symmetric DCC model (Engle 2002). Moreover, to obtain the MES it is necessary to estimate tail expectations. This is performed with a non-parametric kernel estimation method (see Brownlees and Engle 2012).

Open-source Matlab code is available, thanks to *Sylvain Benoit*, and *Gilbert Colletaz*, *Christophe Hurlin*, who developed it in Benoit et al. (2013).

ΔCoVaR

Following Adrian and Brunnermeier (2016) $\Delta CoVaR$ is estimated through a quantile regression (Koenker and Bassett Jr 1978) on the αth quantile, where r_{sys} and r_i are, respectively, market-wide returns on equity and bank i's returns. Quantile regression estimates the αth percentile of the distribution of the dependent variable given the regressors, rather than the mean of the distribution of the dependent variable as in standard OLS regressions. This allows comparing how different quantiles of the regress and are affected by the regressors; hence, it is suitable to analyse tail events. While Adrian and Brunnermeier (2016) employ an estimator based on an augmented regression, we further simplify the estimation of $\Delta CoVaR$ following the approach in Benoit et al. (2013), which is consistent with the original formulation.

First we regress individual returns on market returns:

$$r_{sys,t} = \gamma_1 + \gamma_2 r_{i,t} + \varepsilon_{\alpha,t}^{sys|i}$$

The estimated coefficients (denoted by $\widehat{\ }$) are employed to build CoVaR. The conditional VaR of bank i ($Var_{\alpha,t}^{i}$) is obtained from the quasi-maximum likelihood estimates of conditional variance generated by the same TGARCH model described above (see Benoit et al. 2013, p. 38).

$$CoVar_{\alpha,t}^{sys|i} = \widehat{\gamma_1} + \widehat{\gamma_2} Var_{\alpha,t}^{i}$$

Finally $\Delta CoVar$ is obtained from the difference between the αth and the median quantile of $CoVar$.

$$\Delta CoVar_{\alpha,t}^{sys|i} = CoVar_{\alpha,t}^{sys|i} - CoVar_{0.5,t}^{sys|i}$$
$$\Delta CoVar_{\alpha,t}^{sys|i} = \hat{\gamma}_2 \left(VaR_{\alpha,t}^{i} - VaR_{0.5,t}^{i} \right)$$

References

Acharya, V., Engle, R., & Richardson, M. (2012). Capital shortfall: A new approach to ranking and regulating systemic risks. *The American Economic Review*, *102*(3), 59–64.

Adrian, T., & Brunnermeier, M. K. (2016). Covar. *The American Economic Review*, *106*(7), 1705–1741.

Alter, A., Craig, B., & Raupach, P. (2014). Centrality-based capital allocations and bailout funds. *International Journal of Central Banking* (Forthcoming).

Bardoscia, M., Battiston, S., Caccioli, F., & Caldarelli, G. (2015). DebtRank: A microscopic foundation for shock propagation. *PloS ONE*, *10*(6), e0130406.

Bardoscia, M., Caccioli, F., Perotti, J. I., Vivaldo, G., & Caldarelli, G. (2016). Distress propagation in complex networks: The case of non-linear DebtRank. *PloS ONE*, *11*(10), e0163825.

Battiston, S., Caldarelli, G., D'Errico, M., & Gurciullo, S. (2016). Leveraging the network: A stress-test framework based on DebtRank. *Statistics & Risk Modeling*, *33*(3–4), 117–138.

Battiston, S., Puliga, M., Kaushik, R., Tasca, P., & Caldarelli, G. (2012). DebtRank: Too central to fail? Financial networks, the fed and systemic risk. *Scientific Reports*, *2*, 541.

Benoit, S., Colletaz, G., Hurlin, C., & Pérignon, C. (2013). *A theoretical and empirical comparison of systemic risk measures*. HEC Paris Research Paper No. FIN-2014-1030.

Brownlees, C., & Engle, R. F. (2016). SRISK: A conditional capital shortfall measure of systemic risk. *The Review of Financial Studies*, *30*(1), 48–79.

Brownlees, C. T., & Engle, R. (2012). Volatility, correlation and tails for systemic risk measurement. SSRN: 1611229.

Brunnermeier, M. K., & Sannikov, Y. (2014). A macroeconomic model with a financial sector. *The American Economic Review*, *104*(2), 379–421.

Chun, S. Y., Shapiro, A., & Uryasev, S. (2012). Conditional value-at-risk and average value-at-risk: Estimation and asymptotics. *Operations Research*, *60*(4), 739–756.

Danielsson, J., Valenzuela, M., & Zer, I. (2018). Learning from history: Volatility and financial crises. *The Review of Financial Studies*, *31*(7), 2774–2805.

ECB (2009). Financial stability review.

Engle, R. (2002). Dynamic conditional correlation: A simple class of multivariate generalized autoregressive conditional heteroskedasticity models. *Journal of Business & Economic Statistics, 20*(3), 339–350.

ESRB (2014a). *The ESRB handbook on operationalising macro-prudential policy in the banking sector.*

ESRB (2014b). *Flagship report on macro-prudential policy in the banking sector.*

Gauthier, C., Lehar, A., & Souissi, M. (2012). Macroprudential capital requirements and systemic risk. *Journal of Financial Intermediation, 21*(4), 594–618.

Giglio, S., Kelly, B., & Pruitt, S. (2016). Systemic risk and the macroeconomy: An empirical evaluation. *Journal of Financial Economics, 119*(3), 457–471.

Giudici, P., & Parisi, L. (2018). CoRisk: Credit risk contagion with correlation network models. *Risks, 6*(3), 95.

Gurgone, A., Iori, G., & Jafarey, S. (2018). The effects of interbank networks on efficiency and stability in a macroeconomic agent-based model. *Journal of Economic Dynamics and Control, 28*, 257–288.

Hansen, L. P. (2013). Challenges in identifying and measuring systemic risk. In *Risk topography: Systemic risk and macro modeling* (pp. 15–30). University of Chicago Press.

Kleinow, J., Moreira, F., Strobl, S., & Vähämaa, S. (2017). Measuring systemic risk: A comparison of alternative market-based approaches. *Finance Research Letters, 21*, 40–46.

Koenker, R., & Bassett Jr, G. (1978). Regression quantiles. *Econometrica: Journal of the Econometric Society*, 33–50.

Nucera, F., Schwaab, B., Koopman, S. J., & Lucas, A. (2016). The information in systemic risk rankings. *Journal of Empirical Finance, 38*, 461–475.

Pankoke, D. (2014). *Sophisticated vs. simple systemic risk measures*. Working Papers on Finance 1422, University of St. Gallen, School of Finance.

Poledna, S., Bochmann, O., & Thurner, S. (2017). Basel III capital surcharges for G-SIBs are far less effective in managing systemic risk in comparison to network-based, systemic risk-dependent financial transaction taxes. *Journal of Economic Dynamics and Control, 77*, 230–246.

Rabemananjara, R., & Zakoian, J.-M. (1993). Threshold arch models and asymmetries in volatility. *Journal of Applied Econometrics, 8*(1), 31–49.

Rodríguez-Moreno, M., & Peña, J. I. (2013). Systemic risk measures: The simpler the better? *Journal of Banking & Finance, 37*(6), 1817–1831.

Tarashev, N. A., Borio, C. E., & Tsatsaronis, K. (2010). *Attributing systemic risk to individual institutions*. BIS Working Papers, No. 308.

van Oordt, M. R. (2018). *Calibrating the magnitude of the countercyclical capital buffer using market-based stress tests*. Technical report, Bank of Canada Staff Working Paper.

Webber, L., & Willison, M. (2011). *Systemic capital requirements*. Bank of England Working Papers, No. 436.

Zhou, C. C. (2010). Are banks too big to fail? Measuring systemic importance of financial institutions. *International Journal of Central Banking, 6*(4), 205–250.

The Role of (De-)Centralized Wage Setting for Industry Dynamics and Economic Growth: An Agent-Based Analysis with the Eurace@Unibi Model

Herbert Dawid, Philipp Harting, and Michael Neugart

Abstract In this paper, we employ the agent-based macroeconomic Eurace@Unibi model to study the economic implications of different degrees of de-centralization in the wage setting. We think of de-centralization as wages being a weighted average of an economy-wide 'union wage' and a firm-specific component depending on the firm's productivity and the experienced tightness of the labor market. Starting from a baseline scenario, corresponding to a high degree of unionization, in which wages are fully centralized and indexed on economy-wide productivity gains and inflation, we investigate how an increasing level of de-centralization affects the dynamics of output, employment, inequality, and market concentration. Our findings suggest that stronger centralization of the wage-setting process induces lower wage inequality and stronger concentration on the consumption goods market. Furthermore, due to more physical investments, an economy with more centralized wage setting is characterized by higher productivity and faster economic growth.

Keywords Centralized wage bargaining · Collective agreement · De-unionization · Industry dynamics · Inequality · Growth

JEL Classification C63 · E24 · J50 · L16

This research has been supported by the European Unions Horizon 2020 grant No. 822781—Project GROWINPRO. The authors are grateful for helpful comments of an anonymous referee.

H. Dawid (✉)
Department of Business Administration and Economics, Center for Mathematical Economics, Bielefeld University, Bielefeld, Germany
e-mail: hdawid@wiwi.uni-bielefeld.de

P. Harting
Department of Business Administration and Economics, Bielefeld University, Bielefeld, Germany
e-mail: pharting@wiwi.uni-bielefeld.de

M. Neugart
Department of Law and Economics, Technische Universität Darmstadt, Darmstadt, Germany
e-mail: neugart@vwl.tu-darmstadt.de

H. Dawid and J. Arifovic (eds.), *Dynamic Analysis in Complex Economic Environments*, Dynamic Modeling and Econometrics in Economics and Finance 26,
https://doi.org/10.1007/978-3-030-52970-3_9

1 Introduction

One of the key challenges economic policymakers face is to foster economic growth while at the same time keeping the dynamics of (income) inequality in focus. Clearly, the evolution of income inequality is closely connected to the dynamics of wage distributions, and recent empirical work (e.g., Card et al. 2013; Barth et al. 2016) highlights that the increase in heterogeneity of wages across firms (respectively plants) is the most important factor driving increasing wage dispersion. Concurrently, the last decades have been characterized by a decline in the degree of unionization in many industrialized countries (see, e.g., Ebbinghaus and Visser 1999; Visser 2006; Firpo et al. 2018) and also institutional changes toward more de-centralized wage setting on the firm level in countries like Germany (Dustmann et al. 2014). The general narrative in this respect is that although these developments seem to contribute to an increase in wage inequality, they increase the firms' competitiveness and thereby foster (local) economic growth.

In this paper, we study the effect of a de-centralization of the wage setting both on economic growth and on the evolution of wage inequality in a dynamic macroeconomic model. The model captures the competition between firms, on both the labor and the consumption goods market as well as potential demand effects induced by different wage-setting regimes. Furthermore, productivity dynamics in our model are driven by endogenous technology choices of investing firms, such that we can study how the wage-setting regime influences investment and the speed of adoption of new technologies, and how these processes interact with the endogenously emerging dynamics of industry concentration.

Existing models comparing the implications of centralized versus de-centralized wage setting have to a large extent relied on models with static oligopoly-type product market interaction (Haucap and Wey 2004; Blomgren-Hansen 2012) or have completely abstracted from product market competition between firms (Moene and Wallerstein 1997; Vona and Zamparelli 2014). In an influential early contribution, Calmfors and Driffill (1988) provide an analysis of the effect of (de-)centralization of wage bargaining on employment, in a setting with several industries with perfect competition in each industry and output of the industries being partial substitutes on the product market. They assume that demand is fixed independent from the households wage income and establish that under certain conditions there is a hump-shaped (inverse hump-shaped) relationship between the degree of centralization of wage bargaining and the average wage level (employment).[1] With the exception of Moene and Wallerstein (1997) all the mentioned studies, take a static perspective without considering how different wage-setting regimes influence the firms' investment decisions and technology choices.[2] Moene and Wallerstein (1997), focusing entirely on the competition between firms on the labor market, show that in the

[1] See Driffill (2006) for a survey of the stream of literature building on this analysis.

[2] Several papers have studied from a theoretical perspective the implications of centralization of wage bargaining on firms' innovation incentives (e.g., Haucap and Wey 2004; Mukherjee and Pennings 2011; Basak and Mukherjee 2018); however, this stream of literature focuses on hold-up issues

absence of product market competition more centralized wage setting yields higher firm productivity but lower employment compared to de-centralized bargaining of wages.

Our perspective in this paper is that the dynamics of output and wage distributions are crucially driven by the interplay between technological change, evolution of industry structure, and the dynamics on the labor market. Hence, we aim to gain a better understanding of how different wage-setting regimes influence this interplay. In order to capture these effects, we carry out our analysis in the framework of the macroeconomic agent-based Eurace@Unibi model (see Dawid et al. 2019). This model, building on the original Eurace model (see Deissenberg et al. 2008), combines explicit representations of the dynamic competition between firms on the labor and product market in a closed macroeconomic setting with endogenous technology choices of firms and endogenous determination of demand. It has strong empirical micro-foundations for the agents' behavioral rules (Dawid et al. 2019) and has also been shown to be able to reproduce a large set of empirical stylized facts (e.g., Dawid et al. 2018b). The model has been used as a framework for policy analysis in different policy domains (see Dawid et al. 2018a; Deissenberg and van der Hoog 2011) and has proved useful in understanding implications of different degrees of labor market flexibility (Dawid et al. 2014) and dynamic mechanisms determining wage inequality (Dawid and Gemkow 2014; Dawid et al. 2018b). More generally, our analysis contributes to the growing literature on agent-based macroeconomics (see Dawid and Delli Gatti 2018), in which recently several papers have considered macroeconomic effects of the institutional setup in the labor market (Dosi et al. 2017, 2018; Caiani et al. 2019), and the literature on the agent-based analysis of labor market dynamics (see Neugart and Richiardi 2018).

The starting point of our analysis is an economy with a workforce with (ex-ante) uniform skills. There is a fully centralized wage setting, where workers have a uniform wage, labeled as union wage, which is updated over time taking into account inflation and average productivity growth in the economy. We then compare the dynamics emerging in such a setting with scenarios, in which at some given point in time the binding power of the centrally determined union wage is reduced and firms have the option to offer individual wages, which deviate from collectively agreed wages to job candidates. More precisely, we assume that wage offers made to applicants are a weighted average of the centralized wage and a firm-specific wage offer, which is determined according to a wage-setting rule that takes into account the expected productivity of the worker and the frequency with which the firm has been rationed on the labor market in the past.[3] The weight on the union wage then decreases during a transition phase till a certain long run degree of wage centralization is reached. We interpret this process as a reduced form representation of a de-unionization of the workforce or changes in the institutional setup of the

firms face when bargaining with labor unions after investment and, therefore, is quite distinct from our agenda in this paper.

[3]The rule determining the firm-specific wage component corresponds exactly to the wage-setting rule used in the standard version of the Eurace@Unibi model as documented in Dawid et al. (2019).

labor market, which allows for firm-specific agreements that deviate from outcomes of industry-wide bargaining. The long run weight the union wage has in the workers' individual wages captures how strong the degree of de-unionization, respectively, the flexibility in local firm-level wage agreements are. In our experiments, we vary this long run weight from a value of one, which corresponds to the benchmark of fully centralized wage setting throughout to a value of zero, which implies that in the long run wages are fully de-centralized and firm-specific.

We find that in the considered setting a centralized determination of wages does not only reduce wage and income inequality, but also induces faster growth in output and productivity in the economy, compared to scenarios with more de-centralized wage setting. The main driving force underlying these results is that under centralized wage-setting firms that already perform well profit from a uniform wage in terms of lower unit labor costs. These translate into lower prices they can charge compared to their competitors which increases their market share and spurs further investments. Hence, average productivity and output in the economy grow faster than with a de-centralized wage setting where individual market shares of firms are more volatile and investment behavior is spread among a larger fraction of firms and overall lower.

Generally speaking, in case of a more centralized wage formation the cost and price advantages of high-tech firms are directly driven by their productivity advantage. For a more de-centralized wage setting, the competitive advantage of high-tech firms arises through the competition on the labor market. Now, high-tech firms can offer relatively high wages without substantially impairing their unit costs.

Although these findings about the positive dynamic effects of wage centralization clearly should be seen in the context of the assumptions underlying our experiments, for example, the homogeneity of workers with respect to their general skills, our analysis highlights several channels through which the degree of centralization affects economic dynamics, which so far have not been recognized in the literature.

The paper is organized as follows. In Sect. 2, we give a brief description of the structure of the Eurace@Unibi model with particular focus on the wage-setting mechanism and the aspects that are different in this paper from the standard version of the model. The setup of our simulation experiment as well as the results of our analysis are discussed in Sect. 3. Concluding remarks are given in Sect. 4, and in the Appendix we provide the parameter setting underlying our analysis.

2 The Model

2.1 Overall Structure

In a nutshell, the Eurace@Unibi model describes an economy with an investment and a consumption goods sector, and a labor, a financial, and a credit market in a regional context. Capital good firms provide investment goods of different vintages and productivities. Consumption goods firms combine capital and labor of varying degrees of general and specific skills to produce a consumption good that households purchase. Households' saved income goes into the credit and financial markets through which it is channeled to firms financing the production of goods.

In this paper, we use a one-region setup of the Eurace@Unibi model to analyze the economic implications of different levels of wage centralization, where in the standard version of the model, the wage setting is fully de-centralized. More precisely, the wages of workers are determined at the firm level, on the one hand, by the expectation at the time of hiring the employer has about the level of specific skills of the worker, and, on the other hand, by a base wage variable. The base wage is driven by the (past) tightness of the labor market and determines the overall level of wages paid by a particular employer.

In order to address aspects of wage centralization, we extend the Eurace@Unibi model by modifying the wage-setting protocol of the labor market. In particular, we introduce a labor union that determines a collective wage proposal. This union wage is adjusted over time, on the one hand, in order to compensate for inflation and, on the other hand, to claim a share of the economy-wide productivity gains to the workers. The wage bargaining between firms and the union is modeled in reduced form by assuming that the actual wage that a firm has to pay is a linear combination of the centralized union wage and the firm-specific wage. The weight used in the linear combination is thereby an exogenous model parameter and reflects the power of the union in the wage negotiation. Since it also determines the degree of wage centralization, we will employ this parameter as the policy parameter in our analysis.

A complete description of the model is provided in Dawid et al. (2019). Due to space constraints, here no full treatment of the model is given. Rather, we describe only the main aspects of the model, which are crucial for the understanding of the mechanisms driving the policy results discussed below.[4]

Capital goods of different qualities are provided by capital goods producers with infinite supply. The technological frontier (i.e., the quality of the best currently available capital good) improves over time, where technological change is driven by a stochastic (innovation) process. Firms in the consumption goods sector use capital goods combined with labor input to produce consumption goods. The labor market is populated with workers that acquire specific skills on the job, which they need to fully exploit the technological advantages of the capital employed in the production process. Every time when consumption goods producers invest in new capital goods they decide which quality of capital goods to select, thereby determining the speed by which new technologies spread in the economy. Consumption goods are sold at a central market platform (called mall), where firms store and offer their products and consumers come to buy goods at posted prices.

Labor market interaction is described by a simple multi-round search-and-matching procedure where firms post vacancies, searching workers apply, firms make offers and workers accept/reject. Banks collect deposits from households and firms and give credits to firms. The interest that firms have to pay on the amount of their

---

[4]Note that the description of the model provided here is to a large extent identical to the ones given in Dawid et al. (2018b, c).

loan depends on the financial situation of the firm, and the amount of the loan might be restricted by the bank's liquidity and risk exposure. There is a financial market where shares of a single asset are traded, namely an index bond containing all firms in the economy. The allocation of dividends to households is, therefore, determined by the wealth of households in terms of their stock of index bonds. The dividend paid by each share at a certain point in time is given by the sum of the dividends currently paid by all firms. The central bank provides standing facilities for the banks at a given base rate, pays interest on banks' overnight deposits and might provide fiat money to the government. Finally, the government collects income and profit taxes at fixed rates and pays out social benefits to unemployed households.

Firms that are not able to pay the financial commitments declare illiquidity. Furthermore, if the firm has negative net worth at the end of the production cycle insolvency bankruptcy is declared. In both cases, it goes out of business, stops all productive activities, and all employees loose their jobs. The firm writes off a fraction of its debt with all banks with which it has a loan and stays idle for a certain period before it becomes active again.

The choice of the decision rules in the Eurace@Unibi model is based on a systematic attempt to incorporate rules that resemble empirically observable behavior documented in the relevant literature. Concerning households, this means, for example, that empirically identified saving rules are used. Furthermore, purchasing choices are described using models from the Marketing literature with strong empirical support. In particular, in several parts of the model, decision-makers are described by logit models. These models are well suited to capture decisions where individuals try to maximize some objective function which depends on some variables common to all decision-makers and are explicitly represented in the model, as well as on aspects that are idiosyncratic to each decision-maker and captured in the model by a stochastic term. With respect to firm behavior, we follow the 'Management Science Approach', which aims at implementing relatively simple decision rules that match standard procedures of real-world firms as described in the corresponding management literature. A more extensive discussion of the Management Science approach can be found in Dawid and Harting (2012).

Agent actions can be time-driven or event-based, where the former can follow either subjective or objective time schedules. Furthermore, the economic activities take place on a hierarchy of timescales: yearly, monthly, weekly, and daily activities all take place following calendar-time or subjective agent-time. Agents are activated asynchronously according to their subjective time schedules that are anchored on an individual activation day. These activation days are uniformly randomly distributed among the agents at the start of the simulation, but may change endogenously (e.g., when a household gets re-employed, its subjective month gets synchronized with the activation day of its employer due to wage payments). This modeling approach is supposed to capture the de-centralized and typically asynchronous nature of decision-making processes and activities of economic agents.

2.2 Agents, Markets, and Decisions

2.2.1 Output Decision and Production

Consumption goods producers need physical capital and labor for production. A firm i has a capital stock $K_{i,t}$ that is composed of different vintages v with $v = 1, \ldots, V_t$, where V_t denotes the number of available vintages a time t. The accumulation of physical capital by a consumption goods producer follows

$$K^v_{i,t+1} = (1 - \delta)K^v_{i,t} + I^v_{i,t}, \tag{1}$$

where δ is the depreciation rate and $I^v_{i,t} \geq 0$ is the gross investment in vintage v.

The production technology in the consumption goods sector is represented by a Leontief type production function with complementarities between the qualities of the different vintages of the capital good and the specific skill level of employees for using these vintages. Vintages are deployed for production in descending order by using the best vintage first. For each vintage, the effective productivity is determined by the minimum of its productivity and the average level of relevant specific skills of the workers. Accordingly, output for a consumption goods producer i at time t is given by

$$Q_{i,t} = \sum_{v=1}^{V_t} \min\left[K^v_{i,t}, \max\left[0, L_{i,t} - \sum_{k=v+1}^{V_t} K^k_{i,t}\right]\right] \cdot \min\left[A^v, B_{i,t}\right], \tag{2}$$

where $L_{i,t}$ is labor input, A^v is the productivity of vintage v and $B_{i,t}$ denotes the average-specific skill level in firms as explained in more detail in Sect. 2.2.3. The fact that the considered production function takes into account the vintage structure of the capital stock and that firms select among different available vintages enables us to capture the effect of workers' skills on the incentives of firms to invest into new technologies (see Sect. 2.2.4).

Once every month each firm determines the quantities to be produced and delivered to the mall. Actual demand for the product of a firm in a given month is stochastic (see below), and there are stock-out costs, because consumers intending to buy the product of a firm move on to buy from a different producer in case the firm's stock at the mall is empty. Therefore, the firm faces a production planning problem with stochastic demand and stock-out cost. The simplest standard heuristic used in the corresponding Operations Management literature prescribes to generate an estimation of the distribution of demand and then choose the planned stock level after delivery such that the (estimated) stock-out probability during the following month equals a given parameter value which is influenced by stock-out costs, inventory costs, and risk attitude of the firm (see, e.g., Silver et al. 1998). Firms in the Eurace@Unibi model follow this simple heuristic, thereby generating a target production quantity for the considered month. Based on the target production quantity, the firm determines the desired input quantities of physical capital and labor. Realizing this production plan might induce the need to buy new physical capital, hire new labor, or to obtain additional credit. The firm might be rationed on the labor and credit market, in which case it adjusts its production quantity downward.

2.2.2 Pricing Decision

Consumption goods producers set the price of their products once a year which is consistent with empirical observations (see, e.g., Fabiani et al. 2006). The pricing rule is inspired by the price setting described in Nagle et al. (2011, Chap. 6) a standard volume on strategic pricing in the Managerial literature. Firms seek for a profit-maximizing price taking into account the trade-off between price, sales, and costs.

To obtain an indication of the effect of price changes on sales, the consumption goods producers carry out *simulated purchase surveys* (see Nagle et al. 2011, p. 304). A representative sample of households is asked to compare a firm's product with the set of the currently available rival products for a range of prices. Households' answers are based on the same decision rules they use for their real purchasing decisions. Based on the resulting demand, estimations and cost considerations firms choose the price which maximizes their expected discounted profit stream over their planning horizons.

2.2.3 Adjustment of Specific Skills of Workers

The productivity of a worker h is determined by an endogenously increasing specific skill level $b_{h,t}$. It is assumed that during the hiring process the specific skills of job candidates cannot be observed by potential employers. They become observable during the production process. Workers increase the specific skills over time during production by a learning process. The speed of learning depends on the average quality of the technology $A_{i,t}$ used by employer i:

$$b_{h,t+1} = b_{h,t} + \chi^S \cdot \max[0, A_{i,t} - b_{h,t}]. \tag{3}$$

Here $b_{h,t}$ are the specific skills of worker h in period t and $0 < \chi < 1$ denotes the speed of adjustment of specific skills.[5]

[5]In the general version of the model, heterogeneity of the learning speed across individuals is captured and it is assumed that the speed of adjustment positively depends on the level of general skills (see Dawid et al. 2019). In the context of the policy analysis in this paper, we abstract from the explicit representation of the heterogeneity of general skills.

2.2.4 Technological Change

The supply of the capital goods and the process of technological change is modeled in a very simplified way. We recur to a single capital good producer that offers different vintages of the capital good $v = 1, \ldots, V_t$ that have distinct productivities A^v. Alternatively, our representation of the supply of capital goods can be interpreted as a market with monopolistic competition structure, where each vintage is offered by a single firm, which uses the pricing rule described below.

New vintages become available over time following a stochastic process. To avoid spurious growth effects, due to stochastic differences in the dynamics of the technological frontier between runs, we use identical realizations of the stochastic process governing the emergence of new vintages in all runs.

To keep the description of this sector as simple as possible, no explicit representation of the production process and of the needed input factors is introduced. To account for the cost dynamics, it is assumed that the main factor of production costs is the wage bill and, since wages increase on average with the same rate as productivity grows (see Sect. 2.2.6), the growth rate of productivity is used as a proxy for the increase in production costs of the capital goods.

The pricing of the vintages $p_{v,t}$ is modeled as a combination of cost-based p_t^{cost} and value-based prices $p_{v,t}^{\text{value}}$ (see, e.g., Nagle et al. 2011):

$$p_{v,t} = (1 - \lambda) p_t^{\text{cost}} + \lambda p_{v,t}^{\text{value}}. \tag{4}$$

Due to our assumption above, p_t^{cost} increases with the average productivity of the economy. For the value-based price component the average general and specific skills in the economy are determined first. In a next step, the discounted productivities for each vintage are calculated for a firm that employs workers whose human capital is equal to the average of the economy. The value-based part $p_{v,t}^{\text{value}}$ is proportional to this estimated effective productivity of the vintage. The motivation for this rule is that the capital good producer tries to estimate the value of each vintage, in terms of effective productivity, for its average customer. Furthermore, it is assumed that the capital good producer is able to deliver any demanded quantity of any vintage.

The reason why we choose such a simplified representation of the capital goods sector is our focus on the interaction of labor market and consumption goods market dynamics. Therefore, we try to keep all other sectors as simple as possible. Not explicitly modeling the hiring and firing decisions of the capital goods producer has two main implications. First, there are no wage payments from the capital goods producer to households. However, in order to close the model, all revenues of the capital goods producer are channeled back to the households through dividends on the index bonds. Second, the capital goods producer is never rationed on its input markets, in particular, on the labor market. The qualitative implication of explicitly capturing the capital goods producer's hiring process would be that in periods when labor market tightness is high there would be a relatively high probability that the capital goods producer is rationed on the labor market. Being rationed the firm would not be able to deliver the full amount of capital goods that is demanded by the consumption goods producers. This would slow down the expansion of these consumption goods producers relative to their plans. Such a qualitative effect is already present in the model since consumption goods producers need to hire labor themselves whenever they want to expand their production. Through this channel, a tight labor market has already a hampering effect on firms' expansion and potential rationing of the capital goods producer would not add a qualitatively different effect.

2.2.5 Investment and Vintage Choice

If consumption goods producers have a target output level which cannot be produced with their current capital stock, they acquire new capital. To this end, a consumption goods firm has to choose from the set of available vintages. For the decision in which vintage to invest the complementarity between specific skills and technology plays an important role, due to the inertia of the specific skill adaptation, the effective productivity of a vintage with $A^v > B_{i,t}$ is initially below its quality. It converges to A^v over time as the specific skills of workers at the firm catch up to the quality of the vintage. Therefore, the firm computes a discounted sum of estimated effective productivities over a fixed time horizon S. The specific skill evolution is estimated for each time step within $[t, t+S]$ using (3), where the firm inserts its average-specific skill values. A logit choice model based on the ratio of the estimated effective productivity and price for each available vintage determines which vintage is ordered.

Capital goods are produced on demand, and as consumption goods producers may find it more suitable for their production plans not to employ the latest vintages, the capital good producer keeps on delivering also older vintages as the technology frontier grows. Note that the way we model the capital good producer it is a proxy for a more differentiated market with different firms supplying different vintages. In this sense, we capture vertical differentiation in the supply of capital goods. Having an elaborated vintage supply is crucial for our contribution given that the dynamics of the model unfold through the interaction of heterogeneous labor and capital as inputs to competing consumption goods producers. In particular, our approach allows to capture the effects of the skill endowment in a region on the vintage choice of firms and therefore on local technological change, which is an important mechanism in our analysis.

2.2.6 Labor Market Interaction

If the current workforce of a firm is not sufficient to produce its target output, the firm posts vacancies for production workers. The wage it offers is a combination of a firm-specific wage offer $\tilde{w}^O_{i,t}$ and a centrally determined wage component w^U_t.

The firm-specific wage offer has two constituent parts. The first part is the market-driven base wage $w^{\text{base}}_{i,t}$. The base wage is paid per unit of (expected) specific skills of the worker. If the firm cannot fill its vacancies and the number of unfilled vacancies exceeds some threshold $\overline{v} > 0$, the firm raises the base wage offer by a fraction φ to attract more workers, i.e.,

$$w_{i,t+1}^{\text{base}} = (1+\varphi)w_{i,t}^{\text{base}}. \tag{5}$$

The second part of the firm-specific wage offer is related to an applicant's expected level of specific skills. Since the specific skills represent the (maximal) productivity of the employees, the wage $w_{i,t}$ is higher for higher (expected) specific skills. Because the specific skill level of a job applicant is not observable, firms use the average-specific skills of all their employees to estimate that skill level and offer a wage of

$$\tilde{w}_{i,t}^{O} = w_{i,t}^{\text{base}} \times \min[A_{i,t}\bar{B}_{i,t-1}], \tag{6}$$

where $\bar{B}_{i,t-1}$ are the average-specific skills of all employees in the firm. While a firm can observe the specific skill levels of all its current employees, this information will not be transferred to a competitor in case a worker applies there.

The second wage component w_t^U is determined by a labor union and is, therefore, the same for all firms. The aim of the union is to equalize the wage inequality that emerges from firms' heterogeneity with respect to productivity. Furthermore, the workers should benefit from the productivity gains in the economy and should be compensated for real income losses due to inflation. Altogether, we assume that the union wage is adjusted over time by

$$w_t^U = w_{t-1}^U \left(1 + \max\left[0, \bar{\pi}_t + \bar{g}_t\right]\right), \tag{7}$$

where $\bar{\pi}_t$ is the mean monthly inflation rate and $\bar{g}_t$ the average economy-wide productivity growth per month, both averaged over the last year. The actual wage offer of a firm is then

$$w_{i,t}^{O} = (1-\lambda_t^C)\tilde{w}_{i,t}^{O} + \lambda^C w_t^U, \tag{8}$$

where $\lambda_t^C \in [0, 1]$ captures the level of centralization in the wage determination. Note that this wage setting is a reduced form representation of a bargaining process between firms and the labor union, where λ_t^C is a time-variant policy parameter that represents the negotiation power of the labor union.

Similarly, we assume that the adjustment of wages of incumbent workers depends on the level of wage centralization. Formally, we have for the wage of a worker h that works for employer i in the two consecutive periods $t-1$ and t

$$w_{h,i,t} = w_{h,i,t-1}(1 + \max\left[0, \bar{g}_t + \lambda_t^C \bar{\pi}_t\right]). \tag{9}$$

Thus, if the wages are determined fully de-centralized, then the wages of incumbent workers increase with the speed of productivity growth. If, however, the wages become more centralized, then wage adjustment of incumbent workers better accounts for inflation. In case of full centralization, all wages of incumbent workers correspond to the union wage w_t^U.[6]

An unemployed worker considers the wage offers posted by a random sample of searching firms and compares them with her reservation wage $w_{h,t}^R$. A worker h only applies to firm i if it makes a wage offer $w_{i,t}^O > w_{h,t}^R$.

The level of the reservation wage is determined by the current wage if the worker is employed, and in case of an unemployed worker by her previous wage, where the reservation wage declines with the duration of unemployment. The reservation wage never falls below the level of unemployment benefits. If the unemployed worker receives one or more job offers, he/she accepts the job offer with the highest wage offer. In case he/she does not receive any job offers, he/she remains unemployed.

In case the workforce of a firm is too large relative to its target output level, the firm adjusts its number of workers. The set of dismissed workers is random. Additionally, there is a small probability for each worker–employee match to be separated in each period. This should capture job separations due to reasons not explicitly modeled.

2.2.7 Consumption Goods Market Interaction

The consumption goods market is represented by a mall at which the consumption goods producers can offer and sell their products to their customers. Households go shopping once a week and try to spend their entire weekly consumption budget for one good. The consumption budget is determined using a (piecewise) linear consumption rule according to the buffer stock approach (see Carroll 1997; Allen and Carroll 2001). At the beginning of their shopping procedure, they get information about the prices of all available goods at the mall, but they get no information about the available quantities. The decision which good to buy is described using a logit choice model with strong empirical foundation in the Marketing literature (see, e.g., Malhotra 1984). We assume the most important factor governing the consumers choice is the price sensitivity of consumers and therefore the intensity of competition between the consumption goods producers.

The consumption requests for the different goods are collected by the mall and, if the total demand for one good exceeds its mall inventory level then the mall has to ration the demand. In this case, the mall sets a rationing quota corresponding to the

[6] An upshot of our wage-setting rule is that wages follow productivity. Several studies examined from an empirical perspective how closely wages correlate with productivity, including analyses that try to explain movements in the labor share, see, e.g., Autor et al. (2017). While there is some evidence on a decoupling of productivity and real average compensation presented in Schwellnus et al. (2017) for the years from 1995 to 2013 for 24 OECD countries, the result appears to be somewhat sensitive to the way how wages are measured. Meager and Speckesser (2011), for example, assert, based on data from 25 countries for 1995 to 2009, that wages follow productivity when they are measured as total compensation. Similarly, Stansbury and Summers (2017) present evidence of linkage between productivity and compensation in the U.S. over the years 1973 to 2016. There, a one percentage point productivity growth has been associated with 0.7–1% points higher median and average compensation growth.

percentage of the total demand that can be satisfied with the available goods. Each household receives the indicated percentage of the requested consumption goods.

After the shopping activity, rationed households may still have parts of their consumption budget available. Those households have the opportunity to spend the remaining budget for another good in a second shopping loop. In this case, the shopping process is repeated as described above.

The production of the consumption goods firm follows a fixed time schedule with fixed production and delivery dates. Even if the mall stock is completely sold out, it can only be refilled at the fixed delivery date. Consequently, all the demand that exceeds the expected value of the monthly sales plus the additional buffer cannot be satisfied.

2.3 *Parametrization and Validation*

In order to determine the values and ranges of parameters to be used in the policy experiments, we follow an approach that combines direct estimation of parameters for which empirical observations are available with an indirect calibration approach. This is done in order to establish confidence in the ability of the model to capture economic mechanisms which are relevant for real-world economic dynamics. Standard constellations have been identified, where values of parameters are chosen to reflect empirical evidence whenever possible and where a large set of stylized facts can be reproduced. Furthermore, the fact that the development of the Eurace@Unibi model follows as far as possible the Management Science approach, briefly discussed above, provides empirical grounding to individual decision rules, thereby addressing the important point of empirical micro-foundations for modeled behavior.

The set of macroeconomic stylized facts that have been reproduced by the standard constellations of the Eurace@Unibi model includes persistent growth, low positive inflation, and a number of important business cycle properties: persistent fluctuations of output; pro-cyclical movement of employment, consumption and investment, where relative sizes of amplitudes qualitatively match those reported, e.g., in Stock and Watson (1999), countercyclical movement of wages and firm mark-ups. On the industry level, the model generates persistent heterogeneity in firm size, profit rates, productivity, and prices in accordance with empirical observations reported, e.g., in Dosi et al. (1997). Also, labor market regularities, like the Beveridge curve, are reproduced by the model with benchmark parameter constellations. The reader is referred to Dawid et al. (2012) for a more detailed discussion of this issue. Tables with the list of parameter values used in the simulations underlying this paper are provided in the Appendix.

3 Policy Analysis

3.1 Experimental Setup

Our simulation experiment addresses the long-term economic implications of a de-centralization of the wage formation process. The starting point of our analysis is a baseline scenario that describes an economy with a fully centralized wage setting. Full centralization means that there is a uniform union wage from which firms cannot deviate to pay wages that would take firm-specific characteristics into account. This baseline scenario is contrasted with policy scenarios in which at a specific point in time $t = T^D$ a de-centralization process is initiated that leads to more flexibility in the wage setting, thereby facilitating firms to deviate from the centrally set wage.

The narrative of this experimental setup is that the economy is initially characterized by a centralized collective wage setting and then undergoes substantial changes in the institutional setup of the labor market and/or a de-unionization of the labor force that leads to less centralization in the wage formation process. The policy scenarios we analyze differ from each other in terms of the extent to which reductions in the centralization are realized. In the context of our model, the reductions can be achieved by decreasing the parameter λ_t^C governing the degree of centralization of the wage bargaining process.

In our experiments, we distinguish three time phases. In the pre-policy phase $0 < t < T^D$, we assume that the wage formation is fully centralized with $\lambda_0^C = 1.0$, which corresponds to the situation observed in the baseline scenario. At period $t = T^D$, the de-centralization process starts through which λ_t^C declines from its initial level λ_0^C to a scenario-specific level $\bar{\lambda}^C < 1.0$. In order to capture that it takes some time before the reforms are fully effective, we assume a policy phase in which λ_t^C decreases gradually until it reaches the target level $\bar{\lambda}^C$. We assume that the adjustment is on a yearly base with step size Δ_{λ^C}. Thus, the policy phase covers the period from $t = T^D$ to $t = \bar{T}^D$, where

$$\bar{T}^D = T^D + 12 \cdot \left\lceil \frac{\lambda_0^C - \bar{\lambda}^C}{\Delta_{\lambda^C}} \right\rceil . \tag{10}$$

All following periods $t > \bar{T}^D$ constitute the post-policy phase. Put formally, the evolution of λ_t^C can be described by

$$\lambda_t^C = \begin{cases} \lambda_0^C & t < T^D, \\ \lambda_{t-1}^C & T^D \leq t < \bar{T}^D \text{ and } t \bmod 12 \neq 0, \\ \lambda_{t-1}^C - \Delta_{\lambda^C} & T^D \leq t < \bar{T}^D \text{ and } t \bmod 12 = 0, \\ \bar{\lambda}^C & t \geq \bar{T}^D. \end{cases} \tag{11}$$

Since we focus on a long-term perspective, we consider the effects of a de-centralization of the wage formation emerging after a relatively long time horizon of 1000 months. Moreover, we apply the policy treatment after a pre-policy phase of

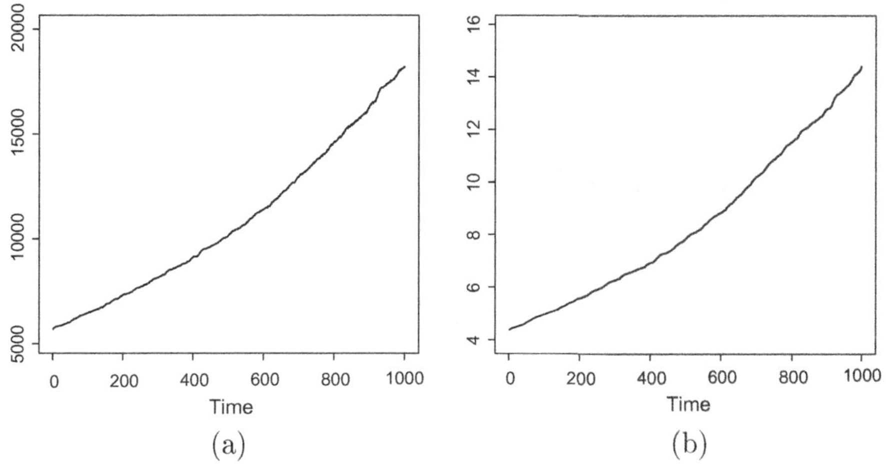

Fig. 1 Time series of total output (**a**), and productivity (**b**) of the baseline scenario

1000 iterations (i.e., $T^D = 1000$) in order to ensure that no transient effects distort our policy analysis. Overall, we consider a time horizon of 2000 iterations where the pre-policy phase is used as transient period and will not be considered in the following analysis.[7]

Besides the baseline scenario in which the wage setting is kept fully centralized over the full-time horizon, we explore 10 policy scenarios with different target levels $\bar{\lambda}^C$. The analyzed values range from $\bar{\lambda}^C = 0$ corresponding to a scenario with full de-centralization to $\bar{\lambda}^C = 0.9$ representing a high level of centralization, with a step size of 0.1 in between. We run for each of the 11 scenarios 100 Monte Carlo simulations.

3.2 *Results*

3.2.1 The Baseline Scenario

We start the discussion of our results with a brief description of some key characteristics of our baseline scenario where the wage setting is kept fully centralized over the full-time horizon. Once the behavior of the baseline model is described, we will go into the policy analysis applying the de-centralization policies to our model.

Figure 1 shows time series for aggregate output (panel a) and productivity (panel b). The economy features an increase in total output driven by a constant increase in productivity. The average annual growth rate is around 1.4% for total

[7]Further simulations disclosed that a too fast transition has negative effects. We observe that low productivity firms exit the market which leads to very high transient unemployment and lower growth.

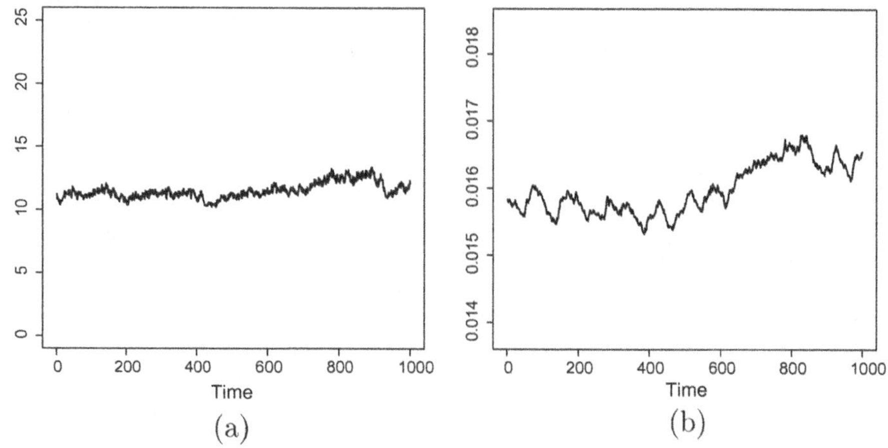

Fig. 2 Time series of unemployment rate (**a**), and Herfindahl index (**b**) for the baseline scenario

output and 1.44% for productivity. Figure 2 shows the time series for the unemployment rate (panel a) and the Herfindahl index (panel b)—a measure for industry concentration. Panel (a) indicates a stationary unemployment rate that fluctuates around a level of 11%. The Herfindahl index stays in a corridor between 0.0155 and 0.017. Given that the model has been set up with 80 firms, the simulated values for the Herfindahl index suggest a competitive industry with only a moderate tendency toward market concentration.[8] Altogether, the baseline scenario with a fully centralized wage formation describes an economy with a competitive industry characterized by technology-driven economic growth and persistent unemployment.

3.2.2 The Long-Term Effects of a De-centralized Wage Setting

Let us first consider the effects of a less centralized wage setting on growth and employment. In order to illustrate the simulation outcomes, we use boxplots where each boxplot represents the distribution of a variable over the 100 batch runs for the considered levels of de-centralization from 0% (baseline scenario) to 100% (full de-centralization). Figure 3 shows boxplots for the average annual growth rate of total output (left panel) and the unemployment rate. The growth rate is computed for the entire time horizon, and the unemployment rate is the average over the last 20 months.[9]

[8]In fact, the smallest possible Herfindahl index in an industry with 80 is 0.0125, describing a situation in which all 80 firms have the same market share.

[9]Note that for expositional convenience the scale used for the boxplots describes a variation from $(1 - \bar{\lambda}^C) \times 100$.

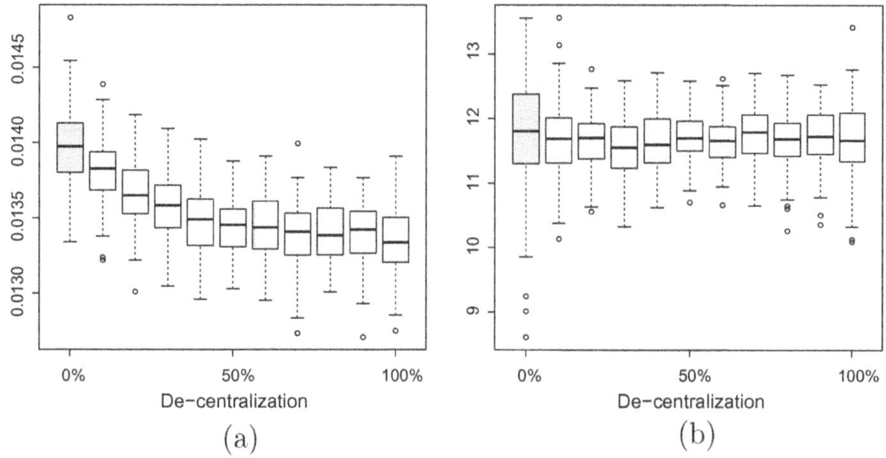

Fig. 3 Effect of a de-centralization on average output growth (**a**), and the unemployment rate at the end of the simulations (**b**)

From Fig. 3a, one can see that a de-centralization of the wage setting results in a negative growth effect. The size of the effect is declining in the degree of flexibility meaning that a small to medium change in de-centralization causes stronger growth reductions, whereas any further flexibility in the wage setting leads only to minor additional losses in output growth. Panel (b) demonstrates that the lower growth is not driven by negative employment effects. The reduction in the centralization of the wage setting does not change the unemployment rate in the long run.

Figure 4 illustrates the effects of an increasing de-centralization on inequality, where panel (a) depicts the effect on wage inequality, and panel (b) the effect on income inequality. Since wage inequality considers only labor income of employed households and, at the same time, we do not distinguish different types of workers, the inequality of wages is zero when wages are collectively negotiated. In fact, every worker receives the same labor income regardless of the characteristics of the employer or the tenure of the job. With an increasing de-centralization of the wage-setting process, however, firms have more scope to offer wages that reflect specific properties of the firm such as the firm-specific productivity profile and the perceived tightness the firm faces on the labor market. Consequently, the more de-centralized the wage setting becomes, the more individualized are the wages resulting in an increasing wage inequality. Qualitatively, there is a similar picture for income inequality, which, besides wages, also includes unemployment benefits and capital income. Income inequality, which is already present in case of fully centralized wages, tends to increase with a higher de-centralization, however, only up to a degree of de-centralization of 60%. After that income inequality slightly decreases as the wage setting becomes more de-centralized.

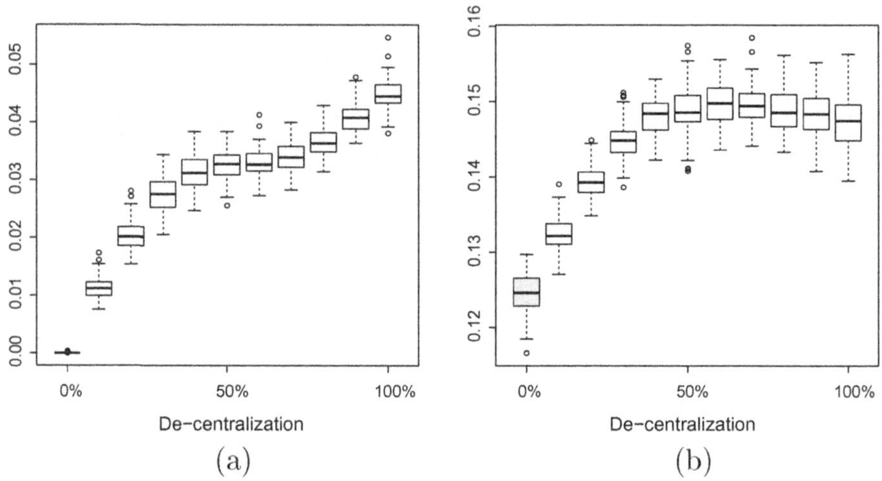

Fig. 4 Effect of a de-centralization on inequality of wages (**a**), and income (**b**) at the end of the simulation (measured as percentage standard deviation)

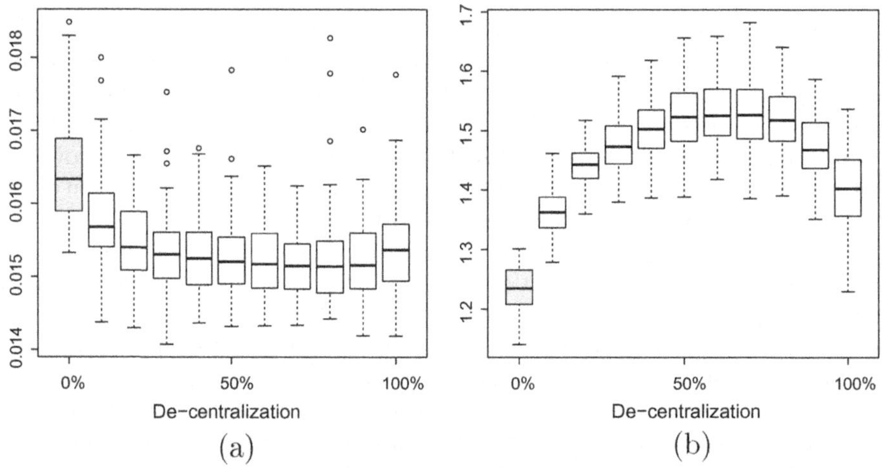

Fig. 5 Effect of a de-centralization on the Herfindahl index at the end of the simulation (**a**), and the firm size dynamics measured by firms' average change per period of ranks in the firm order determined by output size (**b**)

Now, we turn to the implications of a de-centralized wage-setting process for industry dynamics. Panel (a) of Fig. 5 shows how the industry concentration is affected by a change in the wage centralization. One can see that the Herfindahl index is the highest in the baseline scenario and decreases as the wage setting becomes less concentrated. Thus, de-centralization is associated with less industry concentration in the long run. Panel (b) of that figure depicts the average number of ranks a firm moves

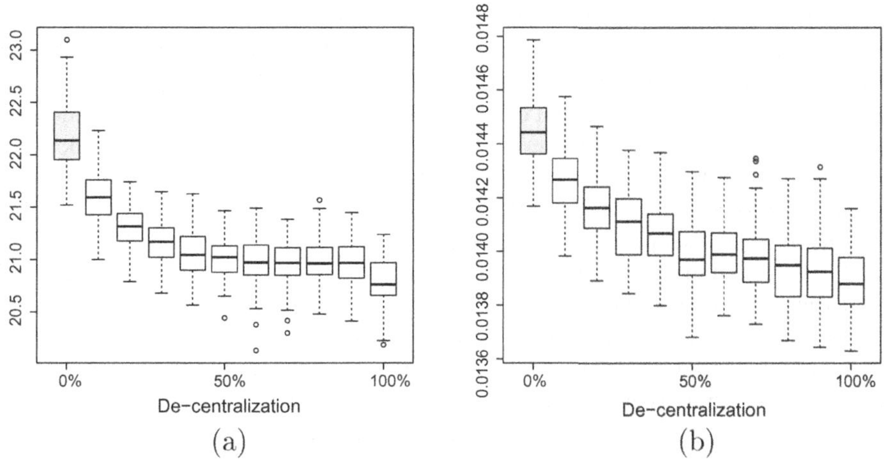

Fig. 6 Effect of a de-centralization on the average size of firms' capital stock (**a**), and the average annual productivity growth in the economy (**b**)

up or down along the order by firm size in each period, which we use as an indicator for the dynamics of market shares. The figure suggests that the firm order shows the highest persistence in the baseline scenario and otherwise follows an inverse U-shaped relation, i.e., the volatility of market shares is the highest at medium levels of wage centralization. This result is robust to using an alternative measure for the volatility of market shares, i.e., Spearman's rank correlation coefficient calculated for the distribution of firm sizes of consecutive periods.

In Fig. 6a, we show the average size of the capital stock of firms at the end of the simulation. Apparently, the average capital stock of firms is the largest in the baseline scenario in which we have observed the highest output growth. This gives a clear indication that the higher long-term growth under a centralized wage setting emerges through heavier overall investments by firms giving rise to larger capital stocks and faster replacement of old vintages. As a result, there is a higher productivity growth in the economy, evidenced in panel (b) where we plot the annual growth rate of the productivity of firms' capital stocks. This plot suggests that the negative effect of a de-centralization on output growth is associated with a slower pace of technical change, which in turn is the consequence of less capital investments of firms.

What stands behind these observations? First of all, it should be noted that firms compete in two markets, the goods market and the labor market. On the goods market, firms compete on prices to generate demand, where the cost structure of a firm eventually determines whether it is profitable to set a higher or a lower price compared to the competitors. On the labor market, firms bid for workers and the main distinguishing feature between firms is the wage that they offer to potential applicants.

A fully centralized wage has two implications. First, the competition on the labor market is turned off as firms can only offer the uniform union wage in the hiring process. In fact, if there are no differences in the wage offer, then job seekers are indifferent between any potential employer and choose the firm to apply randomly. The second implication is that uniform wages give firms with a high productivity a strong competitive advantage in the goods market. If wages are fully equal, the unit labor costs of a firm are entirely determined by its productivity, which enables high-tech firms to set prices more aggressively.

If, in contrast, the wage setting becomes more de-centralized, then wages become increasingly correlated with the productivity level of firms. This, however, weakens the cost advantage of high-tech firms as the higher wages counteract the cost-reducing effects of a higher productivity. At the same time, more flexibility in the wage setting strengthens the importance of base wage offers for the level of unit labor costs. As described in Sect. 2.2.6, the base wage offer reflects the wage a firm is willing to pay per expected unit of productivity and has, therefore, a positive impact on labor unit costs. It is driven by the competition on the labor market and tends to be higher for those firms that have historically faced more problems to fill open vacancies.

Hence, a change in the degree of wage centralization changes the relative importance of two channels driving the unit costs of firms. But how does a shift in the cost mechanisms affect the cost and price advantage of high-tech firms? In order to make a systematic comparison of high- and low-tech firms, we show in the following boxplots for different variables the ratios between high- and low-tech firms. We characterize a firm as high-tech firm if the productivity of its employed capital stock is above the median productivity in the firm population. A ratio above 1.0 implies that the considered variable is on average higher for high-tech firms than for low-tech firms. Figure 7a depicts the price ratio between the two types of firms. One can see that

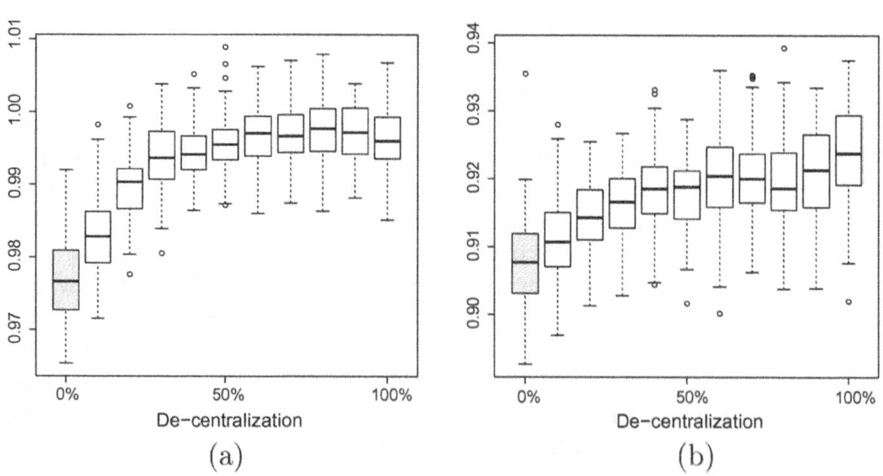

Fig. 7 Effect of a de-centralization on the ratio of high- and low-tech firms for prices (**a**), and unit labor costs (**b**)

high-tech firms set their prices more aggressively in comparison to low-tech firms. The price gap is the largest under a fully centralized wage regime. A qualitatively similar picture can be observed for the relative unit labor costs (panel b). The cost advantage of high-tech firms is also decreasing in the degree of de-centralization. Apparently, high-tech firms forfeit parts of their competitive advantage when the wage setting is shifted from full centralization to more flexible wage regimes.

In Fig. 8a, b, we show the main determinants of the unit labor costs. Panel (a) plots the effect of a de-centralization on the relative productivity, where we consider the effective productivity defined as the minimum of the productivity of a firm's capital stock and the mean-specific skills of workers of that firm. Again, the most pronounced differences between the two types of firms can be found under full centralization, where already a small flexibilization of the wage setting leads to substantial reductions in the productivity gap. In panel (b), we demonstrate the relative base wage offers.[10] Here, one can see that as long as the wages are sufficiently centralized, high-tech firms have on average larger base wage offers than low-tech firms. This can be explained by the productivity-driven cost advantage translating into more labor market activities of those firms which drive up their base wage offers over time. With an increasing de-centralization, however, wages become more heterogeneous among firms introducing the positive correlation between productivity and wages. In this situation, low-tech firms face an inherent disadvantage on the labor market and have to set higher base wage offers in order to still be able to successfully bid for workers. As a result, for higher levels of de-centralization, we observe that the base wage offers are higher for low-tech firms, which in turn contributes to larger unit labor costs in these scenarios.

Overall, one can conclude that in case of a more centralized wage formation the cost and price advantages of high-tech firms are directly driven by their productivity advantage, whereas for a more de-centralized wage setting the competitive advantage of high-tech firms arises through the competition on the labor market in which high-tech firms can offer relatively high wages without substantially impairing their unit costs.

Finally, in Fig. 8c, d, we demonstrate the relative size of the capital stock of high- and low-tech firms as well as their relative outputs. Again, in both figures, the largest difference between high- and low-tech firms can be observed in case of full wage centralization. A notable observation is, however, that under full wage centralization output and capital of high-tech firms are about 50% higher than output and capital of low-tech firms, whereas the productivity of high-tech firms exceeds one of the low-tech firms only by around 8%. This clearly indicates that the higher aggregate growth and the higher market concentration under wage centralization is driven by a relative growth of high-tech firms induced by their productivity-driven cost advantage. This cost advantage enables them to set prices more aggressively compared to their low-tech competitors, which in turn leads to more capital investments and larger output

[10]Note that the base wage offer is not depicted for the baseline scenario as this variable is not determined under full wage centralization.

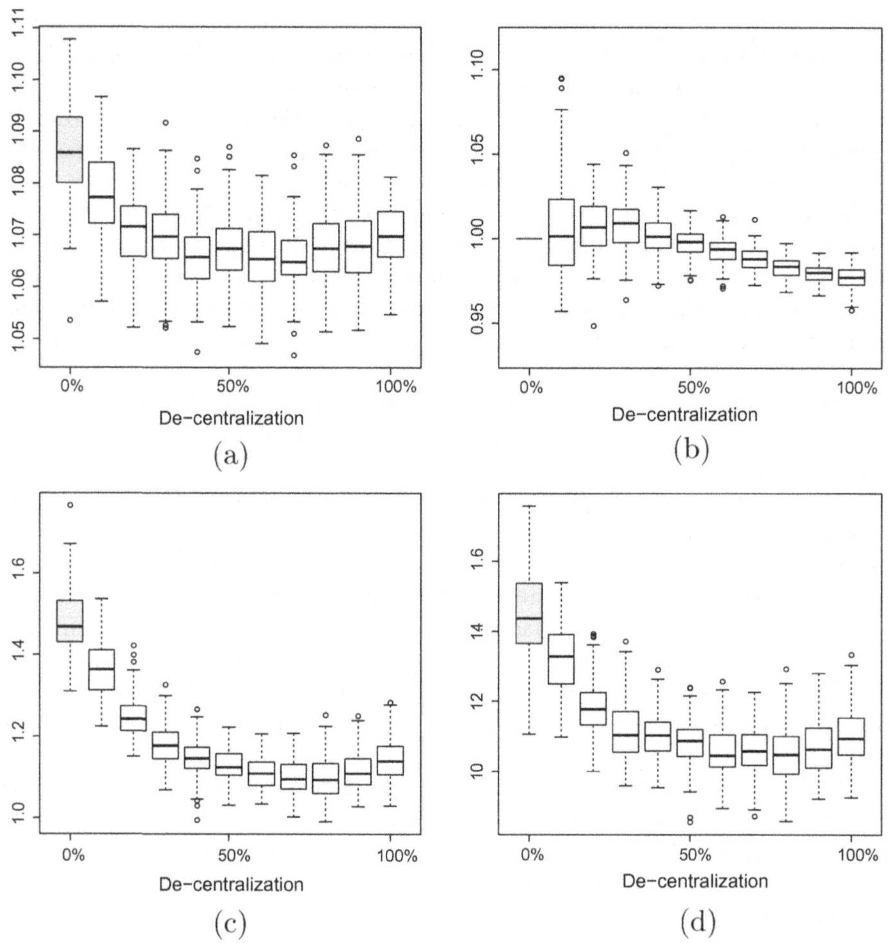

Fig. 8 Effect of a de-centralization on the ratio between high- and low-tech firms for effective productivity (**a**), base wage offers (**b**), size of capital stocks (**c**), and output (**d**)

growth of these firms in the long run. If wages are determined in a de-centralized manner, then high-tech firms have still a cost advantage but it is weaker than the one under full wage centralization. As a result, there is less relative output growth of high-tech firms such that more of the productive resources of the economy are employed by low-tech firms which eventually gives rise to lower long-term growth of aggregate output.

4 Conclusions

There has been a secular decline in the unionization of labor markets and coverage of workers with collective agreements. Moreover, collective agreements have become more flexible in the sense that opening clauses allow firms to deviate from regional or sectoral agreements to a larger extent than previously. It has been argued that while these changes in the wage-setting process of economies have been contributing to larger wage inequality, it should also have increased firms' competitiveness fostering economic growth.

In our contribution, we scrutinize this narrative. To this end, we analyze the effect of centralized versus de-centralized wage-setting arrangements in a closed agent-based macroeconomic model. In contrast to previous analyses, we incorporate not only the effect that de-centralized wage setting has on firms' competitiveness on the labor market, but also look into the effect it has on firms' competitiveness in the product market. We show that more wage flexibility indeed increases wage and income inequality. It has, however, a negative effect on output growth. De-centralized wages curb the cost advantage that high-tech firms have. Under centralized wages, high-tech firms can charge lower prices than their competitors which enables them to capture a larger market share spurring investments in their capital stock. The large and more up-to-date capital stocks of the well-performing high-tech firms in a market with centralized wages lead to higher growth rates than one gets in a market with de-centralized wages in which capital investments are spread among more firms but are overall lower.

We are aware that our analysis rests on a range of modeling assumptions and calibration choices that we had to make. Nevertheless, it suggests that one should be careful with overhasty policy conclusions on the benefits of de-unionized labor markets. More de-centralized wage-setting systems do appear to increase income inequality but they may not necessarily increase growth.

Appendix

Table 1 gives an overview of the most important model parameters. Table 2 shows the setup of the model with respect to different agent types.

Table 1 Values of selected parameters

Parameter	Description	Value
u	Wage replacement rate	0.55
Φ	Target wealth/income ratio	16.67
κ	Adjustment wealth/income ratio	0.01
δ	Capital depreciation rate	0.01
χ	Service level for the expected demand	0.8
γ^C	Intensity of consumer choice	16.0
ρ	Discount rate	0.02
S	Firm time horizon in months	24
Δq^{inv}	Technological progress	0.05
λ	Bargaining power of the capital goods producer	0.5
γ^v	Logit parameter for vintage choice	30.0
φ	Wage update	0.005
$\overline{v}$	Number of unfilled vacancies triggering wage update	2
ψ	Reservation wage update	0.1
α_D	Number applications per day	1
α_T	Total number applications per month	6
χ^S	Specific skills adaptation speed for low skilled workers	0.03703
τ^I	Income tax rate	0.065

Table 2 Number of agents

Agent type	Number
Households	1600
Consumption goods firms	80
Capital good firm	1
Banks	2
Government	1
Central bank	1

References

Allen, T., & Carroll, C. (2001). Individual learning about consumption. *Macroeconomic Dynamics, 5*, 255–271.

Autor, D., Dorn, D., Katz, L. F., Patterson, C., & Van Reenen, J. (2017). *The fall of the labor share and the rise of superstar firms*. IZA Discussion Paper No. 10759.

Barth, E., Bryson, A., Davis, J. C., & Freeman, R. (2016). It's where you work: Increases in the dispersion of earnings across establishments and individuals in the United States. *Journal of Labor Economics, 34*, S67–S97.

Basak, D., & Mukherjee, A. (2018). Labour unionisation structure and product innovation. *International Review of Economics and Finance, 55*, 98–110.

Blomgren-Hansen, N. (2012). Optimum organization of the labor market in a small open economy. *Labour Economics*, *19*, 221–231.

Caiani, A., Russo, A., & Gallegati, M. (2019). Does inequality hamper innovation and growth? An AB-SFC analysis. *Journal of Evolutionary Economics*, *29*, 177–228.

Calmfors, L., & Driffill, J. (1988). Bargaining structure, corporatism, and macroeconomic performance. *Economic Policy*, *6*, 14–61.

Card, D., Heining, J., & Kline, P. (2013). Workplace heterogeneity and the rise of West German wage inequality. *The Quarterly Journal of Economics*, *128*, 967–1015.

Carroll, C. (1997). Buffer-stock saving and the life cycle/permanent income hypothesis. *The Quarterly Journal of Economics*, *112*, 1–55.

Dawid, H., & Delli Gatti, D. (2018). Agent-based macroeconomics. In C. Hommes & B. LeBaron (Eds.), *The handbook of computational economics* (Vol. 4, pp. 63–156). North-Holland.

Dawid, H., & Gemkow, S. (2014). How do social networks contribute to wage inequality? Insights from an agent-based analysis. *Industrial and Corporate Change*, *23*, 1171–1200.

Dawid, H., Gemkow, S., Harting, P., van der Hoog, S., & Neugart, M. (2012). *The Eurace@Unibi model: An agent-based macroeconomic model for economic policy design*. Bielefeld Working Papers in Economics and Management No. 05-2012.

Dawid, H., Gemkow, S., Harting, P., van der Hoog, S., & Neugart, M. (2018a). Agent-based macroeconomic modeling and policy analysis: The Eurace@Unibi model. In S.-H. Chen, M. Kaboudan & Y.-R. Du (Eds.),*The Oxford handbook of computational economics and finance* (pp. 490–519). Oxford University Press.

Dawid, H., & Harting, P. (2012). Capturing firm behavior in agent-based models of industry evolution and macroeconomic dynamics. In G. Bünsdorf (Ed.), *Applied evolutionary economics, behavior and organizations* (pp. 103–130). Edward-Elgar.

Dawid, H., Harting, P., & Neugart, M. (2014). Economic convergence: Policy implications from a heterogeneous agent model. *Journal of Economic Dynamics and Control*, *44*, 54–80.

Dawid, H., Harting, P., & Neugart, M. (2018b). Cohesion policy and inequality dynamics: Insights from a heterogeneous agents macroeconomic model. *Journal of Economic Behavior & Organization*, *150*, 220–255.

Dawid, H., Harting, P., & Neugart, M. (2018c). Fiscal transfers and regional economic growth. *Review of International Economics*, *26*, 651–671.

Dawid, H., Harting, P., van der Hoog, S., & Neugart, M. (2019). A heterogeneous agent macroeconomic model for policy evaluation: Improving transparency and reproducibility. *Journal of Evolutionary Economics*, *29*, 467–538.

Deissenberg, C., & van der Hoog, S. (2011). Energy shocks and macroeconomic stabilization policies in an agent-based macro model. In H. Dawid & W. Semmler (Eds.), *Computational methods in economic dynamics*. Berlin: Springer.

Deissenberg, C., van der Hoog, S., & Dawid, H. (2008). EURACE: A massively parallel agent-based model of the European economy. *Applied Mathematics and Computation*, *204*, 541–552.

Dosi, G., Malerba, F., Marsili, O., & Orsenigo, L. (1997). Industrial structures and dynamics: Evidence, interpretations and puzzles. *Industrial and Corporate Change*, *6*, 3–24.

Dosi, G., Pereira, M., Roventini, A., & Virgillito, M. (2017). When more flexibility yields more fragility: The microfoundations of Keynesian aggregate unemployment. *Journal of Economic Dynamics and Control*, *81*, 162–186.

Dosi, G., Pereira, M., Roventini, A., & Virgillito, M. (2018). Causes and consequences of hysteresis: Aggregate demand, productivity, and employment. *Industrial and Corporate Change*, *27*, 1015–1044.

Driffill, J. (2006). The centralization of wage bargaining revisited: What have we learnt? *Journal of Common Market Studies*, *44*, 731–756.

Dustmann, C., Fitzenberger, B., Schönberg, U., & Spitz-Oener, A. (2014). From sick man of Europe to economic superstar: Germany's resurgent economy. *Journal of Economic Perspectives*, *28*, 167–188.

Ebbinghaus, B., & Visser, J. (1999). When institutions matter: Union growth and decline in Western Europe, 1950–1995. *European Sociological Review*, *15*, 135–158.

Fabiani, S., Druant, M., Hernando, I., Kwapil, C., Landau, B., Loupias, C., et al. (2006). What firm surveys tell us about price-setting behavior in the euro area. *International Journal of Central Banking*, *2*, 3–47.

Firpo, S. P., Fortin, N. M., & Lemieux, T. (2018). Decomposing wage distributions using recentered influence function regressions. *Econometrics*, *6*, 28.

Haucap, J., & Wey, C. (2004). Unionization structures and innovation incentives. *The Economic Journal*, *114*, C149–C165.

Malhotra, N. (1984). The use of linear logit models in marketing research. *Journal of Marketing Research*, *11*, 20–31.

Meager, N., & Speckesser, S. (2011). *Wages, productivity and employment: A review of theory and international data*. Brighton: Institute for Employment Studies.

Moene, K. O., & Wallerstein, M. (1997). Pay inequality. *Journal of Labour Economics*, *15*, 403–430.

Mukherjee, A., & Pennings, E. (2011). Unionisation structure, licensing and innovation. *International Journal of Industrial Organization*, *29*, 232–241.

Nagle, T., Hogan, J., & Zale, J. (2011). *The strategy and tactics of pricing: A guide to growing more profitably*. New Jersey: Pearson Prentice Hall.

Neugart, M., & Richiardi, M. (2018). Agent-based models of the labor market. In S.-H. Chen, M. Kaboudan & Y.-R. Du (Eds.), *The Oxford handbook of computational economics and finance* (pp. 667–687). Oxford University Press.

Schwellnus, C., Kappeler, A., & Pionnier, P.-A. (2017). *Decoupling of wages from productivity: Macro-level facts*. Paris: OECD Economics Department Working Papers No. 1373.

Silver, E., Pyke, D., & Peterson, R. (1998). *Inventory management and production planing and scheduling*. Wiley.

Stansbury, A. M., & Summers, L. H. (2017). *Productivity and pay: Is the link broken?*. NBER Working Paper No. 24165.

Stock, J., & Watson, M. (1999). Business cycle fluctuations and U.S. macroeconomic time series. In J. Taylor and M. Woodford (Eds.), *Handbook of macroeconomics* (Vol. 1, pp. 3–64). Amsterdam: Elsevier.

Visser, J. (2006). Union membership statistics in 24 countries. *Monthly Labor Review*, *129*, 38.

Vona, F., & Zamparelli, L. (2014). Centralized wage setting and labor market policies: The Nordic case. *Eastern Economic Journal*, *40*, 349–364.

Oracle and Interactive Computations, Post-turing Thesis and Man–Machine Interactions

K. Vela Velupillai

Abstract This paper discusses the complexity and computability of the 'Deissenberg Problem' of finding the 'best' point in the efficient set. It is shown that the problem is computably undecidable and that the efficient set of the problem is algorithmically complex.

> Precisely because he is fully aware of a new content, for him content is everything and form nothing, … The basis of life, and therefore of knowledge, is *nosce te ipsum* ….
> Francesco de Sanctis (on Machiavelli)[1]

[1]In 1983 I borrowed a book by a then well-known author from Christoph Deissenberg; unfortunately—or, with hindsight, fortunately—it was taken, *without my knowledge*, by a 'then' friend, from my home library; it was never returned. At some point in 1984, Christophe, in his usual diffident, civilized, way, gently reminded me of having borrowed a book from him. It was then that I had the courage to tell him what had happened—but I offered to buy a new copy of it. He—again, with the utmost politeness—declined the offer, saying that it was a copy presented by the author! I have, since then, familiarized myself with the contents of that book and I prepared *a first draft* of this contribution as a generalization and formalization of Chaps. 5, 6 and 7 of its contents. The 'generalizations' were based on my reading and knowledge of Arrow (1974), March and Simon (1958; 1993), in addition to many of Simon's contribution, from 1947 to his *Raffaele Mattioli Lectures* of 1997. *Fortunately for me*, the author whose book I was guilty of borrowing from Christophe, did *not* refer to, or use, Arrow (*ibid*), March and Simon (*ibid*) and, of course, any of Simon's important work on *Organisations,* particularly in Chap. 7 of the book by *the subsequently 'discredited' author*. This version is on entirely different topics.

A modest contribution to the **Festschrift** in *Honour* of *Christophe Deissenberg*, edited by Herbert Dawid and Jasmina Arifovic, forthcoming in the **Springer Series** on *Dynamic Modeling and Econometrics in Economics and Finance.* The 'Post', in the *Post-Turing Thesis*, above, is a reference to *Emil Post*.

K. Vela Velupillai (✉)
Tottvägen 11, 169 54 Solna, Sweden
e-mail: kvelupillai@gmail.com

H. Dawid and J. Arifovic (eds.), *Dynamic Analysis in Complex Economic Environments*,
Dynamic Modeling and Econometrics in Economics and Finance 26,
https://doi.org/10.1007/978-3-030-52970-3_10

1 Introduction

More than forty-years ago, Deissenberg broached issues in *man–machine interaction* in computation, the difference between efficient sets and feasible sets, their complicated, i.e. complex—structure, multi-agent criteria, reflecting the fact that the information content of the two different sets, from personal perspectives, are distinct, that the seeking of a *unique* solution was akin to the *search for axioms* via an interaction between a person trying to elicit preferences from agents and their decision mechanisms, all these in terms of a computing—i.e., an iterative—process:

> Nevertheless, even when the *computation* of the efficient *set* is possible, the decision-maker is left with the problem of determining the 'best' *point* in the efficient set. Since the efficient *set* is, as a rule, *a complicated*, n-dimensional *structure*, this *reduced problem* is not significantly *simpler* than the original problem of finding the best point in the feasible *set*.
> Deissenberg 1977, p. 2; italics added).[2]

Both, at the time it was written, and today, the issues Deissenberg raises remain important and current, in the literature on modelling economies.

First of all, Ragnar Frisch, in both of his lectures on receiving the first (shared with Jan Tinbergen, in 1969) *Riksbankens Prize in Memory of Alfred Nobel*—for simplicity I shall refer to it as the *Noble Prize in Economics*, in the sequel—(Frisch 1970, 1972) and Johansen (1974), tried to model man–machine interaction in a process of questions and answers by an econometrician trying to elicit the preferences of a politician, in a model where there was a clear difference between a solution in the efficient set, and a feasible one, where—clearly—the former is a subset of the latter.[3]

Secondly, Deissenberg's prescient observations about the 'complicated, n-dimensional structure' of the efficient set, due to the nature of the *information* underpinning this set (and also the feasible set, from which one begins the iteration towards a tentative solution in an optimal model) shows, even at this relatively early stage of his professional career,[4] he emphasized issues that remained of interest to him for over forty of the next years. I summarize these issues as interests in algorithmic

[2]To the best of my knowledge, this paper is *not* listed in Deissenberg's 2017 CV, which was kindly provided by one of the editors; but that does not make it any the less important.

[3]The idea, and its implementation, by Frisch, in a quantitative model of the Indian economy, goes back, at least, to the early 1950s (see, Goodwin 1992, pp. 22–24). The section in Frisch's Nobel Prize Lecture, refer to *The preference function*, p. 23, *ff*., in Frisch (1970); the whole of Frisch (1972) is on the construction of an iterative mechanism to elicit, by way of structured questions—subject to modification in the light of experiences—by an econometrician (as defined 'classically' by Frisch), to elicit answers by politician*s*, to determine their preference functions. Deissenberg's eminently realistic assumption of 'partially conflicting goals' (op.cit, p. 1) by a multiplicity of agents reflects Frisch's considerations of eliciting and revising politicians' preference functions, iteratively, till 'some sort of consistency' is achieved.

[4]He was just over 30 years of age, when the first draft of Deissenberg (1977) was originally prepared. The substance of that paper of the mid-1970s has retained its freshness, relevance and topicality for the ensuing four decades, and some.

information and complexity theories—in addition to dynamic and computational complexity theories (for example, in Barnett et al. 2004 and Deissenberg and Iori 2006).

Thirdly, he has always been interested in (*efficient*) computational processes. All the models he has constructed, whether it be strictly economic, environmental, regional or historical (example, Deissenberg and Nyssen 1998), have emphasized the role, and need for, computation of the solution. However, it is easy to show that computational processes, requiring algorithms for implementing them, are *not necessarily efficient*[5] in the sense in which economists understand them (see the example of pp. 5–7, in Machtey and Young 1978).

Fourthly, he has almost always set up his models in a multi-agent dynamic setting of a variety of optimal control frameworks, to obviate explicit use of analytically difficult differential game assumptions.

Finally, it must be remembered that the classic Arrow and Debreu (1954) model of general economic equilibrium in a multi-agent, multicommodity, exchange economy, is *not* about uniqueness of the existence of equilibria in an efficient set, starting from a feasible set for this economy. Moreover, Arrow states:

> There is another benefit of the existence theorem that I should mention. It turns out that the *existence theorem implies an algorithm for solving general equilibrium*. This is the line that Herb Scarf[6] first took up.
>
> Arrow (1987), p. 198; italics added

From the above five observations, I distill the core analytical aims of Deissenberg (1977)[7] as an attempt to resolve the difference between feasible and efficient sets, by means of man–machine interactions solving the 'multiple-goal problem', in an iterative computational model. The 'best point'—i.e., the optimal point—in the efficient set, which is also an element in the feasible set, because the former is subset of the latter. With these interpretations in mind, I shall outline, in the next section, the kind of computability structure that can solve what I call the *Deissenberg problem*. The third section is a formalization of the *Deissenberg problem*, in terms of the analytical 'ingredients' in Deissenberg (*op.cit*). The concluding final section, briefly, points out that the approximation of the iterative method can stop the computation without ever knowing whether or not it is close—in terms of whatever metric one chooses

---

[5]In the sense of efficient being from a well-defined maximum set. In a choice situation, it is as feasible to choose efficiently as to assume some form of *Zorn's Lemma* (or an unrestricted *Axiom of Choice*).

[6]The model in Arrow-Debreu (*op.cit*) is over the *real numbers*; by the way, for many reasons, Scarf's algorithm is *not constructive*—but it is possible to construct an algorithm over the *reals* so that Arrow's assertion is justified. The computations and optimisations in *all* of Deissenberg's models, to the best of my knowledge, are over the *real numbers*, to which the same comment applies (*cf*. Feferman 2013, Chap. 3 and Fenstad 1980).

[7]This is the 'suggested' bibliographic entry—but the paper itself appeared as a chapter in *volume 2* of **Concepts and Tools of Computer-Assisted Analysis**, Birkhauser Verlag 1977, Basel, edited by H. Bossel. Eden's extensive review of the chapter version in the book, which is 'literally' the same as above.

to use—to a 'true' optimum[8]; in fact, implicitly, the so-called 'best point' *may not exist* in the considered feasible set. In this sense, the next step would be to analyse, in terms of *degrees of unsolvability*, the Deissenberg solution.

I would like to end this section with an entirely apposite remark, in what can only be called a competent review article, Colin Eden (1978, p. 353[9] 'An unfortunate aspect of Deissenberg's presentation, as a part of the complete three-volume text, is that it should be related to the theories which underpin Bossel's description of orientors, values, and norms as a hierarchical system-it would be helpful to see Deissenberg's comments on the multiple-goal problem set outside of the traditional objectivated problem and in the context of *complex policy analysis*'.), has the following observation on Deissenberg (*op.cit*; italics added):

> The third paper, in volume two, which *I found stimulating* is by Christopher [sic!] Deissenberg and presents "some interactive man-machine approaches which can be *effectively* applied in *actual* multiple-goal decision situations to help the decision-maker make his *choice*".

Although Eden does not use effectively in the same sense in which it is used in computability theory, the difference is immaterial; moreover, 'the decision-maker' may be helped, by the 'interactive man–machine approaches' to make a choice, but it does not mean that the choice results in 'the "best" point in the efficient set' being chosen!

2 A Brief Note on *Oracle Computations, Turing Reducibilities, Post-turing Thesis* and *Interactive—Trial and Error—Computation*

These brief notes are a result of the inspiration due to the two classics by Turing (1936–37, 1939) and one (in this context) by Post (1944) and the 'modern' classics of Davis (1958), Soare (2013, 2016) and Putnam (1965).

- On *Oracle and Interactive Computations* (*Relative Computability*, *cf*. Davis 1958, p. 20):
  Turing (1939), Sect. 4, p. 172 (italics added):

  > Let us suppose that we are supplied with some unspecified means of solving number-theoretic problems; a kind of *oracle* as it were.

This is, generally, referred to as an *o-machine*, adjoined to a 'normal' Turing machine—referred to as an *a-machine*; this latter is an entirely 'internal' machine, with no interaction with an outside source, such as, for example, the Internet's World Wide Web and other external sources of data storage, etc. Thus, we can consider a

---

[8]This is the case in Scarf's algorithmic method of finding an approximation to a general economic equilibrium of Arrow-Debreu type (cf., Scarf 1973, p. 52).

[9]Eden does go on, on the next page of his enlightening review article (p. 353; italics added):

generalized Turing machine as consisting of two tapes, or a coupled, *a- & o-machine*, which, from time-to-time, consults an oracle via one of the tapes on which the values of a characteristic function of a given set is written. Soare (2016, p. 52–3, Definition 3.2.1) explicates these ideas as follows (italics in the original):

> … An *oracle Turing machine* (*o-machine*) is a Turing machine with the usual work tape and an extra 'read only' tape, called the *oracle tape*, upon which is written the characteristic function of some set *A*, called the *oracle*, whose symbols {0, 1} cannot be printed over, and are preceded by *B*'s. Two reading heads move along these two tapes simultaneously.[10]

- *Turing Reducibility*, Post (1944, especially p. 289 and p. 312):

Reducibility of a set B to a set A is called (by Post, *ibid*) *Turing Reducibility* and is written as (Soare 2013, p. 231):

$$B \leq_{\mathrm{T}} A$$

Post defines *reducibility* in terms of *problem reducibility* in Post (1944, p. 289) (italics added):

> Related to the question of *solvability* or *unsolvability* of *problems* is that of the reducibility or non-reducibiltiy of one problem to another.

Remark I The reducibility here is (implicitly) defined as the *algorithmic*[11] *solution* of a problem presented in terms of (a generalized, i.e. an *Oracle*) *Turing Machine*. Thus, in the quote from Deissenberg (1977) with which this paper began, he states: *reduced problem*; this means, of course, in the context of this paper, that the *Deissenberg Problem* and the *Deissenberg Solution* are sought with respect to *Turing Reducibilities*.

Kleene (1943, p. 60) began the practice of equating the *intuitive* notion of *effective calculability*, with the formally exact *mathematical* concept of (*general*) *recursive function* as the statement of a *Thesis*. By using the word 'thesis', instead of 'theorem', he meant that it was *not* amenable to (mathematical or mathematical logical) *proof*. It was later (in Kleene 1952, p. 300) called *Church's Thesis*, transmogrified into the *Church-Turing Thesis* (as referred to by all and sundry in recursion or computability theory), and even *Turing's Thesis*.[12]

The *Post-Turing Thesis* relates the computable notion of effectivity with reducibilities and, hence, *Turing Reducibilities*, for given sets (say *B* and *A*[13]), in terms of the computable activities of a *Turing Oracle Machine*:

---

[10]The two reading heads need not move simultaneously; they can move, such that one is a computable function of the other.

[11]Algorithms can be more general than computable functions (See Gurevich 2012).

[12]Except Gandy (1980), and a few others, who referred to Turing's version of it as the *Turing Theorem* (actually as *Theorem T*, on p. 124, Gandy, *ibid*).

[13]As will be made clear in the next section, these are identified, in the *Deissenberg Problem*, with the feasible and efficient sets, respectively.

- *The Post-Turing Thesis* (Soare 2013, p. 227):

> *One set B is effectively reducible to another set A iff B is Turing reducible to A by a Turing oracle machine* ($B \leq_T A$).

Finally, Putnam's classic approach to 'trial and error predicates' in the sequence of solutions to a problem, it is claimed in this paper, is exactly the same—formally—as the iterative procedure used in searching for the rule of termination such that the 'best point' in the efficient set is the final outcome. Putnam allows the iterative procedure used by the decision-maker—or the model builder—to make mistakes to the answers posed to her or him; in the one case, the stopping rule is determinate—whereas in the second case it is not determinate. In Putnam's own words (1965, p. 49):

> But what happens if we modify the notion of a decision procedure by (1) allowing the procedure to '*change its mind*' any *finite* number of times (in terms of *Turing Machines*: we visualize the machine as being given an integer (or an n-tuple of integers) as input. The machine then "prints out" a *finite* sequence of "yesses" and "nos". The last "yes" or "no" is *always to be the correct answer*; and (2) we give
>
> up the requirement that it be possible to tell (effectively) if the computation has terminated? I.e., if the machine has most recently printed "yes" then we know that the integer put in as input must be in the set unless the machine is going to change its mind; but we have *no procedure for telling whether the machine will change its mind or not*.

Remark II Putnam's *Turing Machine* is what we have called, in this paper, the *a-machine*, which does not interact with the 'environment' or with any other aspect of the 'external world'—for example, with the political or economic decision-maker. We shall assume that it is the *Turing Oracle Machine*—the *o-machine*—which can 'change its mind any finite number of times.' Thus, the Putnam observation, that 'we have *no procedure for telling whether the machine will change its mind or not*' becomes syntactically meaningful.[14]

Remark III We will, in this paper, work with the second of the above alternatives—in particular, the idea that 'we have *no procedure for telling whether the machine will change its mind or not*' will turn out to be crucial in the proof of theorem 1, in the next section.[15]

3 Unsolvability of the *Deissenberg Problem*

The main result of this section, stated as a Theorem, is that the *Deissenberg Problem* is (*recursively*) *undecidable* by an *o-machine*. To apply the assumptions and results of the previous section, it is sufficient to identify:

---

[14]I am particularly indebted to item 3, in the anonymous referee's comments, for helping me clarify this point.

[15]For simplicity, and in the interests of conciseness, we shall assume a reader is familiar with the framework and assumptions of Putnam (*op.cit*).

(a) The *feasible* and *efficient* sets with *A* and *B*, respectively;
(b) *Computation* is done by means of a *Turing o-machine*, *interacting* with an external environment (the decision-maker);
(c) The computation is assumed to be done, by the *Turing o-machine*, over the set of integers[16];
(d) The iterative steps of the computation are in accord with Remark III;
(e) It is assumed that *effectivity* is understood in terms of the *Post-Turing Thesis* for the *Turing o-machine*.

These equivalences are sufficient to state, and prove, the following theorem and corollary.

Theorem 1 *The* Deissenberg Problem *is computably—i.e., recursively—undecidable.*

Proof *Turing o-machines*, similar to the Halting Problem for *Turing a-machines*, due to working under the 2nd of Putnam's two assumptions, cannot effectively decide whether terminating a computation is achievable.

Corollary 1 *The* efficient set *of the Deissenberg problem is* algorithmically complex.

Remark IV In the 'original' statement of the *Deissenberg Problem*, it is observed that 'the efficient *set* is, as a rule, a complicated, n-dimensional structure; this 'complicated structure' of the efficient set is captured, in the above corollary, as the algorithmic—or Kolmogorov—complexity of it.

Proof of Corollary 1 A simple application of the *incompressibility theorem* (cf. Li and Vitanyi 1993, p. 96) in conjunction with the result—Proof of Theorem 1.

Remark V Obviously, the efficient set—in view of its algorithmic complexity—is recursively unsolvable (or uncomputable).

Remark VI I conjecture that the properties of the feasible set, viewed from algorithmic information theory, is susceptible to the same kind of results, as for the efficient set.

---

[16]The questions by the model-builder and the answers by, say, the agent—who may be a political or economic decision-maker, are, at best, *rational numbers*, which can be *coded* (for example by *Gödel numbering*) in terms of positive integers. The rational numbers are, in any case, enumerable (cf., for example, Hardy 1908 [1960], p. 1, Example 4). However, as pointed out in footnote 4, above, it is not too difficult to do the same exercise for real number domain and range, as is the case in the case of Deissenberg (1977)—and, in fact, all of the computational examples in the Deissenberg *Oeuvre*.

4 Brief Concluding Notes

Soare (2013, p. 246; first set of italic, added) notes that:

> The field of computability theory deals *mostly* with *incomputable*, not computable objects.

It is in this spirit that I have, in this paper, reformulated the **Deissenberg Problem** in computability terms to obtain incomputable and undecidable results. But Soare is careful in his characterization; he qualifies it by adding 'mostly'! Of course, this means that the general results can be particularized to obtain computable and decidable results. The classic example is the negative solution to *Hilbert's Tenth Problem*—which does not, necessarily, mean that special-purpose Diophantine Relations cannot be solved algorithmically.

The challenge remains, however, to formulate computable and decidable questions, within a mathematical framework where positive answers to questions like the ones Christophe Deissenberg asked—for example, how does one find the 'best point' (read 'optimal point') in an efficient set, when an *Oracle Turing Machine* is implemented for computation.

Herbert Simon, my starting point,[17] always worked with decidable sets,[18] where the completeness theorem (of logic) was applicable. That was why he was able to harvest a rich variety of results in behavioural economics.

Perhaps there is a lesson in this—especially for ordinary mortals like me.

References

Arrow, K. J. (1974). *The limits of organization*. New York: W. W. Norton & Company Inc.

Arrow, K. J., & Debreu, G. (1954). Existence of an equilibrium for a competitive economy. *Econometrica, 22*(3), 265–290.

Barnett, W. A., Deissenberg, C., & Feichtinger, G. (Eds.). (2004). *Economic complexity: Non-linear dynamics, multi-agents economies and learning*. UK: Emerald Group Publishing Limited.

March, J. G., & Simon, H. A. (1958; 1993). *Organizations*, 2nd ed. Oxford, UK: Blackwell Publishers.

Davis, M. (1958). *Computability and unsolvability*. New York: McGraw-Hill Book Company.

Deissenberg, C. (1977). *Man-machine interaction as an answer to the multiple-goal problem*. Diskussionsbeiträge des Fachbereichs Wirtschaftswissenschaften der Universität Konstanz, No. 94, Fachbereich Wirtschaftswissenschaften, Universität Konstanz, Konstanz.

Deissenberg, C., & Iori, G. (2006). Introduction. *Journal of Economic Behavior and Organization, 61*(4), 521–524.

Deissenberg, C., & Nyssen, J. (1998). A simple model of schumpeterian growth with complex dynamics. *Journal of Economic Dynamics and Control, 22*(2), 247–266.

---

[17] I daresay that it was also a starting point for many of Christoph Deissenberg's rich speculations in the decision sciences.

[18] The referee (anonymous) points out that, *delineating decidable and undecidable sets is in itself an (algorithmically) undecidable problem*; this is, strictly speaking, incorrect. The correctness of the assertion depends on the structure of the set(s) under consideration. I have always maintained that Simon worked with sets that were complete (as above) and, therefore all of them were recursive.

Eden, C. (1978). Computer assisted policy analysis: Contributions from Germany. *Policy Sciences, 9*(3), 345–360.
Feiwel, G. R. (1987). Arrow and the ascent of modern economic theory. In K. J. Arrow (Ed.), *Part I: The makers of modern general equilibrium theory, oral history I: An interview* (pp. 191–242). London: The Macmillan Press Ltd.
Feferman, S. (2013). About and around computing over the reals. In *Computability: Turing, Gödel, Church, and beyond* (pp. 55–76). Cambridge, Massachusetts: The MIT Press.
Fenstad, J. E. (1980). *General recursion theory: An axiomatic approach*. Berlin: Springer-Verlag.
Frisch, R. (1970). *From utopian theory to practical applications: The case of econometrics*. Nobel Lecture, 17th June.
Frisch, R. (1972). *Cooperation between politicians and econometricians on the formalization of political preferences*. University of Oslo, Institute of Economics, Reprint Series, No. 90.
Gandy, R. (1980). *Church's thesis and principles for mechanisms*. In J. Barwise, H. J. Keisler & K. Kunen (Eds.), *The Kleene Symposium* (pp. 123, 148). Amsterdam: North-Holland Publishing Company.
Goodwin, R. M. (1992). An eccentric reminiscence of Ragnar Frisch. In *Nonlinearities, disequilibria and simulation: Quantitative methods in the stabilization of macrodynamic systems – Essays in honoour of Björn Thalberg* (pp. 22–24). Houndmills, Basingstoke, Hampshire, UK: The Macmillan Press Ltd.
Gurevich, Y. (2012). Foundational analyses of computation. In S. Barry Cooper, A. Dawar & B. Löwe (Eds.), *How the world computes* (pp. 264–275). Berlin: Springer-Verlag.
Hardy, G. H. (1908, [1960]). *A course of pure mathematics*, 10th ed. London: E.L.B.S, Cambridge University Press.
Li, M., & Vitanyi, P. (1993). *An introduction to Kolmogorov complexity and its applications*. New York: Springer-Verlag.
Johansen, L. (1974). Establishing preference functions for macroeconomic decision models: Some observations on Ragnar Frisch's contribution. *European Economic Review, 5*(1), 41–66.
Kleene, S. C. (1943). Recursive predicates and quantifiers. *Transactions of the American Mathematical Society, 53*(1), 41–73.
Kleene, S. C. (1952). *Introduction to metamathematics*. Princeton, New Jersey: D. Van Nostrand Company Inc.
Machtey, M., & Young, P. (1978). *An introduction to the general theory of algorithms*. New York: North-Holland.
Post, E. L. (1944). Recursively enumerable sets of positive integers and their decision problems. *Bulletin of the American Mathematical Society, 50*(5), 284–316.
Putnam, H. (1965). Trial and error predicates and the solution to a problem of Mostowski. *The Journal of Symbolic Logic, 30*(1), 49–57.
Scarf, H. (1973). *The computation of economic equilibria* (with the collaboration of Terje Hansen). New Haven, CT: Yale University Press.
Soare, R. I. (2013). Interactive computing and relativized computability. In B. Jack Copeland, C. J. Posy & O. Shagrir (Eds.), *Computability: Turing, Gödel, Church, and beyond* (pp. 203–260). Cambridge, Massachusetts: The MIT Press.
Soare, R. I. (2016). *Turing computability: Theory and applications*. Berlin: Springer-Verlag.
Turing, A. M. (1936–37). On computable numbers, with an application to the Entscheidungs problem. *Proceedings of the London Mathematical Society, 42*(2), 230–265.
Turing, A. M. (1937). On computable numbers, with an application to the Entscheidungs problem: A correction. *Proceedings of the London Mathematical Society, 43*(2), 544–546.
Turing, A. M. (1939). Systems of logic based on ordinals. *Proceedings of the London Mathematical Society, 45*(2), 161–228.

The manufacturer's authorised representative in the EU is Springer Nature Customer Service Centre GmbH, Europaplatz 3, 69115 Heidelberg, Germany. If you have any concerns regarding our products, please contact ProductSafety@springernature.com

Printed and bound by CPI Group (UK) Ltd, Croydon, CR0 4YY
28/09/2026
02224086-0004